Dictionary of Latin and Greek Theological Terms

Drawn Principally from Protestant Scholastic Theology

Richard A. Muller

BAKER BOOK HOUSE
Grand Rapids, Michigan 49506

To my Parents,
Alfred and Kathryn Muller,
with love and gratitude

Preface

The ability to work productively in the field of theology, as in any long-established discipline, rests in no small measure upon the mastery of vocabulary. The task is doubly difficult for English-speaking students. In the first place, the technical language of theology is still, frequently, in Greek or Latin. Not only is the precision of the original languages often lost in the transition to English, but many of the standard works in the field of theology continue to use the Greek and Latin terms, assuming that students have mastered the vocabulary. The problem is complicated, in the second place, by the fact that most of the contemporary lexical aids developed for English-speaking theological students are completely in English, including both the terms and their definitions. These considerations alone were enough inducement to lead one toward writing a brief dictionary of Greek and Latin theological terms.

There is one other issue, however, which makes the need for such a lexicon even more pressing: that issue concerns the Protestant heritage and its appropriation in and for the present, for the education of future ministers and teachers, and for the good of the church. Protestants have at their disposal a wealth of finely wrought theological systems, not only from the Reformers, but also from their successors, the theologians and teachers of the late sixteenth and seventeenth centuries. These latter writers took the ideas of the Reformers and, for the sake of preserving Protestantism from external attack and internal dissolution, forged a precise and detailed technical edifice of school-theology, which is now called Protestant orthodoxy or Protestant scholasticism. Not only did these orthodox or scholastic Protestants sustain the historical progress of the Reformation and transmit its theology to later generations, they also clarified and developed the doctrines of the Reformers on such topics as the threefold office of Christ, the two states of Christ, the Lord's Supper, and predestination.

The work of these theologians is well described by the two terms "scholastic" and "orthodox." The former term refers primarily to method, the latter, primarily to dogmatic or doctrinal intention. In the late sixteenth and the seventeenth centuries, both Reformed and Lutheran theologians adopted a highly technical and logical approach to theological system, according to which each theological topic or *locus* was divided into its component parts, the parts analyzed and then defined in careful propositional form. In addition, this highly technical approach sought to achieve precise definition by debate with adversaries and by use of the Christian tradition as a whole in arguing its doctrines. The form of theological system was adapted to a didactical and polemical model that could move from biblical definition to traditional development of doctrine, to debate with doctrinal adversaries past and present, to theological resolution of the problem. This method is rightly called scholastic both in view of its roots in medieval scholasticism and in view of its intention to provide an adequate technical theology for schools—seminaries and universities. The goal of this method, the dogmatic or doctrinal intention of this theology, was to provide the church with "right teaching," literally, "orthodoxy."

I cannot here engage in the debate over the theology of the Protestant orthodox; some have called it dry, rigid, and a distortion of the Reformation; others, among them Karl Barth, have declared it to be a rich and abundant source of theological insight and have viewed it as a legitimate extension of the thought of the Reformers. What is undeniable is the technical expertise of the Protestant scholastics and their impact on modern Protestant theology, as evidenced in the works of Charles Hodge, Francis Pieper, Louis Berkhof, Otto Weber, and, of course, Karl Barth. The problem here is that the theology of the Protestant orthodox is only partially available to students. Standard resources that present orthodox or scholastic Protestantism, such as Heppe's *Reformed Dogmatics* and Schmid's *Doctrinal Theology of the Evangelical Lutheran Church*, give the technical terms, frequently without full definition and, particularly in the case of Heppe, in Latin or Greek without translation. The problem of language carries over into the excellent manuals of Pieper and Berkhof. It is my hope that this dictionary will make this foundational Protestant theology and its terms more accessible and ultimately provide students not only with an incentive to study this essential terminology, but also with a point of entry into Heppe and Schmid and into the great Latin systems of authors like Francis Turretin and Johann Wilhelm Baier.

The use of both Lutheran and Reformed sources in the compilation of this vocabulary has led to a considerable amount of comparison of doctrine in the longer, more substantive definitions, like that of *communicatio idiomatum*. My attempt in all such comparisons has been to draw out in brief the distinctive elements and the common ground of the two positions without making any judgment concerning which holds the better solution to a given doctrinal problem. I would hope that the dictionary will be useful to Reformed and Lutheran alike, without prejudice to either, and that it will provide a useful point of entry into the vocabulary and the thought of the two great representative orthodoxies of the Protestant world.

I should perhaps note at this point that this glossary is neither a complete comparative vocabulary of Protestant orthodoxy nor a complete system of theology arranged alphabetically. The former would be a book many times the length of this one; the latter is rendered unnecessary by the indexes to the standard systems. The object of this volume is to provide an introductory theological vocabulary which will help students to overcome the difficulties inherent in current English-language works that use Latin and Greek terms and even to move somewhat beyond the vocabulary of those works. Students will, I hope, use it with Heppe, Schmid, Pieper, and Berkhof.

The Protestant scholastics had an incredibly rich and precise theological vocabulary. They drew, first, on the heritage of the Reformation, particularly upon the Reformers' reading of the biblical message of salvation by grace alone and justification through faith alone. This first source provided a Latin theological vocabulary that took and modified terms from the medieval and patristic writers in the light of Scripture—and, in addition, a Greek theological vocabulary from the New Testament which was virtually inaccessible before the great development of linguistic scholarship in the age of the Renaissance and Reformation. Second, the Protestant scholastics drew, as the Reformers themselves had drawn, upon those terms from the patristic era and from the Middle Ages that had become the standard currency of theological discussion, such as the terms definitive of trinitarian and christological orthodoxy in the Nicene and Chalcedonian symbols. In this category, however, the Protestant orthodox go far beyond the Reformers in their acceptance and use of terms. The difficult work of rebuilding theological system and of refuting the polemic of their scholastic Roman Catholic opponents led the Protestant orthodox into detailed patristic research and into a careful reading of medieval theology, with the result that a vaster array of technical terms from the fathers and from the medieval doctors appears in their systems than in the works of the Reformers. Third, the Protestant orthodox, in the process of developing systems, and of coming to terms more fully than Reformers with the tradition of the church, drew upon the philosophical vocabulary of the fathers and the medieval doctors. Here especially the Protestant orthodox manifest a concern to broaden and develop the technical capabilities of their theology, but not at the expense of the insights of the Reformers. As a result, they used not only a traditional philosophical vocabulary in connection with theological system, but also developed a vocabulary concerned with the limitation of philosophical and theological knowledge: see, e.g., *usus philosophiae* and *theologia ectypa*. This multiplication of terms available to the theologian relates directly to the precision of thought and expression typical of the scholastic Protestant systems.

In compiling my basic list of terms, I have worked with two ends in view: first, the accurate presentation of the vocabulary of Protestant orthodoxy, and second, the needs of students in their encounter with works currently accessible in which the orthodox or scholastic Protestant vocabulary appears. In order to achieve the first goal, I have consulted Lutheran and Reformed systems of the seventeenth century, principally the systems of Johann Wilhelm Baier and Francis Turretin, together with the standard compendia of Protestant orthodox theology by Heinrich Schmid and Heinrich Heppe. I have extracted all the technical terms from Schmid and Heppe, revising and modifying where necessary on the basis of Baier and Turretin. In order to satisfy the second goal, I have also worked through the systems of two standard exponents of twentieth-century Lutheran and Reformed orthodoxy, Francis Pieper and Louis Berkhof. From these works, I have extracted only terms; I have not translated either lengthy quotations in Latin or Greek or any of the biblical citations given in the original, nor have I included any of the German or Dutch words which appear here and there in Pieper and Berkhof. The resultant list, I hope and believe, will not only be of great service to students in their study of classic works in Protestant theology but will also become, for those same students, a way of entry into the realm of clear and precise theological expression.

This book would not exist, certainly not in its present form, were it not for the encouragement and help of many friends and colleagues. A first word of thanks must go to Allan Fisher of Baker Book House for suggesting this project and for his encouragement throughout the process of writing and editing. I owe a deep debt of gratitude to Pastor Luther Poellot, known to many as translator of an important work of the orthodox Lutheran theologian Martin Chemnitz, for a minute reading of the text, for his careful editorial work both in English and in Latin, and above all for his willingness to share expertise in fine points of Lutheran theology. I owe a similar debt to Dr. Richard Gamble of Westminster Theological Seminary and to Dr. Douglas Kelly of Reformed Theological Seminary, both of whom read the entire manuscript and made several important suggestions. Special thanks of another order go to Jan Gathright of Fuller Theological Seminary, whose expertise at the word-processor made the task of organization and compilation of this dictionary not only feasible, but smooth and virtually free of textual difficulties. Finally, I must express my gratitude to my family—to Gloria, my wife, and to Elizabeth and Karl, our two children—who looked on patiently and encouragingly as I wrote definition after definition on several thousand small file cards. I take responsibility, of course, for any errors or infelicities that remain, and I set the work aside knowing full well that many more definitions might have been included and that many of the discussions of terms might have been expanded.

Note on Style

All definitions begin with the term in Latin or in transliterated Greek. In the case of Greek terms, differences between the

Greek and Latin alphabet, plus the traditional Latinization of some Greek terms (e.g., *hypostasis*), made transliteration necessary for the sake of alphabetization. The Greek form of the term immediately follows the transliteration. The Greek form is followed by a literal translation (in some instances this translation is qualified by the adverb "literally"). Next, where a further explanation is needed, an expanded definition appears, with cross-references to related terms. Cross-references are noted either by "q.v.," when the referenced term is an exact rendering of a phrase in the definition, or by SEE, followed by a term or terms related to the subject of the definition. I have used the terms "Protestant orthodox" and "Protestant scholastic" synonymously, distinguishing where necessary between Lutheran and Reformed orthodox and between Protestant and medieval scholastics. Use of the term "scholastic" without modifier and in a context where the modifiers "Protestant," "Lutheran," "Reformed," or "medieval" have not previously limited the discussion, indicates a term or an idea that is the common property of the several types of scholastic theology.

In addition, I have tried to distinguish between Greek terms drawn by the Protestant scholastics from the New Testament and Greek terms drawn from the writings of the patristic era by the simple expedient of supplying a single Scripture reference with those terms taken from the New Testament. My purpose, here, is not to attempt any analysis of the biblical term but only to indicate which lexicon ought to be consulted for a full description of the meaning and usage of the word: for terms from the New Testament, Bauer's *Greek-English Lexicon;* for terms from the fathers, Lampe's *Patristic Greek Lexicon.* Finally, the dictionary proper is followed by a short English index to key terms. The index will enable those readers who approach the dictionary with an English term or concept in mind to locate the Latin or Greek original and thereby to use the dictionary as a basic theological reference work. The index is not at all exhaustive, but it does list important terms, even when they are cognates, and thereby indicates the location of major definitions in which related terms appear with cross-references.

12

For Further Reading

Those interested in reading further about the historical development of orthodox or scholastic Protestantism should consult the following books and articles for basic definition and discussion and for further bibliography.

Althaus, Paul. *Die Prinzipien der deutschen reformierten Dogmatik in Zeitalter der aristotelischen Scholastik.* Leipzig, 1914.

Beardslee, John W., ed. *Reformed Dogmatics.* Repr. Grand Rapids: Baker, 1977 [1965]. This volume contains a useful introduction plus selections from Wollebius, Voetius, and Turretin; those from Wollebius represent an entire compendium of early orthodox theology.

Dorner, Isaac A. *History of Protestant Theology Particularly in Germany.* Translated by Robson and Taylor. 2 vols. Edinburgh, 1871. Dorner's essay is old and dated but still provides a good beginning survey of the history of Protestant doctrines.

Elert, Werner. *The Structure of Lutheranism.* Translated by Walter A. Hansen. Foreword by Jaroslaw Pelikan. St. Louis: Concordia, 1962. Only volume 1 of the 2-volume German work (*Morphologie des Luthertums*) has been translated to date.

Fatio, Olivier. *Méthode et théologie: Lambert Daneau et les débuts de la scholastique reformée.* Geneva: Librairie Droz, 1976.

Jacobs, Henry E. "Scholasticism in the Lutheran Church," s.v. in *The Lutheran Cyclopedia,* ed. Jacobs and Haas. New York: Scribner's, 1899.

Leonard, Émile. *A History of Protestantism.* 2 vols. Edited by H. H. Rowley. Translated by Joyce Reid. London: Nelson, 1965–1967.

McGiffert, A. C. *Protestant Thought Before Kant.* Repr. New York: Harper & Row, 1961 [1911]. McGiffert devotes chapter 8 to Protestant scholasticism.

Platt, John. *Reformed Thought and Scholasticism: The Arguments for the Existence of God in Dutch Theology, 1575–1650.* Leiden: E. J. Brill, 1982.

Preus, Robert D. *The Theology of Post-Reformation Lutheranism.* 2 vols. St. Louis: Concordia, 1970–1972.

Ritschl, Otto. *Dogmengeschichte des Protestantismus.* 3 vols. Goettingen, 1927. Still a standard work.

Scharlemann, Robert. "Scholasticism (Lutheran)," s.v. in *The Ency-*

clopedia of the Lutheran Church, ed. J. Bodensieck. 3 vols. Minneapolis: Augsburg, 1965.

———. *Aquinas and Gerhard: Theological Controversy and Construction in Medieval and Protestant Scholasticism.* New Haven: Yale University Press, 1964.

Works Consulted

Altenstaig, Johannes. *Vocabularius theologiae.* Hagenau: Heinrich Gran, 1517.

———. *Lexicon theologicum.* Koeln, 1619; repr. Hildersheim: Olms, 1973.

Baier, Johann Wilhelm. *Compendium theologiae positivae. . . .* Edited by C. F. W. Walther. 3 vols. in 4. St. Louis: Concordia, 1879.

Baudry, Léon. *Lexique philosophique de Guillaume d'Ockham: Etude des notions fondamentales.* Paris, 1958.

Bauer, Walter. *A Greek-English Lexicon of the New Testament and Other Early Christian Literature.* Translated, revised, and augmented by William F. Arndt and F. Wilbur Gingrich. 2d ed. revised and augmented by F. Wilbur Gingrich and Frederick W. Danker. Chicago and London: University of Chicago Press, 1979.

Berkhof, Louis. *Introduction to Systematic Theology.* Grand Rapids: Eerdmans, 1932; repr. Grand Rapids: Baker, 1979. This volume is the prolegomenon to Berkhof's *Systematic Theology.* Berkhof's system is not complete without it.

———. *Systematic Theology.* 4th ed. Grand Rapids: Eerdmans, 1939 (frequently reprinted).

Deferrari, Roy, et al. *A Lexicon of St. Thomas Aquinas based on the Summa Theologica and selected passages of his other works.* Washington: Catholic University of America Press, 1949.

Du Cange, Charles. *Glossarium mediae et infimae Latinitatis.* 10 vols. Repr. Graz: Akademische Druck-U. Verlagsanstalt, 1954.

Gerhard, Johann. *Loci theologici.* 9 vols. Edited by E. Preuss. Berlin: Schlawitz, 1863–1875.

Heppe, Heinrich. *Reformed Dogmatics Set Out and Illustrated from the Sources.* Foreword by Karl Barth; revised and edited by Ernst Bizer; translated by G. T. Thomson. Repr. Grand Rapids: Baker, 1978.

Lampe, G. W. H., ed. *A Patristic Greek Lexicon.* Oxford: Clarendon Press, 1961.

Lewis, Charleton T., and Short, Charles. *A New Latin Dictionary:*

founded on the translation of Freund's Latin-German Lexicon, edited by E. A. Andrews; revised, enlarged, and in great part rewritten by Charleton T. Lewis and Charles Short. New York: American Book Company/Oxford: Clarendon Press, 1879.

Niermeyer, J. F. *Mediae Latinitatis Lexicon Minus: A Medieval Latin–French/English Dictionary.* Leiden: E. J. Brill, 1976.

Oberman, Heiko A. *The Harvest of Medieval Theology: Gabriel Biel and Late Medieval Nominalism.* Rev. ed. Grand Rapids: Eerdmans, 1967; repr. Durham: Labyrinth Press, 1982.

Pieper, Francis. *Christian Dogmatics.* Translated by Theodore Engelder, et al. 3 vols. St. Louis: Concordia, 1950–1953.

Polanus von Polansdorf, Amandus. *Syntagma theologiae christianae.* Geneva, 1617.

Schmid, Heinrich. *The Doctrinal Theology of the Evangelical Lutheran Church.* Translated by Charles Hay and Henry Jacobs. 3d ed., rev. Philadelphia, 1899; repr. Minneapolis: Augsburg, n.d.

Seeberg, Reinhold. *Text-book of the History of Doctrines.* Translated by Charles E. Hay. 2 vols. Repr. Grand Rapids: Baker, 1977.

Turretin, Francis. *Institutio theologiae elencticae.* Geneva, 1679–1685; a new edition, Edinburgh, 1847.

Transliteration of Greek

α	a	ξ	x
β	b	o	o
γ	g, n*	π	p
δ	d	ρ	r
ε	e	σ, ς	s
ζ	z	τ	t
η	ē	υ	y, u†
θ	th	φ	ph
ι	i	χ	ch
κ	c, k	ψ	ps
λ	l	ω	ō
μ	m	ʽ	h
ν	n		

* The γ is transliterated by *n* only when γ precedes γ, κ, ξ, or χ.
† The υ is transliterated by *u* only when υ follows α, ε, or o.

Aa

a maximis ad minimis: *from the greatest to the least;* viz., an order of discourse or argument.

a nemine: *from none; from no one;* a term used to describe God the Father, who is neither begotten nor spirated; the Father is *a nemine,* the Son and Spirit both *a Patre,* from the Father. See *agennēsia; filioque; opera Dei personalia; Trinitas.*

a posteriori: *from the latter;* a description of inductive reasoning that moves from effect to cause, from the specific instance to the general principle; specifically, a term applied to those proofs of the existence of God that begin with the finite order and ascend toward the first cause (*prima causa,* q.v.), or first mover (*primum movens,* q.v.). See *causa.*

a priori: *from the former;* a description of deductive reasoning that moves from cause to effect, from the general or principle to the specific; a term applied particularly to the so-called ontological proof of God's existence developed by Anselm, which moves from the idea of God to the actual existence of God. The term can also be applied, although less precisely, to the order of those systems of theology that begin with foundational principles (*principia theologiae,* q.v.), Scripture and God, and then move more or less deductively through the works of God (*opera Dei,* q.v.) to the doctrine of the last day (*dies novissimus,* q.v.). The term is not applied with absolute precision to these systems since they are not purely deductive in structure but frequently pattern themselves consciously on the Apostles' Creed.

ablutio: *a washing* or *cleansing;* a term used as a synonym for *baptismus* (q.v.).

abrenuntiatio: *absolute renunciation;* specifically, the renunciation of Satan and all his works that takes place in the traditional baptismal liturgy. Thus, in Lutheran orthodoxy, one of the effects of baptism signified by the use of water is the deliverance of the infant from the power of Satan by the grace of the Spirit, together with the concomitant gift of spiritual freedom.

absolutio: *absolution* or *acquittal, pardon;* i.e., the pronouncement of the forgiveness of sins following true penitence (*poenitentia*, q.v.) and a genuine confession (*confessio*) of sin. In general both Lutherans and Reformed follow a pattern of corporate confession and general pastoral absolution during the service of worship; Lutherans, however, maintain also a doctrine of private absolution (*absolutio privata*) upon personal confession of sin to a minister of the gospel. *Absolutio* belongs to the church and its ministers according to the power of the keys (*potestas clavium*), i.e., the binding and loosing of sins. Both Roman Catholics and Lutherans affirm fully the churchly power (*potestas ecclesiae*, q.v.) of absolution; the Reformed tend to view the *absolutio* as only an announcement of the forgiveness pronounced by God in Christ.

abstractum: *an abstraction;* i.e., not an existent thing as such, but its essence or one of its attributes considered apart from its existence; also, a non-self-existent nature inhering in another nature. SEE *anhypostasis; communicatio idiomatum; concretum; in abstracto.*

acceptatio: *acceptation;* specifically, an act of grace and mercy according to which God freely accepts a partial satisfaction as fully meritorious. The idea is of particular importance to the Scotist and the Grotian theories of atonement, according to which God accepts as full payment for sin the finite satisfaction offered by Christ. Christ's work, in these theories, does not have infinite value or value commensurate with the entire weight of sin; but God, who is all-powerful, can and does freely accept it as if it were full payment. *Acceptatio,* which abrogates the usual patterns of debt and payment, occurs under the *potentia absoluta* (q.v.), the absolute power of God. In the Grotian theory, the divine acceptation of Christ's work rests primarily upon a view of God as *rector* or governor of the universe and upon a divine exercise of rectoral justice (*iustitia rectoris*, q.v.) rather than of a strict remunerative justice (SEE *iustitia remuneratoria sive distributiva*). SEE *meritum Christi.*

acceptilatio: *acceptation;* basically, a variation of *acceptatio* (q.v.), but having the connotation from Roman law of release from a debt by means of a formal declaration by debtor and creditor that, though there has been no payment, the debt is now considered paid. The term has been used incorrectly as a characterization of the Scotist and Grotian theories of atonement, although both theories presuppose a payment, and Grotius explicitly attacks the theological application of the term.

acceptio personarum: *partiality toward persons;* used with particular reference to the doctrines of predestination, the dispensation of grace, and the just punishment of sin, the phrase is based on the Vulgate text of Rom. 2:11—*Non enim est acceptio personarum apud Deum* ("There is no partiality toward persons with God").

accidens: *accident;* viz., an incidental property of a thing. Thus, an accident is a reality which is conjoined to a thing and which can be withdrawn from the thing without substantial alteration; or, in other words, an accident is a real property contingently predicated of a thing.

accommodatio: *accommodation;* also **attemperatio:** *adjustment* or *accommodation;* and **condescensio:** *condescension.* The Reformers and their scholastic followers all recognized that God must in some way condescend or accommodate himself to human ways of knowing in order to reveal himself. This *accommodatio* occurs specifically in the use of human words and concepts for the communication of the law and the gospel, but it in no way implies the loss of truth or the lessening of scriptural authority. The *accommodatio* or *condescensio* refers to the manner or mode of revelation, the gift of the wisdom of infinite God in finite form, not to the quality of the revelation or to the matter revealed. A parallel idea occurs in the orthodox Protestant distinction between *theologia archetypa* (q.v.) and *theologia ectypa* (q.v.). Note that the sense of *accommodatio* that implies not only a divine condescension, but also a use of time-bound and even erroneous statements as a medium for revelation, arose in the eighteenth century in the thought of Johann Semler and his contemporaries and has no relation either to the position of the Reformers or to that of the Protestant scholastics, either Lutheran or Reformed. SEE *sensus accommodatitius.*

acedia: *despair.* SEE *septem peccata mortalia.*

achōristōs (ἀχωρίστως): *without separation.* SEE *adiairetōs kai achōristōs.*

acroamaticus: *high; of or pertaining to higher things.* SEE *theologia acroamatica.*

actio: *action, activity.* SEE *actus; praedicamenta.*

actio Dei praevia: *prior or preceding act of God.* SEE *causae secundae; concursus.*

actio efficax: *effective action* or *effective act;* especially, the power of *providentia* (q.v.) in its *concursus* (q.v.), or concurrence, with good acts of human beings; i.e., the divine providential support of the good.

actio sacramentalis: *sacramental action or activity;* i.e., the rite (*usus*) of the sacrament as performed by all participants. Thus, in the Lord's Supper, the *actio sacramentalis* consists in the consecration (*consecratio*), distribution (*distributio*), eating (*manducatio*), and drinking (*bibitio*). Neither the Lutherans nor the Reformed allow any continuance of the sacrament beyond the *actio sacramentalis.* SEE *Nihil habet rationem sacramenti extra usum a Christo institutum.*

actiones θεανδρικαί: *theandric activities;* viz., those actions or works of Christ that are the common works of both natures or, more precisely, the conjoint work of the divine-human person. SEE *apotelesma.*

actus: *act, actualization, actuality,* or *reality;* according to the Aristotelian ontology at the root of scholastic language concerning being, *actus* or actuality designates that which exists or that which is actualized (SEE *energeia*), as distinct from *potentia,* that which can exist or has potential for existence. Thus the scholastics can use the concept of *actus,* or actualization, to describe that which is real, existent, perfect, complete, including a perfect or complete action or operation. *Potentia,* by contrast, refers to the possible, to essence (as distinct from existence), to the imperfect and the incomplete, and therefore to the faculty (i.e., *intellectus* or *voluntas,* q.v.) that can perform an action or operation. Thus the *intellectus,* as a faculty, is *in potentia,* in a condition of potency, capable of knowing; while the *intellectus,* in its knowing of an object, is in a condition or state of actualization, so that the knowing or understanding can be called an *actus intellectus,* an actualization or perfecting operation of the intellect. Finally *actus* or actuality can be defined only in relation to *potentia,* or potency, with the sole exception of God, who is fully actualized, or pure actuality (*actus purus*). As Aristotle argues (*Metaphysics,* IX.6. 1048*a*.31–1048*b*.8), not all things exist really or actually in the same sense; their actuality is defined over against a potency, so that seeing is actual in relation to the passive capacity to see. A seed is actual in relation to the matter from which it is formed, but clearly potential in relation to a tree. Thus, *actus* is always logically prior to *potentia* insofar as *potentia* is a potency toward something, even though in some instances potency precedes actuality in time. Thus, the process or motion (*kinēsis; motus*, q.v.) from potency to actuality describes both the continuity and change of the phenomenal world (*natura*, q.v.) and explains the relationship of form (*forma*, q.v.) to matter (*materia*, q.v.). SEE *actus fidei; actus purus; in actu.*

actus apprehendi: *apprehension, the act or actuality of apprehending;* as, e.g., the *apprehensio fiducialis*, or faithful apprehension, which completes faith (*fides*, q.v.). SEE *actus; actus fidei; actus fiduciae.*

actus cogitandi. SEE *substantia cogitans.*

actus consolatorius: *consolatory realization or actualization.* SEE *actus fidei.*

actus depositionis: *act of deposition;* contrasted with *actus propositionis*, an act of presentation. SEE *regnum Christi.*

actus dispositivus sive praeparatorius: *a dispositive or preparatory act or actuality.* SEE *actus; praeparatio ad conversionem.*

actus fidei: *the act, actualization, perfecting operation, or actualizing operation of faith;* in addition to their objective, doctrinal definitions of *fides* (q.v.), the Protestant orthodox also consider faith as it occurs or is actualized in the human, believing subject. In the subject, faith can be considered either as the disposition or capacity of the subject to have faith (*habitus fidei*, q.v.), which in the case of saving faith (*fides salvifica*) is a gracious gift of God, or as the *actus fidei*, the act or actualizing operation of faith, in which the intellect and will appropriate the object of faith (*obiectum fidei*, q.v.). The *actus fidei*, then, can be described by the Lutheran and Reformed scholastics as an *actus intellectus* and an *actus voluntatis*, an operation of intellect and of will. Both *notitia* (knowledge) and *assensus* (assent to knowledge) belong to the intellect, while the *apprehensio fiducialis*, or faithful apprehension, of that knowledge is an act of will. Saving faith in Christ comprises, therefore, the *actus credendi in intellectu*, the actualization of believing in the operation of the intellect, and the *actus fiduciae* (q.v.), or *actus fiducialis voluntatis*, the actualization of faithfulness in the operation of the will. The soul may be considered as the *subiectum quo* (q.v.), or "subject by which," of faith, since soul may be distinguished into the faculties of intellect and will.

The scholastic language of faith as *actus* must not be construed as a description of faith as an activity that accomplishes, for the mind and the will, a saving knowledge of and trust in Christ. Such a view would constitute a denial of the doctrine of justification by grace alone (SEE *iustificatio*). Instead, the language of *habitus fidei* and *actus fidei*, of the disposition or capacity for faith and the actuality or perfecting operation of faith, needs to be understood in the context of the scholastic language of potency (*potentia*) and act, or actuality (*actus*). The disposition, or *habitus*, is a potency for faith that can be actualized as faith. The act or *actus* of faith, although it may be defined as an operation, is not an activity in the sense of a deed or a work, but an operation in the sense of an actualization in which faith comes to be faith or, in other words, moves from potency to actuality.

The Reformed orthodox further distinguish the *actus fidei* into several parts. The first distinction is twofold: an *actus directus* and an *actus reflexus*. The *actus directus fidei*, or direct operation of faith, is faith receiving or, more precisely, having its object. By the *actus directus fidei* an individual believes the promises of the gospel. The *actus reflexus fidei*, the reflex or reflective operation of faith, is the inward appropriation of the object according to which the individual knows that he believes. These two acts can be further distinguished since, in particular, both *notitia* and *assensus* can be considered as *actus directus*. The *actus directus* can be distinguished into (1) an *actus notitiae*, or actualization of knowledge, and (2) a twofold *actus assensus*, or actualization of assent (*assensus theoreticus* and *assensus practicus*), consisting in an *actus refugii*, or actualization of refuge, and an *actus receptionis et unionis*, an actualization of reception and union. By way of explanation, each of these components of the *actus fidei* is direct insofar as it refers to the object of faith as appropriated. This is clear in the case of the *actus notitiae* according to which the *obiectum fidei*, the supernaturally revealed Word of God, belongs to the intellect, and also in the case of theoretical assent according to which the intellect agrees to the certainty of the truth of its knowledge. The *assensus practicus et fiducialis*, or practical and faithful assent, still belongs to the intellect, which here recognizes as certain and as the *obiectum fidei*, not only scriptural revelation, but that revelation of grace and sufficient salvation in Christ which God has promised to believers. The actualization of refuge follows immediately as the realization that Christ himself and union with him provide faith with the means of salvation. This *actus* is primarily of the will but still direct. Finally, on the ground of all that has preceded, but also now as a result of the *actus voluntatis*, or actualization of will toward Christ, there is an *actus receptionis sive adhaesionis et unionis Christi*, an operation of the reception of, adhesion to, and union with Christ. The next operation of faith is the *actus reflexus* in which the soul reflects upon itself and knows that it believes what it believes and that Christ died for it. Whereas the *actus reflexus* is primarily an *actus intellectus*, the final *actus fidei* belongs to the will. The *actus consolationis et confidentiae*, or actuality of consolation and confidence, is an acquiescence of the will to Christ and the knowledge of salvation in Christ. The scholastic analysis of the *actus fidei* is, in short, an attempt to isolate and define the elements of faith which must all be actualized in the believer if the graciously given disposition toward faith, the *habitus fidei*, is to bear fruit in a full realization of *fides*.

actus fiduciae: *the actualization of trust;* actual faith resting on the faithful apprehension by the will (*apprehensio fiducialis* or *apprehensio voluntatis*) of the truth of Christ. The *actus fiduciae* is of the very essence of faith, since it represents the full realization or actualization of all the other elements of the *fides* (q.v.), or faith, in the individual believer. Thus, it can also be called the fiducial actualization of the will, *actus fiducialis voluntatis*, which parallels and completes the actualization of belief in the intellect, the *actus credendi in intellectu*. SEE *actus fidei.*

actus forensis: *forensic act;* i.e., the actualization of a legal state or condition, such as occurs in the justification of the sinner by God on account of faith. The sinner is not made just but is, by the will of God, declared just, legally or forensically, and is thenceforth in a condition of being justified or counted righteous. SEE *actus iustificatorius; iustificatio.*

actus iustificatorius: *justificatory act or operation;* viz., the formal appropriation of the divine *actus forensis* (q.v.) of justification in the believer; the realization or recognition that God no longer counts one as sinful but as righteous in Christ. SEE *iustificatio.*

actus mixtus: *mixed or incomplete actualization;* a term used with reference to a being or substance that is not fully actualized but is not merely potential. SEE *actus; in actu; in potentia.*

actus praeparatorius: *preparatory act;* viz., the fulfillment of the condition or state preparatory to a subsequent condition or state; also **actus praecedaneus**: *preceding act or actualization.* SEE *praeparatio ad conversionem.*

actus primus: *primary actuality;* i.e., the bare existence of a thing distinct from its operations. SEE *in actu.*

actus primus/actus secundus. See *in actu.*

actus purus: *pure or perfect actualization or actuality;* sometimes **actus purissimus:** *most pure actuality;* a term applied to God as the fully actualized being, the only being not in potency; God is, in other words, absolutely perfect and the eternally perfect fulfillment of himself. It is of the essence of God to be *actus purus* or *purissimus* insofar as God, self-existent being, is *in actu* (q.v.), in the state of actualization, and never *in potentia* (q.v.), in the state of potency or incomplete realization. This view of God as fully actualized being lies at the heart of the scholastic exposition of the doctrine of divine immutability (*immutabilitas Dei*, q.v.). Immutability does not indicate inactivity or unrelatedness, but the fulfillment of being. In addition, the full actualization of divine being relates strictly to the discussion of God's being or essence *ad intra* and in no way argues against the exercise of divine *potentia ad extra*, potency or power toward externals (see *opera Dei ad extra*). In other words, God in himself, considered essentially or personally, is not *in potentia* because the divine essence and persons are eternally perfect, and the inward life of the Godhead is eternally complete and fully realized. E.g., the generation of the Son does not imply the ontological movement of the Second Person of the Trinity from a state of incomplete realization to a state of perfect actualization. Nonetheless, the relationships of God to the created order, to the individual objects of the divine will *ad extra*, can be considered *in potentia* insofar as all such relations depend upon the free exercise of the divine will toward an order of contingent beings drawn toward perfection. See *opera Dei ad intra.*

actus secundus: *secondary actuality;* i.e., the existence of a thing in its operations, as contrasted with the bare existence of *actus primus.* See *in actu.*

actus unionis: *the actuality or actualization of union;* specifically, of the *unio personalis* (q.v.), or personal union, of the two natures in Christ. Preferably, the term *actus personalis*, or actualization of the person, should be employed, following the majority of orthodox dogmaticians. The *actus personalis* refers to the *actus primus*, or primary actuality, of Christ's person, which is the actuality of the two natures in the one person or, simply, the existence of the personal union as such. The orthodox note that an *actus naturalis*, or actuality of the nature or humanity, of Christ must logically (but not temporally) precede the *actus personalis.* See *actus; anhypostasis; in actu; natura.*

ad arbitrium: *at one's choice, at will, arbitrarily.*

ad extra: *external, outward, toward the outside.* SEE *opera Dei ad extra.*

ad extremum: *at last, finally; to an extreme.*

ad hoc: *to or for this;* i.e., to or for this case alone, special.

ad hominem: *to the man;* a form of argument that rests on prejudice rather than on proof, designed to influence feelings rather than intellect.

ad intra: *internal, inward, toward the inside.* SEE *opera Dei ad intra.*

ad rem: *to the thing;* i.e., regarding the matter at hand.

adiairetōs kai achōristōs (ἀδιαιρέτως καὶ ἀχωρίστως): *without division and without separation;* a phrase from the Chalcedonian Creed referring to and defining the relationship of Christ's divine and human natures in the *unio personalis* (q.v.), or personal union. Thus Christ's two natures are united in one person without division or separation. The formula is a barrier to the Nestorian heresy, which jeopardized the personal union doctrinally by conceiving of too great a distinction between the natures. SEE *actus unionis; atreptōs kai asynchytōs.*

adiaphora (from the Greek ἀδιάφορα): *things indifferent;* a term deriving from Stoic philosophy, where it indicated the range of morally neutral actions, neither good nor bad. The term figured in two major debates of sixteenth-century Protestantism. In the first, the successors of Luther debated over the reinstitution of papal, conciliar, and episcopal jurisdiction, of the ceremony of the Mass, episcopal confirmation, confession, penance and absolution, chants and vestments. Luther had argued—over against the excessive attachment of medieval theology to such formal and external religious observance and also against the iconoclastic spirits of the early Reformation—for a distinction between the invariable, necessary truths of Christianity and indifferent matters. The Pauline teaching of 1 Cor. 8:1–9:23; Gal. 2:3–5; 5:13–15; and Col. 2:16–20 provides a guide to those seemingly indifferent matters that might create an obstacle or stumbling block to the gospel and to others, truly indifferent, that could be allowed without impeding the gospel. After Luther's death, Melanchthon and his supporters attempted to ensure the peace of the empire and the safety of Lutherans by allowing reinstitution of Roman jurisdiction and practice as *adiaphora*, pro-

25

vided that true doctrine and the preaching of the gospel were not impeded. Opposition to Melanchthon and the admission of such practices into the church of the Reformation coalesced around Flacius Illyricus and his contention that "nothing is indifferent in matters of confession and of inducement to sin" (*scandali*, SEE *scandalum*). The outcome of the debate was the rejection of Melanchthon's conciliatory position on the ground that no practice or jurisdiction implemented or exercised by an enemy of the gospel could be *adiaphora*. The second adiaphoristic controversy occurred in England during the reign of Elizabeth I. Elizabeth insisted on strict conformity in clerical garb. The antivestarian or Puritan party admitted that, theoretically, vestments were *adiaphora* but argued that the association of vestments with popery made their use an obstacle to the promulgation of the gospel. The English antivestarians drew heavily upon continental Protestant sources, including the writings of Flacius. In the end, royal power ended the Elizabethan controversy on the vestarian side. The strict Protestant view, however, as enunciated in both controversies allows only those things to be indifferent that do not impede the gospel but rather serve the glory of God and the good of the church. True *adiaphora* are things neither commanded nor forbidden by the Word of God and which, therefore, concern matters that can be decided in the church by the mutual agreement of the members. *Adiaphora* usually fall into the domain of practice and not the domain of doctrine or conscience. SEE *media*.

adiastasia (ἀδιαστασία): *continuity, absence of separation;* the term is used by the fathers in adjectival form (*adiastatos:* ἀδιάστατος) to indicate the inseparable relation of the Father and the Son and the continuous generation of the Son from the Father.

adidaktos (ἀδίδακτος): *untaught, uninstructed;* used of the Logos in a positive sense, viz., that he knows without having to be taught and knows absolutely. SEE *autodidaktos*.

adikia (ἀδικία): *wrongdoing* or *injustice; wickedness;* e.g., 2 Thess. 2:12.

adminicula: *supports, assistants, auxiliaries;* specifically, spiritual supports leading to illumination (*illuminatio*, q.v.).

administratio foederis gratiae: *administration of the covenant of grace.* SEE *foedus gratiae*.

administratio sacramenti: *administration of the sacrament;* plural, **administratio sacramentorum**: *administration of the sacraments.* SEE *notae ecclesiae; sacramentum.*

adoptio: *adoption;* a corollary of justification in the Reformed doctrine of the *ordo salutis* (q.v.), or order of salvation. The concept does not appear as a formal element in the orthodox Lutheran *ordo salutis.* In the Reformed *ordo,* adoption of the believer as a child of God occurs as the immediate corollary and result of the forensic declaration of righteousness on account of faith. Those justified by the grace of Christ are also made co-heirs with him of the kingdom and are declared sons with Christ, because of their union with him. The concept of *adoptio,* therefore, also rests upon the Reformed teaching of the *unio mystica* (q.v.), or mystical union with Christ: graciously united with Christ, who is Son of God by nature, believers are made sons of God by grace.

adventus Christi: *the advent or coming of Christ;* most frequently a reference to the second visible coming of Christ at the consummation of the age (*consummatio saeculi,* q.v.). On the last day (*dies novissimus,* q.v.) Christ will return in glory and power on the clouds of heaven to redeem his elect and gather them together, both those then living and those then resurrected from the dead, for the final judgment (*iudicium extremum,* q.v.). Following the judgment and the final separation of the righteous from the unrighteous, the elect from the damned, Christ will return all things to the rule of God, Christ will be king forever (the *munus regium;* SEE *munus triplex* and *regnum Christi*), and God will be all in all. The scholastics enumerate several attributes or characteristics of the *adventus Christi.* It will be personal (*personalis*), visible (*visibilis*), blessed (*beatificus*) for believers, terrible or terrifying (*terribilis*) for unbelievers, and glorious (*gloriosus*).

The Protestant orthodox can also speak of three advents of Christ, an advent in the flesh (*in carne*), an advent in grace (*in gratia*), and an advent in glory (*in gloria*). The *adventus Christi in carne* refers specifically to the incarnation, ministry, and work of Christ (SEE *obedientia Christi; officium; satisfactio vicaria*) and to the appearance, or aspect, of Christ during the state of humiliation (*status humiliationis,* q.v.) when his power was revealed in weakness and his divinity, as such, remained hidden from the world except in the performance of miracles and in the transfiguration (SEE *krypsis; ktēsis; occultatio*). The *adventus Christi in gratia* refers to the continuing presence of Christ to his church on earth between his first and his second visible coming, according to his own promise of abiding presence (Matt. 18:20; 28:20). It is an advent *in gratia* since Christ and his grace are present and made available to faith in Word and sacrament. This advent is, of course, invisible. The *adventus in gratia* refers to Christ's state of exaltation (*status exaltationis*, q.v.) and, from the perspective of Lutheran orthodoxy, to the illocal and supernatural mode of presence (*praesentia*, q.v.) of Christ's human nature in the Lord's Supper. The *adventus Christi in gloria* is, strictly speaking, Christ's third coming or second visible coming at the consummation of the age. The Protestant orthodox, both Reformed and Lutheran, are adamant in their rejection of chiliastic beliefs in more than two visible comings of Christ. See *chiliasmus.*

advocatus diaboli: *devil's advocate.*

adynamia (ἀδυναμία): *lack of strength, power, or ability;* in this form, a term from Greek philosophy, e.g., Aristotle (*Metaphysics*, 1019 b. 15–20) in the discussion of potency: *adynamia* is the privation of ability or capacity (see *dynamis*). The fathers know the forms *adynamos* (ἀδύναμος) and *adynatos* (ἀδύνατος), weak or powerless, and deny their predication of God. The Protestant scholastics draw on both usages.

aequipollens: *equivalent, of equal significance.*

aequivocus: *equivocal;* literally, having two *voces,* or voices, that are equally correct; a particularly important issue in the predication of attributes of God, since the equivocal use of a term would make impossible the determination of any meaning. If, as the nominalist perspective in late medieval theology argued, there is no *analogia* (q.v.) between God and the world, then the statement that God is good stands in no relation to the statement that the church is good; the word "good" has been used equivocally, and its usage lies beyond the grasp of reason. Protestant, particularly Reformed, emphasis on the divine transcendence raised the problem of predication of attributes for the Protestant scholastics. See *attributa divina; univocus.*

aeternitas: *eternity;* especially, the *aeternitas Dei,* or eternity of God. By this attribute, the scholastics understand the existence and continuance (*duratio*) of God without beginning or end and apart from all succession and change. Like the medieval scholastics, the Protestant scholastics accept also the definition of Boethius that eternity is the simultaneous and perfect possession of endless life (*aeternitas est interminabilis vitae tota simul et perfecta possessio*). Eternity, therefore, transcends not only limited time but also infinite temporal succession, namely, time itself.

affectio: *affection;* viz., passion or desire, a disposition toward someone or something; synonymous with *passio* and *affectus*. Specifically, the *affectio animi*, or affection of soul, that is the faculty of desire.

affectus voluntatis Dei: *affections of the will of God;* viz., those divine attributes which, according to the strict faculty psychology held by the Protestant scholastics, appear as dispositions or conditions of the divine will; i.e., *amor* or love, *benevolentia* or goodness of will, *clementia* or clemency, *gratia* or grace, *ira* or wrath, *longanimitas* or longsuffering, *misericordia* or mercy, *odium* or hate, and *patientia* or patience. See *attributa divina;* see also *amor; benevolentia; clementia;* etc.

afflatus: *a breathing on someone or something;* hence, inspiration.

agenda: *things to be done;* i.e., the acts or works of the Christian life that spring from faith as it becomes active in love. Thus *agenda* correspond with the Christian virtue of love (*caritas*, q.v.). See *credenda; quadriga; speranda.*

agennēsia (ἀγεννησία): innascibility (*innascibilitas*, q.v.), or *unbegottenness;* the incommunicable property or *character hypostaticus* (q.v.) of the Father that distinguishes his *modus subsistendi* (q.v.), or mode of subsistence, within the divine essence from that of the Son and the Spirit. Whereas both Son and Spirit are from another, either by begetting or procession, the Father is *a nemine* (q.v.), from none, having nothing by communication.

aiōn (αἰών): *eon, aeon, age, era;* in Latin, *saeculum.* See *consummatio saeculi.*

aisthētikon (αἰσθητικόν): *the spiritual faculty of soul;* specifically, the intellect in its role of distinguishing between good and evil, truth and untruth.

akatalēptos (ἀκατάληπτος): *something which cannot be contained or fathomed;* used by the fathers as a term for denoting the immeasurability and incomprehensibility of God, God's utter transcendence, and the absolute mystery of the Son's generation and the Spirit's procession.

alicubitas: *being somewhere;* as opposed to *omnipraesentia* (q.v.), which indicates being everywhere. *Alicubitas* is an attribute of angels, or, as they are frequently called by the Protestant scholastics, *pneumata leitourgika* (q.v.). Since they are spirits, angels do not have local presence, yet they are finite and not omnipresent; they are limited in operation and can therefore be said to be in a place, in a "somewhere," or *ubi*, in a definitive (*definitivus*, q.v.) manner. SEE *ubietas.*

alimonia: *nourishment;* also **alimonium;** a term sometimes applied to the Lord's Supper.

alius/aliud: *another* (masc.)/ *another* (neuter); used by the scholastics to distinguish between another *person* and another *thing,* particularly with reference to intratrinitarian distinctions. Thus the Father and the Son are distinct as *alius* from *alius,* as one person from another person, not as *aliud* from *aliud,* as one thing, or *res,* from another thing, since a distinction between *aliud* and *aliud* or *res* and *res* would deny the oneness of God and point toward tritheism. The natures in Christ, however, are distinct as *aliud et aliud,* one thing and another thing, not as *alius et alius,* one person and another person, since Christ is one person and two natures or, precisely, two natures in one person. The scholastics sometimes use Greek in making the distinction; thus ἄλλος καὶ ἄλλος for *alius et alius,* and ἄλλο καὶ ἄλλο for *aliud et aliud.*

allo kai allo (ἄλλο καὶ ἄλλο): *one thing and another thing;* as opposed to **allos kai allos** (ἄλλος καὶ ἄλλος), *one person and another person.* SEE *alius/aliud.*

alloeosis (from the Greek, ἀλλοίωσις): *interchange or exchange;* viz., a rhetorical figure which permits reference to one thing or nature in terms of, or by means of, another thing or nature. The idea is important to Zwingli's understanding of Christology and of the Lord's Supper, and it identifies the crucial divergence between his theology and that of Luther (the concept is not of particular importance to Reformed theology after Zwingli). Thus, according to Zwingli, one nature of Christ, or its attributes, can be used in speaking of the other nature. The statement that Christ is at the right hand of God refers properly to Christ's divinity, but by *alloeosis,* to his humanity. A similar transfer, or interchange, of meaning occurs in the Lord's Supper where, according to Zwingli, the bread signifies Christ's body and the wine signifies Christ's blood.

allotrioepiskopia (ἀλλοτριοεπισκοπία): *a usurpation of or interference in the business or authority of another.*

alogoi (ἄλογοι): literally, *mindless or reasonless ones;* i.e., irrational creatures.

amanuenses: *secretaries, penmen;* a term applied to the human authors of inspired Scripture who, in writing, acted as the penmen of the Spirit.

ameristos (ἀμερίστος): *incapable of being divided;* hence, inseparable; used by the fathers with reference to the Godhead, specifically, with reference to the inseparability of the persons of the Trinity.

amesōs (ἀμέσως): *immediate; without mediation.*

ametamelētos (ἀμεταμέλητος): *irrevocable; not to be taken away;* used by the Protestant scholastics with reference to Rom. 11:29, where the gifts (χαρίσματα) and the call (κλῆσις) of God are called irrevocable; hence, also a term applied to the decree, or *decretum* (q.v.), upon which both gifts and calling are founded. This latter usage is typical of the Reformed, not of the Lutherans.

amor: *love:* particularly, personal love, love of another person, as of a father, mother, or child; as distinguished from *dilectio* (q.v.) and *caritas* (q.v.). *Amor* can indicate either pure or impure love: e.g., *amor amicitiae,* the pure love of friendship; *amor concupiscentiae,* the impure love that seeks to possess a finite object for enjoyment, i.e., as an end in itself. SEE *amor Dei; uti.*

amor Dei: *the love of God;* i.e., both the love of creatures for God and the divine attribute of love. Considered in the former sense, *amor Dei* is twofold, either *immediatus* or *mediatus,* immediate or mediate. The *amor Dei immediatus* is that love according to which God is loved in and for himself and is the sole object of the love; whereas the *amor Dei mediatus* is that love according to which God is loved in and through the proximate objects of the created order insofar as they ultimately refer to God himself. The distinction between immediate and mediate love thus draws directly on the Augustinian distinction between enjoyment (*frui,* q.v.) and use (*uti*).

Considered as a divine attribute, the *amor Dei* can be defined as the propensity of the divine essence or nature for the good, both in the sense of God's inward, intrinsic, *benevolentia,* or willing of the good, and in the sense of God's external, extrinsic, *beneficentia,* or kindness, toward his creatures. The *amor Dei*, then, is directed inwardly and intrinsically toward God himself as the *summum bonum*, or highest good, and, among the persons of the Trinity, toward one another. Externally, or extrinsically, the *amor Dei* is directed toward all things, but according to a threefold distinction. The *amor Dei universalis* encompasses all things and is manifest in the creation itself, in the conservation and governance of the world; the *amor Dei communis* is directed toward all human beings, both elect and reprobate, and is manifest in the blessings, or benefits (*beneficia*), of God; and the *amor Dei proprius*, or *specialis*, is directed toward the elect or believers only and is manifest in the gift of salvation. The *amor Dei universalis* is frequently called by the scholastics *complacentia*, or general good-pleasure; the *amor Dei communis* is understood to be *benevolentia* in the strict sense of goodwill toward human beings; and *amor Dei specialis*, is termed *amicitia*, i.e., friendship or sympathy toward believers. In the discussion of the divine attributes, the *amor Dei* is considered both as an ultimate essential characteristic of God determinative of the other attributes and as one of the affections of the divine will. In the former sense, resting on the scriptural predication, "God is love" (1 John 4:8), the scholastics can subsume the grace (*gratia*), mercy (*misericordia*), long-suffering (*longanimitas*), patience (*patientia*), and clemency or mildness (*clementia*) of God under the *amor Dei*. In the latter sense, the *amor Dei* together with these related attributes is viewed as an aspect of the divine willing and is juxtaposed with the wrath (*ira*) and hate (*odium*) of God against sin.

anagennēsis (ἀναγέννησις): *regeneration.* SEE *regeneratio.*

anakephalaiōsis (ἀνακεφαλαίωσις): *recapitulation.* SEE *recapitulatio.*

anaktizein (ἀνακτίζειν): *to create anew.*

analogia (from the Greek ἀναλογία): *analogy; the relation of likeness between two things;* a relation which obtains only when the two things are neither totally alike nor totally unlike, but share one or more attributes or have similar attributes. The issue of analogy arises for the Protestant scholastics primarily in their exegesis of difficult texts of Scripture (*analogia fidei, analogia Scripturae,* q.v.) and in their discussion of the divine attributes (*attributa divina,* q.v.).

analogia entis: *the analogy of being;* specifically, the assumption of an *analogia* (q.v.), or likeness, between finite and infinite being which lies at the basis of the *a posteriori* (q.v.) proofs of the existence of

God and at the heart of the discussion of *attributa divina* (q.v.). The *analogia entis* is associated with the Thomist, as distinct from Scotist and nominalist, school in medieval and subsequent theology and philosophy. Since the proofs of God's existence play only a minor role in the Protestant scholastic systems and, when stated, are usually expressed informally and seldom at any length, the *analogia entis* receives little emphasis among the Protestant scholastics. Beyond this, the Protestant scholastic statement of fundamental principles (*principia theologiae*, q.v.), critical of the pure Thomistic approach of the Middle Ages and quite sensitive to the separation of reason and revelation argued by Scotism, recognizes the inability of theology to rest its arguments on a principle of analogy between Creator and creature and, instead, tends to argue the use of ideas and terms on the basis of scriptural revelation. This tendency coheres with the Protestant scholastic view of the use of philosophy (SEE *usus philosophiae*).

analogia fidei: *the analogy of faith;* the use of a general sense of the meaning of Scripture, constructed from the clear or unambiguous *loci* (q.v., *locus*), as the basis for interpreting unclear or ambiguous texts. As distinct from the more basic *analogia Scripturae* (q.v.), the *analogia fidei* presupposes a sense of the theological meaning of Scripture.

analogia Scripturae: *analogy of Scripture;* the interpretation of unclear, difficult, or ambiguous passages of Scripture by comparison with clear and unambiguous passages that refer to the same teaching or event. SEE *analogia fidei.*

anamartēsia (ἀναμαρτησία): *sinlessness;* also **anamartētos** (ἀναμάρτη-τος): *without sin;* terms applied to Christ in his unfallen human nature and perfect obedience. Since Christ's sinlessness, or *impeccabilitas*, is inherent and not due to regeneration and sanctification, it is *anamartēsia inhaesiva.* The Protestant orthodox, both Lutheran and Reformed, insist that Christ was not only sinless but also incapable of sinning because of the *unio personalis* (q.v.), or personal union, of the human nature of Christ with the Word. The temptation of Christ by Satan was nonetheless real, but was also necessarily predestined to fail. Any other view renders the permanence of the incarnation and the efficacy of Christ's saving work merely possible, contingent upon the success or failure of a finite nature rather than grounded on the eternal *consilium Dei* (q.v.), or counsel of God. Nor does the concept of a sinlessness or impeccability of Christ stand in the way of the fullness of Christ's humanity or of Christ's likeness to sinful humanity; in the *status humiliationis* (q.v.), or state of humiliation, Christ was subject to the common infirmities (*infirmitates communes*) of the flesh, such as weariness, physical pain, hunger and thirst, sensitivity to heat and cold, plus spiritual infirmities, anxiety, anger, and grief. The orthodox also refer to these infirmities as *infirmitates naturales* insofar as they belong to the natural state of human beings as they now exist in their fallen condition. The orthodox deny, however, that Christ suffered any *infirmitates personales*, or personal infirmities, such as are caused by personal excesses, congenital defects inherited from parents, sexual promiscuity, or by the divine anger against sin.

anapologētos (ἀναπολόγητος): *without excuse;* from Rom. 1:20, a term applied to fallen humanity which, despite its bondage under sin, remains responsible for its sinful acts because it knows the law of God inwardly and because it sins freely and unconstrainedly against the inward law. SEE *libertas a coactione; liberum arbitrium; libertas naturae; peccatum originalis.*

anarchos (ἄναρχος): *without beginning, without prior first principle;* a term applied to the Father in the Trinity with reference to his *character hypostaticus sive personalis* (q.v.); similar in meaning to *agennēsia* (q.v.).

anathema (from the Greek ἀνάθεμα): *anathema* or *curse;* specifically, an ecclesiastical curse, invariably accompanied by excommunication, frequently leveled against a heretic in condemnation of his doctrine.

ancilla theologiae: *handmaid of theology;* usually applied to philosophy which ought to serve rather than rule or dictate to theology, the queen of the sciences. SEE *usus philosophiae.*

angeloi (ἄγγελοι): *angels;* the official name, or *nomen officii*, given to ministering spirits; e.g., Luke 2:9. SEE *diabolus; pneumata leitourgika.*

angelus Domini: *the angel of the Lord;* a term like *angelus increatus*, or increate angel, applied to the Second Person of the Trinity, the Word, as the subject of the theophanies of the Old Testament, e.g., Exod. 3:2–6, where the "angel of the Lord" is closely identified with God himself.

angelus increatus: *uncreated or increate angel.* SEE *angelus Domini.*

anhypostasis (ἀνυπόστασις): *impersonality* or (more precisely) *non-self-subsistence;* a term applied to the human nature of Christ insofar as it has no subsistence or person in and of itself but rather subsists in the person of the Word for the sake of the incarnation. SEE *enhypostasis; persona.*

anima: *soul;* the spiritual or nonphysical part of the human being (*homo,* q.v.); the *forma corporis,* or form of the body, which provides the pattern and direction of human life and which is therefore called the *entelecheia* (q.v.), or entelechy, of the body, following Aristotle. The soul may be distinguished into two *facultates animae* (q.v.), the *intellectus* (q.v.) and the *voluntas* (q.v.); the will, or *voluntas,* is further subserved by the *affectiones,* or affections; the soul, therefore, thinks, wills, and feels. It gathers, remembers, and interprets the data perceived by the senses and uses its knowledge when making choices. The soul is the entire spiritual part of man and can be called spirit (*spiritus*). As a spirit, moreover, it cannot be divided, augmented, or diminished and is not liable to dissolution, although it is mutable in its knowing and willing. The scholastics conclude from these characteristics of the soul that although created and, therefore, contingent, it is immortal. The majority of the orthodox also concludes, from the relation of the soul to the body, that the soul is a *spiritus incompletus* (q.v.) and that, despite the immortality of soul and mortality of body, embodiment is the proper and natural condition of soul, and the resurrection of the body is necessary to the soul's enjoyment of eternal life. The separation of body and soul in death must, therefore, be viewed as a punishment resulting from the fall. Whereas mortality and natural corruptibility belong to the body as created good, death, the painful sundering of body and soul, is the wage of sin. Hypothetically, had man not fallen, there would have been a passage from mortality and corruptibility to immortality and incorruptibility without any separation of body and soul. Advocates of this argument point to the translations from mortal to immortal existence of Enoch and Elijah and to the transformation of all those believers remaining alive at the final advent of the Lord (1 Cor. 15:52; 1 Thess. 4:17) as exceptions to the rule of death.

On the subject of the origin of individual souls the Lutherans and the Reformed manifest some disagreement. On the ground that the soul is *substantia indivisibilis* or *impartibilis,* i.e., indivisible or non-impartable substance, the Reformed usually argue that souls cannot come into existence *ex traduce,* by transmission, from parents to children, and therefore must be created individually and daily by God. Lutherans tend to argue the opposite, i.e., that souls are generated *per traducem,* through transmission, or transfer, in the act of

35

conception. Orthodox Lutherans argue this point on the basis of the cessation of divine creative work on the seventh day; from the production of Eve entire, both body and soul, from Adam; and from the generation of Adam's son in his image and likeness, which would imply body and soul. In addition, the "creationist" view favored by the Reformed makes God indirectly liable for the sin of infants and fails to take note that the soul is the entelechy or *forma corporis*. Thus their view seems to imply that the human generation does not account for the form of the child, and therefore does not account for the child! The creationists counter with the example of Christ who had no human father from whom he could receive a soul and whose sinlessness could not be accounted for if he had received his soul from a human parent. In addition, the creation of Adam and other biblical references to body and soul seem to indicate their distinction and probably distinct and separate origins (Eccles. 12:7; Heb. 12:9). Finally, the soul is immaterial and the body material, and neither can be derived from the other, either material from immaterial or immaterial from material. This latter point, although it certainly favors the creationist view, also has a problematic tendency toward dualism and ignores the philosophical assumption of the unity of form and matter, body and soul. Neither the Lutheran nor the Reformed orthodox view this doctrinal point as capable of definitive formulation insofar as it cannot be proven directly from Scripture. Nevertheless, creationism is the exception among Lutherans, who tend to weigh the objections to creationism more heavily than those to traducianism. The opposite tends to be true of the Reformed. See *immortalitas; status animarum a corpore separatarum.*

anima naturaliter Christiana: *the soul by nature Christian;* a phrase of Tertullian (d. ca. 220 A.D.) that indicates the natural inclination of the rational soul toward the truth of God as known to Christianity. Not a phrase characteristic of the Protestant orthodox, who held the total inability of fallen man to turn toward God or to know the fullness of divine truth apart from saving revelation. The phrase does, however, find approval among the Arminians who, following Simon Episcopius and Limborch, held the identity of the natural law (*lex naturalis,* q.v.) with the law of Christ (*lex Christi,* q.v.) and who argued the ability of the human reason in its purely natural condition (*status purorum naturalium,* q.v.) to know divine truth and the ability of the human will to do what is in it (*facere quod in se est,* q.v.) and thereby approach God's offer of grace.

annihilatio: *annihilation;* specifically, the final destruction of the world by fire. See *interitus mundi; renovatio.*

anoëtos (ἀνόητος): *without mind, without intellect;* hence, foolish; e.g., Rom. 1:14.

anomia (ἀνομία): *lawlessness, lack of obedience or conformity to the law;* e.g., Rom. 4:7; a term which both Lutheran and Reformed orthodox commonly use to denote sin. See *peccata.*

anomoios (ἀνόμοιος): *unlike;* a term used by extreme Arians of the mid-fourth century, the so-called Anomoeans, to argue that the essence of the Father is utterly unlike that of the Son. This view was so repugnant to the majority of Christians that it served to press the large homoiousian party (see *homoios; homoiousios*) toward alliance with the Nicene or Athanasian theology and toward advocacy of the key-term that identified the Nicene position, *homoousios* (q.v.).

ante rem: *before the thing.* See *universalia.*

antepraedicamenta: *antepredicaments;* i.e., the logical categories representing conditions prerequisite to proper predication (*praedicatio,* q.v.). The scholastics enumerate four *antepraedicamenta:* (1) the distinction between univocity, analogy, equivocity, and denomination. Univocity indicates the identical application of a common name, or term, to two things: i.e., the essence, or *quidditas* (q.v.), of the things, as signified by the name, or term, is identical. Analogy indicates a certain resemblance between two essentially different things, as signified by the use of a common name, or term, with reference to both; i.e., analogy indicates similarity or proportional resemblance. Equivocity indicates the use of a common name, or term, with reference to two essentially different and dissimilar things: equivocals have one name, or term, in common, but no real resemblance. Denomination indicates an accidental or incidental relationship as a result of which the name of one thing is used to describe another. (2) The second of the *antepraedicamenta* is the distinction between complex or compound things and incomplex or simple things. A complex thing is a combination of several individual essences, or quiddities; an incomplex thing (or term) is or signifies a single essence or quiddity. (3) The third of the *antepraedicamenta* is the distinction between substance and accidents, or incidental properties, and between singulars and universals. The issue addressed by this distinction is whether a given predicate exists in a thing or is merely predicated of a thing: e.g., a universal of substance, like "man," can be predicated of an individual—Socrates is a man—but is not *in* the individual; a universal accident, however, like whiteness, can be both predicated of an individual thing—paper is white—and said to be in the thing. (4) The fourth of the *antepraedicamenta* is the distinction of genera and species from their *differentiae*, or bases of differentiation: e.g., the genus "living being" is differentiated from the genus "mineral" by the *differentia* life, whereas the subordinate or subalternate genera "animal" and "plant" are known to be subalternate to the genus "living being" because they have in common the essential *differentia*, life, by which the genus "living being" is identified.

The importance of the *antepraedicamenta* to scholastic theology is most obvious in the discussions of the problem of the predication of divine attributes. Before discussing the attributes, scholastic systems almost invariably set down the presuppositions governing predication, viz., whether it is to be univocal, analogical, or denominative; that God is simple or incomplex; whether the attributes are in God or merely predicated of God (and therefore only rationally distinct); and the fact that there is no genus "God." Thus, the attribute of *simplicitas* comes to the fore as a governing category of predication—i.e., as something more than one attribute among others—because it belongs logically to the *antepraedicamenta.*

anthrōpinon organon (ἀνθρώπινον ὄργανον): *an instrument in human form;* i.e., the human nature of Christ considered as *enhypostasis* (q.v.) and as the means by which the Second Person of the Trinity performs his incarnate work.

anthrōpomorphos (ἀνθρωπόμορφος): *anthropomorphic; having a human form;* denied of God as leading either to trinitarian error or to a materialistic view of the divine being; also applied to figurative language in Scripture which seems to predicate human attributes of God. SEE *anthrōpopatheia.*

anthrōpopatheia (ἀνθρωποπάθεια): *anthropopathy; having human feelings, affections, and passions;* a term only figuratively applied to God, specifically, to the incarnation of the Son and his *exinanitio* (q.v.) and *status humiliationis* (q.v.). But, in general, it is reserved either for the pagan gods as a proper predication or for the explanation of the language of Scripture—i.e., anthropopathic language—when it figuratively predicates feelings, affections, and passions of God.

anthrōpos theophoros (ἄνθρωπος θεόφορος): *a God-bearing man.* SEE *homo Deifer.*

antichristus (from the Greek, ἀντίχριστος): *antichrist;* scriptural use
of the word is confined to the Johannine Epistles (1 John 2:18, 22; 4:3;
2 John 7) where a distinction is made between (1) the many anti-
christs now in the world, who work to deceive the godly and who do
not confess Christ, and (2) the Antichrist who is to come who will
deny Christ and, in so doing, deny both the Father and the Son. John
also speaks (1 John 4:3) of the "spirit ... of the antichrist" which
"even now ... is in the world." Following the fathers, the medieval
doctors, and the Reformers, the Protestant orthodox identify the
final Antichrist of the Johannine passages with the "man of sin" or
"son of perdition who opposeth and exalteth himself above all that
is called God" foretold by Paul in 2 Thess. 2:3–4. The orthodox can
therefore distinguish between (1) the antichrist considered generally
(*generaliter*), as indicated by the plural use of the word in 1 John and
by the "spirit of antichrist" now in the world, and (2) the Antichrist
considered specially (*specialiter et kat' exochēn*), as indicated by
singular usage. The former term indicates all heretics and vicious
opponents of the doctrine of Christ; the latter, the great adversary of
Christ who will appear in the last days. Of the latter, the *Antichristus*
properly so called, the orthodox note several characteristics. (1) He
arises from within the church and sets himself against the church
and its doctrine, since his sin is described as *apostasia* (q.v.), or falling
away. (2) He will sit *in templo Dei*, in the temple of God, which is to
say, in the church. (3) He will rule as the head of the church. (4)
From his seat *in templo Dei* and his position as *caput ecclesiae*, he
will exalt himself above the true God and identify himself as God. (5)
He will cause a great defection from the truth so that many will join
him in his apostasy. (6) He will exhibit great power and cause many
"lying wonders," founded upon the power of Satan, in a rule that will
endure until the end of time. On the basis of these characteristics
the orthodox generally identify the Antichrist as the papacy, the
pontifex Romanus. Some attempted to argue a distinction between
an *Antichristus orientalis* and an *Antichristus occidentalis*, an Eastern and a Western Antichrist, the former title belonging to Muham-
mad, the latter to the papacy; but the difficulty in viewing Islam, or
any form of paganism, as an apostasy, strictly so-called, led the
orthodox to identify Rome alone as Antichrist. They also reject the
identification of Antichrist with the *imperium Romanum*, the Roman
Empire, on the ground that the Antichrist is not a secular power or
a result of pagan history. Finally, they also reject the identification of
any single pope as Antichrist on the ground that Antichrist's rule and
power extend farther and endure longer than the rule and power of
any one man. Thus, Antichrist is the institution of the papacy which
has arisen within the church and which assumes religious supremacy

over all Christians, seats itself in the temple of God, and builds its power on lies, wonders, and apostasy. SEE *adventus Christi; dies novissimus.*

antidosis onomatōn (ἀντίδοσις ὀνομάτων): *mutual interchange of names.* SEE *communicatio idiomatum.*

antilytron (ἀντίλυτρον): *ransom;* e.g., 1 Tim. 2:6. SEE *lytron.*

anypeuthynos (ἀνυπεύθυνος): *not accountable or responsible.*

apeitheia (ἀπείθεια): *disobedience;* viz., a form of sin; e.g., Rom. 11:32, describing the fallen condition of all mankind.

aphormē (ἀφορμή): *occasion, opportunity;* e.g., Rom. 7:8, 11.

aphtharsia (ἀφθαρσία): *incorruptibility, immortality;* e.g., 2 Tim. 1:10, with reference to the postresurrection state of humanity. SEE *immortalitas.*

apocalypsis (ἀποκάλυψις): *apocalypse, revelation, disclosure;* specifically, the revelation of the last things that has been reserved by God for the consummation of the age (*consummatio saeculi,* q.v.); e.g., 1 Peter 1:7, 13; 4:13. SEE *dies novissimus.*

apographa (ἀπόγραφα): *copies of an original;* specifically, the scribal copies of the original *autographa* (q.v.) of Scripture. The Protestant scholastics distinguish between the absolute infallibility of the original copies of the biblical books and the textual imperfection of the *apographa.* Their exegetical method intended, by means of mastery of languages and the comparative study of extant texts, to overcome errors caused by the transmission of the text over centuries and to approach the text and meaning of the original *autographa* critically. They assumed, of course, that the *apographa* were essentially correct; they had high praise, in particular, for the work of the Masoretes. In addition, the Protestant orthodox held, as a matter of doctrinal conviction stated in the *locus de Scriptura sacra* of their theological systems, the providential preservation of the text throughout history. SEE *authoritas Scripturae; variae lectiones.*

apokatastasis (ἀποκατάστασις): *restoration;* specifically, the *apokatastasis pantōn* (ἀποκατάστασις πάντων) or *restoration of all things* (e.g., Acts 3:21). In its context in Acts, the phrase indicates only the fulfillment or establishment of the Old Testament prophecies, but it came to mean, largely through the soteriological speculations of Origen, a doctrine of universal redemption. The Protestant scholastics, following the tradition in general and the Reformers in particular, view such doctrine as false and unscriptural. SEE *damnatio; reprobatio.*

apolytrōsis (ἀπολύτρωσις): *redemption;* specifically, the freeing of a captive by payment of ransom; e.g., Rom. 3:24.

apostasia (ἀποστασία): *apostasy;* a willful falling away from, or rebellion against, Christian truth. Apostasy is the rejection of Christ by one who has been a Christian, the ultimate or final apostasy being the so-called unforgivable sin, the *peccatum in Spiritum Sanctum* (q.v.), the sin against the Holy Spirit; apostasy is also one of the characteristic evidences of the antichrist (*antichristus,* q.v.).

aposynagōgos (ἀποσυνάγωγος): *excommunicated;* e.g., John 16:2.

apotelesma (ἀποτέλεσμα): *a conclusion or completion of a work; accomplishment;* the term was used by the fathers with reference to the hypostatic union (SEE *unio personalis*) and the cooperation of the two natures. It figures importantly in the Lutheran doctrine of the *communicatio idiomatum* (q.v.) and generally in both the Lutheran and Reformed doctrines of Christ's work, which is viewed as brought to completion through the cooperation of the natures, in the case of the Reformed, by special gifts of divine grace, in the case of the Lutherans, by a communication of attributes.

apotelesma theandrikon (ἀποτέλεσμα θεανδρικὸν): *theandric operations;* i.e., the common work of the divine and human natures in the God-man. SEE *communicatio idiomatum; communicatio operationum.*

appetitus: *appetite, desire;* specifically, the appetitive faculty or capacity of a being, which seeks out or inclines toward a good. In all spiritual beings, including God, the exercise of will implies appetite. By extension, the propensities of inanimate objects, and even of matter, can be described as appetite. Thus even primary matter (*materia prima,* q.v.) can be said to have an appetite for form. Scholastic theology and philosophy focus in particular upon the appetites of finite spiritual beings which by nature seek out their own good. Since the fall has caused a deprivation and distortion of desire, a distinction must be made between *appetitus rectus,* right desire, and *appetitus perversus* or *inordinatus,* perverse or inordinate desire. It is characteristic of the desire of sinful beings that it misidentifies the good, particularly ultimate good, and perversely, or inordinately, desires finite things as ends in themselves (SEE *frui*). Thus, *appetitus perversus* and *appetitus inordinatus* (q.v.) are synonyms for sin (*peccata*, q.v.).

Appetite can be distinguished further into natural appetite (*appetitus naturalis*), rational or voluntary appetite (*appetitus rationalis sive voluntarius*), and animal or sensual appetite (*appetitus animalis sive sensualis*). Natural appetite is simply the nature of any existent thing to be what it is and to perform its proper acts or operations; e.g., human beings have a natural appetite for breathing! The rational or voluntary appetite, also called *appetitus intellectualis*, intellectual appetite, is the will. Whereas it is the intellect (*intellectus*, q.v.) that perceives and knows objects, it is the will that chooses. Since choice belongs to the will, the will must be exercised in the choice of even purely intellectual objects—thus *appetitus intellectualis*. In addition, since the will and the intellect are not really, but only formally or rationally distinct (SEE *distinctio*), the appetitive function of will is also rational (*rationalis*). Thus, the will desires the goodness, truth, and justice known by the intellect. Thomistic philosophy places intellect higher than will and therefore argues the cognitive control of rational and voluntary appetite. By way of contrast, the Scotist view places will above intellect and argues, in some sense, the voluntaristic control even of objects and cognition. The debate continued among the Protestant orthodox, with the majority holding the natural priority of intellect over will but arguing that, because of the sinful disorder of man following the fall, intellect subserves will and is controlled by desire or appetite in its perception of the good. The problem of sin is particularly clear in the case of the animal or sensual appetite, i.e., the propensity of animal or carnal beings for the concrete objects of sense. The *appetitus animalis sive sensualis* is, thus, emotion or passion (*affectus, passio*), and may be described in terms of love, hate, joy, anger, desire, aversion, and so forth. This appetite, because of its relation to the body, is usually described as being situated "below" the will in the hierarchy of human faculties. In order for the will to be free, it must be capable of rejecting rationally the irrational desires thrust upon it by sense. The Protestant orthodox can describe sin as a disorder of sense that sets the animal or sensual appetite above the will and intellect and thereby places carnal propensities in control of spiritual. SEE *voluntas*.

appetitus inordinatus: *inordinate appetite or desire;* more strongly, **appetitus perversus:** *a perverse or wrong desire;* terms synonymous with sin (*peccata*, q.v.). The former can indicate an undue desire for otherwise good things, whereas the latter indicates a desire that is, in itself, wrong. SEE *appetitus; septem peccata mortalia.*

appetitus rationalis: *rational appetite, reasonable desire;* i.e., the will in act (*actus*) or volition itself. SEE *voluntas.*

appetitus sensitivus: *sensitive or sensible appetite;* viz., the appetite that relates to the senses as such, as distinct from the *appetitus rationalis* (q.v.).

applicatio salutis: *application of salvation;* viz., the application to the believer of the saving effects of Christ's work, accomplished through the *vocatio* (q.v.), or call, of the gospel and the receiving of Christ by *fides* (q.v.).

applicatio salutis a Christo acquisitae: *application of the salvation acquired by Christ;* a term used synonymously with the more common term *ordo salutis* (q.v.). The distinction between the *salus,* or salvation itself, and its *applicatio* or between its *acquisitio* and *applicatio* is significant in view of the all-sufficiency of the former and the limited efficiency of the latter. SEE *satisfactio vicaria.*

apprehensio fiducialis: *faithful apprehension.* SEE *fides.*

apprehensio simplex: *simple or basic apprehension;* i.e., the mere apprehension by the mind of a datum received by the senses, as distinct from the evaluation of the datum by the intellect.

arbitrium: *choice, decision, judgment.* SEE *liberum arbitrium.*

arbitrium liberatum: *a liberated choice;* viz., the human capacity for choice as liberated by grace for the good, distinguished from *arbitrium servum,* bound choice, the capacity for choice as enslaved to sin. The *arbitrium servum* corresponds with the Augustinian term *non posse non peccare* (q.v.), not able not to sin; *arbitrium liberatum* corresponds with *posse non peccare,* able not to sin. SEE *liberum arbitrium.*

arbor scientiae boni et mali: *tree of the knowledge of good and evil.* SEE *malum.*

arbor vitae: *tree of life.*

archē (ἀρχή): *beginning, origin, first principle;* hence, ordering principle, or rule, particularly from patristic development of Greek philosophical language. The term is sometimes applied to God as the Creator and orderer of all things and sometimes, also, to God the Father, insofar as the First Person of the Trinity is the *fons totius divinitatis* (q.v.), the source or ground of the whole Godhead. SEE *Trinitas.*

archetypos (ἀρχέτυπος): *archetype; pattern in an ultimate sense.* SEE *theologia archetypa.*

argumenta naturae: *arguments from nature;* a reference to the *a posteriori* (q.v.) proofs of the existence of God.

armilla aurea: *a golden chain;* also **catena aurea:** *a golden chain;* terms used among the Reformed orthodox as references to and descriptions of Rom. 8:30, "Whom he did predestinate, them he also called: and whom he called, them he also justified: and whom he justified, them he also glorified." In other words, the *armilla* or *catena aurea* is the unbreakable chain of God's electing grace as it issues forth in the order of salvation (*ordo salutis,* q.v.).

articuli antecedentes/constituentes/consequentes: *antecedent/constituent/consequent articles;* a distinction in doctrines devised by the Lutheran scholastic Calixtus for the sake of promoting church unity. He proposed three categories of doctrine: (1) *Articuli antecedentes,* or antecedent articles, are those known to human reason independent of divine revelation, e.g., the doctrines of the existence of God, of providence, and of the immortality of the soul. (2) The *articuli constituentes,* or constituent articles, are those fundamental truths of the Christian revelation which are distinctive to it and which are doctrinally necessary and normative, e.g., the doctrines of sin, of grace, and of redemption, including concepts like those of original sin, of salvation by grace alone, and of the two natures of Christ. (3) *Articuli consequentes,* or consequent articles, are those doctrines derived by way of logical elaboration from the constituent articles or fundamentals, such as the doctrine of the communication of proper qualities, or *communicatio idiomatum* (q.v.), in the person of Christ and the doctrine of Christ's sacramental presence. Calixtus assumed that agreement among Christians would arise rationally upon the *articuli antecedentes,* and would arise dogmatically on the subjects presented in the *articuli constituentes* on the basis of the *consensus quinquesaecularis,* the consensus of the first five centuries of the church, but would not be needed in the *articuli consequentes,* which were matters capable of argument and difference. Debate between Christians could be reduced to the *articuli consequentes* and reunion of Christendom might become possible. The orthodox Lutherans condemned Calixtus's views and argued that all doctrine given by revelation is in some sense fundamental and that Christian reunion cannot rest upon a willingness to overlook differences in doctrine. See *articuli fundamentales; articuli fundamentales secundarii.*

articuli fidei: *articles of faith; the body of individual doctrines of the Christian faith;* that which is believed, as distinguished from the precepts of love (*praecepta caritatis*, q.v.) which are to be obeyed.

articuli fundamentales: *fundamental articles (of faith or doctrine);* a doctrinal concept originated among the early Lutheran scholastics and later adopted by the Reformed, according to which the basic doctrines necessary to the Christian faith are distinguished from secondary or logically derivative doctrines. Thus *articuli fundamentales* are those doctrines without which Christianity cannot exist and the integrity of which is necessary to the preservation of the faith. This category of fundamental articles includes only articles given by revelation, viz., the doctrine of sin and its consequences; the doctrine of the person and work of Christ; the doctrine of the resurrection; and the doctrine of the scriptural Word as the ground of faith. These *articuli fundamentales* are sometimes called, by the Lutheran scholastics, *articuli fundamentales primarii*, primary fundamental articles, in order to distinguish them from certain highly important derivative articles, like baptism and the Lord's Supper, which treat of the mediation of grace and concerning which the Lutherans had major differences with the Reformed. These latter doctrines the Lutherans refer to as *articuli fundamentales secundarii* (q.v.). See *articuli fidei; fundamentum fidei.*

articuli fundamentales secundarii: *secondary fundamental articles;* a distinction in fundamental articles made by the Lutheran orthodox who recognized that some of the *articuli fundamentales*, such as those concerned with baptism and the Lord's Supper, might be lacking in a person's faith, or at least lacking in correct definition, and that person still be saved by faith in the promises of the gospel, since forgiveness of sins rests on faith in Christ, as witnessed in the Word, and not on acceptance of the doctrines of baptism and the Lord's Supper. A similar generalization can be made in relation to the secondary fundamental article concerning the *communicatio idiomatum* (q.v.). The Lutheran scholastics argued, through use of the distinction, that the Reformed were Christian and participated in the promise of salvation in Christ because of their acceptance of the primary fundamental doctrines of the person and work of Christ but that their doctrinal system was endangered, even their faith in the primary fundamentals, by error in the secondary fundamentals. The distinction was also useful in refuting the Calixtine thesis that Christians need agree only on "constituent" doctrines (*constituentia*) in order to unite and might disagree slightly on "consequent," or derivative, doctrines (*consequentia*). The Lutheran orthodox argued that *consequentia* were not *articuli non-fundamentales* (q.v.) but *articuli fundamentales secundarii* and, therefore, still a major barrier to union. SEE *articuli antecedentes/constituentes/consequentes.*

articuli non-fundamentales: *nonfundamental articles;* articles the denial of which does not endanger salvation since they are not fundamental to the maintenance of Christian truth and are not concerned with the basic objects of faith. Here the Lutheran scholastics include such doctrines as the identity of Antichrist and the nature of angels. Such doctrines, nonetheless, are scriptural and, therefore, if rightly stated, edifying.

articuli puri/mixti: *pure/mixed articles;* articles of doctrine distinguished as to their derivation from the disciplines of theology and philosophy—those deriving from one discipline alone are "pure," and those deriving from both are "mixed." The existence of mixed articles, e.g., the existence and idea of God, demands that theology answer the question of its relation to philosophy. SEE *usus philosophiae.*

articulum omnium fundamentalissimum: *the most fundamental article of all;* a term applied by Lutheran scholastics to the doctrine of justification, also called the *articulus stantis et cadentis ecclesiae* (q.v.).

articulus stantis et cadentis ecclesiae: literally, *the article of the standing and falling of the church;* i.e., the article of Christian doctrine necessary to the life and perpetuation of the church; a phrase used by Luther and thereafter, especially by Lutheran theologians, to describe the doctrine of justification.

asarkos (ἄσαρκος): *without the flesh.* SEE *ensarkos; Logos asarkos.*

asebeia (ἀσέβεια): *impiety, ungodliness;* viz., a specific form or variety of sin; e.g., 2 Tim. 2:16. SEE *peccata; religio.*

aseitas: *aseity, self-existence;* a term derived from the language of self-existence used with reference to God by the scholastics: God is said to exist *a se,* from himself, thus, *a-se-itas.* The term is used synonymously with *autotheos* (q.v.), of himself God. The Reformed orthodox, in their polemical rejection of tritheism, Arianism, Socinianism, the heresy of Valentine Gentilis, and the allied subordinationism of Arminian theology, define the consubstantiality of the Son and the Spirit with the Father as the essential *aseitas* of each of the three persons. In this definition, they distinguish between *aseitas personalis* and *aseitas essentialis,* the former term, personal aseity, involving a trinitarian error and the latter term, essential aseity, interpreting *homoousios* (q.v.) correctly. Thus, insofar as the *deitas,* or divinity, of the Son and Spirit is communicated, which is to say, insofar as they are persons in relation to the Father, they are not *a se,* but *a Patre,* from the Father. *Aseitas,* therefore, does not indicate an *autoprosopon,* a person of itself. Nevertheless, the *deitas* that the Son and Spirit have fully and completely is not a derived deity or divinity. In order to be truly God, the Son and Spirit, considered according to their divinity or according to the divine essence that is theirs, must be *autotheos* and have the attribute of *aseitas.* The Reformed doctrine, then, acknowledges the *aseitas* of the divine essence as such in each of the persons and, consequently, the *aseitas* of the Son and the Spirit considered *essentialiter.* The doctrinal alternative, as found in Socinianism and Arminianism, is the essential subordination of the Son and Spirit on grounds of generation and procession.

assensus: *assent, spiritual acknowledgment,* or *agreement;* a necessary component of *fides* (q.v.). Used without modification, a simple assent to a truth by the intellect. The scholastics distinguish three degrees of assent: *firmitas, certitudo* (q.v.), and *evidentia.* Assent with *firmitas,* or firmness, is full assent without hesitation to something accepted purely on authority. Assent with *certitudo,* or certainty, is full assent founded firmly upon a solid ground of accepted testimony. Assent to *evidentia,* or evidence, rests not on testimony, but on proof drawn either from sense-experience or reason. The Protestant scholastics will argue that the *assensus theoreticus* of faith is assent with *firmitas* and *certitudo* only. *Evidentia,* by way of contrast, belongs to a science (*scientia,* q.v.).

assensus historicus: *historical assent;* viz., assent to the historical veracity of an account. Such assent correlates with *fides historica,* or historical faith, and, like *notitia historica* (q.v.), or historical knowledge, does not belong to the essence of faith and is not saving. See *assensus; fides.*

assumptio carnis: *the assumption of the flesh;* viz., incarnation as described in John 1:14. SEE *incarnatio.*

athanasia (ἀθανασία): *immortality;* e.g., 1 Cor. 15:53. SEE *immortalitas.*

athetēsis (ἀθέτησις): *a setting aside* or *annulment;* e.g., Heb. 7:18; 9:26.

atreptōs kai asynchytōs (ἀτρέπτως καὶ ἀσυγχύτως): *without change and without confusion;* a phrase from the Chalcedonian definition referring to and defining the relationship of Christ's divine and human natures in the *unio personalis* (q.v.). Thus, the natures are united without change or confusion in the person of Christ. The phrase was designed to exclude the Eutychian heresy which had threatened the doctrine of the person of Christ by merging the divine and human natures, i.e., by arguing a communication of divine attributes to the human nature in such a way as to divinize Christ's humanity and, in effect, argue one nature only in the incarnate Word, and that a divine nature. Eutychianism is, thus, a *confusio naturarum*, a confusion of natures. SEE *adiairetōs kai achōristōs; communicatio idiomatum.*

attemperatio. SEE *accommodatio.*

attributa divina: *divine attributes;* viz., the conceptions or designations of the divine essence employed by the finite intellect in its declaration concerning what God is (*Quid sit Deus?*). Since the intellect can conceive of things only by the enumeration of their attributes and cannot conceive of a single designation suitable to the infinite and simple essence of God, it designates the divine essence in terms of a series of *perfectiones* or *proprietates,* which it attributes to or predicates of God; thus, attributes. The scholastics recognize that they must immediately qualify the way in which attributes or properties are predicated of God. (1) The *attributa* are not *accidentia* inhering in and separable from the divine substance but are *attributa essentialia,* i.e., the divine attributes *are* the essence of God himself. (2) Since God is not a composite being, the *attributa* are not parts of God but, in their identity with the divine essence, are also identical with each other. (3) Since there is nothing prior to God and since the divine *essentia* and divine existence (*esse,* q.v.) are inseparable, the attributes are identical also with the existence of God, so that, e.g., in God *being* and *being holy* are identical. (4) The attributes are, nevertheless, truly and properly predicated of God. Thus, the attributes are not distinct from one another or from the divine essence *realiter,* really, as one thing is distinct from another; nor are they distinct merely *rationaliter*, rationally, in the reasoning of the finite subject only (*ratio ratiocinans*, q.v.). In denominating the attributes, the human mind rests its conclusions on the exercise of divine power in the world and on the explicit revelation of God, so that the attributes are predicated of God and distinguished from one another on the basis of a reasoning founded in the reality of the thing under consideration, viz., God (*ratio ratiocinata, cum fundamento in re*). This *distinctio rationis ratiocinatae*, or distinction of ratiocinative reason (SEE *distinctio*), also called a *distinctio virtualis*, is taught by nearly all the Lutheran and Reformed scholastics. It is, incidentally, the solution to the problem of predication proposed by Thomas Aquinas and Henry of Ghent. The Scotist concept of a *distinctio formalis*, or formal distinction, is occasionally used by the Reformed orthodox to explain the distinction of attributes in the divine work *ad extra*.

After propounding these general definitions of *attributa divina*, the orthodox Protestants recognize the need for proper classification of attributes. (*N.B.* All attributes listed in this section are defined individually in the alphabetical order of the lexicon.) On this issue, the Lutherans and the Reformed differ sharply. Reformed scholastics manifest a distinct preference for division of the attributes into *incommunicabilia* and *communicabilia*, incommunicable and communicable attributes, the former category containing those attributes which find no analogy in the finite order and which cannot be conceived as in any way transferable to creatures (*finitum non capax infiniti*, q.v.), and the latter category containing those mirrored in the creature, specifically, in the human being. The *incommunicabilia* are *unitas, simplicitas, aseitas, infinitas, immutabilitas, immensitas, omnipraesentia, perfectio, aeternitas, independentia, necessitas, omnisufficientia*, and *primitas;* the *attributa communicabilia* are *beatitudo, fidelitas, gloria, immortalitas, lux, magnitudo, maiestas, scientia* or *omniscientia, potentia* or *omnipotentia, sanctitas, sapientia* or *omnisapientia, spiritualitas* and its corollary *invisibilitas, vita*, and *voluntas;* plus the so-called *affectus voluntatis Dei*, affections of the divine will, *amor, benevolentia, clementia, gratia, ira, longanimitas, misericordia, odium, patientia;* and also the *virtutes Dei*, divine virtues, *bonitas, felicitas, iustitia*, and *veracitas*. The obvious defect in the classification is that some of the *attributa incommunicabilia* do have analogies in the created order, such as *perfectio* and *independentia* or *simplicitas*, albeit not in an absolute sense, while none of the *attributa communicabilia* are found in creatures in the perfection in which they occur in God—human *scientia* does fall short of *omniscientia!* Under the impact of Cartesianism, some of the Reformed adopted a classification that distinguished *proprietates essen-*

tiales, essential properties, viz., *aseitas, primitas, unitas, spiritualitas, simplicitas, infinitas,* and *perfectio,* as governing categories, from attributes of intellect (*intellectus,* q.v.) and attributes of will (*voluntas,* q.v.). The Lutherans not only perceived the defect of the classification of attributes into *incommunicabilia* and *communicabilia,* but also were bound to reject it totally on christological grounds. According to the Lutheran view of the *communicatio idiomatum* (q.v.) all the divine attributes were communicable, at least in the instance of the divine-human person of Christ. Lutheran orthodoxy, therefore, favored two alternative patterns that produced about the same arrangement. First, division into *attributa positiva* and *attributa negativa,* corresponding to the two ways of denominating divine attributes, viz., by the *via eminentiae* (q.v.), the raising of creaturely attributes to their infinite perfection, and the *via negativa* (q.v.), the negation of creaturely imperfection. Thus, *attributa negativa* are *unitas, simplicitas, infinitas, immensitas, immutabilitas, aeternitas,* and their corollaries; while *attributa positiva* are *sapientia, scientia, vita, sanctitas, veracitas, potentia, bonitas,* and *iustitia.* Second, this division can also be inferred from the consideration of the attributes as either *immanentia* or *operativa,* the former category referring to the inward life of the Godhead that does not relate directly to the *opera Dei ad extra* (q.v.), and the latter category referring specifically to those attributes that are manifest in the *opera ad extra* and that describe the relationship of God to the finite order. SEE *antepraedicamenta; via causalitatis.*

attributa ecclesiae: *attributes of the church;* viz., the attributes named in the Constantinopolitan Creed, *una, sancta, catholica,* and *apostolica.* The Protestant scholastics agree that the church, considered *in se,* is one in an internal unity of faith; is holy in the person of its head, Christ, the *caput ecclesiae,* and holy also in its doctrine, laws, and sacraments; is catholic, or universal, in place or extent, in all time, and in all the faithful everywhere, as opposed to spatially and temporally limited heterodoxy; and is apostolic in its foundation and its doctrines. SEE *ecclesia; notae ecclesiae.*

attributum: *attribute, property, characteristic, proper quality;* synonyms, *proprietas, qualitas.* Since the sum of the attributes of any material or spiritual thing, in their interrelation, is the form or, more strictly speaking, the essence of the thing, the *attributes* identify what the thing is and are inseparable from its substance (*substantia,* q.v.) insofar as any *ens* must have both *esse* (q.v.) and *essentia* (q.v.), or both substance and form (*forma,* q.v.).

attritio: *imperfect contrition, attrition;* i.e., in medieval scholastic and Roman Catholic theology, a sorrow for and detestation of sin arising, not out of the proper ground of contrition, filial fear (*timor filialis*), but rather out of a servile fear (*timor servilis*) of God and his punishment. As such, *attritio* is not sufficient for forgiveness. Nonetheless, the medieval scholastics can argue that attrition is a gift of God insofar as it prepares the soul for true contrition. The Reformers deny any value to *attritio,* particularly in relation to the structure of the Catholic sacrament of penance (*poenitentia,* q.v.) as a preparation for the contrition (*contritio,* q.v.), confession (*confessio,* q.v.), and satisfaction (*satisfactio,* q.v.) of the penitential system.

auctor primarius Scripturae sacrae: *primary author of sacred Scripture, viz., God;* the term recognizes that the human writers of Scripture are authors only in a secondary sense, insofar as the *mandatum scribendi* (q.v.) comes from God.

auctoritas. SEE *authoritas.*

aulos (ἄϋλος): *immaterial or spiritual.* SEE *spiritus.*

autexousion (αὐτεξούσιον): *free will;* also autexousiotēs (αὐτεξουσιότης): *free will;* and adjectivally, autexousios (αὐτεξούσιος): *having free will.*

authentia historica: *historical authenticity or authority;* also authentia historiae: *authenticity of history.* SEE *authoritas Scripturae; historicus.*

authentia normae seu praecepti: *preceptive or normative authenticity or authority.* SEE *authoritas Scripturae.*

authoritas: *authority, originality,* or *genuineness;* the power, dignity, or influence of a work which derives from its *author* or *auctor.*

authoritas divina duplex: *twofold divine authority;* a distinction between (1) the *authoritas rerum,* or authority of the things of Scripture, the *substantia doctrinae* (substance of doctrine), and (2) the *authoritas verborum,* or authority of the words of Scripture, arising from the *accidens scriptionis,* the accident of the writing. The authority of the *substantia,* or *res,* is a formal, inward authority that belongs both to the text of Scripture in the original languages and to the accurate translations of Scripture. The *authoritas verborum* is an external and accidental authority that belongs only to the text in the original languages and is a property or accident lost in translation. Thus the *infallibilitas* of the originals is both *quoad verbum* and *quoad res*, whereas the *infallibilitas* of the versions is only *quoad res*.

authoritas Scripturae: *the authority of Scripture;* viz., the power or genuineness of Scripture which rests on its inspiration (SEE *inspiratio; theopneustos*) and therefore on the absolute authority of God, the primary author of Scripture. The *authoritas* of Scripture can, therefore, be defined in terms of its *authentia,* or authenticity. This *authentia* is distinguished by the Protestant scholastics as twofold. Scripture is authoritative and authentic (1) as the *principium cognoscendi et obiectum formale fidei ac theologiae revelatae,* the foundation of knowing and formal object of faith and of revealed theology; and (2) as the canon or norm, resting on inspiration, for all discernment of truth and falsehood in matters of faith and morals (*in rebus fidei ac morum*). The first category, the authority of Scripture as *principium cognoscendi* (SEE *principia theologiae*), argues the certitude (*certitudo,* q.v.) and infallibility (*infallibilitas*) of Scripture in view of its divine origin. The arguments on which this category of *authoritas* rests are distinguished by the scholastics into internal, intrinsic proofs and external, extrinsic proofs. The former, which argue an *authentia intrinseca,* or intrinsic authenticity, include the material simplicity, dignity, and gravity of the text together with formal attributes of perfect holiness (*sanctitas perfecta*), truth of statement without admixture of error (*veritas assertionum sine admixtis erroribus*), and the sufficiency of the scriptural revelation for salvation (*sufficientia ad salutem*). The latter proofs, which indicate the *authentia extrinseca,* or extrinsic authenticity, point to the antiquity of the Scriptures and their doctrines, the obvious gift of profound knowledge to the human writers of Scripture to which they themselves would have had no natural access, the many miracles attending the production and preservation of the text, and the divine purpose or mission to which the Scriptures testify and to the furtherance of which they contribute. In addition to those extrinsic testimonies drawn from the circumstances of the text itself, the orthodox point to the further extrinsic testimony of the church to Scripture through the holiness and constancy of the martyrs and the conservation and propagation of the Word in history. Some of the Protestant scholastics also distinguish a separate category of *authentia historiae,* or authenticity of history, according to which Scripture is argued to be historically true in its record of words, deeds, events, and doctrines. Generally, however, this historical *authoritas* is subsumed under the attribute of truth belonging to the category of *authentia intrinseca.*

The second major division of scriptural authority, also resting on the divine inspiration of the text, is the *authoritas canonica sive normativa,* the canonical or normative authority, or *authentia normae sive praecepti,* the authenticity of norm or of precept. This authority, or authenticity, of Scripture refers primarily to the actual use in the church of the text as the rule of faith and morals and to the character of Scripture as *axiopistos* (q.v.), trustworthy, or *autopistos* (q.v.), trustworthy in itself (*in se*). The *authoritas canonica* or *normativa,* therefore, is such that it requires assent to the doctrines and demands of Scripture and the use of events and actions in Scripture as moral examples for imitation. Nor is this an authority or authenticity that is subject either to argument or to proof; it rests upon the *res,* or things, given in the text, from their very substance, apart from any collateral or external testimony to them. Whereas the *authentia historiae* and the general *veritas Scripturae* refer to all matters and events given in Scripture, including the words, actions, and teachings of Satan and the godless, insofar as they are reported and stated accurately, the *authentia normae sive praecepti* pertains only to the words, actions, and teachings of God and the godly as presented for edification. Thus, Satan's promises to Christ in the temptation (Matt. 4:1–11) have the *authentia historiae,* but obviously not the *authentia normae sive praecepti* or the *authoritas canonica sive normativa.*

autocheiria (αὐτοχειρία): *murder done with one's own hand;* from **autocheiros** (αὐτόχειρος): *with one's own hand.*

autodidaktos (αὐτοδίδακτος): *self-taught* or *self-instructed;* a term applied to Christ in his human nature, insofar as he was wise apart from human teaching because of the indwelling Logos and through the grace or *gratiae habituales* bestowed on him by the Holy Spirit.

autographa (αὐτόγραφα): *autographs* or *originals;* specifically, the original autograph copies of the books of the Bible as they came from the hands of the inspired authors. The *autographa* are distinguished from *apographa* (ἀπόγραφα) or copies. The Protestant scholastics do not press the point made by their nineteenth-century followers that the infallibility of Scripture and the freedom of Scripture from error reside absolutely in the *autographa* and only in a derivative sense in the *apographa;* rather, the scholastics argue positively that the *apographa* preserve intact the true words of the prophets and the apostles and that the God-breathed (*theopneustos,* q.v.) character of Scripture is manifest in the *apographa* as well as in the *autographa.* In other words, the issue primarily addressed by the seventeenth-century orthodox in their discussion of the *autographa* is the continuity of the extant copies in Hebrew and in Greek with the originals both *quoad res,* with respect to the thing or subject of the text, and *quoad verba,* with respect to the words of the text. In the nineteenth century the issue addressed was primarily the integrity and infallibility of the *autographa* as distinct from and prior to the *apographa,* or scribal copies. SEE *apographa; authoritas divina duplex; Scriptura sacra.*

autopistos (αὐτόπιστος): *trustworthy in and of itself;* specifically, a term used by the Protestant scholastics to denote the self-authenticating character of scriptural authority. *Autopistos* is often paired with *axiopistos* (ἀξιόπιστος), meaning simply "trustworthy." If Scripture is trustworthy in and of itself (*in se* and *per se*), no external authority, whether church or tradition, need be invoked in order to ratify Scripture as the norm of faith and practice. The use of *autopistos* as an attribute of Scripture figured importantly in the Protestant orthodox debate with Rome and with the Roman Catholic concept of the church's *magisterium* (q.v.). SEE *Scriptura sacra.*

autoritas. SEE *authoritas.*

autotheos (αὐτοθεός): *of himself God; i.e., God by nature;* a term applied to each of the persons of the Trinity, in particular to the Son and the Spirit, in order to identify them as divine by nature rather than by grace. The term is specifically applied to the Son to distinguish him from "sons" by creation and "sons" by adoption. SEE *aseitas.*

autozōos (αὐτόζωος): *having life in and of one's self.* SEE *vita Dei.*

auxilium sine quo non: *assistance without which not;* i.e., an assistance without which a desired result cannot occur, as distinguished from an *auxilium quo,* an assistance by which, i.e., an assistance that, in a positive sense, inevitably brings about a result. The former term can be used to describe resistible grace (*gratia resistibilis,* q.v.); the latter, irresistible grace (*gratia irresistibilis,* q.v.). These terms are important in describing the grace present to man prior to the fall as a necessary but resistible assistance, *auxilium sine quo non,* i.e., an assistance unlike the grace of election, which, according to the Reformed, is an irresistible *auxilium quo.* SEE *donum concreatum; donum superadditum.*

avaritia: *greed, avarice.* SEE *septem peccata mortalia.*

axiopistos (ἀξιόπιστος): *trustworthy, worthy of faith;* an attribute of Scripture frequently paired with *autopistos* (q.v.). SEE *Scriptura sacra.*

Bb

baptismus: *baptism;* the first in order of the two sacraments revealed in and enjoined by the New Testament. Baptism is a *sacramentum* (q.v.) because it is a ritual act commanded by God, consisting in a visible sign of God's grace and accompanied by a divine promise. The purpose or goal (*finis*) and the effect (*effectus*) of baptism are, immediately or proximately, the regeneration or renovation (SEE *regeneratio*) of the baptized and, ultimately, their eternal salvation. The scholastics here recognize a distinction between the baptism of infants and the baptism of adults. For infants the sacrament of baptism provides the ordinary or ordained means of regeneration and only secondarily functions as a seal (*obsignatio*) of faith insofar as it is a seal of the *foedus gratiae* (q.v.), or covenant of grace, into which children of believers are born. Lutherans as well as Reformed view baptism as the sign or seal of the covenant of grace, but the Lutherans argue that infants do not belong to the covenant or partake of covenant-holiness (*sanctitas foederalis*) before baptism, whereas the Reformed argue the covenant before baptism. For adults the sacrament of baptism provides principally a seal and a testimony of the grace already bestowed by the Word and, second-arily, an augmentation of the regenerating grace of God. Thus, infants are baptized before hearing the Word, in the expectation that they will receive from their baptism the first-fruits of the gracious work of the Spirit, including faith, whereas adults must first hear the Word and be brought by it to faith and only thereafter are baptized. Against the Anabaptists, who refuse baptism to infants on the ground that infants cannot have faith, both the Lutherans and the Reformed argue the efficacy of divine grace and the fact that faith arises because of grace in the case both of infants and of adults. SEE *abrenuntiatio.*

baptismus flaminis: *baptism of the breath or wind;* i.e., the special gifts of the Spirit poured out on the church (Acts 1:5).

baptismus fluminis: *the baptism of running water,* or simply, *the baptism of water.* SEE *baptismus.*

56

baptismus sanguinis: *the baptism of blood;* i.e., martyrdom.

beati: *the blessed in heaven;* i.e., those who are no longer *in via* (q.v.) but *in patria* (q.v.). The *beati,* because of their purified state—immortality and incorruptibility—are no longer tainted with *concupiscentia* (q.v.) and can now attain the *visio Dei* (q.v.). The knowledge of God accessible to the *beati* is the highest form of human theology except for the theology of the human Jesus in his union with the Word. SEE *theologia beatorum; theologia ectypa.*

beatitudo: *beatitude, blessedness;* specifically, *beatitudo aeterna,* eternal blessedness. The scholastics define *beatitudo aeterna* as the final condition in eternity of all who persevere in faith, consisting in the supernatural perfection of body and soul as bestowed on the faithful after death by the pure grace of God in Christ, to his own eternal glory. The supernatural perfection of the body is the incorruptibility and spirituality of the resurrection (*resurrectio,* q.v.), whereas the supernatural perfection of the soul consists in the intellectual *visio Dei* (q.v.), or vision of God, and the voluntary perfection of love for God, so that the will (*voluntas,* q.v.) can no longer sin. Thus, blessedness consists in the perfect vision and enjoyment (*frui,* q.v.) of God.

Beatitudo consistit in perfecta Dei visione et fruitione: *Blessedness consists in the perfect vision and enjoyment of God.* SEE *beatitudo; frui; visio Dei.*

Bene docet, qui bene distinguit: *He teaches well who distinguishes well;* i.e., good teaching of difficult points depends on the ability to make careful distinctions; a scholastic maxim that illustrates the heart of the scholastic method.

benedictio: *benediction, blessing;* either the blessing of God or the liturgical blessing at the conclusion of the service of worship.

beneficium: *benefit, gift.*

beneplacitum: *good pleasure;* applied restrictively by the Protestant scholastics to God, thus, *beneplacitum Dei,* the good pleasure of God, or divine good pleasure; also, specifically, *beneplacitum voluntatis Dei,* the good pleasure of the will of God, indicating the ground of God's elective choice (Eph. 1:5), principally in Reformed theology, where emphasis is placed on the freedom and sovereignty of the divine purpose. SEE *causa; consilium Dei; decretum; praedestinatio; voluntas Dei.*

benevolentia: literally, *goodwill* or *good willing;* a synonym for *eudokia* (q.v.) and *favor Dei,* related also to the good pleasure (*beneplacitum,* q.v.) of God. The *benevolentia Dei* is one of the affections or attributes of God's will. SEE *amor Dei; attributa divina; bonitas Dei; voluntas Dei.*

bibitio spiritualis et sacramentalis: *a spiritual and sacramental drinking.* SEE *manducatio.*

bonitas: *goodness;* specifically, moral goodness as distinct from *dignitas,* or goodness in the sense of merit. The scholastics also distinguish between *bonitas absoluta,* absolute goodness, and *bonitas dependens ab alio,* goodness dependent on another, or derived goodness; and also between *bonitas essentialis sive substantialis,* essential or substantial good, i.e., the goodness that belongs to the being or essence of things as created by God, and *bonitas accidentalis,* accidental or incidental goodness, i.e., goodness that is in a thing as an incidental property and that can be lost by the thing. *Bonitas essentialis* is also contrasted with *bonitas graduum,* a goodness of degrees. All creatures, insofar as they are created and given being by God, have an essential goodness, but none has a perfect goodness of degrees, since the perfect or highest degree of goodness belongs to God only.

bonitas Dei: *the goodness or moral excellence of God;* a term used by scholastics in arguing that goodness belongs to God in an absolute sense and, with all the divine attributes (*attributa divina,* q.v.), is to be viewed as identical with the divine essence in its perfection. Thus God is good *in se,* in himself, and is the absolute good, the ground and standard of all created goodness. By extension, therefore, God is good respectively or in relation to his creatures. The *bonitas Dei* in relation to creatures is to be considered in three ways: (1) *efficienter,* or efficiently, as the efficient cause that produces all finite or created goodness; (2) as the *exemplar* or *causa exemplaris,* the standard or exemplary cause, of all created good, i.e., as the standard of good according to which goodness is created and judged; (3) as the *summum bonum* (q.v.), the highest good or final cause (*causa finalis,* q.v.), the ultimate end of all good things. Thus the *bonitas Dei* is most clearly manifest in the goodwill (*benevolentia,* q.v.) of God toward his creatures, specifically, in the positive attributes or affections of God's will, grace (SEE *gratia Dei*), mercy (*misericordia,* q.v.), longsuffering (*longanimitas,* q.v.), love (SEE *amor Dei*), and patience (*patientia,* q.v.).

bonum increatum: *uncreated or increate good;* i.e., God, as the self-existent ground of all finite, created good. SEE *bonitas Dei.*

bonum iustificum: *the good or merit that justifies;* viz., the *meritum Christi,* or merit of Christ, which is the object (*obiectum*) of justifying faith.

boulētikōs (βουλητικῶς): *having a will* or *capable of exerting a will;* from **boulēsis** (βούλησις): *will* or *purpose.*

Cc

capacitas nolendi/capacitas volendi: *ability or capacity to refuse or to not will/ability or capacity to will.* SEE *facultas aversandi gratiam; gratia resistibilis.*

capacitas passiva: *passive capacity;* as, e.g., the human capacity for grace according to Lutheran and Reformed monergism. The individual, before grace, cannot seek grace actively but can only receive grace passively. SEE *conversio; gratia.*

caput ecclesiae: *head of the church;* viz., Christ.

caput electorum: *head of the elect;* in Reformed theology, a term applied to Christ as Mediator and second Adam, related to the concept of Christ's federal headship. SEE *foedus gratiae; pactum salutis; primus electorum.*

carentia: *lack, deprivation, privation;* a term used in Augustinian theology to describe sin. SEE *privatio; privatio boni.*

caritas: *love;* particularly love as affection or esteem; self-giving love, synonymous with *benevolentia;* as distinct from *amor* (q.v.) and *dilectio* (q.v.).

castigationes paternae: *paternal castigations;* i.e., limited, temporal punishments, inflicted on believers by God as Father, which have the effect of drawing them away from sin and saving them from the fate of eternal punishment. These punishments are also referred to as *paideia* (παιδεία). SEE *tentatio.*

catena: *a chain;* specifically, a chain of texts excerpted from the fathers for use in exegetical or theological explanation; also a chain of readings from Scripture. Collections of this kind, also called *florilegia* ("gatherings of flowers"), were common in the Middle Ages. Thus, Thomas Aquinas's *Catena aurea* is an extended gloss on the text of the Gospels. The term *catena aurea* is also used as a reference to Rom. 8:30 (SEE *armilla aurea*).

causa: *cause;* that which brings about motion or mutation. Following Aristotle, the medieval scholastics, the Reformers, and the Protestant scholastics held a basic fourfold schema of causality: (1) the *causa efficiens,* the efficient cause, or productive, effective cause, which is the agent productive of the motion or mutation in any sequence of causes and effects; (2) the *causa materialis,* or material cause, which is the substantial basis of the motion or mutation, the *materia* on which the *causa efficiens* operates; (3) the *causa formalis,* or formal cause, which is the *essentia* (q.v.) or *quidditas* (q.v.) of the thing, and which is determinative of *what* the thing caused is to be; (4) the *causa finalis,* or final cause, which is the ultimate purpose for which a thing is made or an act is performed. E.g., in the creation of the world God is the efficient cause; *materia prima* (q.v.), the material cause; the *forma substantialis* (SEE *forma*), or substantial form, which determines the kind of substance drawn out of *materia prima,* is the formal cause; and the glory of God the final cause. Similarly, the Reformed will apply the fourfold causality to the election of believers to salvation, varying occasionally the material and formal causes. Here the *causa efficiens* is the *beneplacitum* (q.v.) or good pleasure of God; the *causa materia* is Christ; the *causa formalis,* the preaching of the gospel; and the *causa finalis,* the praise and glory of God. In the logic of causality, or ordination of a causal sequence, the final cause takes precedence over the material and formal causes; i.e., the ordination of the end (*finis* or *telos*) must precede the selection of means requisite to the achievement of that end. This logic of causality was used by the supralapsarians among the Reformed to argue the correctness of their teaching over the infralapsarian position; i.e., election and reprobation, considered as ends manifesting the final glory of God, stand prior in the order of the decrees (*ordo rerum decretarum,* q.v.) to the establishment of creation and fall as means to those ends. The logic of causality also dictates that proximate or closely related causes produce only proximate or closely related effects. Ultimate ends can be appointed only by the first cause. This means that the realm of finite agents can produce only finite results or effects, whereas an infinite agent or cause, viz., God, is needed for the ordination of ends or goals beyond the finite order. In other words, no effect can be greater than its cause, and there must be a certain proportionality between all causes and their effects. This logic is neatly summed up in the maxim, *Quod non habet, dare non potest* ("What it does not have, it cannot impart"). SEE *supra lapsum.*

causa deficiens: *deficient cause;* a term used with reference to the origin of sin in the Augustinian system held by both Lutheran and Reformed. Since God created all things good, there can be no evil thing that exists as the efficient cause (*causa efficiens*) of sin. Sin must therefore arise, not out of the efficiency of some evil existent agent, but rather out of a deficiency in the willing of something by an otherwise good agent. Thus, the *causa peccati* is a deficient, and not an efficient, cause, a deficient willing rather than an efficient willing, i.e., a willing of something not as it ought to be willed. Neither the will itself, as created, nor the object of its willing is evil. See *causa; malum; peccata; privatio; privatio boni.*

causa efficiens: *efficient cause.* See *causa.*

causa electionis princeps: *the principal cause of election, which is the triune God himself.* See *electio; intuitu fidei; praedestinatio.*

causa finalis: *final cause;* the ultimate purpose of an act or thing. See *causa.*

causa formalis: *formal cause.* See *causa.*

causa formaliter causans: *the formally causing cause;* i.e., the formal cause, or *causa formalis.* See *causa.*

causa impulsiva: *impulsive or impelling cause;* i.e., a cause external to the traditional Aristotelian model of first or efficient, material, formal, and final causes (See *causa*); it moves or provides opportunity for the efficient cause, though not in an absolute or necessary sense, not as a prior efficient cause. Thus, man's misery can be called the *causa impulsiva* or, sometimes more precisely, the *causa impulsiva externa,* the external impelling cause, of the divine mercy. The Protestant scholastics will also use as a synonym for *causa impulsiva externa* the term *causa προκαταρκτική,* a cause that precedes and prepares.

causa instrumentalis: *instrumental cause;* in the realm of *causae secundae* (q.v.), the means, or *medium,* used to bring about a desired effect, distinct from the material and formal causes (See *causa*) as a tool is distinct from both the material upon which it is used and from the form that determines what the material is or will be. See *media.*

causa libera: *free cause;* viz., a cause that operates not out of necessity or compulsion, but freely; specifically, God as the cause of man's salvation insofar as God is in no way constrained to be gracious to his fallen creatures and is not under any external necessity in his ordination of the economy (*dispensatio,* q.v.) of salvation.

causa mali: *cause of evil.* SEE *causa deficiens.*

causa materialis: *material cause.* SEE *causa.*

causa meritoria: *meritorious cause;* i.e., an intermediate or instrumental cause that contributes to a desired effect by rendering the effect worthy of taking place. Thus, Christ's death is the *causa meritoria* of human salvation. The Protestant scholastics, in polemic with Rome, deny that human actions are in any way a *causa meritoria* of the gracious favor of God; salvation is a freely given gift that rests on God's grace alone in Christ. Thus, the idea of the human merits of congruity (*meritum de congruo,* q.v.) to which God graciously responds. SEE *cooperatio; gratia; meritum de condigno.*

causa peccati: *cause of sin.* SEE *causa deficiens.*

causa prima: *first cause.* SEE *prima causa; primum movens.*

causa προηγουμένη: *a cause that precedes or goes before in the sense of preparing or manifesting the way.*

causa propinqua: *a nearby or closely related cause;* as opposed to *causa remota* (q.v.).

causa remota: *remote cause;* viz., a cause not proximate or closely related to an effect; the remoteness may be in time, in space, or in a chain of causality.

causa virtualiter causans: *the virtually or effectively causing cause;* i.e., the efficient cause, or *causa efficiens.* SEE *causa.*

causae secundae: *second causes;* secondary, as distinct from and subordinate to primary causality, viz., the order of finite causality. It is a truism of scholastic theology that God does not act immediately, but mediately, through secondary or instrumental causes. The world does not experience sudden divine interventions but rather the effecting of the divine will in and through the finite order of the universe. Nor does this mean that every finite cause and effect implies a distinct and separate act of God in order to its occurrence, preceding and causing the finite cause and effect. There is no *actio Dei praevia*, no preceding action of God, but a *concursus* (q.v.) of divine primary and creaturely secondary causality or, as the Lutheran orthodox term it, a *continuus Dei in creaturas influxus*, a continuous inflowing or influence of God upon creatures.

causatum: *that which has been caused;* i.e., an effect.

certa persuasio de remissione peccatorum: *the certain persuasion of the remission of sins;* i.e., justifying faith considered subjectively.

certitudo: *certainty, certitude, surety;* specifically, the certainty of knowledge (*certitudo cognitionis*), also termed the certainty of assent or adhesion (*certitudo adhaesionis*). Human knowing is characterized by several distinct kinds of certainty: (1) *Certitudo demonstrativa,* or demonstrative certainty, which is an absolute certainty resting on logical demonstration or proof. This certainty can also be termed *certitudo mathematica,* mathematical certainty, or *certitudo scientiae,* the certainty of rational knowledge. (2) *Certitudo moralis,* a nondemonstrative certainty found in ethical decision and resting on probable arguments. Moral certainty is therefore also termed *certitudo probabilis,* probable certainty. (3) *Certitudo principiorum,* the certitude of principles, i.e., the certainty of basic principles known in and through themselves. This certitude is the foundation of both logical demonstration and moral probability. (4) *Certitudo theologica,* theological certainty, also termed *certitudo fidei,* the certainty of faith. This certainty is not demonstrative, nor does it derive from self-evident principles. Nevertheless, theological certainty is not simply a probable certainty but a *certitudo absoluta et infallibilis,* an absolute and infallible certainty, resting on divine revelation by faith.

certitudo et gratiae praesentis et salutis aeternae: *the certainty both of present grace and of eternal salvation;* i.e., the assurance of salvation that derives from justifying faith. It is characteristic of the early Reformation doctrine of assurance, or certainty of salvation, among both Lutheran and Reformed, that Christ himself, joined to us by grace in the *unio mystica* (q.v.), or mystical union, which results from justification, is the ground of assurance. Luther polemicized against the monster of uncertainty (*monstrum incertitudinis*), and Calvin firmly grounded assurance in faith in Christ, calling Christ the mirror of election (*speculum electionis*). The Reformed orthodox, however, out of a desire to clarify the structure and pattern of assurance, moved away from the simple assertion of union with Christ as the ground of certainty toward the establishment of an inward logic of assurance based on the work of the Holy Spirit. This logic could manifest itself as a simple syllogism arguing the relationship of the believer to the Spirit (SEE *syllogismus practicus*) or as a detailed moral casuistry. The latter pattern is typical of English Puritanism and, via the impact of William Perkins on continental writers like Gisbertus Voetius, of Reformed covenant theology in general. The moral casuistry provided the form for personal regulation of obedience under the covenant of grace. Indeed, neither the moral casuistry nor the basic *syllogismus practicus* could have any application to life outside of the covenant of grace. The problem of assurance arises out of the Christian warfare with sin, death, and the devil, conducted in and through the aid of grace. It is, therefore, an error to view either the *syllogismus practicus* or the casuistry as evidences of legalism associated with the concept of a covenant of works (*foedus operum*, q.v.); instead, both arise out of the Reformed emphasis upon the third use of the law (SEE *usus legis*) under the covenant of grace (*foedus gratiae*, q.v.).

certitudo gratiae et salutis: *certainty of grace and salvation*. SEE *certitudo et gratiae praesentis et salutis aeternae*.

certitudo salutis: *certitude or assurance of salvation;* a certitude that rests, not on reason or proof, but on faith in Christ. SEE *syllogismus practicus*.

cessatio voluntatis: *cessation of will;* in distinguishing human from divine *permissio* (q.v.) the scholastics note that human beings can, in a sense, cease to will and thereby permit something to occur that would be contrary to our willing; since, however, in God there is no *cessatio voluntatis*, the divine permission is always a willing and *efficax* permission.

character: *character; an indelible mark on or quality of the soul;* e.g., the mark or impression made on a soul by sacramental grace, termed *character sacramentalis, character ordinis sive ordinis sacerdotalis, character baptismalis*. In medieval scholastic and Roman Catholic theology, an indelible impression on the soul by baptism and ordination; the doctrinal basis for the unrepeatability of baptism and the indefectibility of ordination; denied by the Protestant scholastics, not only of ordination (to which they deny sacramental status), but also of baptism on the ground that indelible character (*character indelibilis*) rests on the *ex opere operato* conception of sacramental grace. SEE *ex opere operato; gratia; sacramentum*.

65

character hypostaticus sive personalis: *hypostatic or personal character;* specifically, the incommunicable or personal properties (*proprietates personales*) and the personal relations (*relationes personales*) of
the persons of the Trinity as they serve to define and differentiate
the individual persons. In other words, the hypostatic character of
each person is identified or determined by the various personal
characteristics, or *notiones personales,* that describe each of the
persons. Thus, the hypostatic character of the Father, *paternitas,* or
paternity, is defined by the Father's unbegottenness together with his
generation of the Son and his procession of the Spirit. The hypostatic
character of the Son, *filiatio,* or filiation, is defined by his generation
from the Father and his procession of the Spirit. The hypostatic
character of the Spirit, *processio,* or procession, is his emanation or
procession from the Father and the Son or, strictly speaking, his
being proceeded or emanated. SEE *notiones personales; proprietas;
relatio personalis; Trinitas.*

charis (χάρις): *grace.* SEE *gratia.*

cheirothesia (χειροθεσία): *the laying on of hands, particularly in baptism and ordination.*

chiliasmus: *chiliasm or millennialism;* viz., the hope in a future
thousand-year reign of the saints, based on a more or less literalistic
exegesis of Revelation 20. The Protestant orthodox, both Lutheran
and Reformed, denied the notion of an earthly millennium to dawn
in the future and viewed the text as a reference to the reign of grace
between the first and the second visible coming of Christ, the age of
the *ecclesia militans.* The orthodox did distinguish between *chiliasmus crassus,* as taught by the fanatics, and *chiliasmus subtilis*—and
sometimes *chiliasmus subtilissimus,* as found among pietists like
Philipp Spener and Friedrich Lampe. The *chiliasmus crassus* expects
a visible, earthly kingdom of Christ that will last for a literal millennium and accepts the doctrine of one or more resurrections before
the final judgment. *Chiliasmus subtilis* or *subtilissimus* is so called
because it moves subtly, and sometimes most subtly, away from
enthusiastic notions of an earthly thousand-year reign. *Chiliasmus
subtilis* does not hold the establishment of an earthly kingdom of
saints in Jerusalem, but it does argue a conversion of the Jews and
the defeat of Antichrist (*antichristus,* q.v.), two eschatological returns
of Christ, and sometimes two resurrections. *Chiliasmus subtilissimus*
omits all literal detail and looks only toward the hope of better times,
the *spes meliorum temporum,* in a new age of the expansion of the
kingdom through the power of grace. This latter view is now some-

times called postmillennialism because it identifies the final coming as taking place after the millennium. The orthodox sometimes, more polemically, refer to these three grades of chiliasm as *chiliasmus crassissimus,* grossest chiliasm; *chiliasmus crassus,* gross chiliasm; and *chiliasmus subtilis,* subtle chiliasm. SEE *adventus Christi; dies novissimus; ecclesia; spes meliorum temporum.*

chrēsis (χρῆσις): *use, function.* SEE *ktēsis.*

chrēstotēs (χρηστότης): *goodness* or *kindness;* especially, the goodness or kindness of God. SEE *bonitas.*

Christiani sunt in ecclesia: *Christians are in the church.* SEE *Extra ecclesiam non sit salus.*

Christotokos (χριστότοκος): *bearer of Christ;* viz., the Virgin Mary. The term *Christotokos* is not subject to the same objections as the term *Theotokos* (q.v.), bearer of God, since the former can be construed as referring to Christ's humanity.

Christus: *Christ;* literally, *anointed one;* the Latinized form of Χριστός, which is, in turn, the Greek term for "Messiah." The Protestant scholastics universally recognize *Christus* to be the *nomen officii* (q.v.), or official name, of the one anointed to the office of *Mediator* (q.v.). SEE *persona Christi; unio personalis.*

Christus quidem fuit legis doctor, sed non legislator: *Christ was indeed the teacher of the law, but not the legislator;* against the Council of Trent, the Arminians, and the Socinians, both Reformed and Lutheran orthodox argue the perpetuity of the *lex Mosaica* (q.v.) or *lex moralis* (q.v.), the Mosaic law or moral law. They argue also the fulfillment of that law by Christ in such a way that he corrected abuses and perversions of the law and enjoined the fulfilled law upon his church. Christ does not bring a more perfect law. The form of the maxim given above is from the system of the Lutheran scholastic Jerome Kromayer, as cited in Baier-Walther, *Compendium theologiae positivae* (III, p. 57).

circumincessio: *circumincession* or *coinherence;* used as a synonym of the Greek *perichōrēsis* (περιχώρησις), or *emperichōrēsis* (q.v.). *Circumincessio* refers primarily to the coinherence of the persons of the Trinity in the divine essence and in each other, but it can also indicate the coinherence of Christ's divine and human natures in

circumincessio

their communion or personal union. SEE *communio naturarum; unio personalis.*

circumscriptivus: *circumscriptive; capable of being described or judged by physical circumscription.* SEE *praesentia.*

cives: *citizens;* singular, **civis**; Christians are *cives* of the common-wealth of the church, and ultimately of the kingdom of God.

civitas: *commonwealth; body politic;* specifically, the body of citizens (*cives,* q.v.) making up the body politic, as distinct from the collection of buildings making up the city (*urbs*). The term must be correctly understood in relation to the famous usage of Augustine—who wrote, not of the *urbs Dei,* but of the *civitas Dei,* the Christian commonwealth which sojourns here on earth.

clementia: *clemency, mildness;* specifically, **clementia Dei**: *the mild-ness or clemency of God;* viz., that affection of the divine will, related to mercy (*misericordia,* q.v.) and longsuffering (*longanimitas,* q.v.), according to which God is gentle and forbearing toward his crea-tures.

coelum beatorum: *heaven or paradise of the blessed* (*beati,* q.v.).

coelum Dei maiestaticum: *the heaven, or height, of divine majesty;* in Lutheran orthodoxy, the heaven to which Christ ascends, or *terminus ad quem* of the ascension, synonymous with the right hand of God. Thus the ascension is not ascension to a place but the coming of Christ into the fullness of divine glory. This conception of the ascen-sion corresponds to the christological doctrine of the *genus maies-taticum* in the Lutheran teaching concerning the *communicatio idiomatum* (q.v.), or communication of proper qualities. In the exal-tation of Christ (SEE *status exaltationis*), of which the ascension is a stage, the divine majesty and omnipresence possessed by Christ (SEE *ktēsis*), but not used during the state of humiliation (*status humilia-tionis,* q.v.), are exercised in and through the human nature. Ascen-sion to the *coelum maiestaticum,* therefore, indicates the majesty and omnipresence of the risen divine-human person of Christ.

coena Domini: *the Lord's Supper.* SEE *coena sacra.*

coena sacra: *the holy supper;* i.e., the Lord's Supper, also referred to as *coena Domini* and *coena dominica.* The *sacra coena* is the holy rite or action instituted by Christ in which the consecrated bread and wine mediate the body and blood of the Lord both in commemoration of his death and in the sealing of the forgiveness of sins and the impartation of grace by which faith is confirmed to life eternal. Lutherans and Reformed agree that the *coena sacra* is, with baptism, a means of grace and a *Verbum visibile Dei*, a visible Word of God, but differ over the christological foundation of sacramental theory in the *communicatio idiomatum* (q.v.), over the question of the *manducatio indignorum* (q.v.), the eating by the unworthy, and over the definition of the presence of Christ to believers. SEE *communicare Christo; consubstantiatio; impanatio; praesentia illocalis sive definitiva; praesentia localis; praesentia realis; praesentia spiritualis sive virtualis; sacramentum; transubstantiatio.*

coessentialitas: *coessentiality.* SEE *homoousios.*

coetus electorum: *the assembly of the elect;* i.e., the church, specifically, the invisible church. SEE *ecclesia.*

coetus fidelium: *the assembly of the faithful;* a term applied to the church considered as community. SEE *communio sanctorum; ecclesia.*

coetus vocatorum: *assembly of the called;* i.e., the church. SEE *ecclesia; vocatio.*

cognitio: *knowledge in the most general sense of the word;* a term indicating knowledge both of concrete objects and of abstractions, knowledge gained by sense perception, and knowledge of universals, together with knowledge of the objects of the will and the affections. The scholastics can distinguish between *cognitio actualis*, actual knowledge, or knowledge that is presently actualized, and *cognitio habitualis*, habitual or latent knowledge, knowledge that lies inactive as a disposition or capacity of the knower. A further distinction can be made between *cognitio infusa* and *cognitio insita* (q.v.), infused knowledge and implanted knowledge, the former term indicating a knowledge gained by the operation of mind and sense, the latter a knowledge implanted by God. Neither the Reformers nor the Protestant scholastics argue the existence of innate ideas in the Platonic sense; instead, they argue the presence in the mind of certain ideas that arise out of the initial encounter of mind and sense with externals. *Cognitio Dei insita*, implanted knowledge of God, and sometimes even the term *cognitio Dei innata*, innate or inborn knowledge of God, indicate neither an unmediated act of God by which knowledge is implanted nor an inward illumination (*illuminatio*, q.v.), but rather that fundamental sense of the divine mediated by the created order and known by the mind's apprehension of externals, rather than by the process of logical deduction. To these categories of intellectual knowledge, the scholastics also add *cognitio affectiva*, affective knowledge, or knowledge arising out of the affections of the will, principally out of love. The concept of a *cognitio affectiva* as distinct from both rational or intellectual knowledge (*cognitio intellectualis* or *cognitio intellectus sive rationis*) and sense knowledge (*cognitio sensibilis* or *cognitio sensus*) is of paramount importance to the scholastic definition of faith as *cognitio*. The definition does not imply a purely intellectual knowing but includes also the operation of the will and its affective knowing. SEE *fides*.

cognitio abstractiva: *abstract or abstractive knowledge*. SEE *cognitio intuitiva*.

cognitio certa: *certain knowledge or cognition;* consisting in knowledge itself (*notitia*) and assent (*assensus*). SEE *fides*.

cognitio Dei abstractiva: *abstract or abstractive knowledge of God;* viz., that knowledge of God which fallen mankind has through both natural and supernatural revelation. In this life, God is not apprehended directly but rather indirectly through means, so that the knowledge we have of God belongs to the abstractive effort or operation of the intellect as it encounters the forms of revelation. SEE *cognitio Dei intuitiva; cognitio intuitiva*.

cognitio Dei intuitiva: *intuitive knowledge of God;* viz., the direct apprehension of God that is impossible in this life but that is available to the blessed (*beati,* q.v.) in the vision of God (*visio Dei,* q.v.) in the next life.

cognitio Dei naturalis: *natural knowledge of God.* SEE *theologia naturalis*.

cognitio innata: *innate knowledge.* SEE *cognitio; cognitio insita*.

cognitio insita: *ingrafted or implanted knowledge;* especially, *cognitio Dei insita,* ingrafted or implanted knowledge of God. The Protestant scholastics prefer the term *cognitio insita* to the Platonizing language of *cognitio innata,* innate or inborn knowledge. Whereas the concept of inborn knowledge indicates an inward knowledge of eternal truths or universals (*universalia,* q.v.) natural to the mind of man and present from birth apart from any perception of externals, the concept of ingrafted or implanted knowledge, like the idea of a seed of religion (*semen religionis,* q.v.), assumes the beginning of knowledge to be in the most rudimentary apprehension by the intellect of the work of God in creation and providence or, conversely, in the rudimentary knowledge of God implanted in the intellect by God's active presence upholding the created order. Some of the later scholastics speak of the ability of the mind to grasp intuitively or immediately through a *potentia propinqua,* a closely related power of the mind, such revelation of God in nature. See *cognitio intuitiva; theologia naturalis.*

cognitio intuitiva: *intuitive knowledge;* i.e., knowledge that rests on the immediate apprehension of a thing, as distinct from knowledge based on a mediate apprehension by way of demonstration or discourse. In other words, whereas demonstrative knowledge moves from premises to conclusions in a rigorous fashion, and discursive knowledge attains a similar result by less logically rigorous patterns, with the result that the conclusion is not immediately but mediately known, intuitive knowledge moves through no logical development but grasps its object without mediation of argument. *Cognitio intuitiva,* by extension, is a direct knowledge of the existence or nonexistence of things and their qualities; the basis of immediate apprehension is and must be an existent thing or an existent quality in a thing. Such knowledge can be distinguished from abstractive knowledge, or *cognitio abstractiva,* which does not involve the immediate apprehension of existents but rather is a knowledge of the essence or quiddity of things, apart from questions of their individual, concrete existence. *Cognitio abstractiva* can therefore know whether a given thing, granted its existence, is contingent or not, but it cannot know of the actual existence or nonexistence of contingents. Thus, *cognitio intuitiva* knows human beings and their qualities and knows also of the present existence or nonexistence of particular human beings, whereas *cognitio abstractiva* knows about humanity, not individual existent human beings. See *abstractum; concretum.*

cognoscendum: *thing known; object of knowing.* See *cognitio.*

communicare Christo: *to have communion with or join with Christ;* a phrase used synonymously with and in explanation of *libare sanguinem Christi,* to partake of the blood of Christ, and *manducare corpus Christi,* to eat the body of Christ.

communicatio actionum inter se: *communication of activity between themselves;* viz., the common or joint activity of the two natures of Christ in the accomplishment of the work of salvation. SEE *apotelesma; communicatio idiomatum; communicatio operationum.*

communicatio apotelesmatum: *the communication of* apotelesmata *or mediatorial operations.* SEE *apotelesma; communicatio operationum.*

communicatio corporis: *the communication of the body;* i.e., the *corpus Christi,* or body of Christ. SEE *communio corporis.*

communicatio gratiarum: *communication of graces;* the impartation of grace by the Word to the human nature it assumed in the incarnation, consisting in the *gratia unionis,* the grace of union, also termed *gratia eminentiae,* or grace of eminence, which elevates Jesus' humanity above all other creatures; and the *gratiae habituales,* the habitual graces or gracious dispositions conferred by the Holy Spirit on the human nature of Christ. Those latter graces are gifts of true knowledge of God, soundness and perseverance of will, and great power of action, beyond the natural capacity of human beings. Because the *communicatio gratiarum* is a communication of spiritual gifts, it is also sometimes called the *communicatio charismatum.* SEE *apotelesma; dona extraordinaria finita.*

communicatio idiomatum/communicatio proprietatum: *communication of proper qualities;* a term used in Christology to describe the way in which the properties, or *idiomata,* of each nature are communicated to or interchanged in the unity of the person. The *communicatio* can be characterized as either *in concreto* or *in abstracto* (q.v.). The former qualification, *in concreto,* refers to the concretion of Christ's person in the incarnation and personal union; the two natures are here considered as joined in the person, and the interchange of attributes is understood as taking place at the level of the person and not between the natures. This view was typical of the Antiochene Christology and of the Reformed Christology in the sixteenth and seventeenth centuries. The latter qualification, *in abstracto,* refers to the abstractive consideration of the relation of the two natures to each other distinct from their union in the person and to the exchange of properties between the natures, specifically, a communication of divine properties to the human nature. This view was typical of Alexandrian and Cappadocian Christology in the early church. Both views raise doctrinal problems: the Antiochene position, taken to an extreme by Nestorius, threatens the unity of

72

Christ's person; the Alexandrian doctrine, taken to an extreme by Eutyches, threatens the integrity of the natures. In addition, the logic of predication argues the illegitimacy of the use of abstractions as predicates. When the Reformed scholastics accuse the Lutheran orthodox of teaching *communicatio idiomatum in abstracto,* i.e., of using *abstracta,* or abstractions, as predicates, they not only argue a Eutychian tendency but also a logical error in the Lutheran view.

The Lutherans, however, attempt to move beyond the dichotomy between Antioch and Alexandria and, on the supposition that the unity of the two natures in Christ's person demands a real communication or sharing of attributes, formulate a doctrine of the communication of divine attributes to the human nature, not against, but as part of, the *communicatio idiomatum in concreto.* It may be observed that the Lutherans never predicate the *abstractum,* divinity as such, of the *abstractum,* humanity, but instead rest a series of predications on the fact that the *concretum* of the Word is both the divine nature and the person of Christ. The Lutheran orthodox describe three *genera* of *communicatio:* the *genus idiomaticum,* the *genus maiestaticum,* and the *genus apotelesmaticum.* (1) The *genus idiomaticum,* or idiomatic genus, indicates the predication of the qualities or attributes of both natures of the person of the Mediator, so that the God-man can be said, as one person, to suffer and die but also to govern and sustain the whole creation. The qualities of each nature (*idiomata*) belong to the person of Christ, but each nature retains its own *idiomata,* so that the qualities of one nature do not, according to the *genus idiomaticum,* become the qualities of the other. (2) The *genus maiestaticum,* or majestatic genus, indicates the hypostatic relationship of the human nature within the union; since the human nature does not have an independent subsistence, but subsists enhypostatically in the divine person that assumed it, it participates in the divine attributes, specifically in the *gloria* and *maiestas Dei* (hence, *maiestaticum*). This, according to the Lutheran scholastics, does not represent a *communicatio idiomatum in abstracto* between the natures or a transfer of properties from one nature to another. Thus it is *not* a denial of the *genus idiomaticum,* but instead a recognition of the inseparability of person and nature and of the intimate communion between the divine person and his human nature. The human nature, then, partakes of the divine attributes without either losing its own *idiomata* or conferring human, finite *idiomata* upon the divine nature. The *genus maiestaticum* thus accounts for the ubiquity (*ubiquitas,* q.v.), or omnipresence (*omnipraesentia,* q.v.), of Christ's human nature and provides the dogmatic underpinning in Lutheran orthodoxy for the real presence of Christ's body and blood in the Lord's Supper (SEE *Logos non extra*

73

carnem; multivolipraesentia; praesentia). This is the crucial point of contention between Lutherans and Reformed. (3) The *genus apotelesmaticum,* or apotelesmatic genus, refers to the cooperation of the two natures in the union of the person to the end of the completion of the work of the Mediator; nothing is accomplished by either of the natures that is done without the communion and cooperation of the other, including the acts that are peculiar to the natures considered in and of themselves. Thus the divine nature, although it cannot suffer, remains in communion with the human nature through the sufferings of Christ and supports and sustains the humanity through its trials.

Whereas the greatest difference between the Lutherans and the Reformed appears in the *genus maiestaticum,* which the Reformed utterly reject, we note that the Reformed view of the *communicatio,* which tends to be restricted to the *genus idiomaticum,* approaches the communication more as a *praedicatio verbalis,* or verbal predication, of *idiomata* from both natures of the person, whereas the Lutheran view insists that the person actually bears the *idiomata* of both natures. The Reformed, in addition, do not view the *apotelesmata,* or shared operations, of the natures as a *genus* of the *communicatio idiomatum* but as a separate *communicatio apotelesmatum* according to which the distinct operations of both natures are brought to completion in the one work of Christ. Thus, the Lutheran teaching is a real *communicatio* while the Reformed, remaining at the level of a *communicatio in concreto* only, is quite accurately called *antidosis onomatōn* (ἀντίδοσις ὀνομάτων), a mutual interchange or reciprocation of names, rather than a transfer or communication of properties; or a *koinōnia idiōmatōn kata synecdochēn* (κοινωνία ἰδιωμάτων κατὰ συνεκδοχὴν), a communion of proper qualities by synecdoche. Since synecdoche is a figure by which the whole is named for one of its parts, this *communio* is not merely a human invention but a *praedicatio vera,* a true predication of attributes, but of the person only and not between the natures. SEE *abstractum; alius/aliud; communio naturarum; concretum; genus tapeinotikon; ktēsis; unio personalis.*

communicatio operationum: *communication of operations;* also **communicatio apotelesmatum:** *the communication of mediatorial operations in and for the sake of the work of salvation;* terms used by the Reformed to indicate the common work of the two natures of Christ, each doing what is proper to it according to its own attributes. The Lutherans view this *apotelesma,* or divine-human work, as resulting directly from the *communicatio idiomatum* (q.v.) and argue a *genus* *apotelesmaticum* of the *communicatio idiomatum* rather than a separate *communicatio apotelesmatum.*

communio: *communion* or *community;* the Latin equivalent of *koinōnia* (q.v.). SEE *communio sanctorum.*

communio corporis: *communion of the body; i.e., of Christ;* the broken bread of the Lord's Supper, which is the communion of the body of Christ, just as the cup of blessing is the *communio sanguinis Christi,* the communion of the blood of Christ. Thus, in the partaking of and participation in the sacrament, believers have communion or fellowship with Christ (SEE *koinōnia*). This *communio corporis Christi* and *communio sanguinis Christi* points toward the *communicatio corporis et sanguinis Christi,* the communication of the body and blood of Christ, to those who participate in the sacrament. The Reformed confine this *communicatio* to believers, while the Lutherans argue that all who participate receive, since Christ is objectively given. SEE *coena sacra; manducatio.*

communio fidelium: *communion of the faithful;* synonymous with *communio sanctorum* (q.v.).

communio naturarum: *communion of natures;* the intimate and unitive relationship of the divine and human natures in the person of Christ. The term appears in the systems of the Lutheran orthodox as a representation of the *circumincessio* (q.v.), the περιχώρησις, or coinherence of the natures of Christ by which each nature exists or dwells in the other. Specifically, the divine actively indwells the human and the human passively exists in the divine.

communio sanctorum: *communion of saints;* i.e., the Christian community, the church, viewed as the body of believers; also **congregatio sanctorum:** *congregation of the saints.* The members of the church are holy (*sanctus*) and can be called the *communio sanctorum,* (1) because of the righteousness of Christ (SEE *iustitia fidei*), which is imputed to them on account of faith; (2) because of the righteousness of life (*iustitia vitae*) or spiritual righteousness (*iustitia spiritualis,* q.v.) of believers that arises in them because of faith and through the continuing grace of the Spirit (*gratia cooperans* or *gratia inhabitans;* SEE *gratia*); and (3) because of the renovation (*renovatio,* q.v.) and sanctification (*sanctificatio,* q.v.) that occur in believers through the cooperation of the regenerate intellect and will with the grace of the Spirit in Word and sacrament. Among the Reformed the saints are often identified as the elect and the *communio sanctorum* as the invisible body of the elect, or *ecclesia invisibilis* (SEE *ecclesia*). The Lutheran orthodox, too, can identify the church as the body of the elect (*corpus electorum*), but their emphasis lies more on the actuality of faith and the work of grace than on the eternal decree.

communio sanguinis: *communion of the blood; i.e., of Christ.* SEE *communio corporis.*

complacentia rationalis: *rational complacency;* i.e., the condition of fallen man, pleased with himself and his activities.

conceptio miraculosa: *miraculous conception;* viz., the conception of Christ by the power of the Spirit in the Virgin Mary.

concretum: *a concretion;* i.e., a concrete existent as opposed to an abstraction (*abstractum*, q.v.); a subject in which form and substance or essence and existence are conjoined. SEE *in abstracto; in concreto.*

concupiscentia: *concupiscence; profound desire, particularly in a wrongful sense;* specifically, the wrongful desire that is present in the parents during the act of intercourse, which then passes on to the children and which, as an inborn stain, becomes the *fomes peccati* (q.v.), or source of sin, in the succeeding generation. Concupiscence is thus both the *privatio iustitiae originalis,* the privation of original righteousness, and a positive cause of sin.

concursus or **concursus generalis**: *concurrence* or *general concurrence;* a corollary of the doctrines of God as *primum movens* (q.v.) and of providence as *continuata creatio* (q.v.) that defines the continuing divine support of the operation of all secondary causes (whether free, contingent, or necessary). For any contingent being to act in a free, a contingent, or a necessary manner, the divine will which supports all contingent being must concur in its act. This *concursus* is, therefore, *generalis,* or general, i.e., it belongs to the order of creation and providence rather than to the order of grace, and enables all acts of contingent being to occur, whether good or evil. Hence, the *concursus generalis* can be distinguished into a governance (*gubernatio*) *kat' eudokian* (q.v.) and *secundum beneplacitum,* by good pleasure, according to which God works his *opus proprium* (q.v.) in and through the good, and a *gubernatio* that is *kata synchōrēsin* (q.v.), or *secundum permissionem,* by permission, according to which God works his *opus alienum* (q.v.), or alien work, bringing about his ends in and through the evil of creatures.

The *concursus* rests on the *omnipraesentia* (q.v.) and *omnipoten-*

tia (q.v.) of God and can be defined in terms both of God's being or subsistence and of God's effective power or operation. Thus, the scholastics speak of an *immediatio suppositi*, an immediacy of the self-subsistent being of God, filling and supporting the being of all things; and of an *immediatio virtutis*, an immediacy of the effective and operative power of God in and through all things, undergirding, supporting, and sustaining the liberty and contingency of second causes (*causae secundae*, q.v.).

condescentio. See *accommodatio.*

conditio sine qua non: *the condition without which not;* viz., the necessary condition for something.

confessio: *confession; the admission or self-accusation of sin;* in medieval and Roman Catholic theology, a rite done in private before a priest. In Protestant theology it is usually a corporate act of the congregation in worship, although the Lutherans do not exclude private confession. *Confessio* is followed by absolution (*absolutio*, q.v.). In the Roman Catholic sacrament of penance (*poenitentia*, q.v.), contrition (*contritio*, q.v.) precedes *confessio*, and confession is followed both by the priest's absolution and by his imposition of a work of penance, a satisfaction (*satisfactio*, q.v.) to be made for temporal sins in the place of temporal punishment. See *attritio.*

confirmatio: *confirmation;* a rite of the church viewed by the medieval doctors and by the Roman Catholic Church as a sacrament, but denied sacramental status by the Reformers and the Protestant scholastics on the ground that it does not rest on a command of God (see *sacramentum*). Nevertheless, both the Lutheran and Reformed orthodox view *confirmatio*, rightly conceived and performed, as a useful and edifying support of piety. Children baptized in infancy should receive formal instruction in the faith when they have reached an age of discretion. After this instruction they may come publicly before the bishop or pastor in order to make a profession of faith and receive the support of the church's prayers and of the nonsuperstitious laying-on of hands. Such a rite coincides with the teaching of Scripture and the ancient custom of the church. Since, moreover, it is an act of piety and edification and not a sacrament or means of grace, the Protestant scholastics note that it is in no way a completion of baptism.

confirmatio foederis: *confirmation of the covenant;* specifically, the sealing of the covenant of grace to believers through the sacramental signs. See *foedus gratiae; promulgatio foederis; sanctio foederis.*

conformitas voluntatis: *conformity of will;* i.e., the conforming of the human will to the divine.

confusio naturarum: *confusion of natures;* i.e., the Eutychian heresy, which confuses divinity and humanity in Christ by the infusion of divine attributes into the human nature. SEE *atreptōs kai asynchytōs; communicatio idiomatum.*

congregatio sanctorum: *congregation of the saints.* SEE *communio sanctorum.*

conscientia: *conscience;* the application in action of the innate habit of the mind that knows the moral law (SEE *synderesis*). After the Reformation, both Protestants and Roman Catholics developed distinctive literature of conscience in which problems concerning the essentially spontaneous application of the innate knowledge of morality were elaborated in a highly casuistic fashion. Among Protestants, the English Puritans produced the most elaborate literature of "cases of conscience." The Protestant orthodox do not allow, however, that *conscientia* was untouched by the fall but hold that it, together with the understanding and its capacities, has fallen into error; human beings are plagued by *conscientia erronea,* erring conscience, which misidentifies the good.

consecratio: *consecration;* the act of setting aside the sacramental elements from a common or secular use to a sacred use through the statement of the words of institution (*verba institutionis*). Without this first part of the sacramental action (*actio sacramentalis,* q.v.) there can be no sacrament. The Protestant orthodox are careful to point out that the consecration is one and the same as the pronouncement of the words of institution and is, in effect, a prayer of blessing and an announcement of the celebration of the sacrament. Consecration is in no way a magical act that makes Christ's body and blood be present; both the sacrament and Christ's presence are received in the eating and drinking of the consecrated elements. SEE *Nihil habet rationem sacramenti extra usum a Christo institutum; sacramentum; verbum institutionis.*

consensu gentium. SEE *e consensu gentium.*

consensus ecclesiae catholicae: *consensus of the church catholic;* among Protestant theologians, usually a reference to the agreement of the fathers of the early church (*consensus patrum*) on particular points of doctrine, such as the doctrines of Christ and of the Trinity.

Against irenicists like Calixtus, the orthodox, both Lutheran and Reformed, denied the existence of any absolute doctrinal consensus external to and independent from Scripture, and therefore denied a normative status to the tradition of the church even in the more restricted sense of the tradition of the patristic period.

consensus mutuus: *mutual consent.*

consensus patrum: *consensus of the fathers.* See *consensus ecclesiae catholicae.*

consensus quinquesaecularis: *consensus of the first five centuries;* a term used by the Lutheran irenicist, Georg Calixtus, to indicate the fundamental or "constituent" truths of Christianity on which all Christians might agree. See *articuli antecedentes/constituentes/consequentes; articuli fundamentales; consensus ecclesiae catholicae.*

conservatio: *conservation, preservation;* specifically, the preserving or protecting of the created order by its Creator; also **conservatio mundi,** *conservation of the world.* See *providentia.*

consilia evangelica: *evangelical counsels;* viz., the advice or counsel of the church on various moral issues, defined by the medieval scholastics as a higher obedience not commanded in the law. The church counsels, but does not command, vows of poverty and chastity. Those who follow the counsels perform acts of merit and are given a greater certainty of salvation than those who merely follow the commands of the law. The theory of *consilia evangelica* is tied directly to the medieval reverence for the monastic life. On the ground of justification by grace alone, through faith alone, Protestantism, both Reformed and Lutheran, rejects the medieval theory of merit and therefore rejects also the idea of *consilia evangelica.* See *Christus quidem fuit legis doctor, sed non legislator.*

consilium Dei: *counsel of God; in effect, the decision of God;* also **consilium voluntatis Dei:** *the counsel of the will of God; the decision of the divine will;* viz., the *opus Dei essentialis ad intra* according to which God actively, immediately, and eternally wills all things. Considered as essential work, the *consilium* is the act of all three persons; considered as a work *ad intra,* it is the one, undivided, immanent (*inhaerens*) work of the Godhead. *Consilium* in this sense is synonymous with εὐδοκία, *beneplacitum, decretum,* and *voluntas,* and is one with the *essentia* (q.v.) of eternal God. As such, it does not imply decision in the human sense of a choice resting on options or on acquired knowledge; the *consilium*, therefore, is absolute, definite, and inalterable. SEE *aeternitas; beneplacitum; decretum; potentia absoluta; voluntas Dei.*

consilium pacis: *the counsel of peace;* a term used by Reformed theology in the seventeenth century, particularly the Cocceians, for the mutual agreement made in eternity between the Father and the Son, usually termed the *pactum salutis* (q.v.). Since the term *consilium pacis* comes directly from Zech. 6:13, the Cocceians felt they had there found the ideal exegetical basis for their doctrine. Others, including some of the Reformed, felt that this counsel between the Lord and the "Branch" referred, instead, to the earthly designation of the Messiah to his priestly and kingly offices and could not be used as an exegetical basis for the *pactum salutis.*

consolatio fratrum: *consolation of the brethren;* a reference to Matt. 18:20, "For where two or three are gathered together in my name, there am I in the midst of them." Christians gathered as brethren have the consolation and support of Christ's presence.

consubstantialitas: *consubstantiality.* SEE *homoousios.*

consubstantiatio: *consubstantiation;* viz., a doctrine of Christ's sacramental presence in the Eucharist developed in the Middle Ages as an alternative to theories of substantial alteration of the elements either by annihilation or transformation of the substance of the bread and wine. According to the theory of consubstantiation, the body and blood of Christ become substantially present together with the substance of the bread and wine, when the elements are consecrated. The theory is frequently confused with the Lutheran doctrine of real presence. *Consubstantiatio* indicates the presence of Christ's body according to a unique sacramental mode of presence that is proper to Christ's body as such, and is therefore a local presence (*praesentia localis,* q.v.); the Lutheran view, however, argues a real, but illocal presence of Christ's body and blood that is grounded in the omnipresence of Christ's person, and therefore a supernatural and sacramental, rather than a local, union with the visible elements of the sacrament. A concept related to *consubstantiatio* is that of *impanatio,* or impanation, indicating the presence of Christ's body in the bread (*in pane*). Here, too, the bread remains and Christ's body becomes present with it, but, as propounded by its medieval proponent Guitmund of Aversa, *impanatio* implies a hypostatic or personal union of Christ with the bread. With reference to the wine this theory is called *invinatio,* invination. *Consubstantiatio* implies only a presence with and not a union of Christ and the sacramental elements; it was taught as a possibility by Duns Scotus, John of Jandun, and William of Occam. See *praesentia illocalis sive definitiva; praesentia realis; transubstantiatio; ubiquitas; unio personalis; unio sacramentalis.*

consummatio mundi: *the consummation or end of the world.* See *consummatio saeculi; interitus mundi.*

consummatio saeculi: *consummation of the age;* the Latin equivalent of συντέλεια τοῦ αἰῶνος; i.e., the end of the world, consisting in the destruction of the sinful old order by fire and the creation or re-creation of the world in the new age, thus, often, *consummatio huius saeculi,* consummation of this age, indicating the beginning of the next age or *saeculum.* See *adventus Christi; dies novissimus; interitus mundi.*

contemplativus, -a, -um (adj.): *contemplative;* synonymous with *speculativus* (q.v.).

contingentia: *contingency;* i.e., an absence of necessity, not to be equated with chance, but rather to be understood as the result of the free operation of secondary causes (*causae secundae,* q.v.). In a contingent circumstance, an effect results from clearly definable causes, though the effect could be different, given an entirely possible and different interrelation of causes. In short, a contingent event or thing is a nonnecessary event or thing that either might not exist or could be other than it is.

continuata creatio: *continued creation;* the act by which God brought the universe into being provides also for the preservation of the created order. *Providentia* (q.v.) may therefore be viewed as the continuation of the creative act, distinct from creation only from the perspective of time, viz., from the point of view of the creature; providence is a continued act of creation. See *causa secundae; concursus.*

continuus Dei in creaturas influxus: *a continuous inflowing or influence of God on creatures.* See *causae secundae; concursus; continuata creatio.*

contradictio in adiecto: *contradiction in the adjective;* i.e., a contradiction involving the improper pairing of a noun and an adjective; e.g., a square circle, a temporal eternity.

contradictoria: *contradictories; mutually exclusive things or ideas.*

contradictoriae Dei voluntates: *contradictory wills of God;* a term used to indicate the seeming contradiction between the revealed will of God (*voluntas revelata Dei*, q.v.) and the hidden will of God (*voluntas abscondita*) insofar as the former includes the universal offer of salvation, and the latter the salvation of only the elect.

contrarietas: *contrariety;* i.e., a condition of mutual exclusion or incompatibility between things, propositions, or terms. SEE *opposita.*

contrarium: *a contrary;* viz., a thing, a proposition, or a term that is opposite to and logically exclusive of another thing, proposition, or term. SEE *opposita.*

contritio: *contrition;* a genuine repentance (SEE *resipiscentia*) arising out of filial fear (*timor filialis*, q.v.) and love for God (*amor Dei*, q.v.); sometimes distinguished into *contritio activa* and *contritio passiva,* active and passive contrition. The former indicates the active turning of the heart, and even the outward acts of repentance, and is therefore rejected by the Protestant orthodox as works-righteousness. The Lutherans, in particular, stress *contritio passiva,* the inward contrition according to which the heart is broken open by grace and subjected to the *terrores conscientiae,* or terrors of conscience, and thus readied for the positive call of the gospel. *Contritio passiva* is not a work of the inward man but an initial work of the Spirit, effected through the second use of the law and therefore not a contradiction of justification by grace alone. SEE *attritio; lex Dei; ordo salutis; poenitentia; usus legis.*

conversio: *conversion;* viz., the work of the Holy Spirit according to which the intellect and the will of the sinner are turned toward God in contrition and faith. Conversion can be distinguished into: (1) *conversio passiva sive habitualis,* passive or habitual conversion, commonly called regeneration (*regeneratio*), in which the will, passively, without any motion of its own, receives by grace alone the habit or disposition (*habitus*, q.v.) toward repentance and new life in Christ. Because the work of the *conversio passiva* begins in God and passes to the human subject, it is also called *conversio transitiva,* transitive conversion, a conversion that passes over from one being to another. (2) *Conversio activa sive actualis,* active or actual conversion, commonly called conversion (*conversio*) without modifier, in which the regenerated will actually and actively turns toward God; i.e., the human side of conversion, the actual repentance or *metanoia.*

Because the *conversio activa* is confined to the human subject, it is sometimes called *conversio intransitiva*, intransitive conversion, or conversion that does not pass over from one being to another. *Conversio activa* is sometimes also called *regeneratio secunda*, a second or further regeneration, belonging to the renovation (*renovatio*, q.v.) of the individual.

The scholastics also define conversion in relation to its *termini*, or limits. The *terminus a quo* (q.v.) of conversion in a formal sense is sin itself, sin as such, while in an objective sense it is the specific objects of or reasons for sinning peculiar to the individual sinner. The *terminus ad quem* (q.v.) of conversion, formally considered, is faith in Christ; objectively considered, God, to whom the repentant return in and through Christ. The orthodox deny the concept of a *homo renascens* (q.v.), or man in process of being reborn in conversion, and therefore all notion of a middle condition (*status medius*) between the two *termini* of conversion. In other words, conversion is not a process. Thus *conversio transitiva* is immediately effective as *conversio intransitiva*, *conversio habitualis* immediately resultant in *conversio actualis*. The divine work and the turning of the human heart are inseparable and are distinguished only in terms of the subject of the operation. See *conversio continuata; illuminatio; ordo salutis; resipiscentia.*

conversio continuata: *continued conversion;* as distinct from the moment of *conversio* (q.v.) properly so called, continued conversion is the human activity of daily turning from sin in repentance. In this *conversio secunda*, or second conversion, man cooperates with God by means of a renewed intellect and will; it is therefore also termed *illuminatio continuata* and *regeneratio continuata.* Temporally, *conversio continuata* corresponds with *sanctificatio* (q.v.).

conversio reiterata: *reiterated or repeated conversion;* over against the Reformed doctrine of perseverance (*perseverantia*, q.v.), which denies that the elect can finally fall from grace, the Lutheran orthodox argue that believers can fall away from grace as indicated by the loss of the exercise of faith (*exercitium fidei*), but that all such fallen remain subject to the power of grace and may experience a *conversio reiterata.*

cooperatio: *cooperation;* the term usually employed by the Protestant scholastics with reference to the doctrine of human cooperation with divine grace before regeneration, a view also termed synergism (*synergismus*, q.v.).

cor: *heart.*

cor incurvatus ad se: *the heart curved in upon itself;* a description of the sinful tendency of human beings to seek their own good in themselves rather than in God. Luther used the phrase to describe concupiscence or original sin as a positive problem in man rather than simply as a lack of original righteousness.

coram Deo: *before God;* as distinct from *coram hominibus,* before men.

coram hominibus: *before men;* as distinct from *coram Deo,* before God.

corporaliter: *bodily, corporally.* SEE *praesentia illocalis sive definitiva; praesentia localis.*

corpus Christi: *the body of Christ;* by extension, the church, which is the *corpus Christi mysticum.* SEE *coena sacra; ecclesia; unio mystica.*

corpus doctrinae: *body of doctrine;* specifically, the body of doctrine held by the church as true throughout its history and developed systematically during the various ages of the church; therefore, also, a theological system.

corpus electorum: *the body of the elect;* i.e., the church as the communion of saints (*communio sanctorum,* q.v.).

corpus iuris canonici: *the body of canon law;* specifically, the complete collection of ecclesiastical canons or rules that defined the governance of the medieval church and continue to define the governance of the Roman Catholic Church. SEE *forum ecclesiasticum; regimen ecclesiasticum.*

corpus theologiae: *a body of theology;* i.e., a theological system, or *loci communes* (q.v.); also called *corpus doctrinae,* a body of doctrine. SEE *medulla.*

correptio: *accusation* or *rebuke;* viz., an ecclesiastical discipline before *excommunicatio* (q.v.).

corruptio haereditaria: *hereditary corruption* or *inherited sin;* not an actual sin (SEE *peccatum actualis*), but the inherited condition of humanity. The Protestant scholastics view *corruptio haereditaria* as sin *quoad habitum*, sin in the sense of a *habitus* (q.v.), or disposition, as distinct from sin *quoad actum*, sin in the sense of an act, but distinct also from a mere *potentia* or *posse peccare*. See *libertas naturae; peccatum originalis; propagatio peccati*.

creatio: *creation;* distinguished into (1) *creatio activa*, active creation, or the divine creative act in creating the world *ex nihilo;* and (2) *creatio passiva*, passive creation, or the coming to be of the world as created order. The significance of the distinction is the reinforcement of the *ex nihilo* (q.v.) by denying any active role in creation to the materials from which the world is made.

 Creatio can also be distinguished into two stages, (1) *creatio prima*, the first creation, corresponding to Gen. 1:1–2, during which God drew out of nothing the *materia prima*, or *materia inhabilis*, the primary or unformed matter; and (2) *creatio secunda*, according to which God produced individual beings by imparting form and life to the *materia prima*. In Lutheran orthodoxy, the *creatio prima* and *creatio secunda* are sometimes termed *creatio immediata* and *creatio mediata*, since in the *creatio secunda* God arranged previously created *materia*, and the creation was in a sense mediated by the *materia prima*. This arranging of the *materia* consists in the *ordo creationis*, or order of creation, of the *hexaemeron* (q.v.). The Lutherans and the Reformed agree in calling the entire work of creation a free act of God resting solely on the goodness of the divine will. It is therefore neither an absolute necessity (*necessitas absoluta*, q.v.) resting on antecedent cause that God create, nor is it a *necessitas naturae* (q.v.), since God was not bound by his nature to create the world but could have existed without the creation. The Reformed add that creation is a necessity of the consequence (*necessitas consequentiae*, q.v.) since the divine act of creation does result from the eternal and immutable decree of God, or *consilium Dei* (q.v.). See *continuata creatio; operationes Dei externae*.

Crede, ut intelligas: *Believe in order that you may understand.* Augustine's dictum concerning the relationship of belief and authority to reason, from his *Sermon* 43.7 and 9.

credenda; singular, **credendum:** literally, *things to be believed;* thus, beliefs, objects of belief, Christian doctrine. See *agenda; speranda*.

credere/credere in: *to believe/to believe in;* scholastic theology distinguishes three types of believing: (1) *Credere Deo:* to believe God; i.e., to accept as true the revelation or scriptural Word of God. This is not a saving faith but merely *fides historica*, held by good and bad alike. (2) *Credere Deum:* to believe in (the existence of) God; again, not a saving faith, since it implies no loving relationship with God. (3) *Credere in Deum:* to believe in God, in the sense of a close personal love and trust in God and in his mercy; this is *fides salvifica,* or, in the terms of medieval scholasticism, *fides formata* (q.v.). SEE *fides.*

Credo, ut intelligam: *I believe in order that I might understand.* Anselm's statement of his premise concerning the relationship of faith and reason from *Proslogion,* 1; a conscious echo of Augustine's *Crede, ut intelligas.*

crux: *cross.*

crux theologorum: *the cross of theologians;* i.e., the doctrinal question most troublesome to theologians, which cannot be solved in this life, viz., the question concerning the reason for the salvation of some people and not others; a term used by Lutherans to pose the problem of universal and particular grace and to point to the problem inherent both in Calvinism, which must qualify universal grace, and Arminianism, which must deny salvation by (particular) grace alone.

culpa: *guilt, fault,* or *crime;* as distinct from *poena* (q.v.), punishment.

cultus: *an honoring, a reverencing, a veneration of the divine;* a word derived from the verb *colo, colere,* which indicates a caring for, a cultivation of, or an honoring of something. Thus, religion (*religio,* q.v.) is described as *cultus* or as *recta Deum colendi ratio,* a right way of honoring God. *Cultus* may be distinguished into *cultus internus,* or inward devotion, consisting in the Christian virtues of faith (*fides,* q.v.), hope (*spes*), and love (*caritas*); and *cultus externus,* external devotion, consisting in outward worship and Christian service.

cultus vere divinus: *true divine worship;* i.e., worship that is accorded only to God (SEE *latria*). Because of their view of the *communicatio idiomatum* (q.v.), or communication of proper qualities, the Lutheran scholastics argued a *cultus vere divinus* of Christ according to his human nature. The Reformed, by way of contrast, held a *cultus mediatorius,* or mediatorial worship, due to Christ's humanity in its union with the divine nature. SEE *religio.*

cupiditas: *cupidity, passionate desire, lust, wrongful appetite;* in the Augustinian vocabulary, wrongfully and pridefully directed love. SEE *amor; caritas; concupiscentia; dilectio.*

Dd

damnatio: *damnation;* the consignment of individuals to eternal punishment that takes place at the final judgment (*iudicium extremum,* q.v.) and which occurs because of the unforgiven sins and unremitted punishment of the individual; thus, the end of all who, at the judgment, are found to be outside of Christ. SEE *praeteritio; reprobatio.*

Damnatio consistit in aeterna separatione a visione Dei: *Damnation consists in eternal separation from the vision of God.* SEE *damnatio; visio Dei.*

de condigno/de congruo. SEE *meritum de condigno; meritum de congruo.*

de eventu: *as a result; in consequence of an event or action.*

de facto: *in fact;* distinguished from *de jure,* by right or by law.

de fide: *of the faith;* viz., those doctrines which are necessary for salvation and which must be believed. SEE *articuli fundamentales.*

de jure: *by right; by law;* distinguished from *de facto,* in fact, i.e., the actual circumstances, not necessarily by right. SEE *iure divino/iure humano.*

de nihilo: *without cause or reason;* literally, from nothing. SEE *nihil.*

debitio poenae: *an owing of punishment* or *liability to punishment;* i.e., one of the effects of disobedience, specifically, the disobedience of Adam. SEE *reatus.*

debitum: *debt, something that is owed.* SEE *dignitas operum.*

declaratio: *declaration.* SEE *promulgatio.*

decretum: *decree;* specifically, the *decretum aeternum,* or eternal decree, according to which God wills and orders all things; in a restricted sense, the eternal *praedestinatio* (q.v.) of God. The *decretum aeternum* can be distinguished from the counsel of God (*consilium Dei*) only formally, not essentially, since the essential acts of God belong to the divine essence in its simplicity (*simplicitas,* q.v.) and are identical with the essence itself; nevertheless, in a formal sense, the *consilium* is the divine decision, and the *decretum* is the actual willing or expression of that decision. The *decretum,* like the *consilium Dei* (q.v.), is utterly free, absolute, and inalterable, logically antecedent to all things, predicated upon nothing but the nature of the divine essence, which is to say upon the *consilium* or, essentially speaking, on itself. The Reformed scholastics are especially adamant in arguing against the Arminians the absolutely antecedent and unconditional character of the divine decree. They are also adamant in polemicizing against the Socinians, who separate the decree *realiter* from the divine essence. Following the Jesuits, both the Arminians and Socinians posit a *scientia media* (q.v.) and ultimately argue that the *decretum aeternum* does not encompass all things. The Lutheran orthodox also differ with the Reformed concerning the absolutely antecedent character of the decree, but only in its restrictive sense of predestination, with the Reformed insisting that nothing falls outside of the will of God. The decree is commonly distinguished into the *decretum Dei generale,* the general decree of God, according to which all things are ordained, and the *decretum Dei speciale,* the special decree of God, or predestination of mankind to salvation or damnation; i.e., the general decree of *providentia* (q.v.) and the special decree, *praedestinatio* (q.v.), the latter decree often being called *pars providentiae,* a part of providence.

decretum horribile: *terrifying decree;* a much-abused term from Calvin. It does *not* translate "horrible decree" and in no way implies that the eternal decree is somehow unjust or horrifying, but only that the decree is awesome and terrifying, particularly to those who are not in Christ. SEE *decretum.*

definitivus, -a, -um (adj.): *definitive, delimited;* incapable of description or circumscription but nonetheless a finite presence filling or acting within limits and not beyond them. SEE *praesentia.*

deformitas naturae: *deformity of nature;* a result of sin. Note that the term directly reflects the Augustinian view of evil as nonsubstantial and as a defect or deficiency in a thing. SEE *macula; privatio.*

dektikos (δεκτικός): *having the ability or capacity to receive;* specifically, with reference to man's capacity to receive divine gifts or blessings.

dēmiourgikos (δημιουργικός): *formative, creative, having to do with creation;* used by the fathers both with reference to human effort and with reference to the work of God.

descensus ad inferos: *the descent into hell;* viz., that portion of Christ's work that, in the text of the Apostles' Creed, is mentioned immediately after the death and burial of Christ and immediately before the proclamation of the resurrection. The concept was a cause of debate between Lutherans and Reformed and subject to various interpretations on both sides. In general, the Reformed view the *descensus* as the final stage of Christ's state of humiliation (*status humiliationis,* q.v.), while the Lutherans view it as the first stage of the *status exaltationis* (q.v.), or state of exaltation. Among the Reformed, Martin Bucer and Theodore Beza viewed the *descensus* as identical with the burial of Christ, while Calvin referred the *descensus* to the suffering of Christ's soul coincident with the death and burial of the body. The Reformed scholastics tend to draw these themes together and argue that, loosely, the *descensus* refers to all the spiritual suffering of Christ's passion and death and, strictly, to the bondage to death indicated by Christ's three days in the tomb. The Reformed deny both the idea of a local descent of Christ's soul into a place called hell or Hades and the teaching (based on 1 Peter 3:19) that he entered Hades to preach salvation to the patriarchs or to men from the age before Noah. Two sixteenth-century Lutheran theologians, Aepinus and Parsimonius, expressed doctrines similar to the Reformed. Aepinus clearly placed the *descensus* as the final stage of the *status humiliationis* and viewed it as the suffering of Christ's soul in his conquest of hell, parallel to Christ's bodily suffering in his conquest of death. Like the Reformed, Aepinus denied the relevance of 1 Peter 3:19. Parsimonius denied any physical or spatial *descensus* and similarly referred the *descensus* to Christ's suffering. The *Formula of Concord* condemned speculative controversy on the *descensus* and argued that the *descensus* indicated Christ's deliverance of believers from the "jaws of hell" in and through his victory over death, Satan, and hell. This positive, redemptive reading of the *descensus* carried over into Lutheran orthodoxy where the *descensus ad inferos* is interpreted as a *spiritual* (i.e., neither physical nor local) descent to the domain of Satan to announce victory and triumph over the demonic powers. In this interpretation, 1 Peter 3:19 is not an evangelical preaching of salvation to the inhabitants of

Hades but a legal preaching of the just damnation of the wicked. This is an act, not of the humiliated and suffering Christ, but of the exalted Christ. According to the Lutheran dogmaticians, the *descensus* follows the quickening of Christ's body and is the first stage of the *status exaltationis*.

desertio a gratia divina: *desertion by divine grace.*

desiderium gratiae: *the longing or ardent desire for grace;* a characteristic of fully actualized faith in the individual. SEE *actus fidei; fides.*

designatum: *the thing indicated by a sign.* SEE *signum.*

despoteia (δεσποτεία): *lordship* or *mastery.*

Deus: *God, the supreme being and ruler of the universe;* the exact equivalent in Latin of the Greek θεός. As distinct from the various biblical names of God (*nomina Dei,* q.v.), like *Jehovah* or *El Shaddai, Deus* is not a name but a term of reference, indeed, the most general term of reference to the deity. The scholastic doctrine of God distinguishes, for the sake of discussion, between the essence of God (*essentia Dei,* q.v.), the attributes of God (SEE *attributa divina*), the Trinity (*Trinitas,* q.v.) of God, and the works of God (*opera Dei,* q.v.). In brief, the scholastics can define God as the infinite, uncreated, self-existent, and necessary Spirit, one in essence and three in person, Father, Son, and Spirit, the eternal Creator, Preserver, and Redeemer of all things.

Deus ab omni compositione vera et reali liber est: *God is free from all true (i.e., logical) and real (i.e., as between things) composition.* SEE *simplicitas.*

Deus absconditus/Deus revelatus: *the hidden God/the revealed God;* the paradox of God's unknowability and self-manifestation as stated by Luther. The issue is not that God has been hidden and has now revealed himself, but rather that the revelation that has been given to man defies the wisdom of the world because it is the revelation of the hidden God. God is revealed in hiddenness and hidden in his revelation. He reveals himself paradoxically to thwart the proud, *sub contrario,* under the opposite, omnipotence manifest on the cross.

Deus otiosus: *the idle God;* viz., the concept of a God not directly involved with contingent existence. This concept is denied by scholastic theology, both of the Middle Ages and of the sixteenth and seventeenth centuries, whether Roman Catholic, Lutheran, or Reformed. SEE *concursus; continuata creatio.*

Deus propter Christum absolvens sive iustificans: *God absolving or justifying on account of Christ;* i.e., God as revealed in the gospel.

Deus propter peccata damnans: *God damning on account of sin;* i.e., God as manifest in the law.

Deus temporis est expers: *God is destitute of time;* or, more felicitously, *God has no share in time.* SEE *aeternitas.*

deutera gennēsis (δεύτερα γέννησις): *second birth; regeneration.* SEE *regeneratio.*

diabolus: *Satan, the devil.*

diakrisis pneumatōn (διάκρισις πνευμάτων): *the distinction, differentiation, or discernment of spirits;* e.g., 1 Cor. 12:10; a gift given to the church by the Spirit, together with the gifts of prophecy, miracles, healing, and the like. The Protestant scholastics universally recognize the diminution of the more miraculous gifts in the ages of the church, the apostolic and postapostolic era, but the maintenance in the church by the Spirit of the greatest gifts, faith, hope, and love.

diathēkē (διαθήκη): *covenant, testament, pact.* SEE *foedus gratiae; foedus operum; testamentum.*

dichotomia (διχοτομία): *dichotomy; a division into two parts.*

dicta probantia: literally, *statements proving [something];* thus, *prooftexts;* i.e., the texts cited in theological systems as an indication of the biblical foundation of a particular doctrine or doctrinal point; also called *dicta classica*, standard or classic sayings. SEE *locus; locus classicus; sedes doctrinae.*

dies Domini: *day of the Lord;* as in Scripture, the second visible coming of Christ, the final judgment. SEE *adventus Christi; dies novissimus; iudicium extremum.*

dies irae: *the day of wrath;* i.e., the final judgment; a term best known from the hymn in the Latin Requiem Mass which begins, *Dies irae, dies illa, solvet saeclum in favilla* ("Day of wrath, day when the world is reduced to ashes"). SEE *iudicium extremum.*

dies novissimus: *the last day;* viz., the inauguration of the heavenly kingdom of God consisting in the second visible coming of Christ (*adventus Christi,* q.v.), the resurrection of the dead (SEE *resurrectio*), the last judgment (*iudicium extremum,* q.v.), and the ordained ends of the elect in eternal blessedness (*beatitudo aeterna*) and of the reprobate in eternal damnation (SEE *damnatio*). The scholastics also note the *signa diei novissimi* or *signa temporis,* signs of the last day or signs of the time. Although they decry the attempts of the crass or gross chiliasts (SEE *chiliasmus*) to predict the exact date of the end by means of the signs of the last days revealed in Scripture, the orthodox do allow the existence of the signs and permit their careful use for the admonition, edification, and hope of the faithful. They therefore classify the signs into categories of *signa remota,* or remote signs; *signa propinqua,* near signs; *signa propinquiora,* nearer signs; and *signa proxima,* proximate signs. The *signa remota* are often identified as the events connected with the opening of the first six of the seven seals (Rev. 6:1–17): wars and conflict, famine and pestilence, persecution and earthquakes. The *signa propinqua* mark more clearly the approach of the end; chief among them are the great apostasy and the accompanying increase of worldliness and unbelief. These are followed by the *signa propinquiora,* which include the increased lawlessness and indifference to religion resulting from the great apostasy, great political disturbances, and the beginnings of the gathering together of Israel. The *signa proxima,* finally, include the completion of the mission to the Gentiles, the further increase of political disruption accompanying the manifestation of the "beast" of Revelation 13 and 17, the so-called "abomination of desolation" and the great tribulation that lead to the full development of the power of Antichrist (*antichristus,* q.v.), and the last battle, Armageddon. These *signa proxima* immediately precede the *adventus Christi* and the *dies novissimus.* SEE *consummatio saeculi; interitus mundi.*

difformitas naturae. SEE *deformitas naturae.*

dignitas: *goodness* or *dignity;* i.e., goodness in the sense of merit, as distinct from *bonitas,* or moral goodness. SEE *meritum de condigno.*

dignitas operum: *dignity or value of works;* denied specifically by Protestant theology, particularly when construed as the meritorious work of man that places God in the position of debtor and constrains God to reward men with grace. Even in the covenant of works (*foedus operum,* q.v.) the Reformed deny any *dignitas operum* to human obedience that could cause *debitum* or debt to exist on God's part in an absolute sense. Nevertheless, since God, in covenant, has ordained that he will respond graciously to human obedience and faithfulness, God can *ex pacto* (q.v.), on the basis of his own covenant, become *debitor*. This latter qualification is rooted in the late medieval conception of *pactum*, or covenant, in relation to the conception of the *potentia ordinata* (q.v.), though here it is no longer in any relation to the temporal *ordo salutis* (q.v.) or to human works. SEE *meritum de condigno; meritum de congruo*.

dikaiōma (δικαίωμα): *a requirement* or *commandment;* specifically, a requirement or commandment of the law.

dikaiosynē (δικαιοσύνη): *righteousness, uprightness, justice;* both in the sense of human fulfillment of the law (Phil. 3:6) and in the sense of the absolute righteousness of God himself (Rom. 1:17), which makes or declares the faithful to be righteous. SEE *iustificatio; iustitia*.

dilectio: *love;* especially, love in the sense of an attraction as distinct from *caritas* (q.v.) and *amor* (q.v.); the virtual opposite of *cupiditas* (q.v.).

dimensio: *dimension, the size or extension of a thing;* i.e., a property of material things only, since spiritual things, e.g., souls and angels, do not have extension.

dipleuron (δίπλευρον): *two-sided.* SEE *foedus dipleuron*.

disparata: *disparates, opposites;* i.e., terms, ideas, or propositions that are mutually exclusive. SEE *opposita*.

dispensatio: *arrangement* or *dispensation;* the Latin equivalent of *oikonomia;* a term applied primarily to the arrangement of the works of God and specifically by the Reformed to the successive dispensations of the one covenant of grace: there is one covenant from Abraham onward, but it can be separated into several patterns of administration, i.e., Abrahamic, Mosaic, Davidic, and the New Testament. In general, *dispensatio, oikonomia,* or its usual transliteration in the Latin of the scholastics, *oeconomia,* refers to the special saving providence of God.

distinctio: *distinction;* i.e., a logical distinction, of which the scholastics identify four kinds: (1) *Distinctio realis,* a real distinction, such as exists between two independent things; (2) *Distinctio formalis,* a formal distinction, such as exists between two (or more) formal aspects of the essence of a thing; as, e.g., between intellect and will,

93

which are not separate things but which are also distinguishable within the thing, in this case, the soul or spirit of which they are predicated. The formal distinction is also called the *distinctio formalis a parte rei*, the formal distinction on the part of the thing. (3) *Distinctio rationis ratiocinatae*, a distinction by reason of analysis, sometimes qualified or explicated as *distinctio rationis ratiocinatae quae habet fundamentum in re* ("a distinction by reason of analysis that has its basis or foundation in the thing"). Since this distinction is neither between things nor in a thing, it is purely rational; yet it is argued as a distinction expressive of extramental reality since it is grounded on the thing and therefore preserved from being merely a product of the mind. In other words the *distinctio rationis ratiocinatae* represents no distinction in the thing but a truth of reason concerning the thing. (4) *Distinctio rationis rationans*, a distinction by reason reasoning; i.e., a merely rational distinction resting only on the operation of the reason and not on the thing. To these four basic distinctions, a fifth is sometimes added: the *distinctio modalis*, the modal distinction, a distinction between various modes of subsistence of a thing or various ways in which a thing exists. The *distinctio modalis* belongs not so much to the logical spectrum of distinction between the real and the purely rational as to the vocabulary of trinitarian theology, according to which a person can be described as a mode of subsistence (*modus subsistendi*, q.v.). Logically, there is little difference between the *distinctio formalis* and the *distinctio modalis*.

In Protestant scholastic theology, as in the theology of the medieval scholastics, the question of distinctions is of paramount importance in the discussion of the divine attributes (*attributa divina*, q.v.). How can theology make predications of an essentially simple being whose attributes are essentially identical? Most of the Protestant scholastics reject the formal distinction and accept the *distinctio rationis ratiocinatae*.

distributio: *distribution;* in the Lord's Supper, the distribution of the elements and, in the Lutheran doctrine of the real presence (*praesentia realis*, q.v.), the distribution of the body and blood of Christ. SEE *coena sacra; communio corporis*.

distributio meriti Christi: *the distribution of the merits of Christ;* a term used by Luther to distinguish the breaking of Christ's body and the outpouring of Christ's blood on the cross, as belonging to the *meritum Christi* (q.v.), or merit of Christ, from the breaking of the bread and the outpouring of the wine in the Lord's Supper, as belonging to the *distributio meriti Christi*. The Lord's Supper, then, is not a sacrifice; Christ's body and blood are truly present, but the receipt of the grace of Christ by faithful participants rests on the merit of Christ's passion and death once for all on the cross, not on a sacrificial character of the eucharistic presence. The Lutheran orthodox follow Luther's point, but the term *distributio meriti Christi* does not appear to have been commonly used.

doctor: *teacher;* especially, the *doctores ecclesiae,* the teachers of the church or eminent writers of past ages, called professors of doctrine both past and present.

doctrina: *doctrine, teaching.*

doctrina divina: *divine teaching or doctrine;* i.e., the teaching of Scripture, which is the only norm for Christian doctrine, *doctrina Christiana.*

doctrina e Scriptura Sacra hausta: *doctrine drawn from Holy Scripture;* i.e., theology or Christian doctrine as defined by the *sola Scriptura* of the Reformation.

dogma (δόγμα): *requirement, commandment, decree;* hence, a doctrine absolutely necessary to the faith.

dokimasia (δοκιμασία): *a testing or temptation.* SEE *tentatio.*

dominium: *lordship* or *dominion;* specifically, the dominion given to man over the creation in Gen. 1:26–28, associated with the *imago Dei* (q.v.).

dona extraordinaria finita: *extraordinary finite gifts;* viz., powers and attributes bestowed on Christ's human nature by the Holy Spirit for the sake of Christ's mediatorial work. The Reformed scholastics emphasize such gifts in their doctrine of *communicatio gratiarum* (q.v.), or communication of graces, and of *communicatio apotelesmatum* (q.v.), or communication of accomplishment. By way of contrast, Lutheran orthodoxy emphasized the *communicatio idiomatum* (q.v.) and *communio naturarum* (q.v.), the real communication of properties and communion of natures as the basis for the extraordinary powers of Christ. The Lutherans, then, deny extraordinary finite gifts and argue the infinite gifts of the Word in communion with its human nature.

donum concreatum: *concreated gift;* also **donum naturale**: *natural gift;* or **donum intrinsecum**: *intrinsic or inward gift;* terms used by Protestant scholastics in opposition to the medieval scholastic concept of a *donum superadditum* (q.v.). The Protestant argument was that the *donum gratuitum,* the utterly free gift, of *iustitia originalis* (q.v.) was part of the original constitution of man and therefore a *donum concreatum, naturale,* or *intrinsecum* rather than something superadded to the original constitution of man. By extension, the loss of the *iustitia originalis* in the fall was the loss of something fundamental to the constitution of man that could be resupplied only by a divine act and not, as the semi-Pelagian tendency in late medieval Scotism and nominalism indicated, something superadded that could be regained by a minimal act of human obedience. SEE *facere quod in se est; homo; imago Dei; meritum de congruo.*

donum διακρίσεως: *the gift of distinguishing or differentiating;* specifically, the gift of distinguishing between spirits, the *diakrisis pneumatōn* of 1 Cor. 12:10.

donum gratiae: *gift of grace.* SEE *gratia infusa; gratia inhaerens.*

donum superadditum: *superadded gift;* specifically, the gift of grace superadded to human nature after creation but before the fall, a concept debated in the medieval theory of grace and merit and rejected by the Protestant orthodox. The concept arises out of the problem of explaining the hypothetical ability of Adam and Eve to have retained their original righteousness. Augustine recognized (*City of God,* XIV.27) that a finite nature, such as that present in Adam, would be of necessity mutable and liable to fall. Indeed, if Adam were created fully righteous and also mutable (as indeed he was), then any change would constitute a fall. Augustine therefore argued a gift of resistible grace to Adam, before the fall, that made Adam able to choose the good and preserve his will in its pristine integrity. This grace can be described as an *auxilium sine quo non* (q.v.), an assistance without which no continuance of righteousness is possible. The medieval scholastics raised the question of the relation of this superadded grace to Adam's original righteousness. Aquinas maintained that the *donum superadditum* was part of the original constitution of man and that its loss was the loss of the original capacity for righteousness. Since the superadded grace was not merited in the beginning, it cannot be regained by merit after the fall. Franciscan theology, particularly as mediated to the later Middle Ages by Scotus, argued that the *donum superadditum* was not part of the original constitution or original righteousness of man, but was to be considered truly as a gift merited by a first act of obedience on the part of Adam performed by Adam according to his purely natural capacities (*ex puris naturalibus*). Since Adam could, by doing a minimal or finite act, merit the initial gift of God's grace, fallen man might, by doing a minimal act, also merit the gift of first grace (SEE *meritum de congruo*). The Reformers and the Protestant orthodox reject the idea of any remaining ability in man to do good and argue the necessity of an effective *gratia praeveniens* (q.v.), or prevenient grace. In place of the idea of a *donum superadditum*, they argue that the original righteousness of Adam and the *posse non peccare* (q.v.), or ability not to sin, was a *donum concreatum* (q.v.), a gift given in the original constitution of man. SEE *homo; status purorum naturalium*.

ductio per contradictoriam propositionem: *reckoning or argument by means of the contradictory proposition;* an argument that proceeds to prove the truth of the proposition in question negatively, by showing the impossibility of its contradiction, therefore, also called *ductio per impossibile,* argument by means of the impossible.

dulia (from the Greek δουλεία): *veneration or reverence.* SEE *latria.*

duplex cognitio Dei: *twofold knowledge of God;* a distinction emphasized by Calvin in the final edition (1559) of the *Institutes,* and carried over into Reformed orthodoxy as a barrier to the inclusion of natural theology in the orthodox system of doctrine, according to which the general, nonsaving knowledge of God as Creator and as the wrathful Judge of sin, accessible to pagan and Christian alike, is distinguished from special, saving knowledge of God as Redeemer. This latter, saving knowledge is available only in the revelation given in Christ. Lutherans did not enunciate the principle in the same terms; they nevertheless observe it equally rigorously, to the end that neither of the major forms of Protestant orthodoxy has any genuine affinity for natural theology. SEE *theologia naturalis/theologia revelata; theologia naturalis regenitorum.*

duplex providentiae schola: *the twofold school of providence;* a term used by late orthodox writers in the era of rational supernaturalism to distinguish the personal and the general experience of providence in their attempt to prove providence from human experience. SEE *providentia.*

duplex veritas: *double truth;* viz., the theory that a thing can be true in philosophy but false in theology, or be false in philosophy but true

97

in theology. The idea of a *duplex veritas* rests upon the seeming frequent contradiction between revelation and the results of human reason or experience: e.g., the birth of Jesus from a virgin; the doctrine that God is both one and three; the doctrine of creation *ex nihilo* (q.v.). The problem was pressed in the era of orthodoxy by Daniel Hoffmann, who not only insisted on the existence of *duplex veritas* but called theology the *vera veritas*, true truth, as distinct from philosophy, the damnable *falsa veritas*, false truth, which is superseded by theology. The orthodox, both Lutheran and Reformed, responded by carefully delimiting the *usus philosophiae* (q.v.) and by arguing that philosophy or reason and theology, correctly understood, do not contradict each other and do not require a theory of double truth. Thus, the virgin birth proposes a miracle, not a claim that virgins in general can bear; the doctrine of the Trinity shows God to be one in one way and three in another and does not violate the law of noncontradiction; the doctrine of creation *ex nihilo* does not indicate the origin of something from nothing in a general sense, but the active creation of something by the power of absolute being. Protestant scholasticism generally argued, against the *duplex veritas*, that theology never contradicts reason directly but frequently supplies truths of revelation that transcend the powers of reason.

dynamis (δύναμις): *power;* in philosophy, the power to accomplish change, i.e., potency (*potentia*, q.v.); in theology, the power as distinct from the essence, or *ousia* (q.v.), of God; the classic adoptionist Christology proposes the indwelling of divine *dynamis* rather than divine *ousia* in the human Jesus and is referred to as the heresy of dynamic monarchianism. SEE *adynamia.*

Ee

e consensu gentium: *from the consent of mankind;* a form of argument resting, not on logical proof, but on the general agreement of all people and nations; an argument typically added by the Protestant scholastics to the traditional *a posteriori* proofs of God's existence in the refutation of atheism preliminary to the *locus de Deo.*

ecclesia (from the Greek ἐκκλησία): *church;* the orthodox describe the church of all believers in all ages as the *ecclesia universalis,* the universal church, and less frequently as *ecclesia catholica,* catholic church. The universal church is distinguished into two states, the *ecclesia militans,* or church militant, and the *ecclesia triumphans,* or church triumphant. The *ecclesia militans* is the earthly church presently engaged in Christian warfare against sin, death, and the devil. The scholastics distinguish between the *ecclesia militans* defined *proprie et praecise* (properly and precisely), i.e., the congregation of the saints or of believers (*congregatio sanctorum; congregatio credentium*), and the *ecclesia militans* defined *improprie et per synecdochen* (improperly and by synecdoche), i.e., the whole church in which faithful and unfaithful, saints and hypocrites, are mixed. The *ecclesia triumphans* is the church of the *beati* (q.v.), or blessed, both now and in eternity, the church at rest.

The *ecclesia militans* can also be distinguished into the *ecclesia synthetica, or collectiva,* and the *ecclesia repraesentativa* (q.v.). The former term identifies the whole body of believers, including clergy and teachers, while the latter identifies the *ministerium ecclesiasticum,* the ministers of the church concerned to preach the Word and teach sacred doctrine. This distinction is favored by the Lutherans and adapted by the Reformed, who identify the *ecclesia repraesentativa* not simply as clergy and teachers, but primarily as the church gathered in presbyteries and synods for the sake of governance. The church is also distinguished, by Reformed and Lutherans, into the *ecclesia visibilis* and the *ecclesia invisibilis;* the former term refers to all those who belong outwardly to the church, which is to say the *ecclesia militans improprie dicta,* the church of the saints and the hypocrites, the elect and the nonelect together; the latter term refers to the *coetus electorum*, or community of the elect, which is the *ecclesia militans proprie et praecise dicta* and the mystical body of Christ (*corpus Christi mysticum*). See *attributa ecclesiae; notae ecclesiae; regimen ecclesiasticum.*

ecclesia docens/ecclesia discens: *the teaching church and the learning church;* a distinction (used by Roman Catholics but rejected by Protestants) between (1) the teaching church (*ecclesia docens*), consisting in the hierarchy of the pope and the bishops in whom resides the *magisterium* (q.v.), or teaching authority, and (2) the learning church (*ecclesia discens*), consisting in the body of the faithful whose duty it is to accept the truth of the church. Since priests teach only by the authority of the bishop, they belong, with the laity, to the *ecclesia discens.*

ecclesia particularis: *the particular church;* i.e., the individual congregation. See *ecclesia.*

ecclesia repraesentativa: *the representative church;* viz., the ministers and elders who represent the church in its governing bodies. The Protestant orthodox are careful to warn against the identification of the church with a hierarchy as taught by Rome (see *ecclesia docens/ ecclesia discens*) and point out the purely administrative function of such bodies and the subordinate role of all confessions or doctrinal statements produced by ecclesiastical assemblies. The *ecclesia repraesentativa* does not make declarations by divine right (*iure divino*) and must remain obedient to and be itself governed by God's Word. See *ecclesia; norma; potestas ecclesiae.*

ecclesiola: *little church;* the idea of small group meetings of Christians for prayer and study of Scripture; developed by the pietists, who viewed their gathering as an *ecclesiola in ecclesia,* a little church within the church. The Lutheran orthodox opposed such meetings, frequently held without the presence of clergy and without sanction of clergy and church, as fundamentally separatistic, sectarian, and liable to produce distortions and misinterpretations of the church's doctrines.

efficax: *effective, effectual;* sometimes the Greek ἐνεργητικός is used.

eisagōgikos (εἰσαγωγικός): *introductory.*

ekdosis (ἔκδοσις): *taking off* or *putting off;* used by the Protestant scholastics as a term opposed to *endysis* (ἔνδυσις), putting on, in the description of repentance and conversion. SEE *poenitentia.*

ekporeusis (ἐκπόρευσις): *procession.* SEE *processio.*

ekthesis (ἔκθεσις): *exposition* or *explanation; exegesis of a text.*

ektypos (ἔκτυπος): *ectype;* copy or reflection of the archetype or ultimate pattern.

electio: *election;* the positive part of predestination according to which God chooses in Christ those individuals who will be his eternally. The Lutherans and the Reformed both ground *electio* in the love of God but differ in their formulations of election in relation to faith and justification. For the early orthodox Reformed, Christ is the sole *fundamentum electionis* (q.v.), and the ultimate choice of some rather than others is set in the depths of the divine will, apart from any consideration of individuals in order to safeguard the *sola gratia* of salvation; for the Lutherans, the ultimate choice of some rather than others lies in the mystery of justification by faith. Many of the seventeenth-century orthodox describe the divine choice therefore as taking place in view of faith (*intuitu fidei,* q.v.). The language of *intuitu fidei* never intended to make faith a cause of election and, indeed, always stood juxtaposed with the declaration of salvation by grace alone and of the origin of faith in grace. It stands, however, over against the Reformed view according to which faith and justification could be reduced to mere elements in a causally rigid order of salvation (*ordo salutis,* q.v.) resting on election. SEE *praedestinatio; praeteritio; reprobatio.*

electio intuitu fidei finalis, ex praevisa fide finali: *election in view of final faith, through foreknowledge of final faith.* SEE *intuitu fidei.*

elenchticus, -a, -um (adj.): *elenctic* or *elenctical; for the purpose of confutation or logical refutation;* a descriptive adjective frequently used by Protestant scholastics with reference to the polemical section of their dogmatic systems. Whereas *polemic* indicates simple attack, *elenctic* implies refutation leading toward positive statement.

elenchus (from the Greek ἔλεγχος): *a logical refutation;* frequently set in the form of a syllogism.

emanatio: *emanation, an outflow;* a term used by the scholastics to refer to creation, not in the Neoplatonic sense of an actual efflux of the divine being or a differentiation of the divine being into a descending series of lesser spiritual and ultimately material beings (a contradiction of the creation *ex nihilo,* q.v.), but rather in the sense of an outpouring from absolute Being, *primum ens* (q.v.), of the power that brings things into being, or in the sense of the divine *conservatio* (q.v.), or *concursus* (q.v.). The continued existence of the contingent order rests upon the *continuus Dei in creaturas influxus,* the continuous inflowing of God upon creatures.

emmenonta (ἐμμένοντα): *immanent or inward things, belonging to one subject;* opposed to *metabainonta.*

emperichōrēsis (ἐμπεριχώρησις): *mutual interexistence or inexistence* (*mutua inexistentia*); a term applied to the interpenetration of the persons or hypostases of the Godhead, indicating the interrelation of the persons in their very subsistence. SEE *circumincessio; subsistentia; Trinitas.*

emphanismos (ἐμφανισμός): *a disclosure, revelation,* or *manifestation.* SEE *patefactio; revelatio.*

enantion (ἐναντίον): *a real contradiction.* SEE *enantiophanē.*

enantiophanē (ἐναντιοφανῆ): *an apparent contradiction (in Scripture);* a place where the reader of Scripture might assume a contradiction, particularly a contradiction in the divine will, e.g., Exod. 9:1–12 and 10:20–27 where God wills the liberation of Israel but also hardens Pharaoh's heart. The scholastics invariably deny real contradictions and seek exegetically and doctrinally to resolve the apparent ones.

endysis (ἔνδυσις): *putting on;* e.g., Rom. 13:14; Col. 3:10; a scriptural term used in the description of repentance as the vivification (*vivificatio*) of believers, specifically, as "putting on the new man." SEE *poenitentia.*

energeia (ἐνέργεια): *power, operation* (derived from ἐν, *in,* and ἔργον, *work*); in Aristotelian philosophy, the state or condition of actuality or perfect actualization and operation, in Latin, *actus.*

energētikos (ἐνεργητικός): *effective.*

enhypostasis (ἐνυπόστασις): literally, *in-personality;* having one's subsistence in the subsistence of another; usually applied to the human nature of Christ with reference to the identification of the "person" or subsistence of Christ as the eternal person of the Word which has, in time, assumed a non-self-subsistent, or anhypostatic, human nature. The purpose of this formulation, which arose after Chalcedon principally in the thought of John of Damascus, is to safeguard the union of the two natures through affirmation of the oneness of Christ's person: the person is divine and not the sum of the two natures. Less often, the term is applied to the Father, Son, and Spirit in their *circumincessio* (q.v.), since they subsist in one another having the divine *ousia* (q.v.) in common. SEE *anhypostasis; emperichōrēsis; persona Christi; subsistentia.*

ens: *being* (generally); *a being; an existent* or *a thing;* in scholastic theology and philosophy, as distinct from most contemporary, post-Kantian philosophy, *ens* is the most simple predicate. It indicates the reality of a thing, the coincidence of *esse* (q.v.), or the *actus essendi,* the act of existing, with *essentia* (q.v.), the essence or "whatness" of a thing. In the case of the entire finite or contingent order (SEE *contingentia*), *ens* is not a necessary or essential predicate, since there is nothing in the *essentia,* or whatness, of a contingent being to indicate that it must be (that would, of course, be self-contradictory): all finite things can not-be. In the sole instance of God, however, *esse* is an essential or necessary predicate: God cannot not-be since it is of the very essence, or whatness, of God that God always is. By definition, any being that need not exist cannot be God. In God, as distinct from all other beings, *esse* and *essentia* are inseparable. It belongs to the whatness of God that God is fully actualized existence, *actus purus essendi* and *ens necessarium* (SEE *actus purus*).

Ens (or *res,* q.v.) can be distinguished further as either *ens extra mentem,* a being or thing outside of the mind, or *ens rationis,* a being or thing belonging exclusively to the mind, literally, a "being of reason." *Ens rationis* is called *ens* only *improprie* since it has no independent *esse,* whereas *ens extra mentem* or *ens realis* is in the proper sense, *proprie, ens.* Thus, a horse can be called *ens extra mentem,* or *res extra mentem,* whereas a unicorn is only *ens rationis.* This distinction is crucial to the argument over *universalia* (q.v.), since the merely rational, intramental existence of universals would deny to them the status of *ens* in a strict sense.

ens a se: *being from itself;* i.e., self-existent, necessary, noncontingent being, i.e., God. *Ens a se* is thus distinguished from all other *ens* or *entia ab alio,* beings from another. SEE *ens.*

ens perfectissimum: *most perfect being, i.e., God.*

ensarkos (ἔνσαρκος): *in the flesh, i.e., incarnate;* a distinction is frequently made between the eternal Word as Λόγος ἄσαρκος and the Word incarnate, the Λόγος ἔνσαρκος. SEE *incarnatio; Logos asarkos.*

ensarkōsis (ἐνσάρκωσις): *incarnation.* SEE *incarnatio.*

entelecheia (ἐντελέχεια): *entelechy;* i.e., the inner *telos,* that which accounts for form; in the Aristotelian psychology held by the scholastics, the soul. In the basic philosophical sense of inner *telos,* or guiding form, the *entelecheia* is that which mediates between matter and form, potency and actuality. The matter or substance of a thing (*materia, substantia:* Greek ὕλη), as such, conveys the essence of the thing (*essentia,* q.v.; οὐσία) only potentially, whereas the form, as considered in itself as actuality, requires embodiment. The actualization of the thing, the union of matter and form in development and occurrence, the movement from potency to act, rests upon the inner *telos,* the inward principle of self-realization; the motive force of the development is *kinēsis* (κίνησις) or *metabolē* (μεταβολή), the activity or transition from potency to actuality. Description of the soul as entelechy marks an important counter, both for philosophy and for scholastic theology, to the Platonic dualism of soul and body. Just as Aristotelianism allows no separation of form and matter and no independent, extramental existence of *universalia* (q.v.), so does it deny the dualism or separability of soul and body. The body, in the Aristotelianism, is not regarded as the tomb of the soul, but as the natural place of the soul's existence where alone it can exercise its faculties of *intellectus* (q.v.) and *voluntas* (q.v.) and in which alone it can perform its formal function. In this view, the human being is termed a composite substance (*substantia compositiva*) and the soul in itself termed *spiritus incompletus* (q.v.). Thus the Protestant scholastics can call the soul the *forma corporis,* or form of the body, and the *forma informans,* or informing form of the body, defining the body itself as the *formata,* or thing formed. SEE *anima; forma; in actu; mē on.*

enthusiastae: *enthusiasts* or *fanatics* (from the Greek ἐνθουσιασμός, ecstasy or possession by the divine).

entia ab alio: *beings from another;* viz., all contingent being. SEE *ens; ens a se.*

epieikeia (ἐπιείκεια): *forbearance, restraint;* used by the fathers with reference to virtuous men, specifically, with reference to Christ and his teaching of virtue in the face of evil and persecution.

epignōsis (ἐπίγνωσις): *knowledge;* particularly, a knowledge of divine truth.

epilēptōr (ἐπιλήπτωρ): *a person who censures others.*

epiphaneia (ἐπιφάνεια): *epiphany; appearing* or *appearance;* especially, the advent of Christ (*adventus Christi*, q.v.), both Christ's first appearance (2 Tim. 1:10) and Christ's final coming (1 Tim. 6:14).

epistēmē (ἐπιστήμη): *knowledge* or *understanding;* in Aristotelian philosophy, genuine knowledge consisting in an understanding of the reasons or causes of things according to which things are what they are and the way they are; in other words, a science. SEE *sapientia; scientia.*

epizeuxis onomatōn (ἐπίζευξις ὀνομάτων): *the linking together of names or properties.* SEE *communicatio idiomatum.*

equivocus. SEE *aequivocus.*

erotema; plural, **erotemata:** *a question;* specifically, a logical premise stated as a question for the sake of disputation; thus, *erotemata theologiae* as a description of a series of disputations arranged in systematic form. SEE *medulla.*

erōtēsis (ἐρώτησις): *questioning* or *request.*

eschaton (from the Greek ἔσχατον): *eschaton; the end; the end of the world.* SEE *adventus Christi; consummatio saeculi; dies novissimus.*

esse: literally, *to be;* viz., the act of existing (*actus essendi*). Any given individual must have *essentia* (q.v.), or whatness (*quidditas*), and *esse,* the act of existing. E.g., a human being must have both humanity, the human *essentia,* and actual existence, *esse.* Actual existence without *essentia* is nonsense and unidentifiability, while the *essentia* of humanity without the act of existence or actual existence, *esse,* is a mere concept. SEE *ens.*

essentia: *essence;* the whatness or *quidditas* of a being, which makes the being precisely what it is; e.g., the essence of Peter, Paul, and

105

John is their humanity; the essence of God is deity or divinity. SEE *ens; esse; essentia Dei; natura; quidditas; substantia.*

essentia Dei: *the essence or "whatness" of God;* God is the only necessary, self-existent being or, in other words, the only being in whom *esse* (q.v.), or existence, and *essentia* (q.v.), or essence, are inseparable; it is of the essence or "whatness" of God that God exist. Thus the essence of God, as distinguished from the divine attributes (*attributa divina,* q.v.), can be described as independent or self-subsistent spirit. This view of the divine essence coincides, the scholastics note, with the biblical self-description of God (Exod. 3:14) as the one who is.

essentialiter: *essentially;* Latin equivalent of *ousiadōs* (q.v.), as opposed to *personaliter* or *hypostatikōs* (q.v.); specifically, one way of predicating names of God. Thus "Father" can be predicated of God either *essentialiter* or *personaliter.* "Father," predicated of God essentially, indicates the entirety of the Godhead or divine essence, which stands over against the finite order as Creator and Regenerator, i.e., the "one God and Father of all, who is over all and through all and in all" (Eph. 4:6). In this sense, "Father" indicates, according to the scholastics, Father, Son, and Spirit, since the whole of the triune Godhead is over all and through all and in all. When "Father" is predicated personally of the Godhead, however, it refers to the First, Unbegotten Person of the Trinity, not in relation to creatures as such, but rather in relation to the Son and to the Spirit. The name "Father" is predicated of God as Creator, as the unbegotten subsistence in the eternal relation of persons in the Trinity and also as the God who adopts believers as his children. The scholastics also view adoption in Christ as the basis for an essential predication, since the work of salvation is the common work *ad extra* of all three persons of the Trinity. It is thus the whole Godhead, Father, Son, and Spirit, that is called Father by the redeemed.

ethnici: literally, *ethnics;* i.e., pagans.

eucharistia (εὐχαριστία): *eucharist, thankfulness,* or *a giving of thanks;* hence, the Eucharist, the celebration of the Lord's Supper (1 Cor. 10:16). SEE *coena sacra.*

eudokia (εὐδοκία): *goodwill, good pleasure, favor;* used by the Protestant scholastics as a synonym for *benevolentia* (q.v.) or *favor Dei* (q.v.) in their discussions of the *attributa divina* (q.v.) and the *opera Dei ad extra* (q.v.). In Reformed orthodoxy, the *eudokia* or *bene-*

placitum (q.v.) of God is the ground of God's elective choice (Eph. 1:5).

eulogia (εὐλογία): *a praise, blessing, or consecration;* e.g., Heb. 12:17.

eutaxia (εὐταξία): *a good commandment* (Eph. 6:2).

evacuatio: *emptying* or *evacuation;* a Latin word used with *exinanitio* (q.v.) to render the Greek *kenōsis* (q.v.).

evangelium (from the Greek εὐαγγέλιον): *gospel;* literally, *good news;* used throughout the New Testament to indicate the good news of God's gracious offer of salvation. Because of its centrality to the New Testament message, the term is favored by the orthodox as a reference to the promise of salvation offered in Christian preaching.

Evangelium est Deus absolvens et iustificans: *The gospel is God absolving and justifying.*

eventus: *event;* i.e., the result of an action.

ex acceptitatione: *through acceptation;* also **ex acceptatione.** See *acceptatio.*

ex nihilo: *out of nothing;* referring to the divine creation of the world *not* of preexistent, and therefore eternal, materials, but out of nothing. This view is normative for Christian theology and is consonant with the theory of a two-stage creation, i.e., (1) of the material substratum of things and (2) of actual things by the informing or imparting of form to matter. It also implies the denial of nothingness in the sense known to Greek philosophy, the Platonic *mē on* (q.v.), the *nihil* (q.v.), an indeterminacy or plastic, pregnant nothingness that somehow limits the divine creative act. Against the philosopher Lubinus and the mystic Boehme, who revived the Platonic schema and insisted on the limiting reality of *non ens*, the Protestant scholastics argued a *nihil negativum, materiam excludens*, a negative or absolute nothingness, excluding matter, having no characteristics and in no way limiting the work of God; it is pure space and is in no way either a substratum or a precondition for creation. The void or chaos that appears as a first stage of creation stands over against the negative nothingness of space as a *nihil positivum*, a positive nothingness, a material substratum that is as yet no-thing, a primary matter prior to the creation of the substances of things. See *ex nihilo nihil fit; materia prima.*

Ex nihilo nihil fit: *From nothing, nothing comes;* a traditional philosophical maxim frequently employed in relation to the Christian doctrine of creation *ex nihilo* (q.v.) in scholastic debate over the relation of philosophy to theology, specifically in relation to the question of *duplex veritas* (q.v.), or double truth. The Protestant scholastics allow the maxim *ex nihilo nihil fit* as representing the limit of natural reason, and as supplemented without contradiction by the truth of the doctrine of the divine *creatio* (q.v.): no finite creature can create from nothing. The single exception to the rule is the *ens perfectissimum* (q.v.), God, who is *ens* (q.v.) in an absolute sense, without analogy in the finite order and therefore transcendent to, rather than contradictory to, the results of human reason. As *ens perfectissimum*, God can give being to the finite order. In addition, the maxim does not claim *ex nihilo nihil creatur*, i.e., that nothing is created out of nothing, but only *ex nihilo nihil generatur*, nothing is produced out of nothing. Christian doctrine never claims that nothing or nothingness is a positive source or ground of something, but only that God creates out of nothing or, in other words, creates all of existence including the material substratam (SEE *materia prima*).

ex opere operantis: *by the work of the worker;* with reference to the sacraments, the assumption that a proper attitude of the recipient in the act of receiving a sacrament will lead to the bestowal of a grace beyond that received by the mere administration and receipt of the sacrament *ex opere operato* (q.v.). The concept of grace available *ex opere operantis* lies at the heart of the medieval system of merit (*meritum*, q.v.) and is denied by the Reformers and the Protestant orthodox.

ex opere operato: *by the work performed;* with reference to the sacraments, the assumption of medieval scholasticism and Roman Catholicism that the correct and churchly performance of the rite conveys grace to the recipient, unless the recipient places a spiritual impediment (*obex*) in the way of grace. Sacraments themselves, therefore, have a *virtus operativa*, or operative power. This view of sacraments is denied by both Lutherans and Reformed, who maintain that faith must be present in the recipient if the sacraments are to function as means of grace; the mere performance of the rite will not convey grace. SEE *sacramentum*.

ex pacto: *through or on the basis of the pact or covenant;* especially **ex pacto divino**: *on the basis of the divine pact or covenant;* a term related to the concept of a divine *potentia ordinata* (q.v.), indicating a divinely ordained or compacted offer of grace. The term derives from the Scotist and nominalist view of the efficacy of sacraments: the power of the sacrament lies, not in the elements, but in the promised divine work that occurs in and through the celebration. Reformed federal theology continued the use of the term, particularly with reference to the *foedus operum* (q.v.), to indicate the divine ordination of the terms upon which man might fulfill covenant obligations. The human acts of obedience required by the *foedus operum* were not in themselves deserving of eternal life but were considered efficacious *ex pacto*, on the basis of the agreement made by God. Although the conclusion would be denied by the Reformed scholastics, this view of the merit of Adam's obedience approaches very closely the medieval concept of *meritum de congruo* (q.v.).

ex parte Dei: *on the part of God;* a term relating to the stipulations of the covenant relationship between God and man. Under the covenant certain promises are made *ex parte Dei* to be fulfilled contingent upon acts of obedience performed *ex parte hominis*, on the part of men. The two terms used in this manner, paired, indicate a two-sided, or reciprocal, covenant (*foedus dipleuron*, q.v.).

ex parte hominis: *on the part of men.* SEE *ex parte Dei.*

ex praevisa fidei/propter praevisam fidem: *through foreknowledge of faith/according to foreknowledge of faith;* synonymous with *intuitu fidei* (q.v.). SEE *praevisa fidei.*

ex puris naturalibus: *out of or according to the purely natural condition.* SEE *status purorum naturalium.*

ex testamento: *through or on the basis of the testament;* i.e., the *ordo salutis* is made available to man *ex testamento*, on the basis of the testament given in Christ. SEE *ex pacto; testamentum.*

exaequatio naturarum: *an equalization of natures;* viz., the result of a mixture and commingling of the divine and human natures in Christ such as was taught by the heretic Eutyches. The natures are confused, their integrity lost, and their *idiomata*, or proper qualities, merged, ultimately to the loss of the humanity in the infinitude of divinity. SEE *atreptōs kai asynchytōs.*

exclusivae particulae: *exclusive particles.* SEE *particulae exclusivae.*

excommunicatio: *excommunication;* church censure that refuses to the impenitent sinner participation in the Lord's Supper and in the fellowship of the Christian community; the Reformed distinguish between *excommunicatio minor,* disciplinary exclusion from the Lord's Supper, and *excommunicatio maior,* full exclusion from fellowship following admonition by the consistory and discussion of the offense in the congregation.

exercitium: *exercise;* viz., the exercise or act of an ability or capacity either intellectual or physical; e.g., the exercise of understanding.

exercitium fidei: *the exercise of faith.* SEE *perseverantia.*

exinanitio: *self-emptying* or *self-renunciation;* viz., the Latin equivalent of the Greek term *kenōsis* (q.v.). Specifically, the *exinanitio* is the relinquishing of the *forma Dei* (q.v.), or form of God, by Christ and the assumption of the *forma servi,* or form of a servant, as witnessed by Phil. 2:5–7. This text marks a point of major exegetical and christological divergence between Lutheran and Reformed, particularly concerning the identification of the active subject (*subiectum quod,* q.v.) of the *exinanitio.* According to the Lutheran dogmaticians, the active subject of the *exinanitio* is the Incarnate Person of the Word. The incarnation itself is not, therefore, either humiliation or self-emptying, but the prior condition of both *exinanitio* and *humiliatio.* The *exinanitio* pertains to Christ's human nature insofar as the divine majesty and its full use belong to Christ's humanity in the personal union (SEE *communicatio idiomatum*), and therefore Christ relinquishes its exercise according to both natures. The Reformed, by way of contrast, identify the preincarnate Christ, the *Logos* ἄσαρκος and *incarnandus* (q.v.), as the *subiectum quod* of the *exinanitio* and therefore argue that the *exinanitio* consists in the relinquishment of divine glory, the *forma Dei,* by the *Logos* in its assumption of the flesh and the *forma servi.* SEE *anthrōpopatheia; status humiliationis.*

exitium: *destruction* or *cause of destruction* (from the verb *exeo,* to go away or pass away); a term typically used with reference to the *exitium reproborum,* the destruction of the reprobate because of their sins, generally synonymous with the *poena damni,* the punishment of the damned, and not an indication of total or essential annihilation (*annihilatio,* q.v.). SEE *damnatio; interitus mundi; poena; reprobatio.*

exousia (ἐξουσία): *the freedom or right to act, choose, or decide;* thus, ability, authority, or power. The Protestant scholastics use the term in both senses as an attribute of God indicating the unconstrained power of God to act. It can also indicate human freedom of choice, which the scholastics call *autexousion* (q.v.).

expiatio: *expiation;* an act of making amends or of purging by sacrifice (*piaculum*, q.v.). Like *satisfactio*, satisfaction, *expiatio* indicates an act performed because of an offense and directed toward the solution of the problem or toward payment of the debt incurred by the offense. Whereas *expiatio* indicates specifically a sacrificial act or a purgation, *satisfactio* has the connotation of payment or reparation which makes the offended party content or satisfied. SEE *reconciliatio; satisfactio vicaria.*

expromissio: *surety, guarantee.* SEE *fideiussio; pactum salutis; sponsio.*

extra calvinisticum: *the Calvinistic* extra; a term used by the Lutherans to refer to the Reformed insistence on the utter transcendence of the human nature of Christ by the Second Person of the Trinity in and during the incarnation. The Reformed argued that the Word is fully united to but never totally contained within the human nature and, therefore, even in incarnation is to be conceived of as beyond or outside of (*extra*) the human nature. In response to the Calvinistic *extra*, the Lutherans taught the maxim, *Logos non extra carnem* (q.v.). It is clear that the so-called *extra calvinisticum* is not the invention of Calvinists but is a christological concept, safeguarding both the transcendence of Christ's divinity and the integrity of Christ's humanity, known to and used by the fathers of the first five centuries, including Athanasius and Augustine. It is also clear (1) that Reformed emphasis on the concept arose out of the tendency of Reformed christology to teach a *communicatio idiomatum* (q.v.) *in concreto* over against the perceived Lutheran emphasis upon a *communicatio idiomatum in abstracto* and (2) that the polarization of Lutheran and Reformed Christologies owed much to the debate over the mode of Christ's presence in the Lord's Supper, in which the Lutherans emphasized the real but illocal presence of Christ's body and blood by reason of the communicated omnipresence of the Logos (SEE *praesentia illocalis sive definitiva*) and the Reformed emphasized the transcendence of the divine and the heavenly location of Christ's body. Against the Lutherans, the Reformed interpreted the *extra calvinisticum* in terms of the maxim *Finitum non capax infiniti* (q.v.), the finite is incapable of the infinite. In other words, the finite humanity of Christ is incapable of receiving or grasping infinite attributes such as omnipresence, omnipotence, or omniscience. SEE *in abstracto; praesentia spiritualis sive virtualis; unio personalis.*

111

Extra ecclesiam non sit salus: *Outside of the church there may be no salvation;* a maxim from Cyprian (*Epistles,* 73.21) often cited by the scholastics, who accept it as true with the provision that the church is identified as the *communio sanctorum* (q.v.), or communion of saints, and by its marks, Word and sacrament (SEE *notae ecclesiae*). The maxim is also frequently given as *Extra ecclesiam nulla salus* or *Salus extra ecclesiam non est.*

extra enthusiasticum: *the enthusiastic extra;* viz., the teaching of enthusiasts, fanatics, and proponents of the inner light that the grace of the Spirit operates *extra Verbum,* outside of the Word, and *extra sacramentum,* outside of the sacrament. The Lutheran orthodox accuse Zwingli of holding such a doctrine and, less correctly, because of Zwingli, allege it also against the Reformed orthodox. Unlike the Lutherans, the Reformed do allow an immediate work of the Spirit paralleling Word and sacrament, but they continue to affirm Word and sacrament as the chief means of grace.

extra mundum: *outside of or beyond the world;* applied to God as a synonym of *immensitas,* indicating that God, who does not occupy space, is present in but not confined by the world.

extra muros ecclesiae: *outside of the walls of the church;* a characterization of unbelievers.

Ff

facere quod in se est: *to do what is in one's self;* a concept from late medieval scholastic theology returned to Protestant thought by Arminius. According to the medieval scholastics, man could respond to the *gratia universalis,* not with a truly meritorious act (*meritum de condigno,* q.v.), but with an act representative of and flowing from the minimal good that was in him, not a truly good act, but a bare turning toward the divine, a *meritum de congruo* (q.v.). On the basis of this minimal act, God would respond graciously; thus the maxim, *Facientibus quod in se est, Deus non denegat gratiam* ("To those who do what is in them, God will not deny grace"). This view of human ability rests upon the Scotist and nominalist view of the *donum superadditum* (q.v.).

facienda: *things done;* i.e., acts or works of Christian life, usually referred to as *agenda* (q.v.).

facultas aversandi gratiam: *the ability or capacity to turn grace away;* a term related to the Lutheran view of *gratia resistibilis* (q.v.), or resistible grace. Orthodox Lutheranism, as opposed to Reformed orthodoxy, argues the human capacity to resist the saving grace of the Word. Lutheranism also denies the synergistic teaching of a *facultas se applicandi ad gratiam,* an ability or capacity to apply or attach oneself to grace, i.e., a *capacitas volendi,* or ability to will. The *facultas aversandi gratiam* is merely a *capacitas nolendi,* or ability to refuse or not will.

facultas se applicandi ad gratiam: *the ability or capacity to apply or attach oneself to grace;* viz., the assumption of a fully developed synergism. SEE *facultas aversandi gratiam; synergismus.*

facultates animae: *faculties of the soul;* viz., *intellectus* (q.v.) and *voluntas* (q.v.). These two faculties of soul, intellect and will, are not two separate things but are distinct modes of one thing (*modus rei*); i.e., they are not really but modally or formally distinct. The soul is spiritual and therefore indivisible; it can just as accurately be said to understand and to will as to have understanding and to have will.

fatum astrologicum: *astrological fate;* viz., the doctrine that the lives and fortunes of individuals are influenced by the stars. The Protestant scholastics generally argue that *fatum astrologicum,* like *fatum Stoicum* (q.v.), is ruled out by the Christian doctrine of *providentia* (q.v.).

fatum Stoicum: *Stoic fate;* viz., the doctrine that all things occur by a rigid, absolute necessity (*necessitas absoluta,* q.v.), as taught by the ancient Stoic philosophers. The Protestant scholastics take great pains to argue that their doctrine of divine *providentia* (q.v.), particularly the notion of the concurrence (*concursus,* q.v.) of the divine operative will with all finite events, is not equated with the *fatum Stoicum* and, specifically, is not viewed as a denial of the liberty of *causae secundae* (q.v.).

favor Dei: *the favor of God;* viz., the gracious disposition of God toward mankind.

felicitas: *felicity, happiness;* both the *felicitas Dei,* or happiness of God, and the *felicitas beatorum,* or happiness of the blessed who dwell with God in the *coelum beatorum,* or heaven of the blessed (SEE *beati; beatitudo*). Since happiness can be defined as the attainment of the good, God, who is the highest good (*summum bonum,* q.v.) and whose goodness (*bonitas,* q.v.) is eternal and immutable in its perfection, must be eternally happy in himself. In addition, the blessed who have attained the fellowship of God, the *summum bonum,* must also be happy in the fruition of their fellowship. Finally, the happiness of man in this life must be defined in terms of the good toward which the individual is directed, with the result that true human happiness arises only out of the right ordering of life in the recognition that fellowship with God in Christ is the goal of human existence and the glory of God (*gloria Dei,* q.v.) is the ultimate end of all mankind.

fideiussio: *guarantee, surety,* or *bond;* a term used by Reformed theologians as a synonym for *sponsio* (q.v.). *Fideiussio* comes from Roman law and indicates the actual posted bond, or set guarantee, required for the freedom of the accused. The Reformed recognize here a problem related to the eternal nature of the *pactum salutis* (q.v.) and the *sponsio* over against the temporal character of the *satisfactio Christi* (q.v.), but argue that the *fideiussio,* or bond, is effective eternally in its inception insofar as the merit of Christ's work, and, indeed, the work of satisfaction itself, rests upon the decree. Of course, the sinner or debtor remains liable for his sin or debt until the *fideiussio* has been applied to him in time.

fidelitas: *fidelity, faithfulness;* specifically, the *fidelitas Dei,* or faithfulness of God, that communicable or relative attribute according to which God is consistent and constant in his promises and in his grace. The *fidelitas Dei* rests directly on the intrinsic truthfulness of God (SEE *veracitas Dei*) and the absolute immutability of God (SEE *immutabilitas Dei*); in order for God to be faithful, he must be essentially truthful and immutably so. In the theology of the English Reformed and of those continental theologians strongly influenced by the practical thrust of the English theology, the *fidelitas Dei* frequently appears in the practical section of the *locus* on immutability as the "use" to which the notion of divine immutability may be put in Christian piety, i.e., a ground of Christian consolation.

fides: *faith;* the firm persuasion of the truth of God's revelation or that truth itself considered as the object of belief (SEE *fides qua creditur; fides quae creditur*); most frequently the former, as it is manifest in Christians.

Fides may be considered further as (1) *fides historica,* historical faith, which is a mere acceptance of a datum as true apart from any spiritual effect—even devils believe that Christ died to save the world from sin; (2) *fides temporaria,* temporary faith, which apprehends the truth of God as more than mere historical datum but which subsequently dissipates into unbelief; (3) *fides miraculosa,* miraculous faith, a faith directed specifically toward divine promises of supernatural or suprahuman capacities, such as the faith that moves mountains; (4) *fides salvifica,* saving faith, which accepts the promises of God and the truths of God to the salvation of the believer; (5) *fides legalis,* legal faith, which accepts as true the contents of divine revelation apart from the gospel—i.e., faith which accepts the law and its demand for obedience and which could conceivably save under the unabrogated *foedus operum* (q.v.) but which cannot save after the fall; (6) *fides evangelica,* evangelical faith, which accepts the saving revelation of God in Christ as given specifically in the gospel.

Fides salvifica, further defined as *fides propria,* true, personal faith, is usually explained as having three components, the first two belonging to the intellect and comprising the category of *cognitio certa,* certain cognition, the latter one belonging to the will: (1) *notitia,* knowledge, the actual content of the gospel and the promises of God; (2) *assensus,* assent, by which the intellect acknowledges the truth of *notitia,* apart from any personal trust or saving appropriation of that knowledge; (3) *fiducia,* trust, or *apprehensio fiducialis,* faithful apprehension, which appropriates savingly, by an act of the will, the true knowledge of the promises of God in Christ. Saving faith, therefore, cannot be merely intellectual; it must also be volitional. SEE *actus fidei; fides implicita; habitus; habitus fidei; intellectus; voluntas.*

fides actualis: *actual faith* or *actualized faith;* i.e., a faith that truly grasps the grace of Christ, as opposed to temporary or historical faith. SEE *fides.*

fides apprehensiva: *apprehending or appropriating faith;* viz., that faith which apprehends or appropriates Christ; synonymous with *fiducia* (q.v.) or *apprehensio fiducialis.* SEE *fides.*

Fides bonae voluntatis genetrix est: *Faith is the mother of a good will.*

fides carbonaria: *the faith of colliers;* i.e., *of charcoal burners;* viz., *fides implicita* (q.v.), or implicit faith, on the assumption that a collier knows little or nothing of Christian doctrine.

fides caritate formata: *faith informed by love;* i.e., faith that is animated and instructed by love (*caritas*) and is therefore active in producing good works. According to the medieval doctors, *fides caritate formata* could exist only when the believer was in a state of grace, since such *fides* must rest upon a habit or disposition of love supernaturally created in the soul by grace. This conception of faith is denied by the Reformers and the Protestant orthodox insofar as it implies the necessity of works for justification and insofar as it rests on a concept of a created grace (*gratia creata*) implanted or infused into man. SEE *gratia infusa.*

fides directa: *direct faith;* i.e., faith as it lays hold of its object, the promise of salvation in Christ given in the gospel. SEE *actus fidei.*

fides divina: *divine faith;* faith engendered in us by the power of God as distinct from *fides humana,* the natural human capacity to hold convictions concerning things.

Fides filios Dei facit: *Faith makes sons or children of God.*

fides formata: *informed faith.* SEE *fides caritate formata.*

fides humana: *human faith.* SEE *fides divina.*

fides implicita: *implicit faith;* sometimes called blind faith; a faith that is mere assent without certain knowledge, e.g., faith that accepts as true "what the church believes," without knowing the objective contents of the faith. The Reformers and the Protestant scholastics uniformly deny implicit faith; since knowledge is lacking, this is no faith. SEE *fides; fides carbonaria.*

fides informis: *uninformed faith;* in medieval scholastic theology, a faith which has not been informed or animated by love. Such faith can exist outside of a state of grace. SEE *fides caritate formata.*

fides iustificans: *justifying faith;* viz., that faith through or on the basis of which we are justified by grace. Faith does not actively justify but rather is the means of acceptance (*medium ληπτικόν,* q.v.) of the grace that justifies. SEE *actus fidei; fides; iustificatio.*

Fides iustificat non propter se, ut est in homine qualitas, sed propter Christum, quem apprehendit: *Faith justifies not because of itself, insofar as it is a quality in man, but on account of Christ, of whom faith lays hold.*

fides qua creditur: *the faith by which (it) is believed;* i.e., the faith of the believer that receives and holds the revelation of God, *fides* subjectively considered.

fides qua iustificat: *faith insofar as it justifies;* i.e., faith considered as *fides iustificans* (q.v.), justifying faith.

fides quae creditur: *the faith which is believed;* i.e., the content of faith as revealed by God, *fides* objectively considered.

fides quaerens intellectum: *faith in search of understanding;* a dictum concerning the relationship of faith and reason from the *proemium* to Anselm's *Proslogion*, which closely follows the Augustinian model of *Crede, ut intelligas.*

fides reflexa: *reflex or reflective faith;* i.e., faith as it knows subjectively, for itself, the presence of its object to intellect and will in a saving manner. SEE *actus fidei.*

fides specialis: *special or personal faith;* i.e., saving faith, just as *gratia specialis* is saving grace. SEE *fides.*

fiducia: *trust;* the essence of *fides* (q.v.); note that in English the etymological relation between *fides* (faith) and *fiducia* is lost; in the older theology faith and trust are intimately related. *Fiducia,* as the crown of faith, is also called *apprehensio fiducialis,* or faithful apprehension.

fiducia cordis: *the trust or faithfulness of the heart;* i.e., the faithful apprehension (*apprehensio fiducialis*) that grasps the knowledge of Christ and completes faith (*fides,* q.v.). S*ee actus fidei.*

figura: *figure;* specifically, a figure of speech or a sign or symbol. S*ee signum.*

filiatio: *filiation; sonship* or *begottenness;* sometimes called *nativitas.* S*ee relatio personalis.*

filioque: literally, *and the Son;* a reference to an addition in the third article of the Western form of the Niceno-Constantinopolitan Creed. It did not belong to the original ecumenical creed, but derives from the Council of Toledo in a.d. 589. The addition marks the codification of anti-Arian theology in the West by announcing the co-equality of Father and Son in the fact of the Spirit's procession from both, rather than from the Father alone as in the Eastern model. This doctrine of double procession represents the basic thrust of Western trinitarianism from Augustine onward.

filius: *son;* specifically, the *filius Dei,* or Son of God, the Second Person of the Trinity, the eternal *Verbum Dei,* or Word of God. S*ee Trinitas.*

filius patris: *Son of the Father;* i.e., the Second Person of the Trinity. S*ee Deus; Trinitas.*

finis: *goal, end;* frequently, the goal or end of a series of events or of causes and effects. S*ee causa finalis.*

finis creationis: *the end or goal of creation;* viz., according to both Reformed and Lutheran scholastics, the glory of God in the manifestation of his power, wisdom, and goodness.

finis hominum: *the end or goal of man;* the glory of God, not simply in the sense of the attribute, but also in the sense of celebration. The end of man is the glorification and eternal celebration of the goodness of the Creator. To this definition the Reformed usually add the manifestation of God's mercy in the elect and justice in the reprobate as part of the glorification of God.

finis intermedius: *intermediate end or goal;* an end or goal of thought or action which is penultimate and contributory to the *finis ultimus.* In logic, the intermediate ends are subordinate to the final goal; intermediate ends occur first in time, but not in the conceptual ordering of thought or action.

finis legis: *the end or goal of the law;* viz., Christ, in whom the law is fulfilled. SEE *usus legis.*

finis theologiae: *the goal or end of theology;* a term variously applied, depending on whether the intermediate or the ultimate end is in view and whether theology as a whole is viewed as practical or as speculative.

finis ultimus: *the ultimate end or goal;* since the *finis ultimus* always represents the basic reason for a thought or action, it may also be considered as the *causa finalis* (q.v.).

Finitum non capax infiniti: *The finite is incapable of the infinite;* i.e., the finite or finite being is incapable of grasping, comprehending, or receiving the infinite or infinite being; an epistemological and christological maxim emphasized by the Reformed in debate with the Lutherans. Epistemologically it signifies the limitation of the human mind, even the mind of Christ, in the knowledge of divine things. The Reformed thus insist not only that all human theology is *theologia ectypa* (q.v.) and not *theologia archetypa* (q.v.), but also that the *theologia unionis* (q.v.) which is known to Christ according to his humanity must be finite. Christologically, it signifies the finitude of all humanity, including Christ's, and therefore its incapacity for receiving divine attributes, such as omnipresence, omnipotence, and omniscience. The maxim also appears in the form, *Finitum non possit capere infinitum.* SEE *extra calvinisticum.*

foederatus: *a party in covenant, confederate;* plural, **foederati:** *confederates;* a term used by the Reformed covenant theologians to designate Christ as man's partner or confederate in the work of salvation and, in the plural, to indicate the relationship between Christ and believers as confederates, *foederati,* in covenant. SEE *foedus gratiae.*

foedus: *covenant;* synonymous with *pactum.* The use of the concept of covenant, *foedus,* in Protestant orthodox theology is primarily a

Reformed phenomenon. The Lutherans do not deny the importance of the concept to biblical theology and history, but neither do they develop a doctrine of covenant as such. The Reformed scholastics, by contrast, develop the structure of *pactum salutis* (q.v.), *foedus operum* (q.v.), and *foedus gratiae* (q.v.) as one of the central architectonic patterns of their systems. Arminianism retained some of the Reformed covenant structure, but developed it in a synergistic and even semi-Pelagian pattern, with emphasis upon the *foedus naturae* (q.v.). All the following terms that begin with the word *foedus* derive from the Reformed orthodox systems.

foedus dipleuron or **foedus** δίπλευρον: *two-sided or two-way covenant;* at the point at which man enters into God's covenant, receives the terms established by God and, in effect, becomes a partner in covenant with God, the *foedus operum* (q.v.) and *foedus gratiae* (q.v.) can be termed two-sided covenants. *Foedus dipleuron,* therefore, indicates, not the covenant in itself or in its underlying requirements, but rather the further relationship of God and man together in covenant, and particularly the free acceptance on the part of man of the promise of God and of the obedience required by the covenant. When man is faithful and obedient under covenant he, in effect, binds God to the promises, according to God's own ordination. The contrast between *foedus monopleuron* (q.v.), one-sided covenant, and *foedus dipleuron* is particularly clear in the instance of the covenant of grace (*foedus gratiae*). Since the covenant is ordained by God alone and cannot be entered by fallen humanity unless God provides the grace necessary to regenerate the will and draw man into covenant, the covenant is initially one-sided; but once an individual is drawn into the covenant and his will is regenerated, responsibility under covenant and, specifically, faithful obedience to the will of God are required of him—and the covenant appears as two-sided. It is thus an error to oppose *foedus monopleuron* and *foedus dipleuron* as if there were two Reformed covenant theologies, the one predestinarian and the other voluntaristic; the language of *monopleuron* and *dipleuron* describes the same covenant from different points of view. SEE *ex pacto; ex parte Dei; potentia ordinata.*

foedus gratiae: *covenant of grace;* also **foedus gratiae gratuitum**: *gracious or graciously given covenant of grace;* and **foedus gratiae evangelicum**: *covenant of grace concerning the gospel* or *evangelical covenant of grace;* considered, first, as a *foedus monopleuron* (q.v.), or one-sided covenant, the covenant of grace is the pact (*pactum, pactio*) made by God beginning with the *protevangelium* (q.v.), confirmed and revealed more fully in Abraham, and finally fulfilled in

Christ. It is a *foedus monopleuron* because it stands as a gracious promise of salvation given to fallen man apart from any consideration of man's ability to respond to it or fulfill it and apart from any human initiative. Human beings are drawn into covenant by the grace of God alone. Once they enter covenant, however, and become parties to the divine offer of salvation, they take on responsibilities, under the covenant, before God. The *foedus gratiae*, therefore, also appears as a mutual pact and agreement between God and man, a *foedus dipleuron* (q.v.). Following Calvin, the Reformed speak of one *foedus gratiae* in substance (*substantia*), which can be divided or distinguished into several dispensations (SEE *dispensatio*), or temporal administrations. Thus, the covenant of grace does not alter in the substance of its promised salvation from the first announcement of grace to Adam and Eve, to the fuller promise of grace to Abraham and his seed, to the gift of the law in the Mosaic form of the covenant, to the modification of its administration under the Israelite monarchy and during the age of prophets, to its final dispensation begun in Christ and continuing to the end of the world. Viewed in this way, the Reformed doctrine of the *foedus gratiae* has the effect of drawing the Old and New Testaments together and of explaining the moral law (SEE *lex moralis; lex Mosaica*) as belonging to the divine promise of salvation rather than to the abrogated *foedus operum* (q.v.), or covenant of works. The entire biblical history of gracious promise, obedience under covenant, and saving fulfillment in Christ thus becomes a part—a central structure—of theological system and a pattern of salvation directly applicable to the life of God's people in the present. Now, as in all previous dispensations, God requires faith and repentance of those in covenant with him.

The *administratio foederis gratiae*, or administration of the covenant of grace, is described both historically and dogmatically by the scholastics. (1) Historically, the scholastics argue either a dichotomous division into the Old and New Testaments or a trichotomous division into the prelegal *dispensatio* from the *protevangelium* to Moses, the legal *dispensatio* from Moses to Christ, and the evangelical *dispensatio* from Christ to the end of time. The covenant can thus be described as *ante legem* (before the law), *sub lege* (under the law), and *post legem* (after the law). Earlier covenant theology further divided the covenant into Noachic and Abrahamic periods before Moses. (2) Dogmatically, the covenant can be considered in terms of its promulgation (*promulgatio foederis*, q.v.), its legal foundation, the *stipulatio, nomothesia* (q.v.), or *sanctio foederis* (q.v.), and its confirmation in and through covenant signs and seals (*confirmatio foederis*, q.v.). SEE *usus legis*.

foedus monopleuron or **foedus** μονόπλευρον: *one-sided or one-way covenant;* the covenant as bestowed by God and exhibiting his will toward man. Since the foundation of all divine covenants is the eternal will of God, and the purpose of all divine covenants is ultimately the fulfillment of God's will to the glory of God alone, God's covenants, both the *foedus operum* (q.v.) and the *foedus gratiae* (q.v.), are declarations of the divine will toward man and thus one-sided, *monopleuron*, rather than being covenants arranged by the mutual consent of parties for their mutual benefit. Even though the covenants include man and are to his benefit, man has no part in the arrangement of the terms of the covenants, both of which are bestowed, as it were, from above. SEE *foedus; foedus dipleuron*.

foedus naturae: *covenant of nature;* also sometimes **foedus naturale:** *natural covenant;* a designation of the antelapsarian covenant between God and man, predicated on the original integrity of human nature and its capacity for obedience under the terms of the innate moral or natural law. In the seventeenth century, the Reformed tended to replace this term with *foedus operum* (q.v.), whereas the Arminians, with their emphasis on the inborn capacity for obedience, tended to retain it.

foedus operum: *covenant of works;* viz., the first covenant made by God with man, instituted before the fall when man was still in the *status integritatis* (q.v.) and capable of perfect obedience. The doctrine of the *foedus operum* assumes that Adam and Eve knew the moral law either as the *lex naturalis* (q.v.) as yet unimpaired and unbeclouded by sin or as a *lex paradisiaca* (q.v.) revealed by God. Some of the Reformed go so far as to find in the tree of life (*arbor vitae*) and the tree of the knowledge of good and evil (*arbor scientiae boni et mali*, q.v.) sacramental signs of the grace available, on condition of obedience, to the first pair under the covenant of works. Since, moreover, the trees, and therefore the commands to eat and not eat, have a broad federal significance, the Reformed invariably interpret the violation of the covenant of works as more than a violation of a simple token command not to eat, indeed, as a violation of the entire *lex moralis* (q.v.). The Lutherans, who do not argue a *foedus operum*, tend to argue that violation of the divine command was only mediately a violation of the whole moral law and, immediately, a violation of a test that demanded the same obedience if not the explicit behavior stipulated by the moral law. SEE *homo; iustitia originalis; peccatum originalis*.

fomes peccati: literally, *the tinder of sin;* i.e., the fomenter of sin or source of sin; the inborn concupiscence (*concupiscentia*, q.v.) of the newborn child which ultimately will issue in sin. The idea of the *fomes peccati* is crucial to the doctrine of original sin when the creationist option concerning the origin of the soul is accepted, since the concept of *fomes peccati* argues the transmission of sin in and through the body. See *peccata.*

fons: *fount, fountain, source.*

fons omnium bonorum: *the fountain or source of all good or of all good things;* viz., God the Creator considered according to his absolute goodness as the source of all good in the created order. See *bonitas Dei; summum bonum.*

fons primarius: *primary source;* a term applied to Scripture as the foremost or primary source of theology. The term is not intended to rule out ancillary sources of theology entirely but to accord them distinctly secondary status. See *principia theologiae; usus philosophiae.*

fons totius divinitatis: *source or ground of the whole Godhead;* a term applied to the Father as the person of the Trinity who is the ingenerate source of the filiation of the Son and the spiration, or procession, of the Spirit. Similarly, the Father is the *fons actionis*, the source of the activity of the persons of the Trinity in the *opus oeconomicum* (q.v.).

fontes solutionum: *sources of the solution;* frequently, a concluding section of a dogmatic *locus* (q.v.) in late scholastic systems in which the basis of a positive solution to doctrinal debate is set forth.

forma: *form;* i.e., the form as distinguished from the *materia* and the *substantia* (q.v.) of a thing. From the Aristotelian perspective, form and matter are the inseparable components of *substantia;* the realist perspective, derived from Platonism, assumes the independent extramental existence of *universalia* (q.v.), or forms, and therefore the separability of form and matter. Protestant scholasticism, Lutheran and Reformed, follows the Aristotelian model. *Forma* is not synonymous with *essentia*, since *forma* indicates the shape or pattern impressed upon a *substantia*, whereas *essentia* indicates the entire whatness of a thing including the materiality or spirituality of its *substantia.* In scholastic philosophy and theology, *forma*, as pattern or shape, is synonymous with *causa formalis*, the formal cause (see

123

causa), and somewhat more strictly defined as *forma substantialis*, substantial form, the aspect of *substantia* that differentiates it from other substances, from the secondary matter (*materia secunda*, q.v.) of those substances, and from the purely potential primary matter (*materia prima*, q.v.). In any particular instance of a substance, the term *forma* applies in two ways: first, the *forma substantialis* that differentiates *materia prima* into this or that *materia secunda*, e.g., brass or iron or stone; and second, the principle of self-realization of the individual thing (SEE *entelecheia*) in its movement from potency to actuality (SEE *actus; in actu*), e.g., the form of the statue to be made from the brass or the iron or stone, or in a natural process, the form of the tree that grows from the organic substance of trees.

forma conversionis: *the form of conversion;* carefully defined by the Lutheran scholastics as the translation or transference of unregenerate man from the state of sin and wrath and the kingdom of darkness into the state of grace and faith and the kingdom of God's light. Conversion is, therefore, formally considered, an alteration of condition.

forma corporis: *form of the body;* i.e., the soul. SEE *anima; entelecheia; spiritus incompletus.*

forma Dei: *form of God, the appearance or conduct of God;* a term arising from the text of Phil. 2:5–7 where Christ, existing in the *forma Dei*, or μορφὴ θεοῦ, relinquishes his glory to assume the *forma servi*, or μορθὴ δούλου, the form of a servant. Lutherans and Reformed agree that *forma Dei* does not refer to the divine essence or nature, since relinquishing the *forma Dei* indicates a change in condition or state (SEE *status humiliationis*) and hardly a loss of divinity on the part of the Word. Similarly *forma servi* does not indicate human nature as such but the servant condition of the Word incarnate. The conclusion of the state of humiliation and the beginning of the state of exaltation (*status exaltationis*, q.v.) indicate the passing of the condition of servitude, the *forma servi*, not of Christ's human nature. Beyond this agreement, the Lutheran and Reformed orthodox find a major ground for dispute. The Lutherans predicate the *forma Dei* and the self-emptying (SEE *exinanitio*) of the divine-human Christ while the Reformed predicate the *forma Dei* and the *exinanitio* of the preexistent Christ, the *Logos asarkos*. The Lutherans, therefore, do not include incarnation in the *status humiliationis* or *status exinanitionis*, whereas the Reformed do view incarnation as part of the *humiliatio*.

forma informans: *informing form.* SEE *entelecheia.*

forma sacramenti: *form of the sacrament;* i.e., that which is constitutive of the sacrament as sacrament. The Protestant scholastics argue that sacraments are what they are because of divine institution and not because of faith. Thus, although faith is required to receive the benefits of Christ, the sacrament represents apart from faith an objective offer of grace. Ultimately the *forma* of the sacrament is the *unio sacramentalis* (q.v.), or sacramental union itself, since it is the relation of the *signum* (q.v.) to the *res sacramenti* that makes the elements an objective offer of grace and a sacrament.

forma servi: *the form of a servant;* a reference to the result of the *exinanitio* (q.v.) or *kenōsis* of the Word, from Phil. 2:7. SEE *forma Dei; status humiliationis.*

formalis (adj.): *formal;* i.e., with reference to form. SEE *distinctio; forma.*

formaliter (adv.): *formally.*

forum ecclesiasticum: *an ecclesiastical court;* specifically, a court of canon law in the Roman Catholic Church. SEE *corpus iuris canonici.*

frui: *to enjoy;* in the Augustinian vocabulary, *frui* means specifically to love something for its own sake or as an end in itself, as contrasted to *uti,* to love something for the sake of another or as a means to a higher end. In the Augustinian perspective adopted by the medieval and the Protestant scholastics, *frui* applies only to the love of creatures for God (SEE *amor Dei*) since God alone deserves to be loved for his own sake and as an ultimate end. The created order is not to be despised, but rather to be loved (*uti*) as a means to the higher end of the love of God. Thus God is loved for his sake alone, whereas self and neighbor are loved for God's sake because they are God's creatures and reflect the divine love. In this view, sin is easily characterized as an idolatry that loves the finite as an ultimate end in and for itself.

fruitio: *enjoyment, fruition.* SEE *frui.*

fundamentum electionis: *foundation of election;* in early Reformed orthodoxy, a term applied to Christ in whom the elect are chosen. The term was also used by the Arminians with the implication that the human decision to believe in Christ was the *fundamentum*

125

electionis. At the Synod of Dort, the term was debated and then omitted from the canons because of the Arminian usage. Ultimately the term was lost to Reformed theology. The Reformed scholastics could also distinguish between the *fundamentum electionis,* which, strictly speaking, can only describe Christ according to his divinity and in his decretive willing, and the *fundamentum salutis electorum,* the foundation of the salvation of the elect, which can be applied to Christ in his office as Mediator.

fundamentum fidei: *foundation of faith;* i.e., Christ, upon whom the faith and the salvation of mankind rest. In orthodox Lutheran dogmatics, where a major emphasis was placed on the identification of fundamental articles (*articuli fundamentales,* q.v.) of faith, the ground or foundation of those articles, the *fundamentum fidei,* was also identified. Since fundamental articles are those articles necessary for salvation, they all testify to and are founded upon Christ, the *fundamentum fidei* or *fundamentum fidei et salutis.* The Lutheran scholastics further distinguish the *fundamentum fidei* in terms of its essence, or substance, and its *media,* or means, of proclamation and dissemination. Thus (1) the *fundamentum substantiale,* or substantial foundation, is Christ, the substance and object of faith (*obiectum fidei,* q.v.); (2) the *fundamentum organicum,* the organic or instrumental foundation, is the Word of God, the *principium* or principle of faith, and the chief means of faith (*medium fidei*); and (3) the *fundamentum dogmaticum,* or dogmatic foundation, is that basic teaching of the church that comprises the essential *articuli fundamentales fidei* and sustains the faith of the individual Christian, such as the doctrines of Christ's person and work. This threefold division of the *fundamentum fidei* serves to manifest Christ as the basis of the scriptural Word as well as the reliance of Christian doctrine both on the written Word and on Christ himself, the incarnate Word, the ultimate foundation of the entire revelation of God.

fundamentum Scripturae: *the foundation or ground of Scripture;* i.e., Christ, who as Mediator and Savior is the foundation, center, and essential content of the whole of Scripture. A term used particularly by the Reformed who followed Zacharias Ursinus.

Gg

gemina praedestinatio: *double predestination.* SEE *praedestinatio.*

generatio: *generation;* when used in relation to human beings, birth; when used relative to the Second Person of the Trinity, the Son, the eternal and changeless activity in the Godhead by which the Father produces the Son without division of essence and by which the Second Person of the Trinity is identified as an individual subsistence or *modus subsistendi,* mode of subsistence, of the divine essence. The *generatio,* moreover, is not voluntary but natural and necessary. *Generatio* can also be distinguished into *generatio activa,* active generation, which is the active begetting of the Son by the Father, and *generatio passiva,* passive generation, which is the Son's reflexive relation to the Father in the generation. *Generatio passiva* is sometimes used synonymously with *filiatio,* filiation. Thus the generation of the Son can be described as eternal and perpetual (*aeterna et perpetua*) and described also as *hyperphysica* (q.v.), not physical. It is not, moreover, a movement of the Son from potency to actuality or from nonbeing (*non esse*) into existence (*esse*), but an eternal and perpetual relation in the Godhead, an unchanging activity or motion that is in the divine essence according to its very nature. Since *generatio* belongs to the divine nature, it is a necessary, not a voluntary activity. Finally, like the other *proprietates personales* (SEE *proprietas*), *paternitas* and *spiratio* or *processio,* paternity and spiration or procession, the generation or filiation of the Son is entirely internal (*interna et intima*). SEE *persona; processio intellectualis; subsistentia; Trinitas.*

genesis (γένεσις): *birth, beginning,* or *begetting;* the Greek term used synonymously in trinitarian language with *filiatio,* filiation, or *nativitas,* birth or begottenness, as the *character hypostaticus* (q.v.) or personal character of the Son; also synonymous with *generatio* (q.v.).

genitura: *a generation* or *begetting;* either the act of generation or the thing generated; in trinitarian language, the spiritual generation of the Son or the Son considered as generated.

gennèsia (γεννήσια): *begottenness;* the Greek equivalent of the *filiatio,* or filiation, and *generatio,* or generation, of the Second Person of the Trinity. SEE *genesis; Trinitas.*

genus: *genus;* viz., either a number of individual things identified as a group by means of a common concept or universal, or the universal itself as predicated of a group of individual things. In the former view, the universal is merely an abstraction; in the latter, it exists either in the thing or prior to the thing (SEE *universalia*). The idea of *genus* must be further clarified as indicating a universal that does not exhaustively express or describe the essence, or *quidditas* (q.v.), of the individuals in the group. Thus, human beings, horses, and snails all belong to the *genus* animal. By way of contrast, *species* refers to individuals in a group or to the universal predicated of the group in such a way as to express the essence of those individuals fully or exhaustively. Thus "man" as a species indicates all human beings as specifically rational, intellectual animals and therefore distinct from horses and snails.

genus apotelesmaticum. SEE *communicatio idiomatum.*

genus idiomaticum. SEE *communicatio idiomatum.*

genus maiestaticum. SEE *communicatio idiomatum.*

genus tapeinotikon (from the Greek ταπείνωσις): *tapeinotic genus* or *genus of humiliation;* a fourth genus of the *communicatio idiomatum* (q.v.), or communication of proper qualities, argued by the nineteenth-century German kenoticists, according to which the divine nature empties itself in and through the communication of human attributes to it by the human nature. This concept does not form a part of the orthodox Lutheran Christology and was not taught as a positive doctrine in the era of orthodoxy. The Reformed did, in polemic, point out that the logic of the Lutheran *communicatio idiomatum,* with its communication of divine attributes to the human nature, demanded a reciprocal communication of human attributes to the divine nature. The Reformed argument was intended to show the illogic of the Lutheran position, not, of course, to suggest a fourth genus.

genus theologiae: *the genus of theology;* viz., the classification of theological study. The Protestant scholastics raise the question of the nature of the theological discipline in the prolegomena of their systems, specifically, the question of the classification or *genus* of theology among the various types of human study: art (*ars*), science (*scientia*), wisdom (*sapientia*), or prudence (*prudentia*). Most frequently they place theology, with qualification, into the *genus scientia*. SEE *theologia*.

gloria: *glory, brightness, splendor;* specifically, the *gloria Dei*, or glory of God. The scholastics include *gloria* among the divine attributes, usually in close association with *maiestas*, or majesty. Both terms, *gloria* and *maiestas*, indicate the infinite eminence of God, as manifest in the biblical language of the inaccessible light in which God dwells and the inapproachability of the "face of God." *Gloria* indicates, specifically, the brightness or resplendence of God in his perfection and infinite eminence. This brightness and resplendence, moreover, belong to the divine essence and all its attributes, with the result that the *gloria Dei* and *maiestas Dei* are the divine essence itself, God as the absolute resplendence and the ultimate greatness. SEE *attributa divina*.

gradus gloriae: *degrees of glory;* the teaching, based on 1 Cor. 15:41–42, that heavenly gifts will be distributed unequally after the judgment, *without* implying, however, greater or lesser blessedness or a fuller *visio Dei* (q.v.) for some rather than others. The Reformed tend to rest the *gradus gloriae* on the differences between individuals in this life; those who manifest greater fruits of faith and righteousness on earth will inherit greater glory in heaven. The Lutherans, however, argue against any consideration of human merit on the part of God and admit no degrees *in essentialibus*, in essentials, but only *in accidentalibus*, in accidentals, with those degrees having reference only to the freedom of God to bestow different *praemia* (q.v.) on different activities. SEE *dies novissimus; iudicium extremum*.

gradus poenarum infernalium: *degrees of punishment in hell.* SEE *poena*.

gratia: *grace;* in Greek, χάρις; the gracious or benevolent disposition of God toward sinful mankind and, therefore, the divine operation by which the sinful heart and mind are regenerated and the continuing divine power or operation that cleanses, strengthens, and sanctifies the regenerate. The Protestant scholastics distinguish five *actus gratiae*, or actualizations of grace. (1) *Gratia praeveniens*, or prevenient grace, is the grace of the Holy Spirit bestowed upon sinners in and through the Word; it must precede repentance. (2) *Gratia praeparans* is the preparing grace, according to which the Spirit instills in the repentant sinner a full knowledge of his inability and also his desire to accept the promises of the gospel. This is the stage of the life of the sinner that can be termed the *praeparatio ad conversionem* (q.v.) and that the Lutheran orthodox characterize as a time of *terrores conscientiae* (q.v.). Both this preparation for conversion and the terrors of conscience draw directly upon the second use of the law, the *usus paedagogicus* (SEE *usus legis*). (3) *Gratia operans*, or operating grace, is the effective grace of conversion, according to which the Spirit regenerates the will, illuminates the mind, and imparts faith. Operating grace is, therefore, the grace of justification insofar as it creates in man the means, or medium, faith, through which we are justified by grace (SEE *medium* ληπτικόν). (4) *Gratia cooperans*, or cooperating grace, is the continuing grace of the Spirit, also termed *gratia inhabitans*, indwelling grace, which cooperates with and reinforces the regenerate will and intellect in sanctification. *Gratia cooperans* is the ground of all good works and, insofar as it is a new capacity in the believer for the good, it can be called the *habitus gratiae*, or disposition of grace. Finally, some of the scholastics make a distinction between *gratia cooperans* and (5) *gratia conservans*, or conserving, preserving grace, according to which the Spirit enables the believer to persevere in faith. This latter distinction arises most probably out of the distinction between *sanctificatio* (q.v.) and *perseverantia* (q.v.) in the scholastic *ordo salutis* (q.v.), or order of salvation. Lutherans and Reformed differ over the question of the resistibility of grace. The Lutherans argue a *gratia resistibilis* (q.v.), or resistible grace, so that no inalterable or necessary pattern of *actus gratiae* must follow the initial gift of *gratia praeveniens;* indeed, grace may be rejected and subsequently regained in a repeated conversion (*conversio reiterata*, q.v.). The Reformed argue that grace is irresistible (*gratia irresistibilis*) when given effectively to the elect.

gratia communis: *common grace;* i.e., a nonsaving, universal grace according to which God in his goodness bestows his favor upon all creation in the general blessings of physical sustenance and moral influence for the good. Thus, rain falls on the just and the unjust, and all men have the law engraved on their hearts. *Gratia communis* is therefore contrasted by the Reformed with particular or special grace (*gratia particularis sive specialis*, q.v.).

gratia Dei: *the grace of God;* viz., the goodness of God (*bonitas Dei*, q.v.) toward mankind manifest as undeserved favor and, specifically, the cleansing power of God which renews and regenerates sinners.

gratia gratum faciens: *grace making gracious;* in late medieval theology, the habit of grace (*habitus gratiae,* q.v.) infused into the sinner by which the sinner is justified or made righteous. Following the Reformers' forensic conception of justification (*iustificatio,* q.v.), the Protestant orthodox separate justification and sanctification in the *ordo salutis* (q.v.) and, in addition, deny that grace is a quality in man, defining it instead as an effective power of God. The concept of *gratia gratum faciens* is, therefore, replaced by the concept of the *gratia cooperans,* or cooperating grace, of the Holy Spirit. See *gratia; gratia infusa.*

gratia habitualis: *habitual grace;* also **gratiae habituales**: *habitual graces.* See *communicatio gratiarum.*

gratia infusa: *infused grace;* viz., the *donum gratiae,* or gift of grace, bestowed by God upon believers and the *habitus gratiae,* the habit or disposition toward grace, created in believers by the grace of the Holy Spirit. The Protestant scholastics deny that *gratia infusa* or *gratia inhaerens,* inhering grace, is the basis of justification. Rather *gratia infusa* is the result of *regeneratio* (q.v.) and the basis of *sanctificatio* (q.v.), the source of all the good works of believers. The orthodox, in the main, avoid language of a *habitus gratiae* (q.v.) and prefer the terms *gratia inhaerens* or *gratia cooperans* to the term *gratia infusa* in order to retain in their formulations the Reformers' teaching concerning grace as a power of God or a divine favor (*favor Dei* or *gratuitus favor Dei*) that never belongs to man as an aspect of human nature but is always graciously given. See *gratia.*

gratia ingrediens: *grace entering in;* a synonym for *gratia praeveniens* (q.v.). See *gratia.*

gratia inhaerens: *inherent grace* or *inhering grace;* also termed *gratia inhabitans.* See *gratia.*

gratia particularis sive specialis: *particular or special grace;* i.e., the grace of God that is given savingly only to the elect. The Reformed contrast this *gratia particularis* or *gratia specialis* with the *gratia universalis* (q.v.), or universal grace of the gospel promise, and with the *gratia communis* (q.v.), the common, nonsaving grace given to all. Lutheran orthodoxy argues against the concept on the ground of the efficacy of the Word and in the name of universal grace as a *gratia seria,* a serious grace or grace seriously offered to all, and therefore salvific. See *gratia.*

131

gratia praeveniens: *prevenient grace, the grace that "comes before" all human response to God.* A special term is given to the grace that necessarily precedes *conversio* (q.v.), since mankind is universally sinful and incapable of salvation or of any truly good work without the help of God. A fully monergistic theology, Augustinianism or Calvinism, must assume that this grace is irresistible, whereas a synergistic system, semi-Pelagianism or Arminianism, will hold prevenient grace to be resistible. SEE *gratia resistibilis.*

gratia resistibilis: *resistible grace;* a theological concept used by both the Lutherans and the Arminians to argue against the Reformed that *gratia salvifica* (q.v.), salvific or saving grace, is both universally offered and resistible. Whereas the Arminian teaching clearly indicates a *cooperatio* (q.v.), a cooperation or a synergistic relationship, between God and man in the effecting of salvation, the Lutheran teaching observes that only God's grace is *efficax,* or effective, in salvation but that, since it is not an immediate operation of the divine *omnipotentia* (q.v.) but rather a mediate operation of God in and through designated *media gratiae,* or means of grace, it may be resisted. In other words, the Arminian insists that man may both effectively resist and also effectively cooperate with the *gratia praeveniens* (q.v.), prevenient grace, whereas the Lutheran orthodox allow only a resistance to, but not an effective cooperation with, the *gratia praeveniens.* The Reformed, by way of contrast, allow neither resistance to nor cooperation with the *gratia salvifica praeveniens* and insist that it is both an irresistible grace (*gratia irresistibilis*) and a particular grace (*gratia particularis*).

gratia sacramentalis: *sacramental grace;* viz., the grace of God made available in and through the sacramental means of grace to those who have faith in Christ.

gratia salvifica: *saving grace;* specifically, the gracious favor of God on account of Christ: *Gratia salvifica est gratuitus Dei favor propter Christum.* SEE *gratia.*

gratia specialis: *special grace.* SEE *gratia particularis sive specialis.*

gratia Spiritus Sancti applicatrix: *the applicative grace of the Holy Spirit;* viz., that grace applied by the Holy Spirit which works salvation in the *regeneratio* (q.v.), *conversio* (q.v.), and *sanctificatio* (q.v.) of believers. SEE *ordo salutis.*

gratia unionis: *grace of union.* SEE *communicatio gratiarum.*

gratia universalis: *universal grace;* i.e., that grace of God in the universal call of the gospel according to which salvation is offered to all. SEE *gratia; gratia particularis sive specialis.*

gratuitus favor Dei: *the gracious favor of God, i.e., the grace of God.* SEE *gratia.*

gubernatio: *governance, rule;* especially, providential governance. SEE *concursus; providentia; regimen ecclesiasticum.*

gubernatio ecclesiae civilis: *civil government of the church;* viz., that power which the civil magistrate exercises with respect to the church within his jurisdiction; specifically, a responsibility to protect true worship and the law of God. The power of the magistrate is defined as *circa sacra,* around the holy, not *in sacra,* in the holy.

gula: *gluttony.* SEE *septem peccata mortalia.*

Hh

habitus: *disposition;* specifically, spiritual capacity, belonging to either of the faculties of soul, i.e., to mind or to will. The scholastics assumed that, in addition to defining the faculties of the soul, they also had to acknowledge the capacities or dispositions of those faculties. A faculty cannot receive a datum or act in a manner for which it has no capacity. SEE *anima; facultates animae; intellectus; mens; voluntas.*

habitus fidei: *habit or disposition of faith;* the God-given spiritual capacity of fallen human beings to have faith: i.e., if the mind and will are not disposed to have faith, faith is impossible. Since the fall involves a loss of spiritual capacities, the human being will not come to faith unless the *habitus fidei* is once again instilled. SEE *actus fidei; habitus infusa; medium* ληπτικόν; *semen fidei.*

habitus gratiae: *habit or disposition of grace;* a divine gift infused into the soul in such a way as to become a part of human nature. The *habitus gratiae* can therefore also be called *gratia creata*, created grace, as distinct from the uncreated power of God that brings it into existence, *gratia increata*. In addition, according to its function, the *habitus gratiae* can be called justifying grace (*gratia iustificans*) or sanctifying grace (*gratia sanctificans*). This concept, together with the related concept of an infused righteousness (*iustitia infusa*, q.v.), was rejected by the Reformers insofar as it cannot be correlated with the doctrine of a forensic justification (*iustificatio*, q.v.) on the ground of the alien righteousness (*iustitia aliena*) of Christ imputed to believers by grace alone through faith. The *habitus gratiae* implies an intrinsic righteousness in the believer, whereas the Reformers' concept of imputed righteousness is extrinsic. Righteousness is viewed by the Reformers and the orthodox as inherent, or intrinsic (SEE *iustitia inhaerens*), in relation to the work of the Spirit in sanctification (*sanctificatio*, q.v.), but the concept, here, is expressed in terms of cleansing (*renovatio*, q.v.) rather than in terms of an infused disposition or habit.

habitus infusa: *infused habit or disposition;* i.e., a disposition of mind or will not present naturally in a human being, usually because of the loss of the *imago Dei* (q.v.) in the fall, that is graciously instilled or infused in mind or will by God. SEE *gratia infusa; habitus gratiae.*

habitus supernaturalis sive spiritualis: *supernatural or spiritual habit;* a disposition, capacity, or aptitude that does not belong to the natural capacities of man but which rests upon the divine work of grace in us and is therefore both of the Spirit (*spiritualis*) and from beyond our nature (*supernaturalis*). SEE *habitus gratiae.*

habitus vitiosus acquisitus: *an acquired corrupt habit or disposition.* SEE *peccatum habituale acquisitum.*

Hades (ᾅδης): *Hades;* the Greek equivalent of *Sheol,* the abode of the dead. Following the usage of the New Testament, the Protestant scholastics view *Hades* as the abode of the souls of unbelievers between the death of the body (*mors temporalis,* q.v.) and the final resurrection (SEE *resurrectio*). The unbeliever's soul is separated from God and consigned to the punishment of *Hades* according to the particular and hidden judgment (*iudicium particulare et occultum,* q.v.) that occurs at death. The souls of believers are not consigned to *Hades* but rather are brought into fellowship with God in paradise (*paradisio,* q.v.). SEE *anima.*

hagiasmos (ἁγιασμός): *holiness* (Rom. 6:19, 22) or *sanctification* (1 Cor. 1:30). SEE *sanctitas; sanctificatio.*

haplōs (ἁπλῶς): *simply, absolutely, essentially;* also, with reference to exegesis, *literally,* as distinct from "figuratively" or "allegorically."

hēgemonikon (ἡγεμονικόν): *that which has hegemony (over the mind);* i.e., the inmost part of spirit or of mind (Eph. 4:23), which must be regenerated if the *intellectus* (q.v.) is to overcome its blindness and assent to knowledge of God. The *hēgemonikon* is usually seated in the heart and identified by the fathers as the source of free choice and as the seat of the contemplative life, which, as a result of the creation of man in the *imago Dei,* was capable of seeking God and of perceiving the divine light; in the fall, the *hēgemonikon* lost its capability of seeking and finding the divine and thus became the source of man's inability to choose freely for the good. Depending on a philosopher's or theologian's view of the seat of choice, it is variously identified, sometimes as intellect itself, sometimes as the underlying intellective appetite, and sometimes as will.

hekousios (ἑκούσιος): *voluntary.*

henōsis hypostatikē (ἕνωσις ὑποστατική): *hypostatic or personal union.* SEE *unio personalis.*

heteroousios (ἑτεροούσιος): *of a different essence;* a term used by the radical Arians of the mid- and late fourth century, Aetius and Eunomius, similar in implication to the extreme Arian term, *anomoios* (q.v.), unlike. SEE *homoousios.*

heurēma (εὕρημα): *invention;* used by the orthodox as a negative epithet, roughly synonymous with heresy, since, following patristic usage, heresy was innovation.

hexaemeron: literally, *the six days;* from the Greek *hex* (six) and *hēmera* (day); specifically, the six days of creation or six days of divine work as recounted in the first chapter of Genesis.

Hic est sanguis meus: *This is my blood;* i.e., the words of institution of the Lord's Supper, or *coena sacra* (q.v.). SEE *verbum institutionis.*

hilastērion (ἱλαστήριον): *expiation* or *propitation;* specifically, in the objective sense of that which makes expiation or propitiation, e.g., Rom. 3:25; therefore, Christ as the propitiation for our sins. SEE *munus triplex; sacerdotium; satisfactio vicaria.*

historia revelationis: *the history of revelation;* a term applied to the historical course of the revelation and fulfillment of God's law and promises, especially to the historical course of the covenant of grace (*foedus gratiae,* q.v.) from Abraham to Christ.

historicus, -a, -um (adj.): *historical;* also, as an adverb, **historicaliter**: *historically;* by extension, particularly in exegetical usage, *historicus* indicates "literal"; e.g., *sensus historicus,* the historical sense, is the *sensus literalis,* or literal sense, of the text as opposed to the *sensus allegoricus.* SEE *authentia historica; sensus literalis.*

Hoc est corpus meum: *This is my body;* i.e., the words of institution of the Lord's Supper, or *coena sacra* (q.v.). SEE *verbum institutionis.*

holōs (ὅλως): *generally.*

homo: *man;* the Latin generic term corresponding to the Greek *anthrōpos,* as distinct from *vir,* a male, and *femina,* a female. Scholastic theology draws distinctions between the carnal man (*homo carnalis*), the human being conceived as material or fleshly and as given over to things of the flesh or fleshly desires (SEE *appetitus*), and the spiritual man (*homo spiritualis*), the human being conceived as guided by his higher faculties. A similar distinction can be made between *homo exterior,* the exterior or physical man, and *homo interior,* the interior or spiritual man; or again, between *homo infidelis,* unbelieving or unfaithful man, and *homo fidelis,* believing or faithful man. These distinctions, in turn, rest upon the highly developed theological anthropology or doctrine of man held by the medieval scholastics, modified in the light of the doctrine of salvation by grace alone, and refashioned by the Reformers and Protestant orthodoxy. The Protestant orthodox make a basic distinction between the condition of man before the fall (*ante lapsum*) and that of man after the fall (*post lapsum;* SEE *lapsus*). Man, male and female, was created in the image of God (*imago Dei,* q.v.), a creature of body (*corpus*) and soul (*anima,* q.v.), capable by virtue of the liberty of his nature (*libertas naturae,* q.v.) of choosing freely (SEE *liberum arbitrium*) between good and evil, able not to sin (*posse non peccare*) and able to sin (*posse peccare*). Since man was, even in this state, sustained by God's grace (*gratia,* q.v.), the Protestant orthodox deny both the idea of a purely natural condition (*status purorum naturalium,* q.v.) and the idea of a divine grace bestowed on man for initial meritorious acts done on the basis of human will alone (SEE *donum concreatum; donum superadditum; facere quod in se est*). Nonetheless, before the fall, man was capable of relying upon a resistible divine grace and of learning the natural law (*lex naturalis,* q.v.), or law of paradise (*lex paradisiaca,* q.v.), by means of the light of nature (*lumen naturae,* q.v.). The Reformed describe these conditions of obedience before the fall as a covenant of works (*foedus operum,* q.v.). Since man was created good, as were all things made by God, evil cannot be described as a thing (*res,* q.v.) or as a substance (*substantia,* q.v.), but must be understood as a privation of the good (*privatio boni,* q.v.) which results from a defective willing (SEE *voluntas*). Thus sin (SEE *peccata*) is not a substance but a stain (*macula,* q.v.) or a fault (*reatus,* q.v.). Once fallen away from this pristine fellowship with God, man can return to God only through illumination (*illuminatio,* q.v.) by the light of grace and through the work of the Spirit in regeneration (*regeneratio,* q.v.). Human beings regenerated and illuminated by grace can be described as pilgrims (SEE *viator*) on the way (*in via,* q.v.) toward salvation (*salus;* SEE *ordo salutis*). The true knowledge of God necessary for salvation is no longer accessible to man by means of the light of nature: general revelation in nature only leaves man without excuse in sin—a special revelation of saving truth (SEE *revelatio generalis/revelatio specialis*) is required for salvation (SEE *Scriptura sacra*). Since all have sinned and death is the wages of sin, all men must die (SEE *mors*), but the faithful (*fideles*), the members of the church militant (*ecclesia militans;* SEE *ecclesia*), pass, by way of death, into the ranks of the blessed (*beati*, q.v.), illuminated now by the light of glory (*lumen gloriae*), unable to sin (*non posse peccare*, q.v.), in the heavenly homeland (SEE *in patria*), the city (*civitas*, q.v.) or commonwealth of God, the church triumphant (*ecclesia triumphans*). The unfaithful (*infideles*), following the resurrection of the dead (SEE *resurrectio*) and the final judgment (*iudicium extremum*, q.v.), will suffer eternal punishment (SEE *poena*) and destruction (*exitium*, q.v.).

homo Deifer: *a God-bearing man;* a heretical christological position, ascribed to Nestorius because of his assertion of the hypostatic or personal character of Christ's human nature.

homo peccator: *man the sinner; man after the fall;* specifically, man as the one for whom theology exists, insofar as theology is intended to teach the doctrines necessary to salvation.

homo renascens: *man being reborn or in the process of being reborn;* a view of conversion denied by the orthodox who all argue, even those who speak of *praeparatio ad conversionem* (q.v.), or preparation for conversion, and of *terrores conscientiae* (q.v.), or terrors of conscience, leading toward conversion, that the *conversio* (q.v.) itself occurs in the moment of the application of saving grace by the Spirit. There is, then, no *status medius*, or middle state, between the sinful condition in which we are born and the *status gratiae* (q.v.), or state of grace, into which we are drawn by grace in conversion and justification. There is no *homo in statu medio constitutus*, no man established in a middle state or condition.

homoeousios. SEE *homoiousios.*

homoios (ὅμοιος): *like, similar;* a term used by the party which dominated the councils of Nice (Ustodizo, a small city in Thrace—359) and Constantinople (360). It was offered as a term of compromise between the Athanasian and radical Arian positions and indicated that the Son was "like the Father." Although *homoios* may be regarded as less pointedly Arian than the *anomoios* (q.v.), or "unlike," of radical Arianism of Eunomius and the Council of Sirmium (357), it does *not* argue likeness of essence (*homoiousios*, q.v.) and may indicate only a moral or ethical likeness. The so-called homoean position, therefore, not only fails to satisfy Athanasian or Nicene orthodoxy, but also fails to address the views of the true middle-party, the homoiousians. The term is occasionally used by the Protestant orthodox as a characterization of Arian error.

homoiousios (ὁμοιούσιος): *of like substance;* a term used to describe the relation of the Father to the Son by the non-Athanasian, non-Arian party in the church following the Council of Nicaea. The term represents an attempt of the conservative majority of the bishops of the mid-fourth century to avoid the radical distinction, typical of Arianism, between Father as fully God and the Son as creature without adopting the much-debated Athanasian term *homoousios* (q.v.) and the Nicene formula. *Homoousios* seemed to imply a Sabellian, or modalistic monarchian, view of the Trinity, particularly in the light of the theology of Marcellus of Ancyra, one of the advocates of the Nicene formula. The middle position represented by the term *homoiousios* is frequently called semi-Arian because of Athanasius's opposition, but it clearly represents an alternative to both the Athanasian *homoousios* and the Arian *anomoios* (q.v.). Ultimately, the large homoiousian party in the church was reconciled to the Athanasian or Nicene language of *homoousios* through the positive efforts of the Cappadocian fathers and because of the negative impact of the hyper-Arian anomoean party.

homoousios (ὁμοούσιος): *of the same substance; consubstantial;* the term central to the argument of Athanasius against Arius and to the solution of the trinitarian problem offered at the Council of Nicaea (A.D. 325). It ultimately indicates the numerical unity of essence in the three divine persons, Father, Son, and Holy Spirit, against the Arian contention of three distinct substances. The term had been used earlier by Origen and in Greek philosophy to indicate a generic equality or sameness of substance, and even by the Gnostics to indicate the continuity of substance between the emanated aeons that have come forth from the abyss of spiritual being. The Nicene usage of the term *homoousios* was probably limited to the refutation of Arianism and the affirmation of the substantial equality of the Father and the Son. In the theological development of trinitarian theology, however, the Nicene language was rapidly interpreted as pointing to the concept of the oneness and indivisibility of the Godhead; in addition, it was read in terms of the Western, Latin usage inherited from Tertullian, *unius substantiae,* of one substance. Both the Latin understanding of *homoousios* and the development of Greek doctrine typical of the Cappadocian fathers and of the Council of Constantinople (381) argue a numerical unity of indivisible divine essence in which the three divine persons subsist and which is fully present in each of the persons. Thus, *homoousios* indicates

139

the fullness of the indivisible *ousia,* or substance, of the Godhead in each of the divine persons and implies the essential coinherence (*circumincessio,* q.v.) of the three persons. (It was part of the Cappadocian contribution to extend the language of *homoousios* to the Holy Spirit.)

The term also indicates, following the declarations of the Council of Chalcedon (451), the fullness of Christ's humanity: Christ, as Son of God, is *homoousios* with the Father, and as Son of Mary is *homoousios* with mankind. In the Chalcedonian formula, therefore, *homoousios* has the root meaning of consubstantiality or coessentiality. Protestant orthodoxy maintains the patristic usage. SEE *Trinitas; unio personalis.*

honor adorationis: *the honor of adoration;* specifically, adoration accorded to Christ as the Son of God. The whole person of Christ is the object of worship and adoration, but that worship and adoration rests on Christ's divinity, not on his humanity. SEE *latria.*

hyieis basileias (υἱεῖς βασιλείας): *children or sons of the kingdom;* a term applied to the baptized. In Reformed theology it even extends to the nonelect, since by baptism they belong (if only outwardly) to the covenant people.

hyiothesia (υἱοθεσία): *adoption.* SEE *adoptio.*

hylē amorphos (ὕλη ἄμορφος): *formless void, chaos;* used by the Protestant scholastics as a synonym for the *materia prima* (q.v.) or *materia inhabilis* (q.v.) of the *creatio prima.* SEE *creatio.*

hyparktikōs (ὑπαρκτικῶς): *really* or *substantially.*

hyperdulia: *exalted or high veneration.* SEE *latria.*

hypēretikon (ὑπηρετικόν): *a menial person; a servant; a subordinate thing.*

hyperochē (ὑπεροχή): *prominence, superiority.*

hyperphysica (from the Greek, ὑπερφυσικὰ): *hyperphysical; beyond the physical;* a term applied to the eternal *generatio* (q.v.) of the Son in order to emphasize the difference between divine and creaturely generation. The term is also used by orthodox Lutherans to characterize the illocal presence of Christ's body and blood in the Lord's Supper. SEE *praesentia illocalis sive definitiva.*

hyphistamenon (ὑφιστάμενον): *something placed or set under something else; a subordinate thing.*

hypodikos (ὑπόδικος): *guilty; liable to punishment,* e.g., Rom. 3:19. SEE *reatus.*

hyponomos (ὑπόνομος): *under law, subject to law;* this usage does not appear in the standard lexica of classical, New Testament, or patristic Greek.

hypostasis (ὑπόστασις). SEE *subsistentia* and *persona.*

hypostatikōs (ὑποστατικῶς): *hypostatically* or *personally;* as opposed to *ousiadōs* (οὐσιαδῶς), essentially. SEE *essentialiter.*

hypsōsis (ὕψωσις): *exaltation.* SEE *status exaltationis.*

Ii

idiomata: *proper qualities;* the intimate attributes or properties of a thing that identify it in its individuality, i.e., that are proper to it. SEE *attributa divina; communicatio idiomatum; proprietas; proprium.*

idion deipnon (ἴδιον δεῖπνον): *one's own supper or dinner* (1 Cor. 11:21) in contrast to the Lord's Supper, which is not a meal for physical nourishment.

idiopoiēsis (ἰδιοποίησις): *self-appropriation; the act of making something one's own or taking something for one's self.*

idiopoiētikōs (ἰδιοποιητικῶς): *appropriately or peculiarly belonging to a person.*

illocalis subsistendi modus: *illocal mode of subsistence;* viz., a mode or manner of individual existence characteristic of a spiritual being as opposed to a physical thing. SEE *localis subsistendi modus; praesentia.*

illuminatio: *illumination;* viz., the realization or actuality of grace (*actus gratiae*) by which the Holy Spirit instructs the sinner in and through the ministry of the Word, both to convict the individual of sin by means of the law and to convey to him a knowledge of salvation by means of the gospel. *Illuminatio* is an application of grace and is therefore sometimes called an *actus gratiae applicatricis.* This application begins with conversion but continues on through sanctification as the basis of both repentance and assurance in the life of the believer. *Illuminatio* is therefore intimately connected with calling (*vocatio*, q.v.), specifically with the special or direct calling (*vocatio specialis sive directa*) of the Word. This illumination can further be distinguished into *illuminatio imperfecta sive paedagogica*, imperfect or pedagogical illumination, which is an external teaching that prepares the individual for the work of the Spirit, and *illuminatio perfecta sive salutaris*, perfect or salvific illumination, which is the internal teaching of the Spirit in conjunction with conversion. This latter illumination is both *legalis*, by means of the law, and *evangelica*, by means of the gospel. Furthermore, illumination is aided by the *adminicula*, the spiritual supports or auxiliaries, prayer (*oratio*), meditation (*meditatio*), and trial (*tentatio*).

We also note the philosophical meaning of illumination, rooted in medieval Augustinianism, and less typical of the Protestant than of the medieval scholastics. *Illuminatio* here indicates the enlightenment of the mind by the divine light with archetypal ideas of truth, goodness, perfection, and so forth. According to the theory of illumination, finite truth, goodness, or perfection is recognized by means of a disposition or capacity of the mind (*habitus mentis*) that has been graciously instilled in the human reason by the enlightening influence of the divine ideas or *rationes aeternae*, the archetypal forms or universal ideas. In addition, the indirect knowledge that we have of these archetypes is the foundation of certainty. Apart from this illumination of the mind, our knowledge must rest on sense perception of the finite order where no absolutes are given and where there is, therefore, no absolute certainty. This view of illumination belongs to the Augustinian tradition as defined by Bonaventure in the Middle Ages. Its underlying philosophical realism made the theory unacceptable to the more Aristotelian or conceptualist of the scholastics (Thomas and Scotus) and, of course, to the nominalists. The Protestant scholastics tend to inherit the Aristotelian view of truth (*veritas*, q.v.) and a generally Aristotelian epistemology. They therefore tend away from the philosophical use of *illuminatio* but retain the specifically theological form of the theory as related to the internal work and testimony of the Spirit. SEE *actus; conversio; sanctificatio; testimonium internum Spiritus Sancti; universalia.*

imago Dei: *image of God;* sometimes **imago divina**: *divine image;* viz., that likeness or resemblance to God in which man was originally created and which was lost, or at least so vitiated, in the fall that only *vestigia* now remain. The Reformed and the Lutherans agree, against the Roman Catholic (and medieval scholastic) idea of a *donum superadditum* (q.v.), that the *imago divina* was not superadded to human nature, but was a *donum*, or gift, belonging to the original human constitution and intrinsic to it, a *donum concreatum* (q.v.). They also agree as to its nearly complete loss and the present inability of man to regain any of the lost gift by his own efforts. They disagree, however, as to the precise identification of the *imago.* The orthodox Lutheran doctrine was constructed negatively, in reaction to Matthias Flacius's extreme view of the fall, and positively, under the influence of a highly christological definition of the *imago* according to its basic substance or essence. Against Flacius's identification of the *imago Dei* in man as the *forma substantialis* of humanity, the Lutheran orthodox distinguished between the substantial image of God, which is Christ himself, and the accidental image, which is the likeness of the divine in man's original created nature. The *imago substantialis* is the image and essence of the Father, which Christ, as the Second Person of the Trinity, possesses in and of himself. Since the substantial image is the Son of God, then man neither had nor lost the substantial image; indeed, the fall did not destroy the substance of human nature, nor does grace restore or create substance in redemption. Rather the fall brought about the loss of accidental perfections or attributes that are restored to human nature by the grace of redemption. This *imago Dei accidentalis* can therefore be defined precisely in terms of the gifts of grace bestowed on man in the work of salvation, viz., righteousness, holiness, and knowledge of God. The Lutheran dogmaticians conclude that the original *imago Dei* lost in the fall consisted in the "principal perfections" of righteousness, holiness, and wisdom. All three are perfections of soul. To these they add three derivative or secondary perfections that belong to body as well as to soul: impassibility or freedom from suffering; immortality or freedom from dying, not in the sense of *non posse mori*, not capable of dying, but in the sense of *posse non mori*, the ability (through obedience resting on the *iustitia originalis*, q.v.) not to die; and dominion or power over the creation, subsidiary to and derived from the power of God, including the right to enjoy the fruits of the earth.

The Reformed agree that the *imago* is accidental, not substantial, so that it was both capable of being passed on and capable of being lost. They do not, however, emphasize as strongly the christological element of the doctrine of the *imago* in man and therefore tend not to juxtapose the concept of the *imago substantialis* with the *imago accidentalis*. Instead, the Reformed argue that Christ, as Son of God and Second Person of the Trinity, is the *imago Dei invisibilis*, the image of invisible God, and thus may be called the essential or natural image of God (*imago Dei essentialis sive naturalis*) in his equality with the Father, not in the sense of his being an archetype for humanity. In addition, the Reformed do not make the distinction between primary and secondary perfections, but join body and soul together more closely in the definition of the *imago*. Thus the Reformed argue that although the *imago* is not substantial, nevertheless it belongs to the whole essence of man, to the primary faculties of the soul (*intellectus* and *voluntas*, q.v.) and all of their virtues, and, because of the intimate relation of soul to body, to the body as well. The *imago*, then, belongs to the body in a derivative sense, but it is the whole *imago* that pertains to the body in this derived sense and not merely a set of secondary perfections. Rather than a primary attribute of holiness, therefore, the Reformed argue a perfect blessedness of body and soul. To this they add, in agreement with the Lutherans, a high original wisdom, implying both true knowledge of God and true knowledge of self; original righteousness; and dominion over the creation. Beyond this the Reformed also emphasize the *liberum arbitrium* (q.v.), or free choice, of the will as part of the original *imago*. The *liberum arbitrium*, defined as the *posse non peccare* (q.v.), is fundamental to the *imago* since, together with the gracious support of God, it is the freedom of choosing the good that perpetuates (or could have perpetuated) the attribute of original righteousness. This original freedom of choice, then, was the freedom to obey God perfectly. Of course, the will itself considered as a faculty is not lost in the fall; neither is the intellect, the affections, or the basic inward capacity to know the good (SEE *conscientia; synderesis*)—these are merely vitiated, distorted, deprived of righteousness, and enslaved to sin. The sin which brings about the loss or, more precisely, the profound distortion, is not an absolute privation of being (*privatio pura*) but a partial privation of attributes in a substance (*privatio non pura*). The Reformed, therefore, make a further distinction between the *imago Dei intrinseca*, the intrinsic image of God, consisting in the faculties of intellect and will, the affections, and the conscience (or, at least, the capacity to know good, the *synderesis*), i.e., the *imago* abstractly or metaphysically considered, and the *imago Dei extrinseca*, the extrinsic image of God, consisting in these faculties in their righteousness, holiness, and purity, i.e., the *imago* concretely and ethically considered. Whereas the *imago* in the former sense can be said to remain as one aspect of the essence of humanity, the *imago* in the latter sense is clearly lost in the fall. The regenerate (*renati*) do not regain by grace all that was lost in the fall, although the sanctifying grace of the Spirit does restore some of the original righteousness and knowledge of self. The Reformed, therefore, speak of an *imago spiritualis*, or spiritual image, of God in the regenerate.

Finally, the Reformed agree with the Lutherans in allowing that Adam was in some sense immortal and had the *posse non mori*, but they do not include this ability in the *imago* itself; instead it rests on the right exercise of freedom of choice. This immortality, then, is the result of righteousness and, according to the Reformed, does not exclude a physical mortality related to the bodily mutability of man and to man's need for sustenance. This immortality is a derivation from the *imago* rather than an aspect of it. The difference here with the Lutherans consists only in the Lutheran inclusion of derived attributes in the *imago* as secondary perfections belonging principally to the body. SEE *homo; imago Satanae; privatio; privatio boni.*

imago Satanae: *image of Satan;* a term used by the Lutheran theologian Flacius in his extreme view of the fall. He argued that the fall resulted in the loss of the entire *imago Dei* and, therefore, in the alteration of the *forma substantialis* of humanity from good to evil, so that the original righteous *forma* (q.v.) of humanity, the *imago Dei* (q.v.), was replaced by a new utterly depraved form, the *imago Satanae,* which could be saved only through a new creation by grace.

imitatio Christi: *imitation of Christ;* a central theme in Christian piety and spirituality from Ignatius of Antioch in the early second century onward; also the title of a book on this theme, attributed to Thomas à Kempis. The term *imitatio Christi* indicates the form of spirituality which uses the loving, obedient, servantlike life of Christ, including his passion, as the model for Christian living. The early patristic stress on imitation grew out of persecution and emphasized the path to martyrdom and individual acceptance of the cross. The medieval form of the teaching, brought to fulfillment in à Kempis's work, is a form of this-worldly mysticism that describes the spiritual life and the interior discipline necessary to inculcate a Christlike perfection in this life. This model became typical of the *devotio moderna,* or modern devotion, of the fifteenth century.

immaculata conceptio: *immaculate conception;* viz., the doctrine that the Virgin Mary was conceived sinless in order that she be a fitting vessel for the conception of Christ. The doctrine was developed and hotly contested among the medieval doctors; Thomas Aquinas denied the concept; Duns Scotus argued its logical probability and, on the basis of probability, its validity. The immaculate conception is universally rejected by the Reformers as unnecessary to the sinless nature of Christ. Note that the word *immaculata* is used with direct reference to the basic characterization of sin as *macula* (q.v.), or stain.

immediatio suppositi: *the immediacy of the self-subsistent individual or being,* specifically, of God in his *omnipraesentia* (q.v.). SEE *concursus.*

immediatio virtutis: *the immediacy of effective power,* specifically, of the divine *omnipotentia* (q.v.). SEE *concursus.*

immensitas: *immeasurability; immensurability;* especially, the *immensitas Dei,* or immeasurability of God. By this attribute the scholastics indicate the freedom of God from all limit of place. The divine essence is *sine mensura,* without measure, and fills all things repletively (SEE *repletivus*). *Immensitas* can be distinguished from *omnipraesentia* (q.v.), or omnipresence. The freedom of God from all limit of place or measure, i.e., *immensitas,* properly describes God in eternity apart from all created place; *omnipraesentia,* strictly defined, indicates the repletive presence of God in all created places and in relation to the limited presence of all creatures. Of course, place (*locus*) as such is characteristic of the finite, created order, without which there could be no place. The scholastics do not understand either place or space as an absolute. Thus *immensitas* is an immanent, essential attribute of God in his distinction from the world, whereas *omnipraesentia* is a relative attribute that expresses the noncircumscriptive presence of God: God is *illocalis,* or nonlocal, and his presence *intensiva, indivisibilis,* and *incomprehensibilis.*

immortalitas: *immortality;* an attribute or property of all spiritual being that, insofar as it is immaterial and simple, is not subject to the dissolution that affects all material and complex substances. Thus the soul (*anima,* q.v.) is immortal, not only by grace (*per gratiam*), but by its own nature (*per naturam suam*). This immortality of soul is not, however, an absolute immortality. The scholastics note that the soul take its origin from God, is therefore contingent upon the divine will for its existence, and could be destroyed by God, indeed, would cease to be without the continuing providential support of God (SEE *concursus; continuata creatio*). The soul is immortal in the sense that it cannot be destroyed or dissolved by finite or secondary causes. The same considerations apply to angels. Absolute immortality, i.e., absolute, noncontingent, self-existent, and necessary life, belongs only to God. The *immortalitas Dei* can be argued in terms of the immateriality or spirituality (*spiritualitas,* q.v.) and the simplicity (*simplicitas,* q.v.) of God. God as spirit is not subject to dissolution, and as absolute, infinite spirit does not belong, as finite spirits do, to the contingent order. God's immortality is also, and more properly, a function of the divine life (*vita Dei,* q.v.) that God has of himself. This divine life, by virtue of which God is eternally active, is identical with the divine essence. Since it is of the very essence of God that God lives or, in other words, that God exists (SEE *actus purus*), God is immortal in an absolute sense. Conversely any being not absolutely immortal could not be God. SEE *immutabilitas.*

147

immutabilitas: *immutability, changelessness;* especially, the *immutabilitas Dei,* or immutability of God, according to which God is understood as free from all mutation of being, attributes, place, or will, and from all physical and ethical change; or, in other words, the *immutabilitas Dei* indicates the eternal and perpetual identity of the divine essence with all its perfections. Specifically, immutability of *esse* indicates the *immortalitas* (q.v.), or immortality, and *incorruptibilitas,* or incorruptibility, of God; immutability of *attributa* or *accidentia* indicates the changelessness of divine perfections; immutability of *locus,* or place, refers to the *omnipraesentia* (q.v.), or omnipresence, of God that fills all things; and immutability of *voluntas* (q.v.), or will, refers to the divine constancy in all that has been decreed and promised. God, therefore, does not repent; repentance is attributed to God in Scripture by anthropopathy (*anthrōpopatheia,* q.v.) and indicates, not a change in God, but rather a changed relationship between God and man. Neither does creation imply a change in God and a denial of immutability. The scholastics distinguish between the *principium agendi,* or effective principle in creation, which is the divine essence itself, and the *effectum productum,* or produced effect, in creation, which is the created order. In the produced effect there is clearly change or mutation. The creation is a movement from nonexistence to existence. But in the effective principle, God, there is no change or mutation since God eternally and immutably wills to produce the creation. The change that occurs in creation is external to God. SEE *fidelitas.*

impanatio: *impanation;* viz., the presence of the body of Christ *in pane,* in the bread of the sacrament, as opposed both to the theory of *transubstantiatio* (q.v.) and to the theories of illocal and spiritual presence. SEE *consubstantiatio; praesentia illocalis sive definitiva; praesentia spiritualis sive virtualis.*

impeccabilitas: *sinlessness.* SEE *anamartēsia.*

imperium dominicum: *lordly command.* SEE *lex paradisiaca.*

impii: *the impious;* hence, sinners, as in such usages as *iustificatio impii,* the justification of the sinner.

impoenitentia finalis: *final impenitence;* i.e., the condition of those who die unregenerate. SEE *intuitu incredulitatis finalis; peccatum in Spiritum Sanctum.*

impulsum scribendi. SEE *mandatum scribendi.*

imputatio: *imputation, an act of attribution;* specifically, either (1) *imputatio peccati,* the imputation of sin, or (2) *imputatio satisfactionis Christi,* the imputation of the satisfaction of Christ, which are parallel imputations following a pattern reminiscent of the patristic conception of *recapitulatio* (q.v.).

(1) *Imputatio peccati* is distinguished into *imputatio mediata* and *imputatio immediata,* mediate and immediate imputation. Mediate imputation refers to the divine attribution of sinfulness to mankind because of the *corruptio haereditaria,* or hereditary corruption, of all people. The imputation is mediate since it is contingent upon the natural corruption of individual human beings. Immediate imputation, by contrast, refers to the divine attribution of sinfulness to mankind because of the fall; i.e., it is the immediate attribution of the fall itself to all the progeny of Adam and Eve, apart from their hereditary corruption. The imputation is immediate because it is not contingent upon the corruption of individual human beings. Scholastic Lutheranism tended to recognize both an *imputatio mediata* and an *imputatio immediata;* the Reformed, however, in accordance with the principles of covenant theology and their view of Adam as federal head, tended toward *imputatio immediata* to the exclusion of a theory of mediate imputation. Only the renegade school of Saumur tended in the opposite direction, teaching an *imputatio mediata* only. This view was rejected by the orthodox Reformed as standing in conflict with and prejudicial to the *imputatio satisfactionis Christi.* In the era of orthodoxy both the Socinians and the Arminians denied any *imputatio peccati.*

(2) *Imputatio satisfactionis Christi* is the objective basis of justification by grace through faith. Christ's payment for sin is imputed to the faithful, who could not of themselves make payment; the unrighteous are counted righteous on the grounds of their faith. The orthodox Reformed argued that, since Christ's righteous satisfaction was imputed immediately to believers without any righteousness being present in or satisfaction made by them before the imputation, the imputation of sin must also be immediate; if not, injustice would be done to Christ's work. See *peccatum originalis; satisfactio Christi.*

in abstracto: *in the abstract;* with reference to an abstraction, as opposed to *in concreto,* in the concrete, or with reference to a *concretum* (q.v.). In the problem of the *communicatio idiomatum* (q.v.), as debated by the Reformed and the Lutherans, the question arises as to whether or not attributes, considered *in abstracto,* can be predicated of the person of Christ (which is a *concretum*) and referred or communicated from the *abstractum* (q.v.) of one nature to the *abstractum* of the other. The Reformed contend that *abstracta*

149

cannot be predicated of each other or predicated of *concreta*. Thus, divinity (an abstraction) cannot be predicated of humanity (an abstraction), nor can divinity be predicated of the man Jesus (a concretion) or humanity of God (a concretion). Rather the attributes of both natures can be predicated of the *concretum* of Christ's divine-human person, and, because of the *unio personalis* (q.v.), the *concreta* of the natures can be predicated of each other. Thus, the man Jesus is God. The Reformed argue that to predicate divine attributes of the human nature of Christ is to predicate *abstracta* of an *abstractum* and, therefore, an error—a *communicatio idiomatum in abstracto*.

The Lutheran response agrees that predication is correctly made *in concreto* and incorrectly made *in abstracto*, so that it is proper to say that the man Jesus is God and improper to claim that humanity is divinity. They argue, however, that the predication of divine attributes of the human nature arises out of the presence of the human *concretum* in and with the *concretum* of the divine person through the *unio personalis* (q.v.), or personal union. It is therefore incorrect to call the Lutheran view a *communicatio idiomatum in abstracto*.

in actu: *in the state or condition of actualization; in actuality;* a scholastic distinction between an operative faculty in the state of primary actualization, *in actu primo*, and an operative faculty in the state of secondary actualization, *in actu secundo*. There is a sense in which a being or a substance endowed with operative faculties like intellect and will is actualized, or *in actu*, simply by being what it is, apart from the consideration of the operations of the faculties. This condition of simply being what it is with its faculties is the condition of primary actualization; the being or substance is *in actu primo*. The condition of the being in the actual exercise of its faculties is the condition of secondary actualization; the being is considered to be *in actu secundo*. In finite, temporal creatures a real distinction obtains between being *in actu primo* and being *in actu secundo*, since the faculties of intellect and will are not in eternal or perpetual operation. In God, however, the distinction is merely rational or, in the Scotist form of the argument, formal—since there is in God no movement from potency to actuality, no coming into operation of operative faculties, no real distinction between a faculty and its operation, or between an attribute and the divine essence (SEE *attributa divina; distinctio*). With the qualification that it is merely rational or formal, however, a distinction can be made between the mind and will of God as such and the operation or exercise of knowing and willing in God or, further, between the life of God as such and the *ad intra* activity or operations in which that life is eternally expressed. SEE *opera Dei ad intra; vita Dei.*

in carne/in gratia/in gloria: *in the flesh/in grace/in glory;* a way of referring to the three advents of Christ. SEE *adventus Christi.*

in concreto: *in the concrete,* or *with reference to the concrete thing,* as opposed to *in abstracto* (q.v.).

in defectu: *in defect* or *defective;* contrasted with *in excessu* (q.v.).

in excessu: *in excess, excessive;* contrasted with *in defectu,* in defect or defective; terms indicating a misuse or imbalance of ideas or principles in a systematic exposition. The Reformed orthodox speak, e.g., of the medieval scholastic use of philosophy in theological system as *in excessu* and of the Anabaptist scorn of philosophy as *usus in defectu,* contrasting both cases with their own use of philosophy within the proper limits.

in foro divino: literally, *in the divine forum; i.e., before the divine assize;* a metaphorical way of describing the pattern of man's reconciliation before God as *actus forensis* (q.v.), or forensic act.

in patria: *in the fatherland;* viz., in paradise, or in the place and condition of the blessed (*beati,* q.v.), who are no longer wanderers or pilgrims in search of the heavenly city, but who have found the city that is to come. SEE *in via.*

in potentia: *in potency; potential;* i.e., capable of being or becoming but not yet existent or actualized. SEE *actus; in actu; potentia.*

in puncto rationis: *in point of reason.*

in puris naturalibus: *in a purely natural condition.* SEE *status purorum naturalium.*

in re: *in the thing.* SEE *universalia.*

in se: *in itself.*

in subiecto: *in the subject;* specifically, an idea or concept as it appears in a knowing subject, as opposed to the idea or concept given objectively in itself (*in se*).

in via: literally, *on the way;* a term applied to the *viator* (q.v.) or Christian pilgrim in the world on his way to heavenly reward and blessedness. SEE *in patria.*

incarnandus/incarnatus: *to be incarnate/incarnate* or *incarnated;* an important distinction regarding the divine *Logos,* or Word of God. The Word of God (*Verbum Dei,* q.v.), understood as the Second Person of the Trinity, can be considered either in his eternal Godhead, in his revelatory work throughout history before the incarnation, or in his work as the Incarnate Lord. In the first two senses, the Word is not incarnate but is, nevertheless, not ever severed or divorced from incarnation in the eternal plan or purpose of God (*consilium Dei,* q.v.). In particular, the revelatory work of the Word in the Old Testament represents a foreshadowing of incarnation. Thus, both eternally and in the Old Testament history, the Word may be called the *Logos incarnandus,* the Word to be incarnate. Once the *consilium Dei* has been executed in time, and from thence to eternity, the Word is *Logos incarnatus,* the Word incarnate as the divine-human person of Christ. SEE *incarnatio; unio personalis.*

incarnatio: *incarnation;* viz., the unition (*unitio*), or act of uniting, human nature with the Logos or Word accomplished by the Word in his assumption of a human nature, in the womb of the Virgin Mary, into the unity of his person. Like all the *opera Dei ad extra* or outwardly directed works of God, the incarnation is defined as an *opus commune,* or common work, of the Godhead. Thus, the Logos, or Son, does not incarnate himself apart from the will of the Father and the Spirit. Scripture speaks of the sending of the Son by the Father (Gal. 4:4), of the assumption of flesh by the Word, or Son, himself (John 1:14); and of the conception of Christ by the Holy Spirit (Matt. 1:18). The Protestant scholastics distinguish therefore between the *opus,* or work, of incarnation considered efficiently (*efficienter*) and in terms of origin (*inchoative*) and the work of incarnation considered with a view toward its end, or terminatively (*terminative*). Efficiently and inchoatively it is the work of the undivided Trinity; terminatively it is the work of the Son. Thus, incarnation can be called an *opus mixtum,* or mixed work.

The language employed by both Lutheran and Reformed orthodox to describe or define incarnation follows the tradition of the later fathers and medieval doctors in identifying the *persona Christi,* or person of Christ, as the Second Person of the Trinity, or Son, who, in the *assumptio carnis,* or assumption of the flesh, unites with a non-self-subsistent, impersonal, or anhypostatic human nature (SEE *anhypostasis, enhypostasis*); the human nature is assumed into the unity of the person. The scholastics also conclude that incarnation does not, therefore, amount to a denial of divine immutability (*immutabilitas*, q.v.), insofar as the divine person of the Son undergoes no change in himself but rather executes in time his own eternal will. The change lies in the produced effect, in the human nature of Christ and in the relationship between man and God brought about in and through the incarnation.

The orthodox also describe at length the work of the Spirit in incarnation: the Spirit's work is *formativa*, or δημιουργική, in the conception of Christ by the Virgin; *sanctificativa*, or ἁγιαστική, in the cleansing and sanctifying of the human nature of Christ; *coniunctiva*, or τελειωτική, in relation to the incarnating work of the Logos. Thus, the *unio personalis* (q.v.), or personal union, of the divine and human natures occurs according to the will of the Father, through the formative and sanctifying work of the Spirit, in conjunction with the action of the Logos assuming the flesh or human nature.

Within this union, the orthodox describe a *communio naturarum* (q.v.), or communion of natures, resulting from their perfect relation in the *unio personalis*. Lutherans and Reformed disagree radically over the implications of the *communio naturarum* for the human nature: in the Lutheran view, divine attributes are communicated to the human nature without the loss of human attributes; in the Reformed view, no such communication of proper qualities (*communicatio idiomatum*, q.v.) takes place, but rather there is a verbal predication (*praedicatio verbalis*, q.v.) in which the attributes of both natures are predicated of the person only. See *persona Christi.*

inclinatio ad malum acquisita: *an acquired inclination to evil.* See *peccatum habituale acquisitum.*

incrementa fidei: *increments of faith;* viz., the growth and increase of faith following the initial experience of justification; in later pietist orthodoxy, one of the necessary or essential attributes of saving faith, the others being *perseverantia* (q.v.) and *bona opera,* good works springing from a living faith.

independentia: *independence;* specifically, the *independentia Dei,* independence of God. As a divine attribute, independence indicates the ontological independence of God from the created order and stands as a corollary of both the all-sufficiency (*omnisufficientia,* q.v.) of God and the self-existence (*aseitas,* q.v.) of God. God is independent of all created things insofar as he stands in no need whatsoever of the created order; God is self-sufficient or all-sufficient in his being. The concept does not imply a lack of relationship to

153

creation, but rather manifests God as the necessary being on whom all finite things depend. If God were not independent, there would be no ontological or providential ground of the existence of finite, non-necessary, or contingent things. Similarly, God, in order to be God, must be independent in the sense of being self-existent and prior to all other beings and, therefore, not owing his existence to a prior and higher source. If there were such a source of the existence of God, not only would God lack independence, God would not be God. SEE *attributa divina.*

indifferentia: *indifference, arbitrariness;* particularly, *indifferentia voluntatis,* indifference of the will, as an explanation of free choice (*liberum arbitrium,* q.v.).

individuum: *an individual thing, as opposed to a plurality of things;* also, by extension, the term predicated of an individual thing. *Individuum* and *suppositum* are synonymous.

inexistentia: *inexistence* or *mutual interexistence.* SEE *emperichōrēsis.*

infantes fidelium: *children of the faithful;* a term referring to all the offspring of believers; used by the orthodox to identify specifically the unbaptized children of believers, who are recognized, because of the faith of the community into which they have been born, as members of the people of God. The Reformed, in particular, argue covenant-membership for the *infantes fidelium,* and some of the later orthodox Lutherans also use covenantal language in describing the place of newborn and as yet unbaptized children in the church. The concept is of particular importance in arguing the probable salvation of unbaptized children who die in infancy.

infinitas: *infinitude;* especially, the *infinitas essentiae Dei,* or infinitude of the divine essence. By *infinitas Dei* the scholastics understand the limitlessness of the divine essence with regard to two *species* in particular, *aeternitas* (q.v.), or eternity, and *immensitas* (q.v.). The divine *infinitas* can also be described negatively and positively. It is not an infinity of corporeal quantity or extension but rather an infinity defined by the absence of limit; positively it is an infinite superiority over all things. In addition this *infinitas Dei* or *infinitas essentiae* ought not to be viewed as an isolated attribute but as a property of the divine essence that extends to each and every one of the divine attributes, so that the divine knowledge or *scientia* is *omniscientia* (q.v.) and the divine *potentia, omnipotentia* (q.v.), and so forth.

infirmitates communes: *common infirmities;* i.e., the weaknesses or infirmities that after the fall beset the whole human race, such as hunger, thirst, pain, and anxiety; as distinguished from *infirmitates personales,* the personal infirmities resulting from heredity or personal excess or specific disease, which are not common to all human beings without exception. SEE *anamartēsia.*

infra lapsum: *below or subsequent to the fall;* as opposed to *supra lapsum* (q.v.). SEE *praedestinatio.*

inhaerens in re: *immanent;* literally, *inherent or inhering in things.*

innascibilitas: *innascibility;* the condition or property of not being begotten, i.e., unbegottenness, the Latin equivalent of *agennēsia. Innascibilitas* is, therefore, the personal property (SEE *proprietas*) or hypostatic character (*character hypostaticus,* q.v.) of God the Father. SEE *Trinitas.*

inscriptio legis Dei in corda: *the inscription of the law of God upon the heart;* one of the benefits of the new covenant revealed in Jer. 31:33. The term is used in Reformed federalism in its description of the *foedus gratiae* (q.v.) in its evangelical *administratio.*

insitio in Christum: literally, *engrafting into Christ; standing in Christ* or *being in Christ.* SEE *unio mystica; vocatio.*

inspiratio: *inspiration;* a term used to describe the role of the Spirit in composition of Scripture. Since *spiratio,* spiration, is the activity of Spirit, *inspiratio* is an apt term for the in-working of Spirit. The inspiration of human authors, and hence of the text written by them, in no way deprives them even momentarily of their reason, their usual forms of expression, or the thought-patterns typical of their time in history and specific culture. The Protestant scholastics are careful to balance, in their *locus de Scriptura sacra,* the human and divine elements in Scripture. Inspiration provides a guarantee of the truth of the text and of its authority in matters of faith and practice. SEE *spiratio; theopneustos.*

institutio: *instruction; formal basis for education;* a term used in the titles of several important classical works: Quintilian's *Institutio oratoria;* the Roman manuals of jurisprudence, *Institutiones iuris civilis;* Lactantius's *Divinae institutiones,* and Cassiodorus's *Institutiones divinarum et saecularium lectionum.* From these works, the title passes over into the Reformation in Calvin's *Institutio christianae religionis.*

155

It was subsequently used by the early orthodox Reformed theologian Bucanus, *Institutiones theologicae seu locorum communium christianae religionis*—a conscious echo of Calvin—and by the Arminian, Simon Episcopius, *Institutiones theologiae*. In all cases, the term indicates an instruction basic to the discipline.

instrumenta operativa sive effectiva: *operative or effective instruments;* viz., the Word and the sacraments. SEE *media gratiae; organa gratiae et salutis*.

instrumentum: *instrument;* a means, or *medium*, used to bring about a desired effect.

instrumentum ἀεργόν: *an inactive or inoperative instrument;* as distinguished from an *instrumentum* συνεργόν, a cooperative instrument.

instrumentum coniunctum: *a conjoined or conjunctive instrument;* also *instrumentum unitum* (q.v.). In Christology, the human nature of Christ may be called an *instrumentum* of the Word; yet it is not an *instrumentum separatum* (q.v.), or separated instrument, since it is in union with the Word, indeed, personally conjoined (*personaliter coniunctum*) to the Word.

instrumentum iustificationis: *instrument of justification;* i.e., faith. Justification is accomplished by grace in an *actus forensis* on the basis of faith. Both the Lutherans and the Reformed view faith as a passive instrument in justification, since faith does not cause justification but is the *medium* ληπτικόν (q.v.) of justification.

instrumentum separatum: *a separate or separated instrument;* also **instrumentum assumptum sive extrinsecum**: *an assumed or extrinsic instrument;* an implement or tool (*organum*) assumed by an agent for use in an action or work, but which is physically or ontologically distinct from the agent.

instrumentum unitum: *a joined or united instrument;* also *instrumentum coniunctum* (q.v.); i.e., an implement or tool united or conjoined with the active agent in its work or activity.

integritas: *integrity, soundness of health in body and soul, purity, uprightness;* specifically, the condition of man as created in the *imago Dei* (q.v.).

intellectus: *intellect, understanding;* viz., the faculty of the soul that knows and that assents to the truth of what it knows, as opposed to *voluntas* (q.v.), or will, the faculty of soul that chooses. Intellect, like will, is immaterial, though, of course, substantial. A distinction must be made between *intellectus separatus,* a separated intellect that does not exist in union with a body, e.g., an angel, and *intellectus coniunctus,* a conjoined intellect that exists in union with and relation to a body, e.g., the human soul. SEE *spiritus completus; spiritus incompletus.*

intellectus Dei: *the divine intellect or understanding;* viz., the intellect of God. Just as God is described as having a will (SEE *voluntas Dei*), so is he argued by the scholastics to have intellect or understanding, the other faculty of spiritual or rational being. Like all the other divine attributes, the *intellectus Dei* is identical with the divine essence. Thus, it is infinite, perfect, and self-sufficient, absolute, totally free, and necessary. Both the divine knowledge (*scientia Dei,* q.v., or *omniscientia,* q.v.) and the divine wisdom (*sapientia Dei* or *omnisapientia,* q.v.) belong to the *intellectus Dei.* It is of the nature of the divine understanding that it knows all things and knows them wisely.

intercessio Christi: *the intercession of Christ;* specifically, the supplications offered by Christ on behalf of mankind and for the sake of believers in the execution of his *munus sacerdotale,* or priestly office. Christ's intercessory work is distinct from his other priestly work, that of making satisfaction for sin (SEE *satisfactio vicaria*), and is not confined to the *status humiliationis* (q.v.), or state of humiliation, but continues after the resurrection into the *status exaltationis* (q.v.), or state of exaltation. The *intercessio Christi* can also be distinguished into the *intercessio generalis,* or general intercession, in which Christ prays for the forgiveness of the sins of all mankind (Luke 23:34), and the *intercessio specialis,* or special intercession, in which Christ prays for believers only (John 17). In the state of exaltation Christ prays to the Father for the continued gracious application of his satisfaction. The Reformed orthodox tend to argue that the postresurrection work of intercession is a continuing mediation but neither oral nor verbal, whereas the Lutherans leave the question open. The intercession may be verbal but *sola mente,* of the mind only, or it may be only the continued presentation before God of the merit of Christ's satisfaction by Christ himself, as a real act of intercession. SEE *munus Christi; sacerdotium.*

interior Spiritus illuminatio: *inward or inner illumination of the Spirit.* SEE *illuminatio; testimonium internum Spiritus Sancti.*

interitus mundi: *the destruction or annihilation of the world;* specifically, the final purgation by fire that will occur at the end of the age (*consummatio saeculi,* q.v.). Following Johann Gerhard, Lutheran orthodoxy tended to argue a total annihilation (*annihilatio*) of the sinful earth, an *interitus mundi secundum substantiam,* the destruction of the world according to substance. Early Lutheran theologians, including Luther and Johann Brenz, argued a purgation of evil and sin, an *interitus mundi secundum accidentia,* or destruction of the world according to accidents or incidental properties. In this view, the goodness of being as created by God, the substantial goodness of the created order, is preserved in the *consummatio,* whereas the evil that inheres in the world as a defect will be purged away; the evil is accidental, an incidental property of good things. The Reformed agree that the destruction will be *secundum accidentia* and frequently argue that, after the purging away of evil, a refashioning of the world will take place and all things will be made new. This renovation (*renovatio*) of the creation represents the fulfillment of God's original creative purpose and the triumph of God's grace in all things over the effects of the fall.

intuitu fidei: *in view of faith;* a term used by the Lutheran scholastics, beginning with Aegidius Hunnius and Johann Gerhard, to qualify the divine predestination as a *decretum conditionatum,* a conditioned decree, willed by God in view of faith or with respect to faith. The term represents a counter to the Reformed conception of *decretum absolutum* and an attempt to teach predestination and salvation by grace alone without undercutting the universal grace of the gospel. Although it may be argued that this doctrine was derived from Melanchthonian synergism, it in no way reflects or relates to the semi-Pelagian perspective of seventeenth-century Arminianism. This is clearly witnessed by the Lutheran rejection of even a hypothetical universalism (*universalismus hypotheticus,* q.v.) that would make salvation contingent on human decision. Salvation cannot be contingent on something in man (*aliquid in homine*), but must be entirely the gift of God. Thus Lutheranism can argue both the beginning of faith by grace alone and the intimate relation of election to a foreknowledge of final faith (*intuitu fidei finalis* or *ex praevisa fidei finalis*). The divine foreknowledge implied in the latter term is not, of course, a temporal or time-conditioned foreknowledge of future events, but rather an eternal, simultaneous knowledge of all things and of their place in the divine will (SEE *praescientia*). Election *intuitu* *fidei finalis* is a *decretum conditionatum* insofar as it rests on God's eternal knowledge of the effective power of his own grace to produce faith in particular individuals: both the decree and the condition belong to God. Quenstedt argued, therefore, that the form of election (*forma electionis*) is the entire order (τάξις) according to which God ordains that those who apprehend Christ's merits (SEE *meritum Christi*) in faith and who persevere in faith are elect. In this election, the efficient cause (*causa efficiens;* SEE *causa*) is the will of God alone, the internal impelling cause (*causa intera impulsiva*) is the grace of God alone, and the external impelling cause (*causa externa impulsiva*) is Christ's merit in its gracious application. Final faith, as foreknown by God in eternity, appears in this causality as an external, less principal cause (*causa externa minus principalis*), or as a less principal impelling cause (*causa impulsiva minus principalis*), and faith itself appears not as a cause but as instrument or means (SEE *instrumentum; medium* ληπτικόν), or even as a reason (*ratio*) for election, although always with the qualification that it is not a principal or effective cause—indeed, faith does not enter the causality of election apart from Christ's merit and its gracious application; i.e., not apart from the *causa impulsiva externa*, but rather in gracious conjunction with it. Thus, in the divine foreknowledge the external impelling cause of election may also be defined as Christ's merit apprehended by faith. Election remains solely the gracious work of God but is not defined either in such a way as to exclude the possibility that some may fall away from grace and from genuine faith and be lost, or in such a way as to deny that the elect can truly fall away from faith and stand in total need of the gracious calling of the Word to repentance and new faith. The terms *intuitu fidei, intuitu fidei finalis,* and *electio expraevisa fidei finalis* ultimately became a source of concern within Lutheranism. Proponents of the usage felt that it was a necessary barrier to strict Calvinistic predestinarianism; opponents of the usage felt that it could be too easily misconstrued as synergistic in implication. The seventeenth-century orthodox usage, however, is clearly designed to stand between the doctrinal poles: Calov and Quenstedt maintained the *intuitu fidei* while at the same time polemicizing against the synergism of Georg Calixtus's followers, Latermann and Dreier. If the term did become truly problematic for Lutheranism, this occurred in the eighteenth century as orthodoxy declined and rationalist theologians both turned toward synergism and set aside the fine distinctions made during the era of orthodoxy. SEE *conversio reiterata; decretum; electio; intuitu incredulitatis finalis; obiectum electionis; praedestinatio.*

intuitu incredulitatis finalis: *in view of final unbelief;* the negative counterpart to the scholastic Lutheran doctrine of election *intuitu* *fidei* (q.v.), in view of faith. The Lutheran orthodox insist, against the Reformed, that the seriousness and efficacy of God's universal grace (*gratia universalis*, q.v.) must not be denied. The divine decree of reprobation is, therefore, not an absolute decree (*decretum absolutum*), but a *decretum conditionatum*, a conditioned decree, ordained by God in view of final unbelief, i.e., in view of the ultimate resistance of unbelievers to the gracious call of the Word. SEE *praedestinatio; reprobatio; vocatio.*

invidia: *envy, covetousness.* SEE *septem peccata mortalia.*

invinatio: *invination;* the presence of the blood of Christ *in vino,* in the wine of the sacrament, as opposed both to the theory of *transubstantiatio* (q.v.) and to theories of illocal or of spiritual presence. SEE *consubstantiatio; praesentia illocalis sive definitiva; praesentia spiritualis sive virtualis.*

invisibilitas: *invisibility;* a characteristic or attribute of spiritual being. Since the eye, like all other organs of sense, perceives only objects and effects in the physical order, the order of spiritual being transcends its ability to perceive. The soul, angels apart from their occasional self-manifestation in bodily form, and God are therefore all invisible.

ira: *wrath, anger, ire;* specifically, the *ira Dei,* or wrath of God, against sin. The wrath of God may be counted either as a function of the *iustitia Dei* (q.v.), the righteousness of God, and, specifically, of the *iustitia vindicativa sive punitiva* (q.v.), the vindicatory or punitive righteousness of God; or as one of the affections of the divine will (*voluntas Dei,* q.v.) in its relation to human sin. The *ira Dei* is both most clearly manifest and most fully satisfied in the death of Christ. It is also ultimately expressed in the damnation of those who do not have faith in Christ. SEE *poena; septem peccata mortalia.*

ira misericordiae/ira severitatis: literally, *wrath or anger of mercy/ wrath or anger of severity;* a distinction between the divine anger against the sins of those who are in Christ (*ira misericordiae*), in Luther's language, the divine No beneath which there lies the deeper Yes of grace, and the absolute divine anger against unrepentant and unjustified mankind (*ira severitatis*), the absolute No against sin.

iratus, -a, -um: *angry, wrathful.*

isorropia (ἰσορροπία): *equal propensity.*

isotēs (*ἰσότης*): *equality;* used by the fathers to indicate the equality of the First and Second Persons of the Trinity and, because of its patristic usage, adopted by Protestant scholastics in their *locus de Trinitate.*

iudex: *judge;* especially, Christ in the exercise of his kingly office at the end of time in the last judgment (*iudicium extremum*, q.v.).

iudicium: *judgment* or *decision;* specifically, one of the powers belonging to Christ and exercised by him in his kingly rule. See *iudicium extremum; regnum Christi.*

iudicium extremum: *last judgment;* also **iudicium universale et manifestum**: *the universal and manifest judgment;* in contrast to the *iudicium particulare et occultum* (q.v.), or particular and hidden judgment that occurs at the death of the individual. The last judgment, then, is the final, universal judgment of all mankind which will be manifest to all after the resurrection of the dead (*resurrectio mortuorum*). The judge (*iudex*) will be Christ himself, who will come again with glory and visibly, in and through his human nature, pronounce the judgment of the triune God upon the righteous and the unrighteous. The righteous will be rewarded, according to the remuneratory or distributive justice (*iustitia remuneratoria sive distributiva*, q.v.) of God, with life everlasting (*vita aeterna*, q.v.), and the wicked will receive, according to the vindicatory or punitive justice (*iustitia vindicativa sive punitiva*, q.v.) of God, the just recompense of eternal damnation (*damnatio*, q.v.) and eternal death (*mors aeterna*, q.v.). The scholastics also argue that the judgment will bestow, in addition to the blessedness of salvation and the punishment of damnation, distinct rewards and punishments that recompense individuals according to their deeds. Thus there will be degrees of glory (*gradus gloriae*, q.v.) and degrees of punishment in hell (*gradus poenarum infernalium*).

iudicium particulare et occultum: *the particular and hidden judgment;* viz., the judgment of the individual at death, according to which God either draws the souls of the departed righteous into fellowship with himself or consigns the souls of the unrighteous to Hades to await the final judgment and eternal damnation. See *Hades; paradisio; status animarum a corpore separatarum.*

iure divino/iure humano: *by divine right/by human right;* the distinction is used both with reference to the biblically instituted order of the church, as argued by the Reformers against human tradition, and with reference to the political theory of monarchy according to which the authority or rule of the king derives from God, not from man.

iussio: *a mandate, order,* or *command* (from *iubeo*).

iustificatio: *justification, a counting or reckoning righteous;* specifically, that actuality, or act, of grace (*actus gratiae*) in which God forgives sinful individuals, counts them as righteous on the basis of their faith in Christ, and accepts them as his own reconciled children, apart from all human merit and solely because of the superabundant merit of Christ's work of satisfaction (SEE *satisfactio vicaria*). The justification of sinners is also defined as a forensic act (*actus forensis,* q.v.) insofar as it is a legal declaration made, figuratively speaking, *in foro divino,* in the divine assize, and not an infusion of righteousness into the sinner. Since justification is viewed by the Protestant orthodox as a counting righteous rather than a making righteous, it rests not merely on the merit of Christ, but upon the union of the believer with Christ by grace through faith. An individual is counted righteous because he is *in Christo,* in Christ, covered as it were by the righteousness of Christ. This justification is entirely gracious and in no way merited by the believer. Thus the *causa impulsiva,* or impelling cause, of justification is God alone. The scholastics distinguish further between the *causa impulsiva interna,* or internal impelling cause, the love of God; and the *causa impulsiva externa,* or external impelling cause, the merit or righteousness of Christ. Faith is not, therefore, an active cause of justification but rather the means, or medium, that receives the grace of God in justification (SEE *medium* ληπτικόν). (Word and sacrament are also classified as *media iustificationis,* means of justification, specifically, as *media* δοτικά, or given means, since they are instruments of grace bestowed by God and properly received by faith.)

The Protestant scholastics can also distinguish, in accord with the basic definition of justification, between *iustificatio negativa,* or negative justification, and *iustificatio positiva,* or positive justification. These are inseparable, though logically distinct, aspects of the single forensic declaration of the sinner as righteous. The former, *iustificatio negativa,* is the forgiveness of sins; the latter, *iustificatio positiva,* is the imputation of Christ's righteousness to the sinner. This distinction relates directly to the Protestant view of the obedience of Christ (*obedientia Christi,* q.v.) and the fullness of Christ's satisfaction for both punishment (*poena,* q.v.) and guilt (*culpa,* q.v.). The forgiveness of sins and the consequent remission of punishment rest directly on the *satisfactio vicaria,* i.e., on the *obedientia passiva,* or passive obedience of Christ. But justification also entails the setting aside of guilt in the positive fulfillment of the law for sinners by Christ in his *obedientia activa,* or active obedience. Thus sinners are considered positively righteous by the imputation of the active obedience of Christ. This *iustificatio positiva,* or imputed righteousness (*iustitia imputativa*), is the end or goal, the *terminus ad quem,* of justification. Thus the end of justification is not the making righteous of sinners; *iustificatio* is an *actus,* an act or actualization, not a process, and it is forensic, not regenerative. The scholastics therefore tend to place justification after calling (*vocatio,* q.v.), regeneration (*regeneratio,* q.v.), and conversion (*conversio,* q.v.), insofar as these are necessary antecedents to the faith that receives God's gracious justification, but distinct from and prior to sanctification (*sanctificatio,* q.v.) wherein the believer is actually made righteous or holy by the grace of God. Justification is an *actus forensis sive iudicialis,* a forensic or judicial actuality, whereas sanctification is an *actus physicus sive medicinalis,* a physical or medicinal, i.e., a curative actuality. Finally, scholastic Protestantism distinguishes between the *actus gratiae* or *actus forensis* of objective justification (*iustificatio objectiva*) and the *actus iustificatorius,* the justificatory realization, or subjective justification (*iustificatio subjectiva*) of the believer. The former set of terms refers to the objective work of Christ and its effect, the remission of sin and the counting righteous of all who are in Christ; the latter set of terms refers to the inward, subjective recognition on the part of the believer that he is counted righteous in Christ and therefore freed from the condemnation of the law. In Lutheran orthodoxy the distinction is of considerable significance since, like the Lutheran view of election, it attempts to balance the concepts of universal grace and salvation by grace alone. Unlike the Reformed, the Lutherans can argue a universal grace in objective justification such that all who believe—hypothetically all mankind—can be justified. Justification, therefore, in the Lutheran view is limited subjectively but not objectively; the Reformed, however, view justification as limited both objectively and subjectively insofar as it extends in intention as well as in fact to the elect only. SEE *electio; intuitu fidei; ordo salutis; unio mystica sive praesentia gratiae tantum.*

iustificatio peccatoris: *the justification of the sinner;* plural, **iustificatio peccatorum**: *the justification of sinners.* SEE *iustificatio; simul iustus et peccator.*

iustificatus fide sine operibus: *justified by faith without works.*

163

iustitia: *justice* or *righteousness;* **iustitia Dei:** *the justice or righteousness of God.* The Latin word *iustitia* is equivalent to the Greek δικαιοσύνη; the Latin *iustitia Dei* to the Greek δικαιοσύνη Θεοῦ, so that both the Latin and the Greek indicate righteousness, justice, and uprightness. The scholastics distinguish the *iustitia Dei* into *iustitia interna* and *iustitia externa.* The *iustitia interna,* or internal righteousness, of God consists in the holiness of the divine will and its perfect correspondence with the good of God's eternal law. The *iustitia externa* is the righteousness of God as it is manifest *ad extra* (q.v.), or externally, in the *lex Dei,* or law of God (SEE *lex*). This external righteousness can be further distinguished into the *iustitia externa antecedens sive legislativa,* the antecedent or legislative righteousness of God, according to which he makes his laws, and the *iustitia externa consequens sive iudicialis,* the consequent or judicial righteousness of God, according to which God rewards those who keep his law and punishes those who break it. The *iustitia externa consequens* is therefore both a distributive or remunerative righteousness (*iustitia remuneratoria sive distributiva,* q.v.) and a vindicatory or punitive righteousness (*iustitia vindicativa sive punitiva*). In the economy of revelation, the judicial righteousness, with its promise of reward to the obedient and of punishment to the disobedient, is manifest as the legislative or normative righteousness (*iustitia legislatoria sive normativa,* q.v.) of the Mosaic law (*lex Mosaica,* q.v.). The Socinians argued that there was no vindicative or punitive righteousness in God, but the Lutheran and the Reformed orthodox defended the concept as necessary to the divine righteousness and the divine law, both of which would be meaningless without it.

iustitia aequalitatis: *justice of equality;* viz., distributive or remuneratory justice (*iustitia remuneratoria sive distributiva,* q.v.).

iustitia civilis: *civil justice or righteousness;* viz., the righteous acts of unbelievers that oblige the *lex civilis;* the Protestant scholastics argue that this righteousness comes from God as a result of the divine *concursus* (q.v.) and that it is the basis of all human community. Unlike the *iustitia spiritualis* (q.v.), it has nothing to do with redemption, and it falls completely under the *usus legis civilis* (q.v.).

iustitia fidei: *the righteousness of faith;* i.e., the righteousness that is imputed forensically to the believer on the ground of faith. *Iustitia fidei* is therefore not a *iustitia infusa* (q.v.), or infused righteousness, nor a disposition in the believer. Rather it is a *iustitia aliena,* an alien righteousness, a righteousness not our own, which is imputed to us. Ultimately, the *iustitia fidei* is the righteousness of Christ (*iustitia*

Christi). The *iustitia fidei* is also termed *iustitia imputata*, imputed righteousness, or *iustitia fidei imputata*, the imputed righteousness of faith.

iustitia habitualis: *righteousness of habit or disposition;* also **iustitia vitae:** *righteousness of life.*

iustitia imputata: *imputed righteousness;* specifically, the righteousness of Christ which is counted toward or imputed to believers on the ground of faith. This *iustitia* is imputed according to the *actus forensis* (q.v.) of *iustificatio* (q.v.) and merely counts the believer righteous rather than actually making him righteous. *Iustitia imputata* belongs to the *iustificatio peccatoris*, or justification of sinners, by grace, not to the subsequent *iustificatio iusti*, or justification of the just, which implies the gracious gift or impartation of righteousness, a *iustitia inhaerens* (q.v.). Whereas the *iustitia inhaerens*, like the sanctification of believers, must always remain incomplete and imperfect in this life, the *iustitia imputata* is complete and perfect, since it is not ours but Christ's.

iustitia infusa: *infused righteousness;* an actual gift (*donum*) of righteousness infused into the sinner by grace; denied by both the Lutherans and the Reformed. In the sixteenth century, Andreas Osiander (the Elder) argued, following medieval scholastic models, that justification (*iustificatio*, q.v.) was partly a forensic declaration of the sinner as righteous on account of faith but also partly an infusion of the righteousness of Christ (*iustitia Christi*) into the sinner, making the sinner righteous.

iustitia inhaerens: *inherent or inhering righteousness;* viz., the righteousness that is infused into and indwells the believer through the grace of the Holy Spirit following the imputation of righteousness (SEE *iustitia imputata*) in the *actus forensis* (q.v.) of *iustificatio* (q.v.). This *iustitia inhaerens* is a work of grace and rests on Christ's righteousness no less than does the *iustitia imputata*. Since it represents the believer's growth in righteousness it is sometimes called the *iustificatio iusti*, justification of the just, or justification of those declared just through faith. It corresponds with the *iustitia fidei*, or righteousness of faith, that manifests by outward acts the sinner's receipt of the divine act of justification and the accompanying grace of the Spirit. Whereas the Reformed will speak of the *iustitia inhaerens* and *iustificatio iusti* as a second kind of justification and will argue a progress in justification distinct from *sanctificatio* (q.v.), the orthodox Lutherans restrict *iustificatio* to the *actus forensis* and the *iustitia imputata,* reserving the language of actual transformation, *iustitia inhaerens, iustitia habitualis, iustitia vitae,* to the doctrine of *sanctificatio.*

iustitia legislatoria sive normativa: *legislative or normative justice (righteousness);* the eternal and immutable *iustitia; iustitia Dei* (q.v.), or righteousness of God manifest in the revelation of the divine demand of perfect obedience to the law, which is the standard and codification of righteous or just life. Therefore, the law—both the *lex Mosaica* (q.v.), or Mosaic law, and the two great commandments of love of God and neighbor—is called the revelation of the *iustitia legislatoria sive normativa.* In a negative sense, because of human disobedience, the revelation of *iustitia legislatoria* is the antecedent and ground of the *iustitia vindicativa sive punitiva* (q.v.), vindicatory or punitive justice. It is also, because of the grace of God in Christ, the ground of the *iustitia remuneratoria sive distributiva* (q.v.), remuneratory or distributive justice.

iustitia originalis: *original righteousness;* the righteousness of Adam and Eve, as first created by God, which was lost in the fall; also termed **iustitia naturalis:** *natural righteousness,* inasmuch as it was natural to man as originally created. See *imago Dei; peccatum originalis.*

iustitia rectoris: *rectoral or regulative justice;* viz., the legal or governmental justice underlying the Grotian theory of atonement. See *acceptatio; iustitia remuneratoria sive distributiva.*

iustitia remuneratoria sive distributiva: *remunerative or distributive justice.* In their typical division of the external, consequent justice or righteousness of God into *iustitia remuneratoria sive distributiva* and *iustitia vindicativa sive punitiva,* vindicatory or punitive justice, the Protestant scholastics follow closely the model set forth in Aristotle's *Nicomachean Ethics* (1131a–32b), according to which particular or individual justice is declared to be either distributive or rectificatory: distributive justice belongs to those cases in which no wrong has been done and a reward or recompense is to be bestowed in proportion to the value of a deed performed or an obedience rendered; rectificatory justice belongs to those cases in which a wrong has been done and a penalty is to be exacted of the wrongdoer for the sake of vindicating or making restitution to the victim or the wronged party. In the theological adaptation of the Aristotelian model by the scholastics, a dimension of punishment is added to the concept of restitution. Thus, the divine *iustitia remuneratoria sive* *distributiva* is exercised in the just judgment of God on the last day (*dies novissimus*, q.v.) when God graciously rewards those who are justified in Christ, while the *iustitia vindicativa sive punitiva* is exercised in the just judgment of God on the last day when God consigns to eternal damnation the unrighteous who have rejected Christ.

The concept of a *iustitia remuneratoria sive distributiva*, as developed by the Protestant orthodox in relation to their theory of Christ's vicarious satisfaction (*satisfactio vicaria*, q.v.), indicates an exact equivalence between merit offered and salvation bestowed, just as the *iustitia vindicatoria sive punitiva* indicates a strict equality of crime and punishment. Thus the remunerative justice of eternal salvation rests upon the sufficiency of Christ's satisfaction and the fullness of Christ's merit (*meritum Christi*, q.v.) as imputed to believers. This model stands in direct opposition to the *iustitia rectoris*, or rectoral justice, of the Grotian theory of atonement, according to which there is no exact equivalent between the value of Christ's work and the offered salvation, but rather a divine acceptation (*acceptatio*, q.v.) of Christ's death as payment for the sake of providing, not full satisfaction for sin, but rather an example of the divine wrath against sin. The *iustitia rectoris* maintains or regulates the moral government of the world by demanding a payment for sin while at the same time setting aside the universal demand of payment or punishment.

iustitia spiritualis: *spiritual righteousness;* viz., the righteousness of believers accomplished in them by the gracious work of the Spirit, distinct from the *iustitia civilis* since it involves the work of *conversio* (q.v.) and results in a true spiritual good. The *conversio* results in a new spiritual *habitus* (q.v.) and in a *habitus potentiam agendi*, or ability to act, not previously present. See *libertas naturae; posse non peccare*.

iustitia vindicativa sive punitiva: *vindicatory or punitive justice.* See *iustitia; iustitia remuneratoria sive distributiva.*

Iustus fide vivet: *The just will live by faith.*

167

Kk

kakia (κακία): *wickedness* or *depravity;* e.g., 1 Cor. 5:8.

kat' allo (κατ᾽ ἄλλο): *according to* or *as to another thing.* SEE *alius/ aliud.*

kat' eudokian (κατ᾽ εὐδοκίαν): *according to good pleasure or good will;* synonymous with *secundum beneplacitum* or *per benevolentiam;* a term used in the scholastic discussion of *providentia* (q.v.) with specific reference to the way in which God providentially effects his purpose in and through the good acts of finite creatures and in the conservation (*conservatio*) of created good, as distinct from the divine mode of governance *kat' oikonomian* (q.v.) or *kata sunchōrēsin.*

kat' exochēn (κατ᾽ ἐξοχήν): *preeminently, most prominently, par excellence.*

kat' oikonomian (κατ᾽ οἰκονομίαν): *according to the order, plan, or dispensation.* SEE *dispensatio.*

kata charin (κατὰ χάριν): *according to grace; by grace.*

kata dianoian (κατὰ διάνοιαν): *according to the understanding; in accordance with a purpose.*

kata lexin (κατὰ λέξιν): *according to speech or style of speech; in a manner of speaking.*

kata merē (κατὰ μέρη): *in part;* in contrast with the whole (ὅλος).

kata synchōrēsin (κατὰ συγχώρησιν): *by permission;* synonymous with *secundum permissionem;* a term used by the Protestant scholastics to describe the mode of the divine providential care and support of all things according to which God allows and even upholds by his *concursus* (q.v.) actions and things that are contrary to his revealed will; as opposed to divine governance *kat' oikonomian* (q.v.) and *kat' eudokian* (q.v.).

katachrēstikōs (καταχρηστικῶς): *imprecisely* or *loosely;* specifically, with reference to forms or expressions of thought or speech.

katallagē (καταλλαγή): *reconciliation;* e.g., Rom. 5:11. SEE *Mediator; munus triplex.*

kataskeuastikōs (κατασκευαστικῶς). SEE *usus philosophiae.*

kenōsis (κένωσις): *emptying;* specifically, the self-emptying of Christ who was in the form of God and took on himself the form of a servant (*forma servi*) in the accomplishment of the mediatorial office, or *munus triplex* (q.v.), as stated in Phil. 2:5–11. In Latin, *kenōsis* is rendered as *exinanitio* or *evacuatio.* SEE *status humiliationis.*

kinēsis (κίνησις): *process, development, motion, movement.* SEE *motus.*

klēsis (κλῆσις): *position, place,* or *situation.*

koinē dialektos (κοινὴ διάλεκτος): *the common language;* a term applied to the language of international discourse in the Hellenistic world, which is the language of the New Testament.

koinōnia (κοινωνία): *community* or *communion;* sometimes *communication;* a term drawn from the New Testament, particularly from the Pauline Epistles where it indicates the communion or fellowship made possible in Christ through the gospel and by the Spirit (1 Cor. 1:9; 2 Cor. 13:13; Phil. 1:5). *Koinōnia,* therefore, is no worldly or earthly fellowship, nor is it the individual congregation of Christians, but the communion of all Christians, both in their present suffering and in the hope of resurrection. The Protestant orthodox use the term in this particular sense, as the universal communion of Christians with Christ and with one another in Christ. The term is usually rendered as *communio,* communion, or occasionally, in a eucharistic sense, chiefly by the Lutheran orthodox, as *communicatio,* communication, but never as *societas,* society in a general, earthly sense, nor as *ecclesia* (q.v.), church, with its connotations either of local congregation or of earthly institution. Specifically, *koinōnia* refers to the fellowship or communion of believers, the *communio sanctorum* (q.v.), and to the communion of believers with Christ. In the latter sense, both *koinōnia* and *communio* have a eucharistic connotation: the Lord's Supper is the *koinōnia Christi,* or the *communio sanguinis* and *communio corporis* (q.v.) *Christi.* By extension, therefore, the Lutherans also view *koinōnia* as a fellowship resting on the real presence of Christ and the distribution or *distributio* of the body and blood of Christ and as the *communicatio corporis et sanguinis Christi,* the communication of the body and blood of Christ.

koinōnia idiōmatōn (κοινωνία ἰδιωμάτων): *communion of proper qualities.* SEE *communicatio idiomatum.*

kosmos (κόσμος): *world.* SEE *creatio; ex nihilo.*

krasis (κρᾶσις): *composition* or *union;* used by the fathers with reference to the union of natures in Christ, particularly with reference to christological heresy in which the natures are fused in a composite person, e.g., Nestorianism.

kritēria (κριτήρια): *standards, particularly those involving legal decisions.*

krypsis (κρύψις): *a hiding* or *hiddenness;* a term used by the Lutheran scholastics, particularly those of the University of Tübingen, to indicate the nonmanifestation of the divine attributes communicated to the human nature of Christ. During the *status humiliationis* (q.v.), or state of humiliation, Christ's humanity was in full possession (*ktēsis,* q.v.) of the divine attributes but nevertheless appeared weak and finite. The Tübingen theologians argued not only the full possession, but also the full use or exercise (*chrēsis*) of the divine attributes during the state of humiliation to the point of holding that the ubiquity of Christ's humanity indicated by the *sessio Christi* (q.v.), or sitting of Christ at the right hand of the Father, was as true of the *status humiliationis* as it is of the *status exaltationis* (q.v.), or state of exaltation. The weakness and finitude of Christ's humanity were to be explained by the hiding of the exercise of the attributes, by a *krypsis.* This concept must be distinguished from the Reformed idea of an *occultatio* (q.v.), or hiding of the divine nature and attributes under the human nature. Against the Tübingen theologians, the Lutheran faculty at Giessen argued not only a *krypsis,* but also a limitation of the use, or exercise (*chrēsis*), of the attributes given to the human nature. Giessen could then argue a real distinction between the *status humiliationis* and the *status exaltationis.*

ktēsis (κτῆσις): *possession;* a term used by the Lutheran scholastics in their discussion of the communication of omnipotence, omniscience, and omnipresence to the human nature of Christ during the *status humiliationis* (q.v.), or state of humiliation. Since the attributes are communicated in the *unio personalis* (q.v.), or personal union, as a result of the communion of the natures (*communio naturarum*, q.v.), Christ's human nature is in possession (*ktēsis*) of the divine attributes, though in the state of humiliation the attributes are quiescent and their use or function (*chrēsis*, χρῆσις) limited. In the *status exaltationis* (q.v.), or state of exaltation, Christ's *ktēsis*, or possession, of the divine attributes will be fully manifest in their *chrēsis*, or use, in and through his human nature. A distinction can thus be made between the *omnipraesentia intima sive partialis* (q.v.), or secret and partial omnipresence, during the state of humiliation and the *praesentia extima sive totalis* (q.v.), or outward and total presence, exercised during the state of exaltation.

Ll

lacuna: *a gap* or *omission*.

lambanein (λαμβάνειν): *to take or grasp hold of;* e.g., Mark 14:22.

lapsus: *fall, lapse;* specifically, the fall of Adam and Eve from original righteousness (*iustitia originalis,* q.v.) and away from the terms of paradisical law (*lex paradisiaca,* q.v.) and the covenant of works (*foedus operum,* q.v.). The fall is usually described as the result of the sin (*peccata,* q.v.) of pride (*superbia;* SEE *septem peccata mortalia*). Sin, in this primary instance, must be viewed as a privation (*privatio,* q.v.) or, specifically, a privation of the good (*privatio boni,* q.v.) made possible by free choice (*liberum arbitrium,* q.v.) according to the liberty of man's nature (SEE *libertas naturae*). SEE *homo; peccatum originalis*.

lapsus memoriae: *lapse or failure of memory.*

late: *loosely, with latitude.* SEE *stricte*.

latria (from the Greek λατρεία): *worship;* usually contrasted with *dulia,* reverence or veneration. In medieval theology the distinction was made between the *latria* due to God and Christ as the Son of God and the *dulia* due to the saints. Even the Virgin Mary, exalted above the saints as Mother of God, is not worthy of *latria.* After Albertus Magnus, it was customary to distinguish the high veneration, or *hyperdulia,* of Mary from the *dulia* due to saints. In Protestantism, worship of God continued to be described as *latria,* but *dulia* was excluded, since the veneration of saints and of Mary was denied. Christ is worthy of worship, but the basis of that worship or adoration is his divine nature. Prayer is not offered to the human nature of Christ.

Laus Deo: *Praise be to God.*

leitourgia (λειτουργία): *service;* specifically, a ritual, priestly, or sacrificial service; by extension, the high-priestly office of Christ; e.g., Heb. 8:6.

lex: *law;* specifically, the *lex Dei,* law of God, which can be distinguished into (1) the *lex archetypa,* or archetypal law, which is the holiness and righteousness of the divine essence itself and which is the righteous ground of all the *opera Dei ad extra* (q.v.) and of all the promulgated laws of God; and (2) the *lex ectypa,* or ectypal law, which God promulgates in various forms throughout the history of the world for the use of his rational creatures. The *lex ectypa* is, therefore, never an arbitrary law lacking an ultimate, objective foundation, but rather a reflection of the righteous nature of God himself. The *lex ectypa* can be further distinguished into the *lex naturalis* (q.v.), the *lex paradisiaca* (q.v.), and the *lex Mosaica* (q.v.).

lex ceremonialis: *ceremonial law;* specifically, the ceremonial or religious regulations given to Israel under the Old Testament, alongside the moral law of the Decalogue and the civil law of the Jewish nation, such as the Levitical Code. Whereas the *lex moralis* (q.v.) remains in force after the coming of Christ, the *lex ceremonialis* has been abrogated by the gospel.

lex Christi: *law of Christ;* a term used by the Arminian theologians of the late seventeenth century to indicate the precepts of the gospel (SEE *praecepta caritatis*) as the full revelation of the law of life. According to the Arminians, the *lex Christi* was equivalent to the natural law known to Adam before the fall and adumbrated both in the Decalogue (*lex Mosaica,* q.v.) and in the ethics of the great philosophers. This view of the gospel conforms to the synergistic principles of Arminian theology and is rejected by the Protestant scholastics, Reformed and Lutheran alike.

lex Dei: *the law of God.* SEE *lex; lex moralis; lex Mosaica; usus legis.*

Lex est Deus accusans et damnans: *The law is God accusing and damning.*

lex moralis: *the moral law;* specifically and preeminently, the *Decalogus,* or Ten Commandments; also called the *lex Mosaica* (q.v.), as distinct from the *lex ceremonialis* (q.v.) and the *lex civilis,* or civil law, The *lex moralis,* which is primarily intended to regulate morals, is known to the *synderesis* (q.v.) and is the basis of acts of *conscientia* (q.v.). In substance, the *lex moralis* is identical with the *lex naturalis*

173

(q.v.), but, unlike the natural law, it is given by revelation in a form which is clearer and fuller than that otherwise known to the reason. In addition, in its revealed form, the law is connected to distinct promises and sanctions designed to induce righteousness and prevent sin. A *lex moralis primordialis* is sometimes distinguished from the Sinaitic *lex moralis* or *lex Mosaica* on the assumption that God directly revealed the law to Adam and Eve (SEE *lex paradisiaca*).

lex Mosaica: *Mosaic law;* the moral law or *lex moralis* (q.v.) given to Israel by God in a special revelation to Moses on Mount Sinai. In contrast to the moral law known in an obscure way to all rational creatures, the *lex Mosaica* is the clear, complete, and perfect rule of human conduct. The Protestant scholastics argue its completeness and perfection from its fulfillment, without addition, by Christ. Since the law does promise life in return for obedience, the Reformed argue that in one sense it holds forth the abrogated *foedus operum* (q.v.), or covenant of works, if only as the unattainable promise of the righteous God and the now humanly unattainable requirement for salvation apart from grace. In addition, the Reformed can argue that Christ's perfect obedience did fulfill the covenant of works and render Christ capable of replacing Adam as federal head of humanity. Primarily, however, the Reformed view the law as belonging to the Old Testament *dispensatio* (q.v.) of the *foedus gratiae* (q.v.), or covenant of grace. It is the norm of obedience given to God's faithful people to be followed by them with the help of grace. As a norm of obedience belonging to the *foedus gratiae*, the law remains in force under the economy of the New Testament. Lutheran orthodoxy, which does not follow the covenant schema typical of the Reformed, also views the law as the perfect standard of righteousness and the absolute norm of morals, which requires conformity both in outward conduct and inward obedience of mind, will, and affections. In the Lutheran system, however, the law does not appear so much as an adjunct of the gospel as a standard over against the gospel and in dialectical tension with it. The law leads to Christ by humbling the sinner through its condemnation of evils rather than by being subsumed under the promise. This difference between the Lutheran and Reformed views is most apparent in the discussion of the use of the law, the *usus legis* (q.v.).

lex naturalis: *natural law;* also **lex naturae:** *law of nature;* the universal moral law either impressed by God upon the mind of all people or immediately discerned by the reason in its encounter with the order of nature. The natural law was therefore available even to those pagans who did not have the advantage of the Sinaitic revelation and the *lex Mosaica* (q.v.), with the result that they were left without excuse in their sins, convicted by *conscientia* (q.v.). The scholastics argue the identity of the *lex naturalis* with the *lex Mosaica* or *lex moralis quoad substantiam*, according to substance, and distinguish them *quoad formam*, according to form. The *lex naturalis* is inward, written on the heart and therefore obscure, whereas the *lex Mosaica* is revealed externally and written on tablets and thus of greater clarity.

Lex orandi est lex credendi et agendi: *The rule of prayer is the rule of belief and of action;* a maxim usually attributed to Pope Coelestinus or Celestine I (A.D. 422–432).

lex paradisiaca: *law of paradise;* viewed by most Protestant scholastics as identical with the *lex naturalis* (q.v.) and, therefore, by extension, with the Decalogue. In their elaboration of the doctrine of the *foedus operum* (q.v.) the Reformed tended to argue that Adam's violation of the *lex paradisiaca* implied the violation of virtually the whole Decalogue—except the prohibition of adultery—since it involved denial of God's sovereignty, a potential blasphemy, a violation of worship, disrespect to God as Father, murder understood as suicide and the communication of death to all mankind, covetousness, and intended theft. The Lutherans argued differently, assuming that the command not to eat of the tree was an additional stipulation beyond the Decalogue written on the heart. The Lutheran opinion rests on the status of the divine command not to eat as an *imperium dominicum,* a lordly command, designed to test obedience and not as a representation of the *lex naturalis;* the Reformed agree as to the status of the command, but interpret the offense in terms of the law known to the first pair inwardly. SEE *homo.*

Lex praescribit, evangelium inscribit: *The law prescribes, the gospel inscribes;* viz., the law prescribes obedience and points the way toward righteousness, but effects neither; the gospel effects obedience and righteousness by inscribing them on the heart.

lex scripta: *the written law;* the law as embodied in statutes and regulations, as opposed to the *lex non scripta,* the unwritten or customary law.

libare sanguinem Christi: *to partake of the blood of Christ.* SEE *coena sacra; communicare Christo.*

175

liber naturae/gratiae/gloriae: *the book of nature/of grace/of glory;* a figurative way of speaking of the three sources of knowledge of God, nature, grace, and the final vision of God's glory.

libertas a coactione: *freedom from coaction or coercion;* in scholastic thought, the basic criterion for freedom of action or choice. In other words, an individual is considered free to act or choose even if under a necessity of nature (*necessitas naturae,* q.v.), since the act or choice though self-determined or inwardly determined is in no way the result of external compulsion or externally imposed constraint. SEE *necessitas coactionis.*

libertas naturae: *the freedom or liberty of nature;* viz., the liberty that is proper to a being given its particular nature. No being, not even omnipotent God, can act contrary to its nature. In man, this *libertas naturae* can be distinguished into four distinct categories or states: (1) the *libertas Adami,* or freedom of Adam, before the fall—this is the ability or power not to sin, *potentia non peccandi,* and Adam and Eve are described, in the traditional Augustinian terminology, as *posse non peccare,* able not to sin; (2) the *libertas peccatorum,* or freedom of sinners, a freedom that is proper to and confined within the limits of fallen nature and is therefore an absolute *impotentia bene agendi,* inability to do good or to act for the good, with the sinner described as *non posse non peccare* (q.v.), not able not to sin; (3) the *libertas fidelium,* or freedom of the faithful, a freedom of those regenerated by the Holy Spirit that is proper to the regenerate nature and is characterized by the *potentia peccandi et bene agendi,* the ability to sin and to do good; the regenerate, because of grace, can be described as *posse peccare et non peccare,* able to sin and not to sin; (4) the *libertas gloriae,* or liberty of glory, a freedom proper to the fully redeemed nature of the *beati* (q.v.), who, as residents of the heavenly kingdom, as *in patria* (q.v.), are now characterized by *impotentia peccare,* inability to sin, and as *non posse peccare,* unable to sin. SEE *homo; libertas a coactione; necessitas naturae.*

libertatis imperfectio: *imperfection of freedom.* SEE *liberum arbitrium.*

liberum arbitrium: *free choice;* often loosely and incorrectly rendered "free will." Lutherans and Reformed agree that the faculty of will, the *voluntas* (q.v.), is itself free and that the bondage into which humanity has fallen is not a bondage of the faculty of will as such. No human being is compelled to sin; the will is thus free from external constraint (*coactio*) and from an imposed necessity (SEE *necessitas coactionis*). The human predicament is therefore defined neither as the loss of the faculty of will nor of the inward freedom, or *libertas*, of the will. What has been lost is the freedom of choice, specifically, the ability freely to choose the good and freely to avoid that which is evil. The *libertas voluntatis essentialis* (essential freedom of will) remains intact, but the will itself is fallen and suffers from the defect and stain of sin (see *macula*). The Lutheran scholastics argue further that *liberum arbitrium* can be defined in terms of a freedom of contrariety or specification (*libertas contrarietatis; libertas specificationis*); i.e., the freedom to choose one object and to reject another on the assumption that the will itself is not predetermined or predisposed toward any specifics. This freedom can also be stated as a freedom of exercise (*libertas exercitii*), or a freedom to act or not act. The fall, therefore, can be conceived as removing the basic indifference of the will toward sin, with the result that all choices of the will become sinful and the free choice of the good is no longer a possibility. *Arbitrium* has been enslaved to sin and can now be called, as Luther termed it, the *servum arbitrium*, or bound choice. The Reformed similarly maintain the freedom of the faculty of will and the *liberum arbitrium* apart from the disposition of fallen man to sin. Since, moreover, the choice of sin is not the result of an external compulsion but of the inward disposition of the individual resulting from the corruption of his nature, even the choice of sin can be described as *liberum arbitrium*, though in a restricted sense. The Reformed disagree with the Lutheran view of free choice as arising out of an indifference of the will or out of a freedom to act or not act (i.e., a suspension of willing). In the Reformed view, an original indifference to good or evil would have been a defect in the creature. Adam was not therefore indifferent to good and evil, but created good and upright, with the ability to continue in the good. Adam's freedom was a freedom to be obedient, not a freedom to obey or refuse to obey, i.e., not a freedom of acting or not acting. It was a freedom to do the good apart from external compulsion with the will itself as the sole efficient cause of its choice. Nevertheless, the will itself and its power of choice were mutable, capable of rejecting the grace of God, and therefore capable of evil. The Reformed argue, then, that the will is never indifferent, either before or after the fall, and that, consequently, the fall did not result simply from the *liberum arbitrium*. The fall arose neither out of an original imperfection of freedom (*libertatis imperfectio*) nor out of a resident possibility of enslavement (*possibilitas servitutis*), but rather from the *mutabilitas voluntatis*, or mutability of will. See *libertas a coactione*.

limbus: literally, *border; limbo;* in Roman Catholic doctrine, a place of the dead bordering on hell and purgatory to which are consigned those souls that have not been redeemed by grace but that nonetheless cannot be classed either as pagans or as reprobate sinners. *Limbus* can be distinguished into the *limbus infantum,* or borderland of infants, into which unbaptized children who die in infancy are placed, and the *limbus patrum,* or borderland of the patriarchs, in which the saints of the Old Testament must wait until their redemption is completed by Christ, specifically, in and through the *descensus ad inferos* (q.v.), or descent into hell. The medieval scholastics argued that neither *limbus* was a place of torment. Children consigned to the *limbus infantum* or *limbus puerorum* (limbo of children) are subject to the *poena damni,* or punishment of the damned, which is the denial of the *visio Dei* (q.v.), or vision of God, but not the *poena sensus,* or punishment of the senses, inflicted on damned sinners. The patriarchs, moreover, were only awaiting the final announcement of salvation; their *limbus* was considered distinct from the *limbus infantum* and further still from the pains of hell and purgatory. It was often referred to as "the bosom of Abraham." Protestantism rejects the concept of *limbus* just as it rejects the doctrines of degrees of merit and of sin. The *limbus patrum* is explicitly rejected in the orthodox Protestant treatment of the descent into hell. The Protestant scholastics consider all the postmortem *receptacula animae,* or receptacles of souls, viz., *purgatorium, limbus puerorum* or *limbus infantum,* and *limbus patrum* as inventions or fabrications of Rome.

localis inclusio: *local inclusion;* specifically, the inclusion of the body and blood of Christ locally in the bread and wine of the sacrament. SEE *consubstantiatio; impanatio; praesentia localis.*

localis subsistendi modus: *a local mode or manner of subsisting;* i.e., the mode of subsisting characteristic of Christ's body during his earthly life and of Christ's body in its heavenly exaltation when considered according to its own properties, or *idiomata.* The Reformed scholastics insist that this is the sole *modus subsistendi* (q.v.) that can be attributed to Christ's human nature. The Lutherans, however, on the basis of their view of the *communicatio idiomatum* (q.v.), or communication of proper qualities, argue also an *illocalis subsistendi modus,* or illocal mode of subsistence, which belongs to Christ's human nature. The *illocalis subsistendi modus* explains both Christ's appearance to the disciples after the resurrection "when the doors were shut" (John 20:19, 26) and the real presence of Christ in the bread and wine of the sacrament. See *praesentia; praesentia illocalis sive definitiva; ubiquitas.*

localiter: *locally;* i.e., a way of being present that is defined spatially. See *praesentia; praesentia illocalis sive definitiva.*

loci communes: *common places;* the collection of basic scriptural *loci* and their interpretations into an ordered body of Christian doctrine; a standard title for such systems of doctrine. See *medulla.*

locus: *place* or *topic;* the crucial text or place in Scripture at the basis of a particular Christian doctrine; hence, the topical discussion of the doctrine, a chapter in a theological system; also, a term indicating the accident or predicate "place." See *locus classicus; praedicamenta.*

locus classicus: *a standard or classic passage;* literally, a "classic place"; a place or passage in a text, frequently Scripture, traditionally used as the primary ground of an idea or doctrine. See *dicta probantia; loci communes; sedes doctrinae.*

locutio exhibitiva: *exhibitive locution;* viz., a way of speaking which manifests or shows forth something; specifically, the form of speech used by Christ at the Last Supper in the words "this is my body" and "this is my blood," by means of which Christ exhibits his body and blood without reference to the bread and wine. In other words, Christ holds forth the visible means, or visible elements, but refers to and manifests the invisible, heavenly elements. See *coena Domini; praesentia illocalis sive definitiva; res sacramenti; sacramentum; signum.*

logistikōs (λογιστικῶς): *in word or thought, as distinct from in act or in deed.*

Logos (Λόγος): *word* or *reason;* specifically, the Second Person of the Trinity, both in his person, as the perfect image of the Father, and in his office as the revealer and revelation of the Father and as the creative Word uttered by the Father. See *Verbum Dei.*

Logos asarkos (Λόγος ἄσαρκος): *the Word or Logos without the flesh;* a term derived from the fathers used to distinguish the Second Person of the Trinity in his preincarnate mediation from the Word "incarnate," the Word having been made flesh. See *ensarkos; incarnandus/incarnatus; incarnatio.*

179

Logos non extra carnem: *The* Logos *is not beyond the flesh;* a postulate of seventeenth-century Lutheran orthodoxy opposed to the *extra calvinisticum* (q.v.) of the Reformed. The phrase arises out of the distinctive Lutheran view of the *communicatio idiomatum* (q.v.), specifically, the *genus maiestaticum.* As early as Brenz's Christology the Lutherans argued that there is no place where the Logos is present and not also united to the human nature. Since the Logos is omnipresent, the human nature must be everywhere with the Logos; or, more precisely, the Logos, by virtue of its own omnipresence, which has been communicated to the human nature according to the *genus maiestaticum,* has the human nature illocally present to it everywhere. Therefore, the Logos is not beyond or outside of the flesh. See *omnipraesentia intima sive partialis; praesentia; praesentia illocalis sive definitiva; ubiquitas.*

longanimitas: *longsuffering;* the patient bearing of an offense, particularly over a long period of time; thus, the willingness of God to endure the offense of sin rather than immediately annihilate the world in its wickedness. The *longanimitas Dei* is the affection of the divine will according to which God wills to await repentance and to allow millennia to elapse, for the sake of mankind, between the fall and the final judgment. *Longanimitas* is virtually synonymous with *patientia,* indicating the height of patience.

lumen naturae/gratiae/gloriae: *the light of nature/of grace/of glory;* the threefold light by which human beings learn of God, the first two pertaining to this life, the last to the heavenly life. See *liber naturae/gratiae/gloriae; theologia beatorum.*

lux Dei: *the light of God;* occasionally considered a divine attribute, according to which God is defined as absolute light, in which there is no darkness at all. Theologically, the *lux Dei* indicates the truth, wisdom, holiness, and purity of God, and also, preeminently, the divine self-sufficiency. God is light unto himself and the ultimate source of all light just as he is also the ultimate source of all life. *Lux Dei* is therefore a scriptural predication which indicates the *aseitas* (q.v.), or self-existence, of God, the *omnisufficientia* (q.v.), or all-sufficiency, and the essential *necessitas* of God.

luxuria: *lust.* See *septem peccata mortalia.*

lytron: (λύτρον): *ransom;* a term favored by both the Lutherans and the Reformed as a reference to Christ's work on the cross, since the term is found only in Jesus' own words, Mark 10:45 and Matt. 20:28, "the Son of Man came ... to give his life as a ransom (λύτρον) for many."

lytrōsis (λύτρωσις): *redemption; payment of a ransom;* e.g., Heb. 9:12.

Mm

macula: *stain* or *blemish;* specifically, the spiritual pollution (*pollutio spiritualis*) and deformity of nature (*deformitas naturae*), i.e., the defilement of the soul that results from sin. S<small>EE</small> *reatus.*

magister: *master;* in the university, the title of one who has been awarded the first of the teaching degrees above the *baccalaureus.*

magisterium: *teaching authority;* i.e., the authority of the *magister* (q.v.); most frequently, the teaching authority of the church, the *ecclesia docens* (q.v.), according to Roman Catholic doctrine.

magnalia Dei: *the mighty works of God.* S<small>EE</small> *opera Dei.*

magnitudo: *greatness, magnitude;* as an attribute of God, the *magnitudo Dei,* the greatness of God in all his attributes, the greatness or magnitude of the divine essence itself. Specifically, *magnitudo* is used as a synonym for infinitude (*infinitas,* q.v.), both in terms of the divine immensity (*immensitas,* q.v.), or transcendence of space, and the divine eternity (*aeternitas,* q.v.), or transcendence of time. S<small>EE</small> *attributa divina.*

maiestas: *majesty;* i.e., the *maiestas Dei,* or majesty of God, the supreme eminence of the divine essence and attributes, usually paired with *gloria* (q.v.), the glory of God.

male velle: *evil willing;* the act of willing in an evil manner for the sake of doing evil. S<small>EE</small> *velle malum.*

malum; (adj.) **malus, -a, -um:** *evil;* as defined by Augustine and argued by the scholastics, evil is not a thing or a substance. Since all things, as all the substances from which things are formed, are made by God and since God created all things good, evil must be defined as having nonsubstantial existence, or as existing in the form of a defect or a privation in an otherwise good thing. Evil, therefore, cannot be an ultimate opposed eternally to the ultimate good; evil depends for its very existence upon the existence of good. Nor can evil become absolute, since evil is a defect or a privation in and of the good; its increase toward the absolute results in the absolute privation of the good, i.e., in nonbeing or nothingness. Evil can also be defined, therefore, as the privation of being or as the result of a will moving away from being toward nonbeing.

It is also worth noting that the connection traditionally made between the "tree of the knowledge of good and of evil" (Gen. 2:9)—the *arbor scientiae boni et mali*—and the "apple" reputedly eaten by the first pair rests, not on an ignorance of the text, as sometimes assumed, but on a bit of philological humor: the adjective "evil" (*malus, mala, malum*) is identical in its masculine and neuter forms, respectively, with the Latin words for "apple tree" (*malus*) and "apple" (*malum*).

mandatum: *command, mandate.*

mandatum scribendi: *mandate or command to write;* also **impulsum scribendi,** *the impulse to write;* an assumption of the doctrine of verbal inspiration, viz., that the Spirit initiated the writing of Scripture and provided a *mandatum,* or an *impulsum,* to write (2 Peter 1:21).

manducare corpus Christi: *to eat the body of Christ.* See *coena sacra; communicare Christo; manducatio.*

manducatio: *eating;* specifically, in sacramental theology, the eating, partaking, and enjoyment of the Lord's Supper (*coena sacra,* q.v.). This *manducatio* is variously distinguished by the scholastics. The Reformed argue a twofold distinction between (1) a *manducatio sacramentalis* or *symbolica,* a sacramental or symbolical eating, which is given to believers and unbelievers and which involves only the eating of the *signum,* or sign, the bread; and (2) a *manducatio spiritualis,* or spiritual eating, which is possible only for believers, who receive the body of Christ through faith by the agency of the Spirit. The Reformed further speak of a *manducatio indigna,* an unworthy eating, of the sacramental elements by unbelievers; but they deny a *manducatio indignorum,* eating by the unworthy, which implies that unbelievers actually receive the body of Christ. In opposition to this view, which appeared to them to be a denial of the real presence of Christ in the supper (*praesentia realis,* q.v.), the Lutherans argue (1) a *manducatio oralis,* or oral eating, not in the sense of a natural or physical eating, but rather a sacramental eating in the sense of a *manducatio hyperphysica sive supernaturalis,* a hyperphysical or supernatural eating, Christ's body being received through the mouth, but not being digested as bread is digested; and (2) a *manducatio sacramentalis* or *spiritualis*, sacramental or spiritual eating, i.e., appropriating to oneself the merits and blessings of Christ by faith. Further, this emphasis on *praesentia realis* and *manducatio oralis hyperphysica* led the Lutherans to deny a distinction between *manducatio indigna* and *manducatio indignorum* and to argue, on the basis of 1 Cor. 11:27–29, that the unbeliever receives the body of Christ to his judgment or damnation. Lutheran theologians typically point to the *manducatio indignorum* as the key to understanding the difference between Lutheran affirmation of *praesentia realis* and Reformed use of the term. Note further that the language of *manducatio spiritualis, sacramentalis*, etc., equally applies to the spiritual and sacramental drinking of Christ's blood: thus *bibitio spiritualis, bibitio sacramentalis*, and the like.

manifestatio: *manifestation*. SEE *patefactio; revelatio*.

manutenentia: *maintenance* or *preservation;* synonymous with *conservatio*, conservation; one aspect of *providentia* (q.v.).

massa perditionis: *mass or lump of perdition;* i.e., the universally fallen humanity out of which God elects some to salvation; an Augustinian term associated particularly with the infralapsarian form of the doctrine of predestination. SEE *infra lapsum; praedestinatio*.

mater fidelium: *mother of the faithful;* a designation of the church considered as institution. SEE *ecclesia*.

materia: *matter;* i.e., the corporeal substratum of things. Substance (*substantia*, q.v.) is the union of *materia* and form (*forma*, q.v.). SEE *essentia; materia prima; materia secunda; natura*.

materia coelestis: *heavenly material* or *heavenly element;* i.e., the *res coelestis*, or heavenly element in the Lord's Supper. Rather than use language of sign and thing signified (*signum* and *res signata*) and imply a sacramental theology of mere representation or spiritual presence, the Lutheran orthodox speak of the visible, corporeal, or sensible element and the invisible or intelligible element of the sacrament, or to the earthly material (*materia terrestris*) and heavenly material (*materia coelestis*) of the sacrament. Thus, in the Lord's Supper there is a sacramental union (*unio sacramentalis*, q.v.) of earthly material, bread and wine, with heavenly material, the body and blood of Christ. Whereas the *materia* or *res* of the Lord's Supper is easily identified as the person of Christ, the *materia* or *res* of baptism was the subject of some discussion among the Lutheran scholastics. Some identified it as the Holy Spirit, others as Christ or the blood of Christ, but most argued the Trinity, as indicated by the baptismal formula. Nevertheless, it is Christ and his blood which make the sacrament possible and provide the objective ground of the salvation therein offered (SEE *res sacramenti*), so that Christ remains the *res signata*, or thing signified, by the sacrament from one point of view, while the Father, Son, and Spirit, who, as one God, dwell in the heart of believers, are clearly the ultimate ground and the source of baptismal grace and, therefore, from another view are equally well called the *materia* or *res coelestis*. Later orthodox Lutherans thought it better to refrain from final decision on the point at issue. SEE *baptismus; coena sacra; sacramentum.*

materia inhabilis: literally, *undisposed matter;* the formless mass of the first act of creation, also called *materia prima* (q.v.). Not only is *materia inhabilis* undisposed or unformed, it is also incapable of forming or giving disposition to itself. SEE *creatio.*

materia prima: *prime matter* or *first material;* also termed *materia inhabilis* (q.v.), undisposed or formless matter; in theology, the formless earth of the first act of creation which God informs in the second act of creation in order to bring forth the individual species of the created order; in scholastic philosophy, the underlying unformed material substratum of all things, identified by Aristotle as the basis of continuity and change beneath the transitory substances of temporal things. The *materia prima*, as the absolutely generalized basis of all subsequent individuation, is utterly potential and is devoid of all attributes or qualities. Individuation rests, first, on the informing of prime matter with the *forma substantialis*, or substantial form, that distinguishes the substance of one species of thing from the substance of another species. This union of *materia prima* with *forma substantialis* results in *materia secunda*, second matter, the basis of all material existence. The way in which this *materia secunda* is further differentiated into individuals of a species was a matter of dispute among the scholastics. The Thomists argued that the principle of individuation is not the form, or universal, in things but the matter itself of things insofar as matter is that out of which quantity arises. Scotus argued that prime matter itself cannot be the principle of individuation, since matter apart from form is entirely undetermined and undifferentiated. Scotus identifies the principle of individuation as a formally distinct (SEE *distinctio*) individual entity of a thing, i.e., as a principle that is really the thing as a composite of form and matter but that is formally distinguishable in the thing as an individuating principle neither purely material nor purely of the universal. Scotus refers to it as the *haeccitas* or "thisness" of the thing.

Among the Protestant orthodox, the Lutherans tend to follow the medieval doctors more closely than the Reformed concerning *materia prima*, identifying it as chaos, i.e., as *materia* lacking *forma substantialis*. Some of the Reformed argue, against this, that the *materia prima* or *inhabilis* of Gen. 1:1 is the mingled earth and water of the unarranged mass of the universe, i.e., *materia* with substantial form but not yet separated out into a coherent world order.

materia secunda: *second matter;* viz., substance at the basis of existent things, the combination of *materia prima* (q.v.) and substantial form or *forma substantialis*.

materia terrena: *earthly material or substance;* i.e., the bread and wine of the sacrament as distinct from the *materia coelestis* (q.v.), or heavenly material, with which they are united; also called *materia terrestris*. See *coena Domini; unio sacramentalis*.

mē on (μὴ ὄν): *nonbeing;* specifically, in Platonic philosophy, a plasticity of space or an indeterminacy upon which the ideas or forms (ἰδέαι or εἴδη) are impressed. This nonbeing accounts for the imperfection and transience of all embodiments of the eternal forms. Over against this theory, Aristotle argued that space, nothingness, or nonbeing in this absolute sense cannot be the foundation of the corporeal order. In other words, Aristotle argued against an absolute dualism of form and matter, being and nonbeing. In his *Metaphysics*, Aristotle argued an eternal material substratum, μή πω ὄν, a not-quite-nothingness of pure potency (*potentia*, q.v.) or unformed matter (ὕλη). In addition, he assumed the union of form and matter, denying the incorporeal existence of ideas or universals (*universalia*, q.v.). Form is the principle of self-realization (*entelecheia*, q.v.) in all things. Thus, formless matter or pure potency does not exist as such; rather potency always exists in relation to some actuality (*actus*, q.v.; SEE ALSO *in actu*). The scholastics adapt the Aristotelian model insofar as it is more susceptible of a Christian construction. The μὴ ὄν is, therefore, *non-ens*, nonbeing, in an absolute sense, a *nihil negativum materiam excludens*, a negative nothingness excluding matter, pure space not susceptible of form. Formless matter or pure potency is a *nihil positivum*, a positive nothingness, or material no-thing, usually identified as *materia prima* (q.v.), primary matter, the void or chaotic earth of the first day of creation. SEE *ens; forma; nihil.*

media: *means;* singular, **medium;** the instrumentality through which an end, or goal, is accomplished, sometimes termed instrumental cause (*causa instrumentalis,* q.v.), or second cause (*causae secundae,* q.v.). It is characteristic of means that they are passive in the order of causes and are utilized by the efficient cause. The value, positive or negative, of means derives, therefore, from the end achieved, the means in themselves being neutral. When, however, means are used in such a way as to have value in themselves and, in effect, attain the status of a proximate end, they not only cease to be neutral but also affect the achievement of the final end. A related problem concerning the particular status of churchly rites and practices considered as means led to the use of *media* as a synonym for *adiaphora* (q.v.) in the discussions of so-called things indifferent.

media communicationis remissionis peccatorum: *means of the communication of the remission of sins;* i.e., the Word and the sacraments viewed causally or *ex parte Dei,* on the part of God, as means of offering or bestowing (*media oblativa sive dativa*) grace, or as instruments (*instrumenta*) of grace that are operative and effective (*operativa et effectiva*). SEE *organa gratiae et salutis.*

media δοτικά: *given or received means;* in the justification of the sinner, the means of grace given by God, Word and sacrament, as distinct from faith, the *medium* ληπτικόν (q.v.), or receiving means.

media gratiae: *means of grace;* i.e., Word and sacraments as the means by which the grace of God is operative in the church. The term is used by both Lutheran and Reformed orthodox, although the Lutherans often substitute a stronger term, *organa gratiae et salutis* (q.v.), instruments of grace and salvation. The identification of Word and sacraments as *media gratiae* does not intend to exclude a general or common operation of grace but rather to indicate the function of both Word and sacraments in the regeneration (*regeneratio,* q.v.) and sanctification (*sanctificatio,* q.v.) of man as the instruments or objective channels of special or saving grace (*gratia specialis*). Word and sacraments are thus instrumental both in the inception of salvation and in the continuance of the work of grace in the Christian life. In addition, Word and sacraments are the sole officially ordained or instituted instruments or means of grace. God has promised the presence of his grace to faithful hearers of the Word and faithful participants in the sacraments. Thus the right preaching of the Word and right administration of the sacraments are the marks or identifying features of the true church (*notae ecclesiae,* q.v.). The Lutherans differ with the Reformed in rooting saving grace more totally in Word and sacrament. Without denying the efficacy of grace in Word and sacrament, the Reformed can argue the nonreception of that grace and also the ineffectual calling of the external Word (*Verbum externum,* q.v.) in the case of the nonelect or reprobate.

media iustificationis: *the means of justification;* i.e., Word and sacrament, the *media* δοτικά (q.v.), or given means; and faith, the *medium* ληπτικόν (q.v.), or receiving means. See *fides; iustificatio; organa gratiae et salutis.*

media remissionis peccatorum: *means of the remission of sins;* i.e., the means of grace, or Word and sacrament. See *organa gratiae et salutis.*

Mediator: *Mediator, Reconciler;* viz., Christ in the exercise of his threefold office (*munus triplex,* q.v.). Christ, as the God-man, is the person who fulfills the conditions requisite to the reconciliation of God and sinful mankind. His human nature is capable of performing a redemptive act representative of and in the place of mankind, and the divine nature is capable both of sustaining the human nature throughout the ordeal of its saving work and of rendering the work performed through the instrumentality of the human nature of infinite value by reason of the infinite worth and power of his divinity. Following Augustine's reading of 1 Tim. 2:5 (*Confessions* 10.43), the medieval doctors argued that Christ was Mediator according to his humanity, in which and through which the work of mediation was performed and without which the divine nature could not have been a mediator. The Reformers, and after them the Protestant scholastics, argue that neither nature by itself could mediate between God and man and that both natures, together, perform the one *opus theandricum* (q.v.), or divine-human work; therefore, Christ is Mediator according to both natures. See *medius; unio personalis.*

meditatio: *meditation.*

medium: *means.* See *media.*

medium cognoscendi: *means of knowing;* in theology the *media cognoscendi* are reason (*ratio*) in the case of natural theology, and

Scripture (not, of course, without the use of our rational faculties) in revealed theology. SEE *principia theologiae; theologia naturalis.*

medium λητττικόν: *the accepting or receiving medium or means;* viz., faith, the *medium iustificationis*, characterized as a passive means, disposed to accept, rather than actively or synergistically searching out the grace of God. The adjective λητττικός is not biblical, but rather was drawn by the Lutheran scholastics from Aristotelian philosophy; in the present usage, it has the effect of describing faith as a *habitus* (q.v.), or disposition. Faith is, therefore, not the cause, but the condition of justification, graciously instilled in man apart from works. The Protestant scholastics use the term *medium receptivum*, or receptive means, as a synonym of *medium* λητττικόν. SEE *iustificatio; media* δοτικά.

medius: *between, in between;* a term applied to Christ who, as one person in whom the divine and human natures are joined, stands directly between God and man. In the medieval scholastic vocabulary, Christ is *medius* or in between God and man according to both natures, and, because of his middle position, capable of being *Mediator* (q.v.) according to his human nature. The Reformers and Protestant scholastics argue that Christ is *medius* and also *Mediator* according to both natures, though they continue to distinguish between *medius* as a neutral term indicating the position of Christ as God-man between God and man, and *Mediator* as an official term pointing toward Christ's work of reconciliation.

medulla: *marrow, central core;* thus, the primary or central issues in a body of knowledge, e.g., *medulla theologiae*, the marrow of theology—the title of a brief, tightly organized theological system by William Ames. SEE *corpus theologiae; erotema; loci communes; theologia acroamatica.*

membra ecclesiae militantis: *members of the church militant;* viz., the members of the earthly and struggling church who, in death, will become *membra ecclesiae triumphantis*, members of the church triumphant. SEE *ecclesia.*

mens: *mind; intellect.* SEE *intellectus.*

mensura: *measure.* SEE *immensitas.*

merita supererogationis: *merits of supererogation.* SEE *opera supererogationis.*

meritum: *merit;* viz., the value or worth of a good or obedient act or the act itself; by extension, the just desert of the person performing the act. According to the medieval scholastic doctrine of salvation, human beings, with the aid of grace (*gratia*, q.v.), are required to live a life of active obedience and thereby be worthy of salvation. Considered in themselves as human acts, acts of obedience are half-merits that do not earn in an ultimate sense the gift of eternal salvation (*meritum de congruo*, q.v.). Considered, however, as works of the Spirit in us, these acts are fully meritorious (*meritum de condigno*). The Christian sinner, moreover, is required to perform acts of penance (*poenitentia*) which, because penance is a sacrament and a means of grace, both convey grace to the sinner through the performance of the sacrament (*ex opere operato*, q.v.) and, insofar as the sinner willingly performs the act and receives further grace (*ex opere operantis*, q.v.), are themselves meritorious acts or merits. Over against this view, the Protestant scholastics, both Lutheran and Reformed, hold that no human acts, whether before or after grace, have merit. The human being, justified by grace through faith alone, in standing before God is counted both righteous and personally sinful (*simul iustus et peccator*, q.v.). The good acts which flow from grace are divine acts in us and contribute nothing at all to man's salvation. Since, in this view, only perfect righteousness can be meritorious, only Christ merits life in and of himself, not for himself, but vicariously for us. This merit of Christ (*meritum Christi*, q.v.), the value or worth of Christ's righteousness or obedience, is the superabundant ground of salvation and is the sole true merit allowed in the Protestant orthodox system. SEE *poenitentia.*

meritum Christi: *the merit of Christ;* a term understood in two ways: the medieval scholastics, in accord with their view of the obedience of Christ (*obedientia Christi*, q.v.), divided the merit of Christ into the merit acquired by Christ for himself through his perfect obedience, as a result of which he was worthy of life and could accept death voluntarily (i.e., not as the wages of sin), and the merit of Christ's passive obedience to death, which can be graciously applied via the sacraments to believers. The Protestant scholastics, on the basis of the unity of the *obedientia Christi* and the application of the entirety of Christ's work to believers, argue that Christ merited nothing for himself. Equally important to the concept of the *meritum Christi* is the question of the source and the extent or value of Christ's merit. The argument most often found among the Protestant scholastics, both Lutheran and Reformed, received its clearest medieval formulation in the thought of Thomas Aquinas. The source of the *meritum Christi* is the *persona Christi* who performs the work of satisfaction (*satisfactio vicaria*, q.v.). Since the person is the divine Word, the infinite Second Person of the Trinity, the work performed by that person, even though accomplished through the instrumentality of his human nature, must be infinite. Against this view, Duns Scotus argued that Christ's work was in and of itself of finite value, since the source of the value or worth of the work must be the human nature of Christ in and by which the work was accomplished. The infinite sufficiency of Christ's merit arose, according to Scotus, from the divine acceptation (*acceptatio*, q.v.) of the finite *meritum Christi* as payment in full for sin. This counterargument became significant for Protestant orthodoxy in the seventeenth century when it was adopted by Hugo Grotius and ultimately became the normative view in Arminianism—the so-called moral government theory of atonement (SEE *acceptilatio*). A third view was stated by Calvin, most probably as an intensification of the Scotist view. The value of Christ's merit rests upon the divine decree (*Institutes*, II.xvii.1). Unlike the Scotist view, Calvin's doctrine argues the infinite merit or all-sufficiency of Christ's satisfaction, but on the same basis as the Scotist acceptation, the absolute will of God. Although Calvin's view is probably more in accord with the Reformed teaching concerning the *communicatio idiomatum* (q.v.), or communication of proper qualities, in the person of Christ, the orthodox Reformed tend not to follow Calvin, but rather to agree with the Lutheran scholastics in grounding the infinite worthiness of Christ's satisfaction in the divinity of Christ's person (Turretin, *Institutio theologiae* XIV.xii.7).

meritum de condigno: *merit of condignity* or *condign merit;* also called full merit as opposed to a half-merit or *meritum de congruo* (q.v.).

meritum de congruo: *merit of congruity;* a so-called half-merit, or proportionate merit. In late medieval scholastic theology a distinction was made between a *meritum de condigno*, a merit of condignity or full merit, deserving of grace, and a *meritum de congruo*, a half-merit or act not truly deserving of grace, but nevertheless receiving grace on the basis of the divine generosity. Aquinas had argued that meritorious acts of the regenerate could be considered either in terms of the merit of the Holy Spirit's work in the individual or in terms of the merit of the individual's own effort. In the former case, the act could be viewed as a *meritum de condigno*, a full merit, inasmuch as the work of the Spirit is absolutely good and is the ground of a truly and justly deserved salvation. In the latter case, the act is only a *meritum de congruo*, a half-merit, inasmuch as no human act can justly deserve the reward of salvation. Nevertheless,

191

the half-merit can be viewed as receiving a proportionate reward in the gift of salvation. In response to a finite act in which the individual does what he is able, God who is infinite responds by doing as much as he is able—which, of course, is infinitely greater. The gift is not equivalent in an absolute sense, as in the case of *meritum de condigno*, but it is proportionately just. Whereas Aquinas allowed no merit, either *de congruo* or *de condigno*, before the work of grace in man, late medieval theology, following Scotus, argued a *meritum de congruo*, before saving or operative grace (SEE *gratia*), in the purely natural condition (*status purorum naturalium*, q.v.). According to Scotus, the fall had merely resulted in the loss of a superadded gift (*donum superadditum*, q.v.) of grace that Adam had earned by doing a meritorious work on the basis of his natural ability. After the fall, Scotus argued, this grace could be once again earned; a man could merit grace by doing what was in him, i.e., by performing a half-merit, thereby earning a proportionate reward. In other words, a person need not be capable of earning salvation by a fully meritorious act, which, of course, is impossible for fallen mankind. The concept of a *meritum de congruo*, or proportionate merit, allowed late medieval scholastics to argue that a minimal act might be performed and, because of it, first grace conferred. SEE *facere quod in se est.*

mesitēs (μεσίτης): *mediator*. SEE *Mediator.*

metabainonta (μεταβαίνοντα): *things that have passed over from one condition or one subject to another.*

metameleia (μεταμέλεια): *feeling of regret.* SEE *metanoia.*

metanoia (μετάνοια): *repentance, change of mind;* e.g., Luke 15:7. The Protestant scholastics will frequently conjoin *metanoia*, defined as a change of mind, with *metameleia* (μεταμέλεια), defined as the feeling of regret or anguish over sin, in their definitions of repentance (*resipiscentia*, q.v.; ALSO *poenitentia*) and conversion (*conversio activa sive actualis*, q.v.).

metaphysica: *metaphysic* or, in common English usage, *metaphysics;* literally, *beyond the physics;* a term arising from the placement of Aristotle's treatise on first philosophy, or first principles, in the ancient collection of Andronicus—after the treatises on physics. Aristotle himself did not use the term *metaphysica.* Metaphysics is by definition the philosophical knowledge (SEE *epistēmē; scientia*) concerned with the first principles of knowing and being. It is the discussion of universals, or essences, as the ground of the knowledge and existence of particulars. As such, it represents an area or interest of philosophy that overlaps the domain of theology (SEE *articuli puri/mixti; usus philosophiae*). Metaphysics deals with God as first mover (*primum movens*, q.v.), with primary efficient causality (SEE *causa*), and with the relationship of form (*forma*, q.v.) and matter (SEE *materia prima; mē on*) and, therefore, with questions relating to the origin of the world. SEE *creatio; essentia; ex nihilo; universalia.*

metaphysicus, -a, -um (adj.): *metaphysical;* beyond the physical. SEE *metaphysica.*

microcosmos (from the Greek μικρόκοσμος): *microcosm* or *miniature world, tiny universe;* a term applied to man as the pinnacle and sum of creation in whom the entirety of the created order is mirrored. The scholastics refer to the human being as a chart, or compendium, of creation that, in small compass, recapitulates the creation.

millennium: *a thousand years;* viz., the thousand-year reign of the saints. SEE *chiliasmus.*

ministerium: *the body of ministers or pastors charged with the work of maintaining pure worship and true doctrine;* also the work of service in which the *ministri* engage. SEE *regimen ecclesiasticum.*

ministrantes inter Christianos: *ministers or servants among Christians;* i.e., the clergy. The Reformers and the Protestant orthodox are adamant in their argument against Rome that a minister or pastor is not a priest (*sacerdos*) but rather an official of the church distinguished from laity only by office or work and having no special powers.

ministri ministrantes: *ministering or serving ministers;* among the Reformed a term used to designate the presbyters and deacons who support the work of the clergy. As the *ecclesia repraesentativa*, the presbyters join with the pastor in governing the church. SEE *ecclesia.*

mirabilia; also **mira**: *wonders, wondrous things;* amazing, and even seemingly inexplicable, occurrences that are not, however, in the category of miracula (q.v.). Angels and devils have the power to perform *mirabilia* but not *miracula.*

193

miracula: *miracles, strange or marvelous things or occurrences brought about by the divine omnipotence;* as distinct from *mirabilia* (q.v.), miracles can be done only by God. Specifically, God is the first or primary cause of all miracles, although some miracles occur through the activity of instrumental causes and not by direct divine intervention. In addition, a miracle is not an extramundane intrusion or a violation of the laws of nature, but a divine work accomplished in the world in a manner beyond or superior to the regular order of things. Miracles are possible because of the absolute power (*potentia absoluta,* q.v.) of God as the free and first efficient cause of all things, including the laws of the natural order. God is the Creator of all things and of all laws. As the Lord of his creation, he can use the created order in ways not possible for the order in and of itself (see *omnipotentia*).

misericordia: *mercy, compassion;* specifically, the *misericordia Dei,* or mercy of God, according to which God has compassion on his fallen creatures in their inability to return to him; one of the affections of the divine will. See *bonitas Dei; voluntas Dei.*

missa: *Mass;* i.e., Holy Communion (*communio,* q.v.), the celebration of the Lord's Supper (*coena Domini;* see *coena sacra*) in Roman Catholic worship. Use of the term *missa* with reference to the Eucharist implies, therefore, the doctrine of transubstantiation (*transubstantiatio,* q.v.).

missio: *a sending forth* or *mission;* specifically, the *missio Spiritus Sancti,* the sending forth of the Holy Spirit, distinct from, and not to be confused with, the *processio* (q.v.). The *missio* of the Spirit is the activity of the Spirit, according to the *modus agendi* of the persons in the *opera Dei essentialia* (q.v.), by which and through which the Father and the Son act in the world, both in general and in the special economy of salvation.

mixtio: *mixture;* also **commixtio:** *mixture* or *commixture:* a term used to describe the Eutychian heresy. See *atreptōs kai asynchytōs.*

modus: *mode, method,* or *pattern;* used as a synonym for *ratio* in its sense of method or rationale.

modus agendi: *mode or manner of working.* See *opera Dei essentialia.*

modus loquendi: *manner of speaking.*

modus procedendi: *mode or manner of proceeding.*

modus subsistendi: *mode of subsistence;* used in trinitarian language as a synonym for *subsistentia* (q.v.) and as a Latin equivalent for *hypostasis; modus subsistendi* is more technical and precise than *persona* (q.v.). The Reformed in particular prefer to say that the persons of the Trinity are distinguished, not merely *rationaliter* or *formaliter,* but *modaliter,* according to their distinct modes of subsistence. The term can be used generally to indicate the mode or manner of the individual existence of any thing and, in this general sense, plays a role in Lutheran and Reformed christological debate over the manner of Christ's presence in the Lord's Supper and the mode or modes of the subsistence of Christ's body in its union with the divine person of the Word. SEE *distinctio; localis subsistendi modus; praesentia; praesentia illocalis sive definitiva.*

monopleuron (μονόπλευρον): *one-sided.* SEE *foedus monopleuron.*

monstrum incertitudinis: *the monster of uncertainty.* SEE *certitudo et gratiae praesentis et salutis aeternae.*

mors: *death;* defined by the Protestant scholastics as threefold: *mors temporalis sive corporalis* (q.v.), *mors spiritualis* (q.v.), and *mors aeterna* (q.v.).

mors aeterna: *eternal death;* the punishment (*poena,* q.v.) that follows *mors temporalis* (q.v.) at the final judgment in the cases of those whose guilt (*culpa*) has not been covered by the *satisfactio Christi.* Both Lutherans and the Reformed deny the doctrine that *mors aeterna* is an annihilation and define it as an eternal punishment and an eternal separation from fellowship with God, in short, an endless torment for the damned.

mors Christi: *the death of Christ.* SEE *obedientia Christi; passio; satisfactio vicaria.*

mors spiritualis: *spiritual death;* the condition of the unregenerate in this life.

mors temporalis sive corporalis: *temporal or bodily death;* i.e., physical death as the result of sin. The scholastics argue that God is not the cause of death except in the sense that he is the righteous judge who pronounces judgment on sin. Death itself is the privation, or *deprivatio,* of the natural life of man (*privatio vitae hominum naturalis*)

195

by the dissolution of the union of body and soul. As such it derives directly from the fall, which is the impelling cause, or *causa impulsiva*, of death. Since all have fallen in Adam, death occurs in all human beings as part of the *reatus* (q.v.), or liability to punishment, inherited by all of Adam's progeny. The work of salvation accomplished in Christ has, however, altered the meaning of death for Christians; it is now the transition to life eternal. The church, thus, bestows pleasant names upon death, the *mortis dulcia nomina* (q.v.).

mortificatio: *mortification;* also **mortificatio carnis:** *mortification of the flesh;* viz., the putting off of the old man, the dying to the world and the flesh, that marks the beginning of true repentance. SEE *poenitentia; sanctificatio.*

mortis dulcia nomina: *agreeable or pleasant names of death;* e.g., the passage from death to life, being with Christ, and the like. Christians can, in faith, apply these *dulcia nomina* to death, since they know from the promises of the gospel that death has no sting and that life eternal (*vita aeterna*) follows death. SEE *mors.*

motio: *motion* or *movement.* SEE *motus.*

motivum credibilitatis: *a motivation toward belief;* in particular, the authority of the church that testifies to the authority of Scripture. The Reformers and the orthodox allow this authority to the church but insist on the priority of Word over church and on the derivative authority of the church. SEE *potestas ecclesiae; Verbum Dei.*

motus: *motion* or *movement;* either in the sense of an activity or operation, or in the sense of a process or development from potency to actuality. Thus (1) the activity or operation of the soul (*motus animae*) in its faculties of intellect (*intellectus*, q.v.) and will (*voluntas*, q.v.) or in its desire or appetite (*appetitus*, q.v.): the *motus intellectualis sive cogitationis;* the *motus voluntatis;* and the *motus appetitus.* In each of these motions, the basic capacity or faculty of intellect, will, or desire moves from its existence as such, or primary actuality (*in actu primo*), to its fulfillment or realization in operation, or secondary actuality (*in actu secundo;* SEE *in actu*). The sense of *motus* as activity or operation therefore points toward the underlying meaning in Aristotelian metaphysics: (2) the process or development (*kinēsis* or *motus*) from potency to actuality. In the Aristotelian schema adopted by most of the medieval scholastics and by the Protestant orthodox, the potential dualism of form (*forma*, q.v.) and matter (*materia*, q.v.) is avoided by the assumption of a union of matter and form in all things (SEE *universalia*). The material substratum of the thing is a potency, or potential, for form or, more precisely, for the actualization of form—while the form is an inner principle of self-realization (*entelecheia*, q.v.), an inner goal toward which the process or development, the *motus*, of the thing is directed. *Motus*, therefore, is the principle of development which unites form and matter in a thing. Since Aristotelian physics assumes rest unless motion is introduced, the *motus* or *kinēsis* in finite things always requires a prior efficient cause (*causa*, q.v.) or a mover for its existence. Ultimately, since all finite movers both move and are moved, the chain of causality demands a first mover (*primum movens*, q.v.) who moves without himself being moved, i.e., God, the self-existent, necessary, fully actualized being. SEE *actus purus; Deus; ens.*

motus praeparatorii: *preparatory motions or movements;* e.g., the terrors of conscience (*terrores conscientiae*, q.v.) before conversion. SEE *homo renascens.*

multivolipraesentia: *multivolipresence; presence in many* (multi) *places according to the will* (voli) *of God;* specifically, the presence of Christ's humanity in the Lord's Supper according to scholastic Lutheranism. SEE *omnipraesentia generalis; ubivolipraesentia.*

munus Christi: *office of Christ.* SEE *munus triplex.*

munus triplex: *threefold office;* a christological term referring to the threefold work of Christ as prophet, priest, and king. The doctrine of a *munus triplex*, as opposed to a *munus duplex* (priest and king), was taught by Calvin and became standard among the Reformed in the sixteenth century. Following Johann Gerhard, the Lutherans of the seventeenth century tended to adopt the *munus triplex* also. The doctrine assumes that Christ fulfilled in his work all the anointed offices of the old covenant. Although the scholastics will speak of a *munus propheticum, munus sacerdotale,* and *munus regium,* a prophetic, priestly, and kingly office, there is but one office (*munus*), just as there is but one work (*officium*) of Christ. The office is a single threefold function of the Mediator. It is also an eternal office that belongs to the preexistent Word in his mediatorial work during the Old Testament dispensation and to the Word incarnate during both his earthly work and his eternal reign from the resurrection to the *eschaton* (q.v.) and beyond. Thus, the *munus regium,* or kingly office, does not begin at the resurrection or ascension, but has always belonged to Christ as Logos, and even to the incarnate Word according to his human nature, which exercised the *munus regium,* albeit in a hidden form, even during the *status humiliationis* (q.v.). Similar

197

statements can be made of the prophetic and priestly offices. The orthodox also recognize that an office is not something which belongs to a person by nature but is something conferred upon a person. Thus, the baptism of Christ can be viewed as the temporal designation of Christ to his office and as the beginning of his official ministry. The Reformed go further than the Lutherans in elaborating this point and, early on in the era of orthodoxy, speak of the designation or self-designation of the Word to the office of Mediator, a concept that leads ultimately to the doctrine of the *pactum salutis* (q.v.). Finally it should be noted that *munus* and *officium* are not always strictly distinguished and that, as the *munus triplex* became more and more a central structural feature of the doctrine of the work of Christ, the orthodox would also refer to an *officium triplex*. SEE *prophetia; regnum Christi; sacerdotium.*

mutabilitas: *mutability, changeability, the ability to change or alter in form;* ultimately, the capability in all finite things of ceasing to be through defect or corruption; a specifically theological problem is the instance of the mutation of will that is *peccatum originalis* (q.v.).

mutari posse: *the ability to change*. SEE *mutabilitas.*

mysteria fidei: *mysteries of the faith;* i.e., the doctrines known by revelation that transcend the grasp of reason.

Nn

natura: *nature;* a term having three primary meanings in scholastic theology and in Protestant orthodox usage: (1) essence; (2) a particular kind or species of essence in its actual existence; (3) the entire physical universe and its phenomena. In the first sense, *natura* simply means the character or quiddity (*quidditas,* q.v.) of a thing as defined by its primary qualities. Like *essentia* (q.v.), *natura* in this sense can be separate from the actual existence (*esse,* q.v.) of a thing. It indicates the genus, e.g., the *humanitas,* or humanity, of human beings, human nature in the most general sense. In the second sense, *natura* identifies the concrete substance (*substantia,* q.v.) of a species both in essence (*essentia*) and existence (*esse*): e.g., not merely *humanitas* or *natura humana* as the quiddity of human beings, but *natura humana* as the substance of a particular human being, such as that nature assumed by the person of Christ (SEE *persona; persona Christi*). In the third sense, *natura* simply refers to the order of nature and is used in such terms as *lex naturalis* (q.v.), natural law, or *theologia naturalis* (q.v.), natural theology—the law implicit in the order of the phenomenal world and the knowledge of God obtainable from examination of the physical universe.

natura integra: *uncorrupted nature;* i.e., human nature before the fall. SEE *in puris naturalibus.*

necessitas absoluta: *absolute necessity;* viz., simple necessity, or necessity simply and properly so called. *Necessitas absoluta* indicates something that is necessary in such a way that its opposite is contradictory. God's existence is, thus, an absolute necessity, since the nonexistence of the self-existent, necessary being is a contradiction.

necessitas coactionis: *necessity of coaction or compulsion;* a necessity imposed on a thing, an agent, or an event by an external cause not in accord with the will of the thing or agent on which it is imposed. *Necessitas coactionis,* of course, applies only to created beings and not to God. When God is bound to his promises, he is so bound by his own freely willed decree. SEE *necessitas consequentiae.*

necessitas conditionata: *conditioned necessity;* i.e., a necessity of the consequences; SEE *necessitas consequentiae.*

necessitas consequentiae: *necessity of the consequences;* i.e., not an absolute necessity (*necessitas absoluta*, q.v.), but a necessity brought about or conditioned by a previous contingent act or event so that the necessity itself arises out of contingent circumstance; thus, conditional necessity. *Necessitas consequentiae* is also called *necessitas ex suppositione*, necessity on account of supposition, or *necessitas ex hypothesi*, necessity on account of hypothesis, or hypothetical necessity, and sometimes *necessitas ex hypothesi dispositionis*, or necessity on account of a hypothesis of disposition. Each of these latter terms indicates a necessity that arises out of a set of circumstances or out of a disposition or capacity hypothetically rather than absolutely or necessarily conceived; i.e., the conditions that create the necessity are themselves a matter of contingency and are therefore only hypothetically or suppositionally the ground or reason for a necessity. The *necessitas consequentiae* occurs continually in the finite order and, unlike *necessitas absoluta*, is applicable to God in terms of his *potentia ordinata* (q.v.), or ordained power. There is no necessity that God decree what he decrees; but, granting the divine decree, God is bound to his own plan and promises. Therefore, the fulfillment of the divine plan and the divine promises is necessary, but by a *necessitas consequentiae.*

necessitas consequentis: *necessity of the consequent;* i.e., the necessity of something that cannot be other than what it is, which is to say, a simple or absolute necessity. A necessity of the consequent arises out of the connection of necessary causes with the effects that must follow from them. SEE *necessitas absoluta.*

necessitas ex hypothesi or **necessitas ex hypothesi dispositionis**: *hypothetical necessity* or *hypothetical necessity of disposition;* synonymous with *necessitas consequentiae* (q.v.).

necessitas naturae: *necessity of nature;* viz., the limit of thought and action, not imposed from without, but belonging to the nature of the thing or being itself. No being, not even omnipotent God, can act against its own nature. This necessity, since it is not a necessity imposed from without or a necessity that arises out of previous external circumstance, in no way conflicts with the *libertas naturae* (q.v.) of a being.

nekrōsis (νέκρωσις): *mortification;* e.g., 2 Cor. 4:10. SEE *mortificatio.*

Neque carno extra λόγον **neque** λόγος **extra carnem:** *Neither is the flesh beyond the Logos nor the Logos beyond the flesh;* a more elaborate form of the Lutheran christological maxim, *Logos non extra carnem* (q.v.).

nihil: *nothing; nothingness;* also **nihilum;** the form *nihil* is indeclinable; *nihilum* is a regular second declension noun. Theologically and philosophically, *nihil* is sometimes distinguished into the *nihil positivum,* or positive nothingness, i.e., pure potency or potential (*potentia*), and the *nihil negativum,* negative or absolute nothingness, a total absence of both potency and act. SEE *ex nihilo; in actu; mē on.*

Nihil habet rationem sacramenti extra usum a Christo institutum:
Nothing has the nature of a sacrament outside of the exercise instituted by Christ; i.e., there is no sacrament apart from the rite. A maxim from the *Formula of Concord* (Solid Declaration, VII.85) used frequently by the Lutheran orthodox (Baier, *Compendium theologiae positivae,* III, 504–5). The full statement reads, *Nihil habet rationem sacramenti extra usum a Christo institutum seu extra actionem divinitus institutam* (adding the phrase, "or outside of the divinely instituted action"). A variant form is given by Baier, *Nihil habeat rationem sacramenti extra usum, qui institutus est a Deo* (p. 504). The Lutheran orthodox here express a rule for the Protestant interpretation of the sacrament in opposition to the medieval scholastic and continuing Roman Catholic veneration of the host. The Roman Catholic view, based upon the doctrine of transubstantiation (*transubstantiatio,* q.v.), was that the converted elements remained body and blood after the celebration of the sacrament. Consecrated bread, in particular, was reserved and venerated beyond the rite (*extra usum*). The Lutheran orthodox insist on the real illocal presence of Christ's body and blood only for the duration of the sacramental action (*actio sacramentalis*). The real presence is indicated though not controlled by the words of institution, "This do" and "As often as you do this," so that the cessation of the mandated action is also the cessation of the sacramental union. Thus the aphorism, *Unio sacramentalis fit, quando fit manducatio et bibitio,* "The sacramental union occurs when the eating and drinking occur." More precisely, the *unio sacramentalis* is not caused by human act or speech; the words of institution only set apart the visible means for sacramental use. These words do not bring about the real presence or mark a point in time at which the real presence occurs or begins. Nonetheless the words, "This do in remembrance of me," indicate the rite (*usus*) and the

action (*actio*) of the sacrament and therefore indicate the presence of Christ in the consecration (*consecratio*), distribution (*distributio*), eating (*manducatio*), and drinking (*bibitio*). By the same token, there is no real presence during the last part of the rite after the last person has communed. Thus, an eating and drinking that takes place without the consecration or words of institution is not a sacrament, nor is there any real presence; but, equally so, a consecration not followed by sacramental eating and drinking is an empty act, and a piece of consecrated bread or a drop of consecrated wine fallen on the floor does not indicate a desecration of the real presence. The same argument obtains in the definition of baptism. If the water is not consecrated, there is no baptism, and if consecrated water is put to any use other than the baptism instituted by Christ, there is no sacrament. SEE *verbum institutionis.*

nihilum: *nothing.* SEE *nihil.*

nomen officii: *official title;* i.e., a name deriving from one's work or office rather than from one's nature (*nomen naturae*); e.g., *angeloi* (q.v.), *Christus* (q.v.).

nomina Dei: *names of God;* a term reserved by the Protestant scholastics for the specifically biblical appellations of God, such as *Jehovah, Elohim, El, El Shaddai, El Elyon.* The Protestant scholastics often distinguish between the *nomina Dei* and the divine attributes (*attributa divina,* q.v.) and develop a separate *locus* or separate section of a general *locus de Deo* on the subject of the biblical names as an issue to be considered prior to the attributes in the identification of God and his ways.

nomos (νόμος): *law.* SEE *lex Dei.*

nomothesia (νομοθεσία): *legislation, promulgation of law;* e.g., Rom. 9:4. SEE *foedus.*

non-ens: *nonbeing, nothing.* SEE *ens; ex nihilo; mē on; nihil.*

non-impeditio peccati: *the nonprevention of sin;* i.e., the divine *permissio peccati,* or permission of sin. The language of *non-impeditio* is used by the scholastics to indicate that God's active or willing *permissio* (q.v.) of sin in no way entails even a momentary moral approval of the sinful act. God merely does not act to remove the conditions of free will (*liberum arbitrium,* q.v.) and of the operation of secondary causes (*causae secundae,* q.v.) in general according to which sin is physically possible. This *permissio,* however, does not indicate that the punishment (*poena,* q.v.) of such sins is removed, since they occur by the effective will of the sinner. Indeed, the *non-impeditio* implies a withholding of grace and illumination and a giving-over of the sinner to his own sinful willing and ultimately to eternal damnation.

non posse non peccare: *not able not to sin;* viz., the condition of fallen humanity according to the Augustinian perspective; also described as *impotentia bene agendi,* the inability to do good. This condition does not imply an absence of moral responsibility since it arises, *not* from a loss of the *libertas naturae* (q.v.), but from loss of the *potentia bene agendi.* The nature, as such, remains free to act according to the limit of its abilities, apart from any external coaction or coercion, and has lost only the ability to make a choice (*arbitrium,* q.v.) of the good. In addition, since the loss of that ability is the result of the original sin of Adam and not of any act of the divine Law-giver, the responsibility of man before the moral law and the divine promise of fellowship in return for perfect obedience remain unblemished despite human inability.

non posse peccare: *not able to sin;* the condition of humanity in the final state of glory. See *beati; in patria; libertas naturae.*

norma: *norm* or *standard;* variously distinguished as (1) *norma absoluta,* absolute norm, applicable only to Scripture as *principium theologiae* (q.v.); (2) *norma causativa,* causative norm, again applicable only to Scripture; (3) *norma normata,* a standardized norm, applied to churchly confessions, particularly by the orthodox Lutherans, insofar as they set forth the truths of Scripture; and (4) *norma normans,* the standardizing norm, applied to Scripture as that norm standing behind the standardized confessions, or *norma normata.* See *ecclesia repraesentativa; potestas ecclesiae; testes veritatis.*

notae ecclesiae: *marks of the church;* sometimes **notae verae ecclesiae**: *marks of the true church;* the distinguishing features by which the church can be identified: (1) the preaching of the Word (*praedicatio Verbi*) or profession of true doctrine; (2) the valid administration of the true sacraments (see *administratio sacramentorum*); and (3) disciplined Christian life in obedience to Word and sacrament. The Reformers and the Lutheran orthodox generally argue the first two *notae,* Word and sacrament, and assume the third as a by-product or effect. The Reformed scholastics generally argue Word, sacrament, and discipline as the *notae*. SEE *attributa ecclesiae; ecclesia; sacramentum; Verbum Dei.*

notae personales: *personal marks or characteristics;* SEE *character hypostaticus sive personalis.*

notio personalis: *personal notion or conception;* SEE *relatio personalis.*

notiones personales: *personal characteristics or "notions";* specifically, the personal characteristics of the three persons of the Trinity that determine the hypostatic or personal character (*character hypostaticus sive personalis*, q.v.) of each of the persons. The *notiones personales* are identical with the personal relations plus the unbegottenness (*innascibilitas* or *agennēsia*) of the Father; i.e., the *notiones* are the personal relations (*relationes personales*) and the personal properties (*proprietates personales*) of the Trinity. SEE *proprietas; relatio personalis; Trinitas.*

notitia: *knowledge;* synonymous with *cognitio* (q.v.). SEE *fides; scientia.*

notitia Dei acquisita: *acquired knowledge of God.*

notitia Dei insita: *implanted or ingrafted knowledge of God.* SEE *cognitio.*

notitia historica: *historical knowledge;* especially, in theology, the knowledge of the events and the substance of the biblical history; while it pertains to the knowledge-content of faith, it does not itself constitute faith or belong to the essence of faith. SEE *fides.*

Novum Testamentum: *New Testament.* SEE *foedus gratiae; Scriptura sacra; testamentum.*

numen: *a divine spirit, a presiding deity;* a term from Roman religion used to indicate the divine presence.

Oo

obedientia; also **oboedientia**: *obedience.*

obedientia Christi: *obedience of Christ;* viz., Christ's obedient work as the Mediator; performed for our redemption, it was distinguished by the scholastics into *obedientia activa* and *obedientia passiva,* active and passive obedience. The *obedientia activa* describes the life of Christ from his birth to his passion, and particularly his ministry, during which Christ acted sinlessly and in perfect obedience to the will of God. The *obedientia passiva* refers to Christ's passion, during which he accepted passively, without any resistance, the suffering and cross to which he was subjected for the satisfaction of sin. According to the medieval scholastics, following Anselm, the *obedientia activa* was not of a vicarious or substitutionary nature, but rather was Christ's own necessary obedience under the law, the ground of Christ's own merit and therefore of his aptitude for the work of satisfaction. Had the Mediator *not* been meritorious before God, the payment of the *obedientia passiva* would have been exacted of him for his own disobedience and could not have been applied to believers. This view of his obedience relates directly to the medieval theory of penance and to the distinction between punishment (*poena,* q.v.) and guilt (*culpa*). *Poena* accrues to anyone who is not actively obedient, while *culpa* is the result, qualitatively speaking, of sin. Since Christ's *obedientia passiva* accomplished the remission of sin (*remissio peccatorum*), those saved by grace through Christ have their *culpa* removed, but since Christ's *obedientia activa* was accomplished in order to constitute Christ as the worthy Mediator and not applied to sinners, the *poena* of sin remains and must be suffered temporally through the sacrament of penance. Following Luther, the Protestant scholastics, Lutheran and Reformed alike, argued that both the *obedientia activa* and the *obedientia passiva* were accomplished in the place and on behalf of believers and together constituted the one saving work of Christ, satisfying for both the *poena* and *culpa* of sin. Christ's obedience, then, according to the Protestant scholastics, remits sin in such a way as to make unnecessary the sacrament of penance. Note that this view of Christ's obedience conforms to the doctrine of justification *sola fide,* apart from the works of the law. Since the Protestant scholastics are adamant that the *obedientia Christi* was totally soteriological in purpose, they often refer to it as a single obedience with two aspects rather than as an *obedientia activa* and an *obedientia passiva.* Thus the *obedientia Christi* is both an *actio passiva,* a passive action, and a *passio activa,* an active passion. *Actio passiva* refers to Christ's subjection to the law, while *passio activa* refers to the real obedience of his life and death. SEE *imputatio; poenitentia; reatus; satisfactio vicaria.*

obex: *hindrance; impediment;* specifically, a spiritual obstacle in the way of sacramental grace. SEE *ex opere operato.*

obiectum: *object;* in grammar and in logical predication, the thing or concept toward which the action of the verb is directed; in theology or philosophy, the thing or concept toward which the thinking subject, i.e., the mind or intellect, directs its thought, or the thing toward which the senses are directed in perception. SEE *antepraedicamenta; praedicamenta; praedicatio; subiectum.*

obiectum electionis: *the object of election;* viz., the human beings who are numbered as the elect in the eternal decree of God. Lutheran and Reformed scholastics agree that the *obiectum electionis* is neither the whole human race nor the visible church (SEE *ecclesia*) nor all believers, those who will persevere and those who will have faith only temporarily and who ultimately fall away. The object of God's election is the finite number of those who are actually saved, since the elective decree itself, whether defined as a conditional decree or an absolute decree, is inalterable. SEE *decretum; electio; praedestinatio.*

obiectum fidei: *object of faith;* distinguished by the scholastics into two categories: the *obiectum formalis fidei,* or formal object of faith, which is Scripture, and the *obiectum materialis fidei,* or material object of faith, which is Christ, or more precisely, the whole revelation of God as it is fulfilled and given in Christ. Scripture, as the formal object of faith, is also the formal object of theology (*obiectum formalis theologiae*) and the foundation of theological knowing. SEE *obiectum theologiae; principia theologiae.*

obiectum theologiae: *the object of theology;* as defined by the Protestant scholastics, the object of theology is twofold (*duplex*), material and formal. The *obiectum materialis theologiae,* or material object of theology, is the material or substance of revelation, the *res revelatae,* or things revealed. The *obiectum formalis theologiae,* or formal object of theology, is the foundation or method of knowing (*principium sive ratio cognoscendi*) on which our knowledge of the *res revelatae* depends, i.e., the revelation itself as given in Scripture. Therefore, the *obiectum theologiae* is God in his self-revelation and, by extension, Christ as the *fundamentum Scripturae* (q.v.) and the focus of saving truth. SEE *authoritas Scripturae; principia theologiae; revelatio generalis/revelatio specialis; veritas.*

obsessio corporalis: *bodily possession;* also **obsessio spiritualis**: *spiritual possession;* an activity of the devil or of evil angels, entering a human being and using him as their instrument.

obsignatio: *an act of sealing or certifying;* a term from Roman law which specifically refers to the witnessing and sealing of a will or testament (*testamentum,* q.v.) and is therefore used with reference to the sealing of the New Testament by Christ. SEE *foedus gratiae.*

occultatio: *hiding* or *veiling;* a term used by the orthodox Reformed in their doctrine of the *status humiliationis* (q.v.), or state of humiliation, to describe the relation of the *humiliatio* or *exinanitio* (evacuation or *kenōsis*) to the divine nature of Christ and its attributes. The divinity of Christ is hidden under the flesh as by a veil. Some of the Lutherans use similar terminology, speaking of a *krypsis* (q.v.) of the divine attributes, i.e., a hiding, but with a different implication, since the Lutheran "kryptics" did hold to a communication of divine attributes to the human nature.

odium: *hatred, animosity, aversion;* especially, the *odium Dei,* the hatred or aversion of God, which the Protestant scholastics frequently list among the affections of the divine will as indicative of the feeling of God toward sin and disobedience. The term *odium Dei* is recognized as an anthropopathism (SEE *anthrōpopatheia*).

oeconomia: *the usual transliteration of the Greek οἰκονομία found in the writings of the Protestant scholastics.* SEE *dispensatio.*

officium: *work;* also, particularly among the later Protestant scholastics, *office;* used as a synonym for *munus* in discussions of the *munus Christi* or *officium Christi.* Strictly speaking, *officium Christi* ought to refer to the work of Christ, his obedience both active and passive and his satisfaction for sin, whereas *munus Christi* ought to refer primarily to the prophetic, priestly, and kingly office of Christ, the "official" or appointed tasks to which Christ was anointed as Mediator. See *munus triplex; obedientia Christi; satisfactio vicaria.*

oikonomia (οἰκονομία): *economy.* See *dispensatio.*

Omne peccatum in Deum committitur: *All sin is committed against God;* i.e., since all sins violate the divine law, even when their immediate result is the suffering of other human beings, they are ultimately sins against God himself.

omnipotentia: *omnipotence, having all power and potency, being all-powerful;* an attribute of God; *omnipotentia* indicates the power, or *potentia,* of God *ad extra* by virtue of which he can do all things that are not contrary either to his will or his knowledge. In other words, the *omnipotentia Dei* is limited only by the essence or nature of God himself and by nothing external to God. Thus, the fact that God cannot do evil, cannot die, and cannot cease to be Father, Son, and Spirit is not a limit on or a contradiction of his *omnipotentia.* The scholastics agree with Augustine that all such hypothetical acts as would diminish God would be signs of weakness or of a defective willing, not evidences of omnipotence. Since, moreover, God himself is eternally fully actualized (*in actu,* q.v.) and *never* in process or in potency (*in potentia*), the *potentia Dei,* the potency of God, or *omnipotentia Dei,* refers to the divine activity *ad extra* and never to a change or a potential for change in the divine essence, which is, by definition, both perfect and immutably so (see *immutabilitas*). Further, since God's omnipotence is a *potentia* it cannot be a capacity for self-privation; i.e., a deficiency or deficient cause. The divine omnipotence may further be defined as the divine power or potential for the conferring of being and the active governance of all that is. In the former instance, which is the work of creation, the power of God is *omnipotentia absoluta* or *potentia absoluta* (q.v.), since it observes no prior condition apart from the divine essence itself. This *omnipotentia absoluta* can be referred also to miracles. In the latter instance, which is the work of providence or continued creation (see *continuata creatio; providentia*), the power of God is *omnipotentia relativa sive ordinata,* relative or ordained omnipotence, or *potentia ordinata* (q.v.), since it is bound by laws of its own making.

omnipraesentia: *omnipresence;* frequently paired with *immensitas,* which indicates, literally, "without measure" (*sine mensura*). God is everywhere present in the sense of being unbounded by space or measure. God is everywhere present because he is an infinite spiritual, immaterial being who cannot be contained or restricted by physical dimensions. SEE *immensitas.*

omnipraesentia generalis: *general or generalized omnipresence;* specifically, the omnipresence or ubiquity (*ubiquitas*, q.v.) of Christ's human nature, i.e., the illocal, supernatural presence as explained in the Lutheran doctrine of the communication of proper qualities (*communicatio idiomatum*, q.v.). An unqualified assertion of *omnipraesentia generalis* was made by Johann Brenz prior to the *Formula of Concord;* the concept was subsequently modified by Martin Chemnitz, who argued an *ubivolipraesentia* or *multivolipraesentia.* The idea of *ubivolipraesentia* does not limit the presence of Christ's exalted human nature but rather stresses that it is a communicated omnipresence, the purpose of which lies in the divine will and the ground of which is the omnipresence of the Logos. *Multivolipraesentia* stresses, not generalized omnipresence, but the specific presence of Christ's humanity in the Lord's Supper. With this qualification, the *omnipraesentia generalis* does not threaten the *praesentia localis* (q.v.), or local presence, of Christ's human nature according to its own attributes. Indeed, the Lutheran orthodox argue the physical locality of Christ's humanity on the basis of the first *genus* of the *communicatio idiomatum* while arguing ubiquity only on the basis of the second *genus.* In the seventeenth century, it was argued that Christ's humanity *in actu primo,* in its primary actuality or existence as such, remains local or localized always; whereas Christ's humanity *in actu secundo,* in its secondary actualization, is not always localized but partakes of the divine *omnipraesentia* as *omnipraesentia generalis.* SEE *actus; in actu.*

omnipraesentia intima sive partialis: *secret or partial omnipresence;* a term used by Lutheran scholastics to describe the omnipresence of Christ's human nature during the *status humiliationis* (q.v.), or state of humiliation. Christ's divine attributes are then hidden or secret (*intima*) because they are not in use (*chrēsis*) in and through the human nature, even though possessed by the human nature (SEE *ktēsis*). Since this is an omnipresence only in terms of possession and not use, it is termed partial or *partialis,* or, more clearly, *nuda adessentia,* a mere being present, as opposed to an active or effective being present, the *praesentia extima sive totalis* (q.v.). This *omnipraesentia intima sive partialis* must also be distinguished from the *praesentia intima sive personalis,* the intimate or personal presence, i.e., the presence of the *Logos* to the flesh and the flesh to the *Logos* by reason of the *unio personalis* (q.v.). In both cases, *intima,* secret or intimate, indicates the special relationship between the *Logos* and

209

the assumed human nature—in the former term, *omnipraesentia* refers to the real but not manifest communication of proper qualities (*communicatio idiomatum*, q.v.); in the latter term, *praesentia* refers to the communion of the natures (*communio naturarum*, q.v.) one with the other and to the fact that the person of the *Logos* is never and nowhere separated from the human nature. Thus the Lutheran aphorism, *Logos non extra carnem* (q.v.): "The *Logos* is not beyond the flesh."

omnisapientia: *omnisapience; having all wisdom and being all-wise;* specifically, the *omnisapientia* or *sapientia Dei*, the wisdom of the divine counsel (*consilium Dei*, q.v.) by virtue of which God knows all causes and effects and ordains them to their proper ends and by which he ultimately accomplishes his own end in and through all created things. *Omnisapientia* can, therefore, be defined as the correspondence of God's thought with the highest good, or *summum bonum*, of all things. Since, of course, God is himself the *summum bonum* toward which all things ultimately tend, the definition can equally well read, the correspondence of God's thought with God's essence considered as the *summum bonum. Omnisapientia*, furthermore, can be distinguished from *omniscientia*. Whereas *omniscientia* (q.v.) refers to the knowledge that God has as *prima causa efficiens*, or first efficient cause, *omnisapientia* refers to God as *causa finalis*, final cause or goal. Thus, *scientia* and *omniscientia* indicate a pure or theoretical understanding, while *sapientia* and *omnisapientia* denote a practical understanding, a wise knowing that directs the ordering of ends and goals.

omniscientia: *omniscience, having all knowledge and being all-knowing;* specifically, the attribute of God by which God knows all things, all events, and all circumstances of things and events perfectly and immediately in his timeless eternity (SEE *aeternitas*). The *omniscientia Dei* is therefore described by the scholastics as absolutely true (*verissima*), absolutely clear (*distinctissima*), simultaneous (*simultanea*), and immediate or intuitive (*intuitiva*). It is *verissima* because it is all-encompassing, complete, and without defect; *distinctissima* because it lacks no detail, either concerning things possible or things actual or concerning which possibilities will be actualized and which will not; *simultanea* because eternal God is free from succession, not only in being, but also in knowing, and therefore knows all things at once, including the order and temporal succession of things; *intuitiva* because it knows all things by immediate apprehension rather than by discourse or demonstration. SEE *intellectus Dei; scientia Dei.*

omnisufficientia: *all-sufficiency;* a divine attribute derived from the absolute life of God (*vita Dei*, q.v.) and the divine self-existence (*aseitas*, q.v.), indicating the absolute self-sufficiency of God. As self-existent life, God stands in need of nothing but is totally sufficient in and of himself. SEE *attributa divina.*

opera Dei: *the works of God;* without modifier, a term usually applied to the creation and to the providential preservation of creation; more precisely, all the activities of God, distinguished into *opera Dei essentialia* and *opera Dei personalia, opera Dei ad intra* and *opera Dei ad extra.*

opera Dei ad extra: *the outward or external works of God;* the divine activities according to which God creates, sustains, and otherwise relates to all finite things, including the activity or work of grace and salvation; sometimes called *opera exeuntia,* out-going works. SEE *operationes Dei externae.*

opera Dei ad intra: *the inward or internal works or activity of God;* also termed **opera Dei interna**. In contrast to the *opera Dei ad extra,* the internal works of God are accomplished apart from any relation to externals and are, by definition, both eternal and immutable. The internal works of God are either essential or personal, i.e., *opera Dei essentialia* (q.v.), essential works of God, or *opera Dei personalia* (q.v.), personal works of God. The *opera Dei ad intra* can also be termed *opera immanentia,* immanent or inward works, in which case the *opera essentialia* and *opera personalia* are distinguished as (1) *opera immanentia donec exeunt,* immanent works before their going out or efflux, since the *opera essentialia* ground all *opera ad extra;* and (2) *opera immanentia per se,* immanent works of themselves, since the *opera personalia* do not go forth from the divine essence.

opera Dei essentialia: *the essential works of God;* the works of God performed by the Godhead in its oneness; i.e., the common works (*opera communis*) of the divine persons as distinguished from the *opera Dei personalia* (q.v.); specifically, the eternal decree and its execution in time. Although the three persons work as one, there is nevertheless a *modus agendi,* or manner of working, that corresponds with the interpersonal relations of the Father, Son, and Holy Spirit. The Father acts or works through the Son and in the Spirit. Thus the Father is the *fons actionis,* or source of activity, who works of himself and from none (*a nullo*); the Son is the *medium actionis,* or means of action, who works not of himself but from the Father (*a Patre*); and the Spirit is the *terminus actionis,* or limit of activity, who works not of himself but from both (*ab utroque*) Father and Son.

The *opera Dei essentialia* are further distinguished into the *opus Dei essentialis ad intra*, which is the eternal *decretum* (q.v.) or *consilium Dei* (q.v.) willed by the entire Godhead as the foundation of all *opera ad extra*, and the *opus Dei essentialis ad extra*, which is the execution or enactment of the divine decree, both in the general work of *creatio* (q.v.) and *providentia* (q.v.), i.e., the economy or arrangement of salvation. Because of the intimate relationship of the *opus essentialis ad intra* to the *opus essentialis ad extra*, they are sometimes called by the scholastics *opera immanentia donec exeunt*, immanent works preceding external act, and *opera exeuntia*, outgoing acts or external works. SEE *opera Dei ad extra; opera Dei ad intra.*

opera Dei personalia: *the personal works of God;* a term applied to the *ad intra* operation of the individual persons of the Trinity. (While all works of God *ad extra* are by definition the common work of the three persons in the Godhead, *opera personalia* occur only *ad intra*.) The *opera personalia* are restricted, therefore, to the activities of and relations between the persons: the activity of the Father in begetting the Son; the activity of the Father and the Son in spirating the Spirit; the relation of the Son to the Father by being begotten (passive generation); and the relation of the Spirit to the Father and the Son by being spirated (passive spiration). The *opera personalia* are also called *opera divisa* since they identify and distinguish the persons; in contrast, the *opera ad extra* are, by definition, *indivisa.* The *opera personalia* are also called *opera immanentia per se*, immanent works of themselves, since they do not issue forth from the Godhead, in contrast to the *opera essentialia*, which ground all *opera ad extra*. SEE *Opera Trinitatis ad extra sunt indivisa; Trinitas.*

opera supererogationis: *works of supererogation; works beyond those required for salvation;* also **merita supererogationis:** *merits of supererogation;* a concept in medieval and later Roman Catholic theology according to which the saints were believed to have performed works of full merit (SEE *meritum de condigno*) beyond those enjoined by commands of God in the law. Their further obedience was defined in terms of the holy life held forth by the counsels of the gospel (*consilia evangelica*, q.v.). The concept of *opera supererogationis* lies at the foundation of two elements of Roman Catholic piety: indulgences and the rigors of monastic life. On the one hand, it was argued that the supererogatory merits of the saints could be dispensed by the church from its treasury of merits and bestowed as indulgences on those whose lives did not fulfill the legal requirements of salvation.

On the other hand, it was assumed that the saints' *opera supererogationis* were a model for human conduct and that the religious were capable of fulfilling both the commands of the law and the *consilia evangelica* under the conditions of the monastic life.

Opera Trinitatis ad extra sunt indivisa: *The external or* ad extra *works of the Trinity are undivided;* specifically, since the Godhead is one in essence, one in knowledge, and one in will, it would be impossible in any work *ad extra* (q.v.) for one of the divine persons to will and to do one thing and another of the divine persons to will and do another. All the *opera ad extra* or *opera exeuntia* are *opera Dei essentialia* (q.v.). Sometimes the Protestant scholastics will speak of the *opera ad extra* as *opera certo modo personalia,* personal works after a certain manner, because the undivided works *ad extra* do manifest one or another of the persons as their *terminus operationis,* or limit of operation. The incarnation and work of mediation, e.g., terminate on the Son, even though they are willed and effected by Father, Son, and Spirit.

operationes Dei externae: *the external operation or works of God;* distinguished into (1) the *opus naturae* and (2) the *opus gratiae.* Both of these *operationes* consist in the outward, or *ad extra,* exercise of divine will and power, resulting in definite temporal effects in conformity with and as the execution or enactment of the eternal *decretum* (q.v.) or *consilium Dei* (q.v.). (1) The *opus naturae* consists in the *creatio* (q.v.) of the world and the *continuata creatio* (q.v.) or divine *providentia* (q.v.). Although this work of creation and providence is a gracious work of God, it must be distinguished from (2) the *opus gratiae,* or work of special grace, for the sake of the redemption of believers. The *opus gratiae* comprehends the entire saving work of God from the *protevangelium* (q.v.) to the *consummatio saeculi* (q.v.).

opheilēma (ὀφείλημα): *a debt, something owed;* hence, sins or trespasses as in the form of the Lord's Prayer in Matt. 6:12.

opinio: *opinion;* i.e., teaching that does not rest on true knowledge (*scientia,* q.v.) or on wisdom (*sapientia,* q.v.) but on unfounded assertion.

opposita: *opposites* or *contraries;* thus, things, propositions, or terms that are mutually exclusive. Opposite or mutually exclusive things cannot exist together at the same time in the same subject, but only at different times or in separate subjects. Opposite or contrary propositions and terms are such that they negate one another. Thus, a universal positive proposition is contrary to the universal negative proposition which treats of the same subject; likewise, a term that has a positive significance is opposite to a term that expresses its negation, e.g., presence and absence.

oppositio adaequata: *exact or direct opposite.*

opus alienum: *alien work,* as opposed to *opus proprium* (q.v.).

opus oeconomicum: *economic or administrative work;* specifically, the work of the Godhead in the economy of salvation. SEE *opera Dei ad extra; opera Trinitatis ad extra sunt indivisa; operationes Dei externae.*

opus operatum: *the work performed.* SEE *ex opere operato.*

opus proprium: *proper work,* as opposed to *opus alienum,* or alien work. An important distinction in the *opera Dei ad extra* (q.v.) typical in late medieval theology and highly influential among the early Reformers. The divine *opus proprium* is the work of God, such as creation, providence, and grace, that can be considered as proper to God considering his nature as good, just, merciful, and so forth. By contrast, the divine *opus alienum* is the work of God that, in view of the goodness and justice of God, does not seem proper or properly attributed to God, such as the exercise of the divine will in and through human sin, in effect, without the will of the sinner, for the sake of God's ultimate purpose. The *opus alienum* is always the penultimate, never the ultimate work of God.

opus theandricum: *the theandric work;* viz., the work of Christ as *theanthrōpos* (q.v.), or God-man. The term *opus theandricum* considers the result of the divine-human activity of Christ rather than the activity itself (*actiones θεανδρικαί,* q.v.).

oratio: *prayer.*

Oratio, meditatio, tenatio faciunt theologum: *Prayer, meditation, and trial make the theologian;* a maxim from Luther.

ordinatio: *ordering, ordinance, arrangement;* also the ordination of a priest or minister. SEE *sacramentum.*

ordo antecedentium et consequentium: *order of antecedents and consequents.*

ordo causarum et effectum: *the order of causes and effects.* SEE *causa; ordo rerum decretarum; ordo salutis.*

ordo rerum creatarum: *the order of created things;* viz., the fixed order ordained by God that governs the course of all things in creation, under providence, in the work of salvation, and in the final glorification. Like the idea of an *ordo rerum decretarum,* it is typical of Reformed orthodoxy, and it underlies the so-called synthetic order of system that is typical of seventeenth-century scholasticism.

ordo rerum decretarum: *the order of decreed or ordained things;* also **ordo decretorum Dei**: *the order of the decrees of God;* the former term refers to the arrangement (*ordo*) of the entire causality of salvation under the divine *decretum* (q.v.); the latter, more specifically, to the problem of the infralapsarian versus the supralapsarian view of the decree. Both terms arose out of the concern of the Reformed to construct an order of divine saving causality resting upon the logical priorities in the eternal decree as they arise out of the nature and purpose of God. The Lutheran scholastics do not manifest any similar interest in or emphasis on an *ordo rerum decretarum* and view the Reformed structure as excessively speculative and rationalistic. The Reformed, for their part, assume a biblical basis for the entire *ordo.* The *ordo* is also determinative, together with the concept of an *oeconomia* or *dispensatio* (q.v.) of the *foedus gratiae* (q.v.), of the structure of scholastic Reformed systems of theology. SEE *intuitu fidei; praedestinatio.*

ordo salutis: *order of salvation;* a term applied to the temporal order of causes and effects through which the salvation of the sinner is accomplished; viz., calling, regeneration, adoption, conversion, faith, justification, renovation, sanctification, and perseverance. Because of their emphasis upon the eternal decree and its execution in time, the Reformed developed the idea of an *ordo salutis* in detail in the sixteenth century, before the development of a similar structure in Lutheranism. In the seventeenth century, however, under the impact of the precise definition of the Lutheran view of predestination following the *Formula of Concord,* a carefully defined *ordo salutis* did appear in the Lutheran systems. The actual arrangement of the several elements of the *ordo,* i.e., calling, and so on, varies from system to system. SEE *adoptio; conversio; fides; gratia; homo; illumi-*

natio; intuitu fidei; iustificatio; perseverantia; praedestinatio; regeneratio; renovatio; sanctificatio; vocatio.

organa gratiae et salutis: *implements or instruments of grace and salvation;* viz., the *media gratiae,* or means of grace, the Word and the sacraments. Whereas the Reformed tend to use almost exclusively the term *media gratiae,* the Lutherans also use *organa gratiae* to reinforce the concept of Word and sacraments as effective means or instruments through which grace operates for the sake of salvation. The implication of the term is *not* a doctrine of sacramental efficacy *ex opere operato* (q.v.), by the mere performance of the rite, but rather of the guarantee of the effective gift of grace and operation of grace to be received by faith, the *medium ληπτικόν,* or receptive means of grace. Thus, the Lutherans argue that failure to hear the Word or to rightly receive the sacraments arises, not out of an ineffectual offer or an offer of grace not made with equal seriousness to all, but out of an absence of faith and a resistance to grace on the part of the individual. They declare that the Word is an "operating instrument" in conversion: *Verbum Dei est organon operandi.* The sacraments also are "effective means and instruments," *organa ac media efficacia.* SEE *media gratiae.*

organon (ὄργανον): *instrument.* SEE *causa instrumentalis; instrumentum; media.*

otiosus, -a, -um (adj.): *idle, unoccupied;* frequently in the expression *Deus otiosus,* an idle God, explicitly denied by the Reformers and the Protestant scholastics in the doctrines of *continuata creatio* (q.v.) and *concursus* (q.v.).

otiosus habitus: *an idle or disengaged disposition or capacity;* i.e., a capacity not operative, thus a capacity or disposition *in actu primo,* in its primary actuality. SEE *in actu.*

oudeneia (οὐδένεια): *worthlessness* or *nothingness.*

ousia (οὐσία): *essence; substance.* SEE *essentia; essentia Dei; substantia.*

ousiadōs (οὐσιαδῶς): *essentially;* Latin *essentialiter* (q.v.); one way of predicating names of God, as opposed to *hypostatikōs* (ὑποστατικῶς), hypostatically, or *personaliter,* personally.

Pp

pactum: *pact* or *covenant;* also **pactio**. See *foedus; pactum salutis.*

pactum salutis: *covenant of redemption;* in Reformed federalism, the pretemporal, intratrinitarian agreement of the Father and the Son concerning the covenant of grace and its ratification in and through the work of the Son incarnate. The Son covenants with the Father, in the unity of the Godhead, to be the temporal *sponsor* of the Father's *testamentum* (q.v.) in and through the work of the Mediator. In that work, the Son fulfills his *sponsio* (q.v.) or *fideiussio* (q.v.), i.e., his guarantee of payment of the debt of sin in ratification of the Father's *testamentum*. The roots of this idea of an eternal intratrinitarian *pactum* are clearly present in late sixteenth-century Reformed thought, but the concept itself derives from Cocceius's theology and stands as his single major contribution to Reformed system. Although seemingly speculative, the idea of the *pactum salutis* is to emphasize the eternal, inviolable, and trinitarian foundation of the temporal *foedus gratiae* (q.v.), much in the way that the eternal decree underlies and guarantees the *ordo salutis* (q.v.). See *opera Dei ad intra.*

paedagogus ad Christum: *guide to Christ;* i.e., the law. See *usus legis.*

paenitentia. See *poenitentia.*

paideia (παιδεία): *teaching, instruction, discipline,* or *correction, especially of children.* See *castigationes paternae.*

panarmonikos (παναρμόνικος): *complex; embracing a vast array of things.*

parabasis (παράβασις): *sin considered as a transgression against or violation of the law.*

paradeigma (παράδειγμα): *paradigm; idea; concept.*

paradisio: *paradise;* viz., the dwelling-place of the souls of the blessed between the death of the body (*mors temporalis,* q.v.) and the final resurrection (SEE *resurrectio*). *Paradisio* is not to be confused with eternal life (*vita aeterna,* q.v.). SEE *Hades; iudicium particulare et occultum; status animarum a corpore separatarum.*

parangelia (παραγγελία): *a command* or *advisement;* e.g., 1 Thess. 4:2. SEE *foedus.*

paraphysica (παραφυσικά): *beside (or beyond) the physical;* the term does not appear in standard classical, New Testament, or patristic lexica. The usual term is *hyperphysica* (q.v.).

paraptōma (παράπτωμα): *transgression;* specifically, a transgression against God; e.g., Rom. 4:25.

parousia (παρουσία): *parousia, advent;* especially, the second visible coming of Christ as Judge; e.g., Matt. 24:3. SEE *adventus Christi; dies novissimus; iudicium extremum.*

pars providentiae: *a part of providence;* viz., predestination considered as *decretum Dei speciale* under the larger category of providence, the *decretum Dei generale.* Similarly, the *favor Dei* in providence and the *gratia universalis* by which God works for good in all things stand as larger categories behind the *gratia specialis* of salvation. SEE *decretum; praedestinatio; providentia.*

partes animae: *parts of the soul;* not a preferred term, since the soul, as spiritual, cannot be divided in a physical sense. SEE *anima; facultates animae.*

particulae distinctivae: *distinctive particles or units of speech;* especially, phrases or attributions made possible by the union of natures in the person of Christ. SEE *propositiones personales.*

particulae exclusivae: *exclusive particles;* i.e., units of speech indicating mutually exclusive categories. The term is used in orthodox Lutheranism of words indicating the radical exclusion of works from salvation by grace and the radical exclusion of merit by the gracious application of Christ's merit to believers; e.g., grace *without* works.

partim: *partly;* often in comparisons, e.g., *partim bonum, partim malum:* partly good, partly evil.

218

passio: *passion;* the experience of suffering; especially, the *passio Christi,* the passion or suffering of Christ. Broadly conceived, the *passio Christi* extends to the entire *status humiliationis* (q.v.), or state of humiliation, i.e., from Christ's birth to his death, during which he suffered all the common infirmities (SEE *infirmitates communes*) of the human race. More strictly, the *passio Christi* is the *passio magna,* or great suffering, of the final trials and crucifixion. SEE *obedientia Christi.*

passiones: *passions, emotions;* roughly synonymous with the Greek παθήματα; SEE *affectio.*

patefactio: *disclosure, manifestation, a making known.* In general, the Protestant scholastics use *patefactio* to indicate the self-disclosure of God in Christ, and *revelatio,* which implies an uncovering for someone or an impartation of knowledge to someone, to indicate the scriptural or verbal revelation of God. Thus *patefactio* serves more generally as a synonym for *epiphaneia* (ἐπιφάνεια) and *revelatio* as the equivalent of *apocalypsis* (ἀποκάλυψις). SEE *revelatio.*

pater: *father;* specifically, *Deus Pater,* God the Father, the First Person of the Trinity. SEE *Trinitas.*

paternitas: *paternity;* specifically, the paternity of the First Person of the Trinity, the Father in his relation to the Son and Spirit. SEE *relatio personalis.*

pathēmata (παθήματα): SEE *passiones.*

pathētikōs (παθητικῶς): *subject to passions or suffering; passible;* thus, subject to change.

patientia: *patience;* in God, *patientia* is synonymous with longsuffering (*longanimitas,* q.v.).

peccata: *sins;* once actual sin (*peccatum actualis,* q.v.) is distinguished from original sin (*peccatum originalis,* q.v.), it must be further defined according to the kinds of actual sin that are committed. A basic distinction can be made between (1) *peccata voluntaria,* voluntary sins, which are the result of positive human willing, and (2) *peccata involuntaria,* involuntary sins, which do not arise out of malice but out of ignorance, fear, and the like. The Protestant scholastics, following the Reformers, reject the medieval and Roman Catholic distinction between *peccata mortalia* (q.v.) and *peccata venialia.* In place of these, they distinguish sins further into *peccata commissionis* and *peccata omissionis*, sins of commission and omission, and *peccata cordis, oris, et operis*, sins of heart, mouth, and action (i.e., thought, word, and deed). SEE *homo*.

peccata clamantia: *sins that cry out;* i.e., sins not protested by mankind that nonetheless "cry out for vengeance" to Almighty God: e.g., the murder of Abel and by extension the oppression of widows, orphans, strangers, and others who cannot defend themselves and can only cry out to God for help.

peccata enormia: *unusually great sins.*

peccata mortalia: *mortal sins;* viz., sins that result in damnation and eternal death because their commission so denies faith and the work of the Spirit that salvation becomes impossible, as distinguished from *peccata venialia*, venial sins, which are merely weaknesses. Against the medieval scholastics, both the Lutherans and the Reformed deny the distinction, at least in the sense that venial sins must also be recognized as damnable and as worthy of eternal punishment if the sinner perseveres in them to the point of *impoenitentia finalis* (q.v.). Medieval scholastic theology distinguished seven deadly or mortal sins: *superbia, avaritia, luxuria, ira, gula, invidia, acedia:* pride, greed, luxury, anger, gluttony, envy, morosity. The Protestant scholastics more frequently speak of *peccata cordis, oris, operis*, sins of heart, mouth, and action or, as often rendered, thought, word, and deed. SEE *Omne peccatum in Deum committitur; septem peccata mortalia.*

peccata venialia: SEE *peccata mortalia.*

peccatum actualis: *actual sin;* viz., an actual transgression of the law, as opposed to *peccatum originalis* (q.v.), which is inherent in fallen human nature. *Peccatum originalis* is a corruption present in every human being at birth; *peccatum actualis* is the sinful activity which, in the absence of any external coercion, springs from the sinful nature. SEE *arbitrium; voluntas.*

peccatum habituale acquisitum: *an acquired sinful disposition* or *an acquired disposition to sin;* a term used to designate patterns of human sinfulness which are created by the repetition of sinful acts. Against both Lutheran and Reformed orthodoxy, seventeenth-century Arminianism denied *peccatum originalis* (q.v.) and explained all resident human sinfulness as *peccatum habituale acquisitum*. The orthodox accept the concept of *peccatum habituale acquisitum*, but only as a secondary or derivative cause of sin itself resting upon both original sin and the continual commission of actual sins.

peccatum in Spiritum Sanctum: *sin against the Holy Spirit;* the so-called unforgivable sin committed against the work of the Spirit: blasphemy against the truth of salvation conveyed to the heart and mind by the Spirit. Both Lutherans and Reformed distinguish between the *peccatum in Spiritum Sanctum* and mere *impoenitentia finalis,* or final impenitence, arguing that the former is not simply impenitence but the ultimate apostasy from and conscious rejection of the obvious truth of the gospel, despite the work of the Spirit, by one who remains convinced of that truth and cannot deny it, but still maliciously assaults it and rejects it. Since the work of the Spirit is the one path toward remission of sin, ultimate rejection of the Spirit in this blasphemous manner is the sole *peccatum irremissibilium,* or unforgivable sin.

peccatum inhaerens: *inherent sin;* viz., the sinfulness that inheres or resides in the heart and mind of fallen man.

peccatum originalis: *original sin;* not a substance or a positive attribute, but a defect in human nature caused by the fall and consisting in the loss and consequent absence of original righteousness, *iustitia originalis* (q.v.), and of the *imago Dei* (q.v.). This *peccatum originalis* is (1) the *culpa haereditaria,* or hereditary guilt, which is imputed to all mankind because of the sin and guilt of Adam—in Reformed theology this imputation rests on the federal headship of Adam. It is also (2) the *corruptio haereditaria* (q.v.), or hereditary corruption, which, because of the guilt and corruption of Adam and Eve, is transmitted to all their descendants by generation. SEE *culpa; imputatio; macula; propagatio peccati; reatus.*

per consequentiam: *by consequence.* SEE *necessitas consequentiae.*

per se: *by or through itself.*

perfectio: *perfection;* viz., the highest or most complete condition of any thing or attribute; thus the fullness or complete actuality of a thing or attribute. Perfection indicates both a transcendence of mutation and a fulfillment of all potential or potency (*potentia*). The *perfectio Dei,* or perfection of God, is the absolute, unchanging excellence of God in his being and in all his attributes. SEE *in actu; in potentia.*

perfectio essentialis: *essential perfection;* an attribute of Scripture. SEE *perfectio integralis.*

perfectio integralis: *integral perfection;* entire perfection in the sense of a fullness or completeness that lacks nothing; a term applied to Scripture as a whole. Whereas *perfectio essentialis* applies to the content of the text, to what the text says, *perfectio integralis* refers to the completeness of Scripture—it needs no addition. The former term is definitive, the latter circumscriptive.

perichōrēsis (περιχώρησις): SEE *circumincessio; emperichōrēsis.*

permissio: *permission;* specifically, permission as distinct from active or effective willing. The concept of a divine *permissio* was denied by Calvin but accepted by virtually all later Reformed theologians, including Beza and Zanchi, as a means of explaining the origin of sin and the continuing instances of sin in the course of human history. God does not will positively that sins occur but permits creatures to exercise their will in a sinful way. The concept appears also in the Lutheran scholastic systems, though Lutheran opposition to the doctrine of a *decretum absolutum,* or absolute decree, of predestination rendered the origin of sin and the continuing presence of sin less of a problem for Lutheran than for Reformed orthodoxy. SEE *decretum; permissio efficax; praedestinatio.*

permissio efficax: *effective permission* or *willing permission;* especially, the providential *concursus* (q.v.) underlying evil acts of human beings; a concept typical of Reformed theology, which will not allow a bare or ineffectual permission on the part of God and which will acknowledge no realm of activity outside of the will of God. God therefore is viewed as positively willing to permit the free agency of human beings and as supporting their acts with his providential *concursus* even when those acts go against his revealed will. SEE *non-impeditio peccati.*

perseverantia: *perseverance;* also **perseverantia sanctorum:** *perseverance of the saints;* a term used by the Reformed to indicate the final indefectibility of the elect, who, although they continue after justification to experience temptation and sin, will ultimately never fall beyond the power of God's grace. Even if the exercise of faith (*exercitium fidei*) ceases, the cessation will be only temporary. The Lutherans do not deny the necessity of *perseverantia,* but they hold the possibility of apostasy and sinful loss of faith after the effectual hearing of God's Word. When believers do persevere, they do so by means of God's grace; when they fall away, they do so by their own fault. The difference between Lutheran and Reformed here arises in part out of Lutheran insistence on the efficacy of the Word and consequent refusal to allow the typical Reformed distinction between effectual and ineffectual calling (SEE *vocatio*). SEE *conversio reiterata; incrementa fidei; ordo salutis; sanctificatio.*

persona: *person;* the equivalent in Latin patristic theology of the Greek term *prosōpon* (q.v.). The term *persona* received its first major use in Tertullian's refutation of the Sabellian heresy. Like *prosōpon, persona* had the connotation of a dramatic role or, more precisely, a mask worn by an actor in playing a role. From that basic meaning it had, by Tertullian's time, developed two further implications. In the first place, it had come to indicate the individual character in the play and thereby to have a certain objective significance. In the second place, crucial for Tertullian, it had come to indicate in Roman law an objective individual capable of having property or substance (*substantia,* q.v.). Tertullian found the terms *persona* and *substantia* ideal for identifying an objective threeness and an objective oneness, respectively, in God. In addition, the definition of three *personae* sharing one *substantia* made sense using legal analogies. It is clear from Tertullian's works, however, that he pressed beyond the limitations of the dramatic and legal metaphors toward a metaphysical equation of *substantia* with the indivisible divinity of God and viewed *persona* as a term capable of indicating distinction within the divine substance without separation or division of substance. This usage prevailed in the Latin West and settled the trinitarian question there until the time of the councils of Nicaea, Constantinople, and Chalcedon, at which point the ability to translate the Western language into terms of *prosōpon* and *ousia* and, finally, of *hypostasis* and *ousia,* contributed greatly to the establishment of a standard orthodox terminology in both East and West. Nevertheless, the Western theologians of the fourth and fifth centuries, particularly Hilary of Poitiers, Marius Victorinus, Jerome, and Augustine, noted problems in the terminology. Jerome was suspicious of the term *hypostasis,* viewing it as virtually synonymous with *ousia,* and therefore as a cause of Arian tendencies in trinitarian thinking. The others recognized the orthodox character of Cappadocian usage (SEE *hypostasis*) but noted the difficulty of rendering the Greek terminology into Latin. *Ousia* had been rendered *substantia; hypostasis* ought to indicate, therefore, *persona,* but it too had been translated, prior to its redefinition by the Cappadocians, as *substantia.* In addition, the Latin term *persona,* like the Greek *prosōpon,* was imprecise in its application to theology. Both Hilary and Victorinus, in order to provide a

223

more precise term, used the word *subsistentia,* subsistence, to indicate the individual instances of the divine *substantia,* the persons of the Trinity. Despite these problems, which were echoed at length by Augustine in *Of the Trinity, persona* remained the standard term in Western orthodox definition and was given ecumenical credal status at the Council of Chalcedon in the council's acceptance of Leo I's "tome" as an expression of orthodox Christology.

In the early sixth century, *persona* was finally given metaphysical and philosophical definition by Boethius. In this classic definition, a person is "an individual substance of a rational nature" (*rationalis naturae individua substantia*). Boethius and his contemporary, Cassiodorus, were also responsible for the determination of *subsistentia* as the proper translation of *hypostasis.* Whereas this latter point of definition would ultimately clarify trinitarian usage, the definition of *persona* retains, now at a metaphysical level, the original problem of the Western reaction to the theological use of *hypostasis.* The latter term had caused discussion because of its original translation as *substantia;* and, here, *persona,* which Latin usage had juxtaposed with *substantia,* is defined as an individual *substantia* rather than as the Cappadocians had defined *hypostasis,* an individual instance of a substance or essence. This definition, with its internal problems, was inherited by the medieval doctors as the normative philosophical meaning of *persona.*

The depth of the problem is clearly seen in the medieval scholastic attempts to cope with both Boethius's definition and the Greek trinitarian language. Anselm, for example, generally used *substantia* as an equivalent for *essentia,* but was led by the problem of the definition and the problem of orthodox Greek trinitarian language to speak of one *essentia* and three *personae sive substantiae.* A person, in Anselm's approximation of the Boethian definition, is an individual rational nature (*individua rationalis natura*), while "substance" is used with reference to individuals, particularly to those which subsist in plurality. Thus, person and substance may be used interchangeably. Nonetheless, continues Anselm, since individuals are called substance because they substand (*subjacent*) accidents, the term *substantia* is applied only with difficulty to God insofar as there are no accidents in God. In the case of God, *substantia* must indicate *essentia* (*substantia ponatur pro essentia*). The problem is insoluble; the language is adopted of necessity (*Monologium,* c. 78).

Among the medieval doctors, Richard of St. Victor and Alexander of Hales sought modification of the definition. Because no "person" of the Trinity is an individual substance separate from the *substantia* of the other persons, and because the rational nature of God is the divine substance that belongs inseparably to all the persons, Boethius's definition applies equally well to either the Godhead or the three *hypostases*, though not perfectly in either case. A similar problem arises when the definition is used christologically. Christ is one *persona* but not one *substantia*, not, at least, in the traditional Latin christological language! Richard proposed that in trinitarian and christological usage, *persona* be defined as *divinae naturae incommunicabilis existentia*, the incommunicable existence of a divine nature. For general philosophical usage, he proposed: *persona est existens per se solum juxta singularem quemdam rationalis existentiae modum* ("A person is a thing existing by itself alone according to a certain singular rational mode of existence"). Alexander proposed a similar modification of Boethius: *Persona est existentia incommunicabilis intellectualis naturae vel existens per se solum secundum quemdam modum existendi* ("A person is the incommunicable intellectual existence of a nature, or a thing existing by itself alone according to a certain mode of existing"). In both of these definitions, the term "mode of existing," *modus existendi*, points toward the idea of a subsistence defined by its way or manner of being what it is, an approach in both cases to the patristic concept of *hypostasis*.

Thomas Aquinas followed the more cautious path of accepting Boethius's definition while recognizing that the language of three *substantiae* in God could be construed as tritheistic heresy: the term *substantia* in the basic definition of *persona* must not be understood as indicating a separate *essentia* but rather a *suppositum* (q.v.), a distinct individual. Thus qualified, the definition serves also as a definition of *hypostasis*. Aquinas proposes also his own explanation of the term "person": *Persona significat in divinis relationem, ut rem subsistentem in natura divina* ("Person signifies a relation in the divine, as a thing subsisting in the divine nature"). These *relationes* or *res subsistentes* can be defined as really distinct from one another (SEE *distinctio*) but as only rationally distinct from the divine *essentia* (*Summa Theologiae*, I.ae, qq. 29–30). In effect, Aquinas salvaged the Boethian definition by removing the underlying problematic of the early translation of *hypostasis* as *substantia: persona, hypostasis*, and in this particular instance, *substantia*, refer to subsistent individuals, to real subsistent relations. This solution to the problem, with its use of the term *suppositum*, or as frequently given, *suppositum intelligens*, an intelligent individual, becomes typical of medieval discussion of *persona*.

In the Reformation, although there was little debate over the terms of trinitarian theology, Calvin in particular saw the limits of the term *persona* and, though he certainly knew Boethius's definition, did not follow it specifically. A person, he wrote, is a subsistence in the essence of God, *subsistentia in Dei essentia* (*Institutes*, I.xiii.6).

The term is a direct reflection of patristic usage, particularly that of Augustine and Hilary. The Protestant scholastics tend to refer to Boethius's definition but also to recognize its limitation and to offer alternatives such as *suppositum intelligens* or *suppositum intellectuale,* a self-subsistent intelligence; *quod proprie subsistit,* that which properly or of itself subsists; or *modus subsistendi,* a mode of subsisting. This last term reflects the Protestant scholastic interest in patristic theology, specifically in the trinitarian vocabulary of Hilary, Victorinus, and Augustine, all of whom had used the verb *subsistere* to indicate the threeness of the divine *essentia* or *substantia,* and who had tended toward a modal language of person and personal distinctions in the Trinity. Thus Francis Turretin can define *persona* and *hypostasis* as *suppositum intellectuale* and *subsistentia* and argue that the three *personae* are distinct from the divine *essentia* or *substantia,* not really (*realiter*) or essentially (*essentialiter*) as one thing is distinct from another (*ut res et res*), but rather modally (*modaliter*) as a mode of being is distinct but nonetheless in a thing (*ut modus a re*; SEE *Institutio Theologiae,* III.xxiii.6–7; xxvii.3). The Lutheran orthodox have reservations concerning the use of modal language to describe even the immanent Trinity and therefore argue that the three divine *subsistentiae* or *supposita* can be distinct only rationally (*rationaliter*) from the divine essence (Baier, *Compendium* II, 62–63). There is agreement, however, that the *personae* are distinct *realiter* from one another (SEE *distinctio*). Both the Lutheran and the Reformed discussions manifest careful reading of the medieval systems, with the Reformed drawing more broadly on medieval reformulations and the Lutherans following the more conservative path marked out by Thomas Aquinas.

In none of these usages does the term *persona* have the connotation of emotional individuality or unique consciousness that clearly belongs to the term in contemporary usage. It is quite certain that the trinitarian use of *persona* does not point to three wills, three emotionally unique beings, or, as several eighteenth-century authors influenced by Cartesianism argued, three centers of consciousness; such implication would be tritheistic. It is equally certain that contemporary theological statements to the effect that the God of the Bible is a "personal" God point not to the Trinity, but to the oneness of the divine will in loving relation to creatures. In other words, despite the variety of usages and implications we have noted, the patristic, medieval, Reformation, and Protestant scholastic definitions of the term *persona* are united in their distinction from colloquial modern usage. In brief, the term has traditionally indicated an objective and distinct mode or manner of being, a subsistence or subsistent individual, not necessarily substantially separate from other like *personae*. Thus, in trinitarian usage, three *personae* subsist in the divine *substantia* or *essentia* (q.v.) without division and, in christological usage, one *persona* has two distinct *naturae*, the divine and the human. This can be said while nonetheless arguing one will in God and two in Christ—since will belongs properly to the essence of God and to the natures in Christ, and in neither case to *persona* as such. Thus, in the language of the scholastics, *persona* indicates primarily an *individuum* (q.v.), an individual thing, or a *suppositum* (q.v.), a self-subsistent thing, and, more specifically still, an intelligent self-subsistent thing (*suppositum intelligens*). See *modus subsistendi; natura; persona Christi; persona Deitatis; subsistentia.*

persona Christi: *the person of Christ.* General agreement exists among Protestant scholastics, Lutheran and Reformed, on the basic principles of Chalcedonian orthodoxy: (1) Christ is the true God (*verus Deus*), *homoousios* (q.v.), or consubstantial with God the Father; (2) Christ is true man (*verus homo*), consubstantial with us in his humanity; (3) these two natures (*naturae*) are united in one person, the human nature being assumed by the person of the Son or Word. Thus Christ can be called one person in two natures (*una persona in duabus naturis*), or considered as having a unity of person (*unitas personae*) and a duality of natures (*dualitas naturarum*). The two natures, therefore, are distinct as one thing from another thing, each having its own attributes or proper qualities, but they are not distinct as one person from another person (see *alius/aliud*). Since Christ is one person in two natures and that person or subsistence (see *subsistentia*) is the divine person, Christ's humanity is viewed as impersonal (see *anhypostasis*), or as subsistent in and through another (see *enhypostasis*). See *incarnatio; Mediator; natura; unio personalis.*

persona composita: *composite person;* also *persona σύνθετος;* the term used with reference to the person of Christ by John of Damascus (*De Fide Orthodoxa*, III.3) and debated by the Protestant orthodox, many of whom viewed it as too easily capable of a Nestorian interpretation; i.e., the person of Christ as constituted by the union of the two natures. Such an interpretation was uniformly rejected. See *anhypostasis; unio personalis.*

persona Deitatis or **persona divina**: *person of the Deity* or *divine person;* i.e., one of the three persons, or hypostases, of the Godhead, each of which has by nature the whole, indivisible divine essence, and who are distinguished from each other by the incommunicable personal attributes, unbegottenness, begottenness, and procession. SEE *persona.*

persona publica: *public or representative person;* in Reformed covenant theology, a term applied to Adam as the federal head of humanity. In entering the covenant, Adam acted not only for himself, but for the entire human race which was then, as it were, in his loins and represented by him before God. In short, when Adam and Eve fell, the whole of human nature, which was summed up in them, fell. SEE *foedus operum.*

personalis unio. SEE *unio personalis.*

personaliter: *personally* or *hypostatically;* as opposed to *essentialiter* (q.v.).

perspicuitas: *perspicuity, clarity of thought, lucidity;* one of the traditional attributes of Scripture.

petitio principii: *begging the question;* a fallacy in logic involving the assertion of an unwarranted premise or an unproven conclusion as if it were a datum of argument.

Philosophus: *the Philosopher;* i.e., Aristotle.

physikē (φυσική): *natural, physical, according to nature.*

physis (φύσις). SEE *natura.*

piaculum: *an expiation* or *expiatory sacrifice;* i.e., a sacrifice that satisfies or atones for an offense; thus the death of Christ. SEE *expiatio; satisfactio vicaria.*

pietas: *piety;* the personal confidence in, reverence for, and fear of God that conduces to true worship of and devotion to God. Thus, piety together with devotion (*cultus,* q.v.) constitutes true religion (*religio,* q.v.).

pignus: *pledge* or *assurance;* a term used with reference to the sacraments. SEE *sacramentum; signum.*

plena possessio: *full possession;* as distinguished from *plenarius usus,* full use. SEE *ktēsis.*

pleonektēma (πλεονέκτημα): *an excess, a covetous act.*

pneuma (πνεῦμα). SEE *spiritus.*

pneumata leitourgika (πνεύματα λειτουργικά): *ministering spirits;* i.e., angels. By definition angels are immaterial, of spiritual substance, endowed with intellect, reason, and will, created by God for his service as ministers or messengers. Angels are not eternal, but created *ex nihilo.* Some fell away from God of their own free will, before the fall of Adam; the others, who persevered in righteousness, are now held by grace in their communion with God.

Since they are finite, angels do not have the attribute of omnipresence; though, as spirit, they are not, strictly speaking, *in* a place. They are limited, not by physical space, but by power of operation upon things. Thus they are localized definitively but not circumscriptively. SEE *alicubitas; praesentia; spiritus.*

poena: *punishment;* as a concept in medieval scholastic theology, *peccatum originalis* (q.v.), original sin, entailed both *culpa,* fault or guilt, and *poena,* punishment. Through the sacrificial work of Christ, remission of *culpa* was made possible for participants in the sacraments of baptism and the Eucharist. In the sacrament of penance, the eternal *poena* due to sin was transformed into temporal acts of satisfaction capable of performance in this life. The Protestant scholastics, because of their view of the *obedientia Christi* (q.v.), would argue that Christ's work removed both *culpa* and *poena.* They further distinguish eternal punishment into *poena damni,* the punishment of the damned, which is the pain of eternal separation from God, and *poena sensus,* the punishment of the senses, which is the actual torment in body and soul suffered by those who are denied the fellowship of God in eternity. The scholastics will distinguish, in the *poena sensus,* various *gradus poenarum infernalium,* degrees of punishment in hell, meted out according to the quality and measure of sins committed. Thus the unbaptized children of heathens will suffer less than heathen parents who had a lifetime of sin and less also than sinful hypocrites in the bosom of the church.

poenitentia: *penitance, penance, repentance,* or *contrition;* specifically, in medieval and Roman Catholic theology, the sacrament of penance (*sacramentum poenitentiae*) consisting of (1) acts of the penitent: sorrow for sin (*contritio,* q.v.), confession of sin (*confessio,* q.v.), and desire for atonement or satisfaction (*satisfactio,* q.v.); and (2) the acts of the priest: absolution (*absolutio,* q.v.) and the imposition of works of penance (which are, technically, extrasacramental). Preparation for penance may begin in *attritio,* an imperfect contrition preceding true contrition. The medieval scholastics argue that the sacrament of penance itself is effective *ex opere operato* (q.v.), while the extrasacramental works of penance are effective *ex opere operantis* (q.v.). The sacrament of penance was overthrown by the Reformers as a denial of salvation by grace alone and justification by faith. In addition, the biblical command, *metanoeite,* was recognized by the Reformers as demanding repentance, not penance. The Vulgate translation, *poenitentiam agite,* could not stand, at least in the technical, sacramental sense given to the term *poenitentia*—rather, the command was translated *resipiscite* (SEE *resipiscentia*), "repent." Protestant theology retains the term *poenitentia,* but only in its root meaning of penitance leading to, or consisting in, repentance or contrition. The Protestant orthodox tend to view *poenitentia* as a broad category descriptive of the putting off of the "old man" and the putting on of the "new man" (Col. 3:9–10), which begins in *contritio passiva* and moves to *contritio activa* (SEE *contritio*), to *fides* (q.v.), and to *nova obedientia,* or new obedience. Similarly, *poenitentia* can be described as the *mortificatio* or νέκρωσις of the old man and the *vivificatio* or ζωοποίησις of the new man. This latter usage of mortification and vivification was favored particularly by the English Reformed or Calvinistic Puritans. SEE *conversio; regeneratio; renovatio.*

poenitentia stantium: *repentance of those who stand or remain standing;* as distinguished from the *poenitentia lapsorum,* the repentance of those who have fallen away from faith.

politeuma (πολίτευμα): *commonwealth* or *nation;* hence, the kingdom of God as the commonwealth or heavenly country of Christians; e.g., Phil. 3:20.

pollutio spiritualis: *spiritual pollution or corruption;* a result of sin. SEE *macula.*

posse non peccare: *able not to sin;* i.e., the condition of Adam before the fall. SEE *libertas naturae.*

possibile: *a possible thing;* most simply, something that is not impossible, something that involves no contradiction. More precisely, the category of possibles comprises the things that are necessary and therefore are actual or actualized (*in actu,* q.v.) and the things that are contingent (SEE *contingentia*) and that therefore can exist or be actualized but that do not exist necessarily. A further distinction can be made concerning possible things according to the theological distinction between the divine *potentia absoluta* (q.v.), or absolute power, and the divine *potentia ordinata* (q.v.), or ordained power. Under the *potentia absoluta* anything is possible that does not involve a contradiction; God's absolute power comprehends the broadest category of possibility. But under the *potentia ordinata* only those things are possible that do not conflict with the divinely established order of nature.

possibilia: *possibles* or *possible existents;* viz., things that do not have to be but that are not impossible. Aristotelian philosophy therefore distinguishes between necessary, possible, and impossible things. The scholastics further distinguish between the merely possible and the actual, the latter representing the contingent order of actual things. These distinctions are significant to scholastic discussions of and distinctions in the *scientia Dei* (q.v.).

possibilitas servitutis: *the possibility of servitude or subjection;* i.e., the possibility of change or mutation of the will toward bondage in sin. This possibility, latent in man as originally created, was capable of being actualized by the wrongful exercise of free choice (*liberum arbitrium*, q.v.). SEE *mutabilitas; peccata.*

post rem: *after the thing.* SEE *universalia.*

potentia: *power*, in the sense of efficacy or efficiency in action; also potency or potential (SEE *in potentia*). In Aristotelian philosophy, *potentia* or *dynamis* (δύναμις) is, specifically, potential being (μή πω ὄν), the capacity or power to accomplish change, to come into being. SEE *actus; in actu; mē on.*

potentia absoluta: *absolute power;* the omnipotence of God limited only by the law of noncontradiction. According to his *potentia absoluta*, God can effect all possibility, constrained only by his own nature. Things which are by nature evil and either impossible or noncomposible things (like square circles) fall outside of the realm of God's power. The term emphasizes the transcendence and omnipotence of God by setting God even above and beyond the laws he has ordained for the operation of his universe. In a more restricted sense, therefore, the *potentia absoluta* can be appealed to as the basis of the miraculous and can be called an extraordinary power (*potentia extraordinaria*) of God, in contrast with the ordinary or usual exercise of divine power (*potentia ordinaria*). SEE *miracula; omnipotentia; potentia ordinata.*

potentia credendi: *the potential for or power of believing.* SEE *actus; in actu; in potentia; potentia.*

potentia ordinata: *ordained power;* the power by which God creates and sustains the world according to his *pactum* (q.v.) with himself and creation. In other words, a limited and bounded power that guarantees the stability and consistency of the orders of nature and of grace; distinct from the *potentia absoluta* (q.v.) according to which God can exercise the entirety of his power and effect all possibility. When contrasted with the miraculous, as accomplished by the divine *potentia extraordinaria,* the ordained power of God is also termed *potentia ordinaria,* ordinary or usual power.

potestas: *authority, rule;* power in the sense of rule or dominion, particularly in relation to law or legal jurisdiction. *Potestas* must be distinguished from the power, or potency (*potentia,* q.v.), to become something or to effect something. The *potestas Dei,* the dominion of God, and the *potestas Christi,* the rule of Christ, exercised according to his *munus regium,* or kingly office, are references to just and rightful governance and not, generally, to creative power (i.e., *potentia*). The Protestant scholastics, therefore, refer to churchly powers not as *potentia,* but as *potestas,* derived from the dominion of God in Christ. See *potestas ecclesiae; potestas interpretandi sive iudicandi.*

potestas ecclesiae: *the power of the church;* specifically, the power of the church's ministry and work, distinguished by the Lutheran scholastics into *potestas ordinis,* the power of order, according to which the church teaches the Word and administers the sacraments; and the *potestas clavium,* or power of the keys, also called *potestas jurisdictionis,* power of jurisdiction, according to which the church forgives sin through absolution or refuses forgiveness through excommunication. The Reformed, in accordance with their greater emphasis on polity, follow a threefold division of church power into (1) *potestas dogmatica sive docendi,* the dogmatic or teaching power, according to which the church preaches the Word, administers the sacraments, and declares true doctrine in its confessions; (2) *potestas gubernandi,* the power of governing, which is both a power of ordering or ordaining (*potestas ordinandi*), and a power of adjudication (*potestas iudicandi*), according to which the laws of the church are established and enforced and church discipline is maintained; and (3) the *potestas misericordiae* or *potestas ministerium,* the power of mercy or power of the ministry, by virtue of which the clergy engage in the Christian work of forgiveness and benevolence. The Reformed also tend to view the pronouncement of forgiveness (an aspect of the *potestas clavium*) as part of the teaching ministry, while they speak of the refusal of forgiveness and excommunication as a *potestas disciplinae* or *potestas correptionis,* a power of discipline.

All *potestas ecclesiae* or *potestas ecclesiastica* (ecclesiastical power) subserves and derives from Christ's *potestas dominica*, dominical or lordly power, which he exercises as the sole Lord and Head of the church. Thus the *potestas dogmatica sive docendi*, the dogmatic or teaching authority of the church, rests on the authority of Christ, its Lord and Head, and on the scriptural revelation of God in Christ. Although both Lutherans and Reformed recognize the derivative and dependent nature of this authority to declare and teach dogma (*dogma*, q.v.), the Reformed are more willing than the Lutherans to allow the church meeting in council to declare doctrine, even at the level of the local congregation. Lutheranism specifically disavows the claim of congregations and synods to pronounce what must be believed, except in churchly, standardized norms (*normae normatae*). See *ecclesia repraesentativa; norma*.

potestas interpretandi sive iudicandi: *the power of interpretation or judgment;* specifically, the power or right to interpret Scripture, distinguished by the Protestant scholastics into *potestas privata*, the power of private judgment, according to which all believers have the power and the right to interpret Scripture for personal edification and the building-up of faith, and the *potestas publica*, the power of public interpretation, which is not given to all Christians but accompanies a special calling to public ministry and which is supported by special gifts. The *potestas interpretandi*, either *privata* or *publica*, is always subject to Scripture and to the *testimonium internum Spiritus Sancti* (q.v.). See *authoritas Scripturae*.

practicus, -a, -um (adj.): *practical; leading or tending toward a goal.*

praecepta caritatis: *precepts or commands of love;* viz., the rules of Christian obedience, and therefore the substance of Christian ethics, as distinguished from the *articuli fidei* (q.v.), or articles of faith. *Praecepta caritatis* is a broader term than *praecepta Decalogi*, insofar as it comprehends the Decalogue, the Two Great Commandments, and the Sermon on the Mount. It also emphasizes love (*caritas*), as springing from grace and faith, as the ground of true obedience. When the literal *sensus* of Scripture contradicts both the articles of faith and the commands of love, then, and only then, must it be given up for an allegorical reading. See *evangelium; lex; quadriga*.

praecepta Decalogi: *the precepts of the Decalogue or Ten Commandments;* viz., the moral law. See *lex; lex moralis; lex Mosaica; praecepta caritatis*.

praecognitio: *foreknowledge or precognition.* See *praescientia*.

praedestinatio: *predestination, foreordination;* viz., the prior appointment of a thing to a specific end. Thus, the eternal foreordination of

God by which all rational creatures, angels and men, have been appointed to their ends, either to eternal life or to eternal death; or, the eternal and immutable decree of God to manifest his mercy and justice in the salvation of some and the damnation of other of his creatures. *Praedestinatio*, moreover, implies not only the *praefinitio*, or appointment to a fixed end or *finis*, but also *ordinatio*, the ordination or appointment of means to that end; i.e., creatures are predestined both *ad media* and *ad finem*. The Reformed, as opposed to both the Lutherans and the Arminians, define the *praefinitio* as absolute; which is to say, *praedestinatio* is a *decretum absolutum*, or absolute decree, in its underlying intention and in its determination of ends. Nevertheless, the Reformed allow that predestination considered as *ordinatio ad media* is not absolute but respective (*respectivum*), i.e., having regard for or giving consideration to the variety of means in the order of free and contingent *causae secundae* (q.v.). In contrast to this the Lutheran orthodox define predestination, not as a *decretum absolutum*, but as a *decretum conditionatum*, a conditioned decree, ordained by God *intuitu fidei* (q.v.), in view of faith. This definition is not intended to make faith the effective or impelling cause of God's decree, and in fact denies that view explicitly; it intends only to preserve the *gratia universalis* (q.v.) of the gospel, which Calvinism appears to restrict. At the same time, the Lutheran view preserves the *sola gratia* of the divine promise by firmly resting faith upon grace. In sum, the scholastic Lutheran view argues a coordination of predestination and faith, on the ground of the atemporal nature of the decree, in order to allow that all who come to faith will be among the elect.

The Arminian view of predestination departs from both the Reformed and the Lutheran views in that it adopts a fully synergistic perspective with the human will preceding God's actual decision to elect any individual. The Arminians divide the decree into parts, corresponding with the *voluntas antecedens*, or antecedent will, and *voluntas consequens*, or consequent will, of God. In exercising his antecedent will, God ordains the means of salvation for all mankind; in exercising his consequent will, God decrees to save or elect all those who choose to have faith in Christ. Unlike the Lutheran *decretum conditionatum*, the Arminian concept of *voluntas consequens* makes the freely willed faith of individuals the effective cause of divine election; election is grounded on a foreknowledge of faith. In preserving and emphasizing *gratia universalis*, the Arminian view sets aside the *sola gratia* of the Reformers. Whereas the Lutherans could accuse the Reformed of teaching an arbitrary predestination, they could accuse the Arminians of a lapse into semi-Pelagianism.

The decree of predestination is further distinguished into *electio* (q.v.) and *reprobatio* (q.v.). Both the Lutherans and those among the Reformed who adopted the infralapsarian (from *infra lapsum*) perspective define *electio* as that positive decree of God by which he chose in Christ those who will be his eternally, but they view *reprobatio* as a negative act or passing over of the rest of mankind, leaving them in their sins to their ultimate *damnatio* (q.v.). Those among the Reformed who adopted the supralapsarian (from *supra lapsum,* q.v.) perspective define *electio* and *reprobatio* as positive, coordinate decrees of God by which God chooses those who will be saved and those who will be damned, in other words, a fully double predestination, or *praedestinatio gemina.*

Finally, as a special and foundational category of predestination, the scholastics argue a *praedestinatio Christi,* or predestination of Christ, resting on texts like 1 Peter 1:20 and upon the definition of election as occurring in Christ. Technically, such a predestination must refer to the human nature of Christ only or to the man, Jesus of Nazareth, since the divine nature of Christ is electing God. Thus, Christ is said to be predestinate according to his humanity for the sake of the salvation of the elect who are predestinate in him. The Reformed scholastics also argue that the divine nature of Christ, the eternal Son, if not predestined in the strict sense of the term, was nonetheless designated or self-designated to incarnation and to the mediatorial office. This view ultimately led to the development of the concept of an eternal *pactum salutis* (q.v.) between the Father and the Son. In Scotist theology, this predestination of Christ is an absolute predestination and is prior to the creation and fall of man. The Protestant orthodox, both Reformed and Lutheran, disavow any speculation concerning incarnation and the *praedestinatio Christi* and therefore deny the Scotist conclusion of incarnation apart from sin. In this the Protestant scholastics agree with the majority of the medieval doctors. SEE *fundamentum electionis; obiectum electionis; Si homo non periisset, Filius hominis non venisset; voluntas Dei.*

praedestinatio ad salutem: *predestination to salvation;* viz., election. SEE *electio; praedestinatio.*

praedestinatio Christi: *the predestination of Christ.* SEE *fundamentum electionis; praedestinatio.*

praedicamenta: *predicaments;* i.e., the categories or general concepts governing the operation of predication or attribution. In the Aristotelian logic followed by the scholastics, there are ten categories of predication: substance, quantity, quality, relation, action, passivity, place, time, posture or situation, and habit or state. The latter nine of the categories, of course, are accidents (SEE *accidens*) and are distinguished from substance (*substantia,* q.v.) by the third of the *antepraedicamenta* (q.v.), or prerequisites to predication. *Quantitas,* or quantity, is the accident or property of extension and enumeration. *Quantitas continua*, or continuous quantity, is the property of size, length, and depth; *quantitas discreta*, or discrete quantity, is the property of number, i.e., of extension into parts that can be enumerated. *Qualitas* is an accident that modifies substance in itself. *Quantitas* is extension without substantial modification and is therefore distinct from *qualitas*, which is concerned with intrinsic disposition and alteration in terms of the fundamental and inalienable dispositions or habits of a thing, its intrinsic potency or capability of operation, and its passibility or capacity for change. (Considered extrinsically, habit, operation, and passibility, or passivity, are distinct *praedicamenta;* SEE BELOW). *Relatio* is the attribution of order and arrangement to things either transcendentally, really, or rationally. Transcendental relation is a relation that belongs to the very essence of a thing and is therefore more than an incidental property or accident, such as the relation of soul to body (SEE *spiritus incompletus*). Real relation is an accident in a thing that refers or relates the thing to another thing. Rational relation is neither of the essence of a thing nor an accident in a thing but is a mental description of the arrangement of essentially unrelated things. *Actio*, or action, indicates an operation, or operative power, considered either immanently, as the faculty or disposition of an agent (e.g., intellect or will in itself in its inward actuality), or transitively, as an action directed externally toward a desired effect. *Passio*, or passivity, identifies an agent or a thing as the mere recipient of an action, apart from any action of its own. *Ubi* or *locus*, place, is the simple accident of location. It is distinguished from posture or situation, *situs* or *dispositio*, which represents an added qualification or the relation or ordering of the parts of a thing within its place. *Quando* is the attribute "when," i.e., the time (*tempus*) of a thing. Finally *habitus*, or habit, is the accident of an added disposition or capacity, such as the accident of a body being clothed. This meaning of *habitus* is distinct from the meaning of the term in faculty psychology (SEE *habitus*).

praedicatio: *predication; by extension, preaching;* in its basic sense, the activity or operation by means of which something is affirmed of or attributed to a subject. Aristotle distinguished three kinds of predication: univocal, equivocal, and denominative. To these, Aquinas added a fourth, analogical. Since the distinction of these four kinds of predication is the necessary prerequisite for beginning to divide things into their proper categories and classifications (*praedicamenta*, q.v.), they are referred to, together with other logical prerequisites of proper predication, as *antepraedicamenta* (q.v.). Preaching is a *praedicatio*, or predication, because it affirms something of God and of God's promises.

236

praedicatio evangelii: *the preaching of the gospel.*

praedicatio identica: *identical predication;* a term used by Lutheran orthodoxy to indicate the identity of bread with body and wine with blood in the Lord's Supper. The bread and the wine are visible to believers; but through and in these elements, Christ's body and blood are manifest in the predications, "This is my body" and "This is my blood." See *locutio exhibitiva.*

praedicatio verbalis: *verbal predication;* used to distinguish between a predication that is merely verbal, i.e., a figure of speech, and a real predication. See *praedicatio.*

Praedicatio Verbi Dei Verbum Dei est: *The preaching of the Word of God is the Word of God;* a phrase from Bullinger's *Confessio Helvetica Posterior* that points to the importance of strictly scriptural preaching in the Reformed Church.

praedicationes inusitatae: *unique predications;* specifically, the predications that occur because of the *unio personalis* (q.v.), or personal union, of the divine and human in Christ. See *propositiones personales.*

praefinitio: *the prescription, ordination, or prior appointment of things to their end.* See *praedestinatio.*

praemia; singular, **praemium**: *rewards, prizes;* a term used in medieval theology to indicate various rewards for merit, and adopted by some of the Protestant orthodox in their discussions of *gradus gloriae* (q.v.), degrees of heavenly glory, but without the connotation of a merit system or of any human ability to earn divine favor.

praeparatio ad conversionem: *preparation for conversion;* a term used in Reformed dogmatics, particularly by the English, to indicate the terror of heart, the deep remorse, and the fear of hell brought on by the elenctical use of the law (See *usus legis*) that precede conversion and can be viewed as a preparatory work of the Spirit, which subdues pride and opens the will for grace. The Reformed are anxious to preserve their doctrine from synergism and argue that the *praeparatio* is itself a work of grace, an *actus praeparatorius,* or preparatory work, an *actus praecedaneus,* or work preceding, that involves the inward life of sinners but does not constitute a human merit. Among the Lutherans this *praeparatio* is referred to under the term *terrores conscientiae* (q.v.).

praeparatio evangelica: *preparation for the gospel;* specifically, the work of the *Logos* in and through providential revelation, human reason, and even pagan philosophy, which instilled in the pagan mind belief in the oneness of God and the desire for both pure worship and higher morality in the centuries prior to the coming of Christ and the apostolic mission. The apologetic tradition of the early church used the concept of a *praeparatio evangelica* to explain the presence of truths in paganism and the relationship of those truths to the Christian revelation. Some of the fathers, like Eusebius of Caesarea in his *Praeparatio evangelica,* parallel the Old Testament revelation to the Jews with the truths known to pagan philosophy and religion, and argue that both of these preparations for Christianity belong to the old covenant. The Old Testament contains revelation given by the *Logos asarkos* (q.v.), or *Logos incarnandus,* the Word to be incarnated (SEE *incarnandus/incarnatus*), while the gift of divine knowledge to the pagans, technically general revelation (*revelatio generalis,* q.v.), was defined by the apologists of the early church as the work of the *logos spermatikos,* the spermatic or seed-logos, present in the mind of man (SEE *semen religionis; sensus divinitatis*). By extension, *praeparatio evangelica* can indicate the truths concerning God known to any nation or in any religion prior to the coming of the gospel.

praescientia: *foreknowledge;* i.e., the knowing of a thing or an event before its occurrence. *Praescientia* is predicated of God who knows our words before they are on our tongues (Ps. 139:4). The scholastics recognize, however, that the *praescientia Dei* is a function or aspect of the divine omniscience (*omniscientia,* q.v.) and is not to be understood in a temporal sense as meaning that God would know in time something that is going to occur at a subsequent time. "Foreknowledge is thus not claimed with respect to God, but with respect to things": *praescientia dicitur non respectu Dei, sed respectu rerum* (J. A. Osiander in Baier, *Compendium,* II, p. 30). God eternally knows all things that are in time, so that the things which are in our future and which are said to be foreknown with respect to us are known by God simultaneously with our past and our present. The scholastics also note that *praescientia* defined in this manner does not compromise the contingency of events or the freedom of the will. God's eternal knowledge of things and events is not itself the cause of those things and events but is rather a knowledge both of things and events and of their causes. (This conclusion, of course, in no way contradicts the ultimate causality of God undergirding all things or the eternal decree of God that does ordain some things as necessary.) Foreknowledge of contingent things and events indicates a certainty on the part of the knower just as immediate, direct knowledge of an event by a finite being indicates certainty—in both instances, without a causal connection. The scholastics recognize, further, that there is a certain kind of necessity resident within the contingent event or thing. But this is no absolute necessity, or necessity of the consequent (*necessitas absoluta* or *necessitas consequentis*, q.v.) arising out of the relation of a necessary cause to its effects; rather it is a conditioned necessity, or a necessity of the consequences (*necessitas consequentiae*, q.v.), arising *a posteriori* in view of a previous series of contingent events or causes. Since *praescientia* indicates not only a knowledge of events, but also of their causes, and thus of the entire operation of the contingent order, it indicates a certain knowledge of this *a posteriori* necessity resident in events and things, but again without necessary causal relation between the knower and the thing known.

praesciti: *the foreseen.* SEE *reprobi.*

praesentia: *presence; nearness or closeness, whether physical and spatial, temporal, or spiritual and nonspatial; proximity.* The scholastics distinguish a series of ways of being present or modes of presence: (1) *Praesentia localis sive corporalis*, local or bodily presence, is also termed *praesentia circumscriptiva*, circumscriptive presence. These terms all denote the mode of presence of physical, finite things. They are present locally, i.e., in a finite place; they are present bodily, i.e., in a finite physical shape within physical boundaries; and therefore they are present in a circumscribed way, i.e., they can be described or demarked by circumscription, which is to say, by drawing a line around them. A human body, e.g., is present locally, corporally, and circumscriptively. (2) *Praesentia spiritualis sive virtualis*, spiritual or virtual presence, is a term applying to any spiritual being which, since it is immaterial, does not occupy space, but rather manifests its presence by a power (*virtus*) of operation. The term is vague, because it can be applied to souls, to angels, to the body of Christ in the Lord's Supper, and even to God. Therefore a distinction must be made between the presence of finite spirits and the presence of an infinite spirit: thus (3) *praesentia illocalis sive definitiva* (q.v.), illocal or definitive presence, and (4) *praesentia repletiva*, repletive presence. Illocal or definitive presence is the presence of a finite spiritual being which cannot be circumscribed or assigned to a spatially defined *locus* because of the immaterial or nonphysical nature of the being, but which, nevertheless, is limited or defined (*definitiva*) by the finitude of the being in its power and operation. Souls and angels are present illocally and definitively, as are, according to most of the orthodox, the bodies of the blessed (*beati*, q.v.). Repletive presence, however, is the presence of a spiritual being that fills a place without being contained or defined in any way by that place. Ultimately God alone, who is unlimited in his power and operation, has repletive presence. Finally, there is (5) *praesentia temporalis,* temporal presence. This term can be applied to all created beings since their presence, local or illocal, circumscriptive or definitive, has duration.

To this set of terms, which is governed by philosophical and ontological considerations, the Protestant scholastics add a set of primarily theological terms related to the problem of the eucharistic presence of Christ. The most general of these terms is *praesentia sacramentalis,* or sacramental presence. It is used by Reformed and Lutherans alike to indicate a mode of presence unique to the person of Christ in the sacrament. Both Lutherans and Reformed argue that this sacramental presence results in a communication of the substance of Christ's body and blood (BUT SEE *manducatio indignorum*) and is therefore a *praesentia substantialis,* a substantial presence. Nevertheless, both deny a *praesentia corporalis* or *localis et circumscriptiva* such as indicated in the Roman Catholic doctrines of transubstantiation (*transubstantiatio,* q.v.) and consubstantiation (*consubstantiatio,* q.v.) on the assumption that Christ's sacramental presence is not the physical mode of presence or local mode of subsistence (*localis subsistendi modus,* q.v.) typical of physical objects or bodies. Christ's eucharistic presence falls, therefore, into the category of a *praesentia spiritualis sive virtualis* (q.v.). This term is favored by the Reformed who argue a presence made possible by the power (*virtus*) of the Holy Spirit. Although this activity of the Spirit is argued to communicate the substance of Christ, the Reformed refuse to attribute any mode of subsistence other than the *localis subsistendi modus* to Christ's body and therefore argue that Christ's body, as such, remains entirely in heaven.

Lutheran orthodoxy, true to the position of Luther in his debate with Zwingli, could view this Reformed teaching only as a denial of *praesentia realis,* or real presence. The term *praesentia realis,* as used in orthodox Lutheranism, indicates the real but supernatural and illocal presence of the true body and blood of Christ in the Lord's Supper over against the virtualism of the Reformed. Specifically, it indicates the illocal mode of subsistence (*illocalis subsistendi modus*) of the body of Christ that is distinct from the omnipresence (*omnipraesentia,* q.v.) of Christ's divine person and from the ubiquity (*ubiquitas,* q.v.) of Christ's human nature resulting from the communication of proper qualities (*communicatio idiomatum,* q.v.) inasmuch as it is an illocal or definitive presence (*praesentia illocalis sive definitiva*) in, with, and under the visible elements of the sacrament. This *praesentia sacramentalis* is real, resting on the promise of Christ (Matt. 26:26–28) that the bread is his body and the wine his blood and on the personal union (*unio personalis,* q.v.), the communion of natures (*communio naturarum*, q.v.) in the union, and the communication of proper qualities. Nevertheless, it is a hyperphysical (*hyperphysica*, q.v.), not a physical, corporeal, or local presence such as occurs naturally and is described in terms of bodily, physical attributes of extension. In addition, since the real presence finds its dogmatic explanation in the power given to Christ in the exaltation of his human nature to the right hand of God (Augustine, *Confessions*, III), and therefore in the full exercise (*chrēsis;* SEE *ktēsis*) of the attribute of omnipresence that belongs to the human nature by virtue of the majestatic genus of the *communicatio idiomatum* (as distinct from the idiomatic genus), it cannot be viewed as a denial of natural attributes or qualities to Christ's human nature. Thus the Lutheran orthodox insist that the body of Christ has not lost the attribute of place—it was present circumscriptively on the cross and is now present definitively in a heavenly somewhere, i.e., it has an *ubi*, a "where" or whereness (*ubietas*). This *praesentia definitiva* is proper to a glorified body and may also be termed a glorious presence, *praesentia gloriosa*. It is, like the real presence, illocal and definitive, but it is nonetheless distinct since it is not sacramental. SEE *immensitas; multivolipraesentia; omnipraesentia intima sive partialis; praesentia extima sive totalis.*

Praesentia bonorum operum ad iustificationem necessaria est: *The presence of good works is necessary to salvation;* a Majorist maxim cited by Francis Pieper (*Christian Dogmatics*, III, pp. 25–26). Orthodox Lutheranism refuses steadfastly to prejudice the *sola gratia* and *sola fide* by any statement of necessary relation between justification and works. The Reformed agree that the presence of good works is in no way requisite to justification, but they add that works must follow justification. The difference arises out of a stronger emphasis among the Reformed on the third use of the law. Both affirm the need for sanctification as evidenced by good works. SEE *iustificatio; usus legis.*

praesentia corporalis: *corporal or bodily presence.* SEE *praesentia.*

praesentia extima sive totalis: *outward or total presence;* a term used by the Lutheran scholastics to describe the manifest omnipresence of Christ's human nature during the *status exaltationis* (q.v.), or state of exaltation. It is *praesentia totalis* since Christ in his human nature both possesses and uses his omnipresence. *Praesentia extima sive totalis* is also termed *omnipraesentia extima.* SEE *ktēsis; omnipraesentia intima sive partialis.*

praesentia illocalis sive definitiva: *illocal or definitive presence;* viz., the mode of presence characteristic of an immaterial but finite being, which by its nature is not confined dimensionally to a given *locus,* or place, but which in its power and operation is nevertheless delimited or defined. The term is used by the Lutheran orthodox as an alternative to the *praesentia spiritualis sive virtualis* (q.v.), spiritual or virtual presence, used by the Reformed in describing Christ's eucharistic presence. A distinction must therefore be made between the communicated *omnipraesentia* (q.v.) of Christ's human nature and the illocal and supernatural presence of Christ's body and blood in the Lord's Supper. Whereas the sacramental presence can be grounded dogmatically on and understood in terms of the *communicatio idiomatum*, the primary intention of the Lutheran orthodox in arguing the illocal and supernatural presence of the body and blood in, under, and with the bread and the wine is to explain the words of institution and thereby indicate a presence of Christ peculiar to and appropriate to the sacrament. The omnipresence or ubiquity (*ubiquitas*, q.v.) of Christ's human nature is a repletive presence (*praesentia repletiva*); Christ's humanity, because of its union with the *Logos*, is present in, through, and to all creatures, filling all things just as the *Logos* fills all things (SEE *Logos non extra carnem*). The illocal presence of Christ's body and blood in the sacrament, however, is a definitive presence (*praesentia definitiva*), not because of any limitation of finitude, but because it is a presence specific to the sacrament. That presence is bound to a particular promise of God given in the words of institution. Thus, Christ is present, repletively, in every place and at every meal, but present definitively and sacramentally only in the consecrated elements of the Lord's Supper. SEE *coena sacra; praedicatio identica; praesentia; unio sacramentalis.*

praesentia intima sive personalis: *intimate (secret) or personal presence.* SEE *omnipraesentia intima sive partialis.*

praesentia localis: *local presence;* also **praesentia circumscriptiva**: circumscriptive presence. SEE *praesentia.*

praesentia realis: *real presence;* a term used in particular by the orthodox Lutherans to indicate the real, illocal presence of Christ's true body and blood in the Lord's Supper. SEE *coena sacra; praesentia; unio sacramentalis.*

praesentia sacramentalis: *sacramental presence.* SEE *coena sacra; consubstantiatio; praesentia; transubstantiatio; unio sacramentalis.*

praesentia spiritualis sive virtualis: *spiritual or virtual presence;* in general, the mode of presence that is characteristic of a spiritual or immaterial being (e.g., an angel or a soul) as opposed to *praesentia* *corporalis* or *praesentia physica,* corporal or physical presence. More specifically, the mode of presence of Christ's body in the Lord's Supper as taught by the Reformed. According to the Reformed doctrine, the body of the ascended Christ, which remains locally or physically present in heaven, is substantially given in the Lord's Supper to those who receive the elements in faith. This communication of the substance of Christ's body and blood occurs by the power of the Holy Spirit to join together two physically separate things. Since believers are thus joined with Christ by the Spirit, the presence is *spiritualis,* or spiritual; since the union occurs by the power (*virtus*) of the Spirit, the presence is *virtualis,* or virtual. The Reformed orthodox tend to describe this spiritual presence and union in terms of the liturgical phrase, *sursum corda,* "lift up your hearts": the glorious body of Christ is not returned from heaven to earth, but rather the hearts and souls of believers through faith and by the Spirit are raised to union with Christ where he dwells, in heaven. SEE *praesentia.*

praesentia substantialis: *substantial presence;* i.e., a real or true presence. Depending on the substance and its attributes, *praesentia substantialis* can be either circumscriptive (local, physical) or definitive (spiritual) or repletive (illocal). SEE *omnipraesentia; praesentia.*

praestantia: *superiority* or *excellence;* specifically, the superiority or excellence of man in his original created state, viz., the untarnished *imago Dei* (q.v.).

praeteritio: *preterition; a passing over* or *passing by;* a term used by the infralapsarian Reformed (SEE *infra lapsum*) to indicate the non-election of those left by God in the condemned mass of mankind. The divine *praeteritio* is a negative willing as contrasted with the positive willing of *electio* (q.v.), or election, and is intended by the infralapsarians to rest all the efficient causes of damnation (*damnatio,* q.v.) in man. Orthodox Lutheranism rejects the concept of *praeteritio* inasmuch as it denies the efficacy of the universal call and grace of the Word (SEE *gratia universalis*). Damnation must ultimately rest on the sinner's final and impenitent resistance to grace and reprobation on the eternal divine foreknowledge of final impenitence in the face of the gracious calling of the Word. SEE *intuitu fidei; intuitu incredulitatis finalis; reprobatio.*

praeveniens: *coming before.* SEE *gratia praeveniens.*

praevisa fidei: *foreknowledge of faith;* in Arminian theology, the ground and impelling cause (*causa impulsiva*) of election; in scholastic Lutheranism, not the impelling cause, but the occasion or reason (*ratio*) for election inasmuch as the apprehension of Christ's merit is eternally foreknown by God. See *intuitu fidei; praedestinatio; synergismus.*

praevisio Dei: *the foresight or prevision of God.* See *praescientia.*

praxis: *praxis, practice;* since theology is a discipline taught and studied with an end in view, viz., the salvation of mankind, it can be called a *praxis,* i.e., a practical discipline. Protestant scholastics, like their medieval predecessors, raised the question in their theological prolegomena whether theology is purely practical, purely speculative, or some combination of the practical and the speculative. All the Lutheran and Reformed orthodox assumed that theology is, at least in part, a *praxis.* See *practicus; speculativus.*

pretium: *price* or *ransom;* a term used to describe the death of Christ. See *lytron; satisfactio vicaria.*

prima causa: *the first cause;* viz., God as the cause of all things, i.e., the uncaused cause or noncontingent, necessary being whose causal activity sets in motion all contingent causes and their effects. See *causa; ens; essentia Dei; primum movens.*

primitas: *primacy;* also **principitas:** *being of the highest order of importance;* the *primitas Dei* or *principitas Dei* arises as a corollary of the absolute life (*vita Dei,* q.v.) and necessary self-existence (*aseitas,* q.v.) of God. Since God alone exists of himself and is the sole ground of all non-necessary or contingent things (*contingentia,* q.v.), God is also first or ultimate, the foundation of all things, the being of the highest order, the *primum ens,* or first being, and the *ens perfectissimum,* the perfect being.

primo loco: *in the first place.*

primum ens: *first being* or *first existent;* viz., God. See *Deus; ens; primitas.*

primum mobile: *the first movable sphere;* i.e., the tenth and outermost of the series of concentric spheres of the Ptolemaic universe. The *primum mobile* is set in motion by God, and its motion is conveyed to the lower spheres. The fixed stars are situated on the *primum mobile,* and its motion accounts for their daily revolution.

primum movens: *the first mover; viz.*, God as the first, efficient cause of all things. The Aristotelian metaphysics underlying scholastic thought, both medieval and Protestant, assumes the basic inertia of matter (*materia*, q.v.) and the state of rest as the basic condition of all things. Thus, for any event to occur or any individual thing to come into existence it must be moved from potency (*potentia*, q.v.) to actuality (*actus*, q.v.). In other words, for natural processes of development or motion (*motus*, q.v.) to occur, there must be a cause, a mover, external to the process that sets it in motion. It is also clear that no purely potential thing can be a mover. For a thing to act as a mover of another thing, as the efficient cause of a particular effect, it must exist in actuality. A mover, therefore, must itself have been moved from *potentia* to *actus*, from potential to actual existence. But there cannot be an infinite regress of finite movers; motion must begin somewhere. Therefore, just as the Aristotelian metaphysics requires the pure potency of a material substratum (*materia prima*, q.v.) from which all finite things are moved toward actual existence, so does it also require a pure actuality (*actus purus*, q.v.), a fully actualized being in which there is no potency. This being is capable of exerting potency, or power (*potentia*), toward externals (*ad extra*, q.v.). In other words, the *motus* of the finite order requires a first mover who brings about all finite motions but who is not himself moved. It is worth noting that this concept of an "unmoved mover" does not at all imply immobility or unrelatedness, as is sometimes alleged against it. Indeed, in the scholastic view, God as unmoved *primum movens* is causally related to all things and to all movements, not merely in the sense of the beginning of motion, but in the sense of the continued and continuing ontological support of all things and movements (SEE *concursus*). SEE *causa.*

primus electorum: *first of the elect;* in Reformed theology, a term applied to Christ according to his human nature, indicating his designation to the office of Mediator. SEE *caput electorum; fundamentum electionis.*

principia per se nota: *self-evident principles;* the foundations of demonstrative knowledge (*scientia*, q.v.).

principia theologiae: *fundamental principles or foundations of theology.* According to the Protestant scholastics, theology has two *principia*, Scripture and God, i.e., the revelation and the one who reveals himself. The scholastic systems frequently begin with a definition of theology followed by a statement of its *principia*, viz., a *locus* on Scripture and a *locus* on God.

245

Thus, (1) the *principium cognoscendi*, the principle of knowing or cognitive foundation, is a term applied to Scripture as the noetic or epistemological *principium theologiae*, without which there could be no true knowledge of God and therefore no theological system; it is sometimes further distinguished into the *principium cognoscendi externum*, the external, written Word, and the *principium cognoscendi internum*, the internal principle of faith which knows the external Word and answers its call, i.e., faith resting on the testimony of the Spirit. (2) The *principium essendi*, the principle of being or essential foundation, is a term applied to God considered as the objective ground of theology without whom there could be neither divine revelation nor theology. SEE *testimonium internum Spiritus Sancti*.

principium agendi: *principle of motion; effective principle.*

principium quo: *the basis by or from which;* as distinct from the **principium quod:** *the basis which.* The former term implies an active principle or basis for an event or effect, a causative principle, while the latter term implies a passive principle that is acted on.

principium unicum: *sole or only principle;* a term applied to Scripture as the sole source of theology. The term *principium cognoscendi*, principle of knowing, is better inasmuch as God himself is also a principle or foundation of theology. SEE *principia theologiae*.

privatio: *privation, deprivation, the loss of a positive attribute or characteristic;* specifically, the loss of original righteousness (*iustitia originalis*, q.v.) in the first sinful willing of Adam. The consequent absence or deprivation of that righteousness is not, however, mere privation (*mere privatio*) but, as sin, is an active opposition to God and to the good, termed by the scholastics *actuosa privatio*, an actualized or active privation, a *vitiositas*, an active corruption or viciousness. A further distinction can be made between *privatio pura*, pure or complete privation, and *privatio non pura*, incomplete privation. The former is a privation of existence (*esse*), i.e., an absolute privation; the latter is a partial privation, or partial loss, a damage caused to the subject. Sin must fall into the latter category since it is only a partial privation of the good; it does not abolish the human will but consists in defective willing. SEE *privatio boni*.

privatio boni: *privation of the good;* the theological assumption that God created all things good, together with the philosophical principle that the actuality (*actus*, q.v.) of a thing is better than its potential existence (*potentia*, q.v.), leads directly to the question of the origin and nature of evil (*malum*, q.v.). Since God did not create evil and since evil is not an actuality but a falling-short of actuality, it cannot be a substance (*substantia*, q.v.) or a thing (*res*, q.v.) but, if it exists in any sense, must be in a substance or thing. In other words, evil is not a created thing or an actual substance but rather wrongness or distortion in a thing or substance. Furthermore, if evil is neither a thing nor a substance, it cannot be an efficient cause (*causa efficiens;* SEE *causa*) but must be termed a deficiency or a deficient cause (*causa deficiens,* q.v.). Evil occurs when an otherwise good thing turns or is turned from a higher to a lower good. Thus, the fall (SEE *lapsus; peccatum originalis*) was not a turning from God to some intrinsically evil thing, but rather from God, the highest good (*summum bonum,* q.v.), toward self wrongfully considered as the highest good. The will toward self rather than toward God is deficient rather than efficient and represents a wrongful and incomplete actualization of will. The result of deficient willing is the loss of full actualization of will and, thus, a privation (*privatio*), or deprivation, of the actualization of will (*actus voluntatis*). Since the actuality of will and the actuality of the human being of whom the will is a faculty (SEE *voluntas*) are goods intended by God the Creator, the evil that arises as a result of sinful or deficient willing is a privation of the good, a *privatio boni.* This argument was first fully developed by Augustine in his *Enchiridion* and is definitive for virtually all subsequent theology—medieval, Reformation, and post-Reformation. Finally, we note that Augustine's argument concerning evil as the *privatio boni,* for all that it derives from Neoplatonism, is an example of the impact of Aristotelian thought upon the classic mind, indeed, a point at which the claim of Neoplatonism to be a synthesis of Platonism and Aristotelianism is most evident. Plato (*Republic,* 476 A; *Theaetetus,* 176 E) seems to argue the real extramental existence of bad and injustice as well as good and justice. Against this, on the basis of his conceptions of actuality and potency, Aristotle had argued that bad things are in fact perverted actualities, things that are in fact lower than their own potency; the bad is not a thing, therefore, but must exist in a thing (*Metaphysics,* IX. 9, 1051a.4–22).

proairesis (προαίρεσις): *the capacity for or faculty of free choice;* synonymous with *arbitrium* and used to denote moral choice and the responsibility for sinful acts. SEE *liberum arbitrium.*

processio: *procession;* the personal property and relation (SEE *relatio personalis*) of the Spirit to the Father and the Son, synonymous with *spiratio* (q.v.). SEE *Trinitas.*

processio intellectualis: *intellectual or intellective procession;* viz., the internal activity or operation of the Godhead by means of which the Father produces the *Verbum internum,* the internal Word or Son, the Second Person of the Trinity; most frequently termed *generatio* (q.v.). Scholastic theology frequently speaks of two emanations, or processions, in the Godhead, the one of intellect or of nature (*processio naturalis*) and the other of the will (*processio per voluntatem*), the former being the generation of the Son and the latter being the procession of the Spirit. Thus the generation or procession of the Son is described as an *actio intellectus,* an action or activity of the divine intellect, on the analogy of the intellective production of a word in the mind. The procession of the Spirit is described as an *actio voluntatis,* or activity of the will, on the analogy of the will inclining toward an object willed or loved. The former analogy is in keeping with the designation of the Second Person of the Trinity as Word, the latter with the Augustinian view of the Spirit as the bond of love between Father and Son.

proemium: *that which comes first;* viz., a preface to a book; also a reward or gift. The latter meaning, reward or gift, obtains in medieval scholastic theology; also spelled *praemium,* plural, *praemia* (q.v.).

prognōsis (πρόγνωσις): *foreknowledge* or *predestination;* e.g., Acts 2:23; 1 Peter 1:2. SEE *praedestinatio; praescientia.*

progressus in infinitum: *progress or advance to infinity;* the alternative to the postulation of an uncaused first cause in the proofs of God's existence; a logical impossibility on the assumption of the mutually contingent existence of all finite causes. Also termed *progressio causarum in infinitum,* a progress or advance of causes to infinity.

prolegomenon: *prolegomenon; introductory remarks;* i.e., the introductory section of a treatise or system of thought in which basic principles and premises are enunciated. One of the most important contributions of Protestant scholasticism to the theology of Lutheranism and Calvinism was the development of theological *prolegomena* in which the fundamental principles of doctrine (*principia theologiae,* q.v.) were enunciated. In most of the orthodox systems, therefore, the reader encounters a *prolegomenon* before either the *locus* (q.v.) on Scripture or the *locus* on God. The *prolegomena* are also the place where the discipline of theology (SEE *theologia*) itself is defined.

promissio: *promise;* plural, **promissiones;** specifically, the *promissiones Dei,* or promises of God, given in Scripture concerning the salvation of mankind. The Protestant scholastics distinguish between the *promissiones conditionales,* or conditional promises, of the law and the *promissiones gratuitae,* or gratuitious, i.e., unconditional promises, of the gospel.

promulgatio: *promulgation;* specifically, the promulgation or declaration (*declaratio*) of the divine promises. SEE *promulgatio foederis.*

promulgatio foederis: *promulgation of the covenant;* in Reformed federalism, the divine declaration of the covenant of grace, beginning with the *protevangelium* (q.v.) and confirmed in the promise to Noah and the promise to Abraham. SEE *confirmatio foederis; foedus gratiae; sanctio foederis.*

pronoia (πρόνοια): *providence, foresight,* or *provision;* e.g., Rom. 13:14. SEE *providentia.*

proorismos (προορισμός): *foreordination, predestination* (Rom. 8:29–30; Eph. 1:11–12). SEE *praedestinatio.*

propagatio peccati: *the propagation of sin;* distinct from the *imputatio peccati* (q.v.), which is a divine act only. The propagation of sin arises both from the divine act of imputation and from the human act of generation. Adam's progeny receive, by imputation, his transgression; they receive also, as a matter of heredity, the privation of righteousness caused by the fall. Sin is thus transmitted by the descent from Adam in the general sense of imputation and, through conception of children, in the specific sense of heredity. Both the Lutherans and the Reformed tend to emphasize the latter and speak of the impure seed, or *semen impurum,* as the source of individual corruption. The Lutherans, for the most part traducian in their theory of the origin of the soul, can more easily explain the *propagatio* as occurring by transmission (*per traducem*); while the Reformed, for the most part creationist, must argue the immediate corrupting of the soul in its contact with a body produced by the *semen impurum.* SEE *anima.*

propheta omnibus excellentior: *a prophet more excellent than all others;* also **propheta** κατ' ἐξοχήν: *the preeminent prophet;* terms applied to Christ in his *munus propheticum,* or prophetic office. SEE *munus triplex; prophetia.*

prophetia: *prophecy;* specifically, the prophetic office or prophetic work of Christ, distinguished into *prophetia legalis* and *prophetia*

evangelica, legal and evangelical prophecy. The Reformed in particular insist on the *prophetia legalis* in view of the inclusion of the law
within the *foedus gratiae* (q.v.). Christ, as Logos *incarnandus* (q.v.),
reveals the Word of the law as his "legal prophecy," just as he reveals
the Word of the gospel as his "evangelical prophecy" both in the Old
Testament and, after the incarnation, in the New. SEE *munus triplex.*

propositio: *proposition;* specifically, a formal statement consisting in
a subject, a verb (most frequently the verb "to be"), and a predicate
which either expresses a truth or denies a falsehood about the
subject. SEE *praedicatio.*

propositiones idiomaticae: *idiomatic propositions;* i.e., the propositions concerning the person of Christ that arise from the properties
or *idiomata* belonging to the person by reason of the *communio
naturarum* (q.v.), or communion of natures. SEE *propositiones personales.*

propositiones personales: *personal propositions;* a term used by the
Lutheran scholastics to indicate the unique propositions or predications (*propositiones sive praedicationes inusitatae*) that are made
possible by and are descriptions of the *unio personalis* (q.v.), or
personal union, of Christ; e.g., God is man; man is God. Reformed
and Lutheran orthodoxy agree in these predications, since a *concretum* (q.v.), or concrete existent, is predicated of another *concretum.*
Both deny the predication of one *abstractum* (q.v.) of another—as,
e.g., divinity is humanity or humanity is divinity. There is profound
disagreement, however, between Lutherans and Reformed concerning the actual communication of proper qualities (*communicatio
idiomatum,* q.v.).

proprie: *properly, strictly.*

proprietas: *property;* specifically, an intimate, incommunicable property; thus the incommunicable attributes of God and the personal
properties (*proprietates personales*) of the Father, Son, and Holy
Spirit, *paternitas* (paternity), *filiatio* (filiation), and *processio* (procession), which belong to the persons of the Trinity individually. Considered as descriptions of the relations between the persons, these
personal properties are termed personal relations (SEE *relatio personalis*). SEE *attributa divina; attributum; notiones personales; Trinitas.*

proprium: *intimate property or attribute;* that which is proper to or
properly predicated of an individual.

propter: *because of, on account of;* **propter quod**: *on account of which.*

proskynēsis (προσκύνησις): *worship, obeisance.*

proslēmma (πρόσλημμα): *an addition* or *acquisition;* used by the fathers with reference to the human nature assumed by the Word.

prosōpon (πρόσωπον): *person;* a less technical term than *hypostasis* or *subsistentia* used to refer to the persons of the Trinity or the person of Christ. By the time that the Greek fathers appropriated the word for use in trinitarian theology, *prosōpon* had taken on, in addition to its original meaning of "face" or "expression," the connotation of a "role," as in a play, and of the individual person indicated by the role. In its theological usage it points toward an individual existence or subsistence, but without any philosophical or metaphysical overtones. Like its Latin equivalent, *persona* (q.v.), it suffers from a certain imprecision and, in the company of terms like *ousia* (q.v.) or "essence," which do have metaphysical import, would ultimately need clarification through use of the term *hypostasis* as defined by the Cappadocian fathers. SEE *subsistentia.*

protevangelium: literally, *the protogospel;* the first announcement of the redemption to be effected in and through Christ, given figuratively to Adam and Eve in the words of God to the serpent, "I will put enmity between you and the woman, and between your seed and her seed; he shall bruise your head, and you shall bruise his heel" (Gen. 3:15); in Reformed federalism, the inception of the covenant of grace.

prothesis (πρόθεσις): *purpose* or *plan; the divine purpose;* e.g., Rom. 8:28; 9:11.

prothymia (προθυμία): *willingness* or *goodwill;* e.g., 2 Cor. 8:12.

prōton pseudos (πρῶτον ψεῦδος): *false fundamental;* i.e., a doctrinal position held as basic by an errorist.

providentia: *providence;* the continuing act of divine power, subsequent to the act of creation, by means of which God preserves all things in being, supports their actions, governs them according to his established order, and directs them toward their ordained ends. Since God is eternal, this distinction between creation and providence results primarily from our temporal view of God's work. In terms of the eternal *decretum* (q.v.) and the *voluntas Dei* (q.v.), creation and providence are one act. The scholastics, therefore, often refer to providence as *continuata creatio* (q.v.). Providence is further defined as the *decretum Dei generale,* or general decree of God, comprehending all things, as distinct from the *decretum Dei speciale* or *praedestinatio* (q.v.); and it is distinguished into *conservatio, concursus* (q.v.), and *gubernatio. Conservatio* (conservation or sustenance) refers to the maintenance of the *esse* (q.v.), or being, of contingent things; *concursus* (concurrence) to the support of the *operationes,* or activities and actions, of contingent beings; *gubernatio* (governance) to the ordinance of God that governs or directs all things. These three aspects of providence, though distinct, are not at all separate, but occur simultaneously in, for, and through all things. Because of the immediacy of the divine providential activity, providence is known from *revelatio generalis* (q.v.) or *theologia naturalis* (q.v.) and not only from *revelatio specialis* or *theologia supernaturalis.* The late Protestant scholastics, under the influence of rationalist philosophy, argued a personal and general experience of providence as a proof of God's *conservatio, concursus,* and *gubernatio* of the world, the so-called *duplex providentiae schola* (q.v.). A further distinction can be made between (1) *providentia ordinaria,* ordinary or general providence, by means of which God conserves, supports, and governs all things through the instrumentality of secondary causes in accord with the laws of nature; and (2) *providentia extraordinaria,* extraordinary or special providence, according to which God performs in his wisdom special acts or miracles (*miracula,* q.v.) that lie beyond the normal possibilities inherent in secondary causality and that can, therefore, be termed either *supra causas,* beyond or above causes, or *contra causas,* against or over against causes. *Providentia ordinaria* corresponds with God's ordained power (*potentia ordinata,* q.v.) and *providentia extraordinaria* with God's absolute power (*potentia absoluta,* q.v.). See *lex naturalis.*

proximus, -a, -um: *proximate; very near; immediately related or following;* the superlative form of the adjective *propinquus, -a, -um,* "near."

prudentia: *prudence;* viz., the form of knowledge (see *cognitio, notitia*) that guides practical judgment by means of universal principles of conduct and action; thus, more generally, the form of knowledge according to which actions are regulated.

psychē (ψυχή): *soul.* See *anima.*

psychopannychia: *the sleep of the soul;* viz., the teaching that the soul lapses into a state of unconsciousness or semiconsciousness between the death of the body (see *mors temporalis*) and the resurrection (*resurrectio,* q.v.) to judgment. The defenders of this doctrine are called *Psychopannychitae. Psychopannychia* is denied by both Lutheran and Reformed orthodox. See *status animarum a corpore separatarum.*

puncta vocalia: *vowel points;* i.e., the signs indicating vocalization of words in the Masoretic text of the Old Testament. In the seventeenth century, Protestant scholastics debated the issue of the date of the pointing of the text, on the assumption that a postcanonical dating might add a human, uninspired element of interpretation and thereby jeopardize the doctrine of the authority of Scripture. Mosaic origin, or at least origin in the time of Ezra, was argued by most of the orthodox Lutheran and Reformed, with the definitive confessional statement being made by the Reformed in the *Formula Consensus Helvetica* (1675), viz., that if not the actual points, then the sounds indicated by the points, are coeval with the consonants. See *authoritas Scripturae.*

purgatorium: *purgatory, cleansing fire;* according to the later fathers, the medieval doctors, and Roman Catholic doctrine, a place and condition of temporal, purgative punishment reserved for those Christians who die with the stain of venial sin still on them or who die without having completed temporal satisfaction or penance for their sins. What occurs in purgatory is a final contrition and penance performed with the aid of grace. The doctrine of purgatory conforms to the structure of the medieval sacramental system and the related views of the obedience of Christ (*obedientia Christi,* q.v.) and of the necessity of merit on the part of man (see *meritum de condigno; meritum de congruo*). The Reformers and the Protestant scholastics reject the idea of purgatory as having no scriptural foundation and as unnecessary in view of justification by grace through faith alone and in view of their conception of the obedience of Christ. The primary biblical ground for the doctrine of *purgatorium* is 2 Macc. 12:42–46, which is deutero-canonical, or apocryphal, and therefore rejected by Protestants.

Qq

quadriga: *the fourfold pattern of medieval exegesis;* a pattern which viewed the text as having a literal or historical, a tropological or moral, an allegorical or doctrinal, and an anagogical or ultimate, eschatological meaning. This fourfold pattern had its beginnings in the patristic period when the fathers—under the impact of established Jewish exegesis of the Old Testament, the allegorical tendencies of the New Testament itself (e.g., Gal. 4:22–26; Heb. 5:5–10), and the unacceptable literal readings of the Old Testament used by the Gnostics to argue its rejection—moved beyond the letter of the text, particularly in their reading of the Old Testament, to what they considered to be the "spirit," or spiritual meaning. Origen codified the approach by distinguishing the literal or somatic, bodily reading of the text from a higher moral or pneumatic meaning and a still more profound doctrinal or psychical meaning. A less rigid pattern, which distinguished the literal, moral, and doctrinal meanings and which pointed toward Christian hope was developed by Augustine in *On Christian Doctrine*, the volume which was to be the basic hermeneutical manual of the Middle Ages.

The carefully enunciated fourfold pattern of the Middle Ages was based upon the association, already made by Augustine and Gregory the Great, between the three Christian virtues, faith (*fides*, q.v.), hope (*spes*), and love (*caritas*, q.v.), and the meaning of the text of Scripture as it speaks to Christians. The church does not, then, disdain the *sensus literalis* or *sensus historicus*, the literal or historical meaning, but learns of it and uses it as the point of departure for searching out the relation of the text to the Christian virtues. When the literal or historical sense includes details concerning human conduct, it bears a lesson for *caritas* and issues forth in the *sensus tropologicus*, or tropological meaning. The trope, related to *caritas*, manifests the Christian *agenda* (q.v.), work to be done. Similarly, the literal sense may include details which point toward Christian faith: thus, the *sensus allegoricus*, or allegorical meaning, which has reference to *fides* and to the *credenda* (q.v.), or things to be believed, by the church. Finally, the literal sense may point beyond the history it narrates to the future of the church. This is the *sensus anagogicus*, the anagogical sense, which relates to *spes* and teaches of *speranda* (q.v.), things to be hoped for. Although this fourfold pattern was subject to abuse and excess, the medieval doctors generally used it in such a way as to find all meanings of a text expressed literally somewhere in Scripture, particularly in the New Testament fulfillment of the Old Testament promises. In addition, the method did not ignore the literal meaning of the text, as sometimes alleged, but used it as the basis for each of the other meanings (SEE *Theologia symbolica non est argumentativa*). The method, moreover, did not demand that all four meanings be found in each text. The *quadriga* was summed up in the following mnemonic couplet taught in the medieval schools: *Litera gesta docet, quid credas allegoria;/moralis quid agas, quo tendas anagogia* ("The letter teaches of deeds, allegory of what is believed;/morality of what is done, anagoge of things to come").

Even before the Reformation, the fourfold method began to be set aside in favor of simpler patterns stressing a more or less unitary meaning of texts. Nicholas of Lyra proposed a double-literal meaning of the Old Testament, which operated along lines of promise and fulfillment, while the humanist scholar Lefèvre d'Etaples proposed a spiritual-literal meaning of the Old Testament, which placed the literal meaning of the text in its New Testament fulfillment. With the Reformation and the increasing impact of linguistic and grammatical studies on the part of both Reformers and humanists, the meaning of the text became more and more firmly lodged in literal and grammatical understanding of texts. Nevertheless, the Reformers maintained the medieval concern for the direct address of the text to the church; the living voice (*viva vox*, q.v.) of God speaks in the Scriptures. Luther maintained to the end of his days a strong tendency toward tropology, particularly in his reading of the Old Testament, and Calvin used a hermeneutic of promise and fulfillment to present the direct address of the Old Testament to his own time—paralleling the interest of the allegorical and anagogical reading of the text. These concerns remain among the Protestant orthodox. We must, therefore, make a distinction not only between the medieval *quadriga* and Reformation exegesis, but also between Reformation exegesis and the modern critical exegesis which severs meaning from application.

qualitas: *quality.* SEE *praedicamenta.*

quantitas: *quantity.* SEE *praedicamenta.*

Quantum credis, tantum habes: *To the extent that you believe, to that extent you possess;* i.e., theology cannot be possessed by those who have no faith.

quidditas: *whatness (of a thing);* the answer to the question *Quid est?* "What is it?"; synonymous with *essentia* (q.v.).

quoad nos: *as far as us;* i.e., as far as we are concerned.

quoad res/quoad verbum: *as far as or concerning the thing/as far as or concerning the word.* SEE *authoritas divina duplex.*

Quod non est biblicum, non est theologicum: *What is not biblical is not theological.*

Quod non habet, dare non potest: *What it does not have, it cannot communicate or impart;* a maxim of causality indicating the necessity of a proportion obtaining between a cause and its effect. No cause can have an effect greater than itself. SEE *causa.*

quod ubique, quod semper, quod ab omnibus creditum est: *which has been believed everywhere, always, and by all;* the so-called canon of Vincent of Lerins (d. ca. 450), which measures universal or catholic orthodoxy.

Rr

raptus in coelum: *a carrying off into the heavens.*

ratio: *reason, both as the mental capacity for reasoning and as a motive, premise, or ground of argument;* sometimes a theory or structure of knowledge.

ratio consequendi salutem: *the schema of attaining to salvation.* SEE *ordo salutis.*

ratio consequentia: *reason or conclusion from the consequences;* i.e., a conclusion based on inference.

ratio Deum colendi: *manner of worshipping God;* a partial definition of religion in general. Religion also includes knowing God, *Deum cognoscendi.* SEE *religio.*

ratio ratiocinans/ratio ratiocinata: *reason reasoning/reason having considered;* a distinction between mere reasoning (*ratio ratiocinans*) and rational analysis of a thing (*ratio ratiocinata*). SEE *distinctio.*

rationalis (adj.): *reasonable; rational.* SEE *distinctio.*

rationaliter (adv.): *rationally; reasonably.*

rationes aeternae: *eternal or divine ideas;* i.e., the eternal archetypal ideas or universals which exist in the mind of God and which, according to the scholastic and Augustinian theory of illumination (*illuminatio,* q.v.), are the foundation of human certainty. SEE *universalia.*

rationes probabiles: *probable reasons.*

realis (adj.): *real;* particularly with reference to the reality of a thing. SEE *distinctio.*

realis communio naturarum: *real communion of natures;* a term used for emphasis by Lutheran dogmaticians to describe their view of the relationship of the natures in Christ's person over against the Reformed definition of the *communio naturarum* (q.v.).

realiter (adv.): *really, in reality.*

reatus: *liability;* **reatus poenae**: liability to punishment; specifically, one of the two effects of sin. Sin (SEE *peccata*) has two immediate effects, (1) *macula* (q.v.), or deformity of soul, and (2) *reatus*, liability under the transgressed law. Man is liable to *poena* (q.v.), since *peccatum* and the resultant *macula* constitute him as guilty before God. The medieval scholastics distinguished between *reatus poenae* and *reatus culpae*, liability to guilt, on the assumption that the *obedientia Christi* (q.v.) satisfied for and removed only the *culpa*, or guilt, of sin, leaving to man the work of temporal satisfaction of the *poena*. The Protestant scholastics refuse to separate *poena* and *culpa* in this manner, and therefore refuse to make a distinction between *reatus culpae* and *reatus poenae*. Instead, they argue a single *reatus*, or liability, on the basis of the fall, a liability to both guilt and punishment. This Protestant view rests on a revision of the doctrine of the *obedientia Christi*. The language of *macula* and *reatus* also appears in the doctrine of baptism. Baptism removes the *reatus* of original sin, rendering the baptized no longer liable to punishment, but does not remove the *actus*, or actuality, of sin, which is to say the *macula*, or deformity of soul, resulting from the fall. Baptism is therefore not a magical act which prevents sin, but merely a beginning of the work of the Spirit. SEE *baptismus*.

recapitulatio: *recapitulation;* the Latin equivalent of the Greek term ἀνακεφαλαίωσις, which, like the Latin, indicates literally the provision of a new "head" or a new "headship." Specifically, the new headship of Christ that supersedes the old headship of Adam and, in the work of salvation, undoes the sin and fall of Adam. The term is best known from its use in the central exposition of the work of Christ in Irenaeus's *Against Heresies*.

reconciliatio: *reconciliation;* viz., the saving work of Christ viewed as the restoration of harmony or agreement between God and man. The term therefore relates specifically to the office of Christ as the Mediator between the two parties in covenant, God and man, and indicates the result of Christ's mediatorial work of satisfaction (*satisfactio*) and expiation (*expiatio*, q.v.), which is to say the restoration of the original relationship between God and man that had been destroyed by the fall of Adam. See *Mediator; medius; satisfactio vicaria.*

recta Deum cognoscendi et colendi ratio: *the right manner of knowing and worshipping God;* viz., religion, or more precisely, true religion. See *religio.*

rectitudo: *rectitude, uprightness;* in particular, the condition of man as created according to the *similitudo,* or likeness, and *imago Dei* (q.v.), image of God.

rector: *rector;* viz., governor, with the connotation of a judicial or legal function. Thus, a term applied to God in the Grotian theory of atonement. Also, *rector mundi,* governor of the world.

redargutio: *refutation, conviction;* especially, the inward conviction or refutation of sin that occurs by the work of the Spirit testifying inwardly to the truth of Scripture, specifically, to the truth of the law in its *usus elenchticus.* See *testimonium internum Spiritus Sancti; usus legis.*

redemptio: *redemption;* specifically, the work of salvation described as a rescue from bondage to sin, a rescue accomplished by the payment of a price; deliverance considered as ransom or repurchase. See *satisfactio vicaria.*

regeneratio: *regeneration;* the rebirth of mind and will accomplished by the gracious work of the Holy Spirit at the outset of the *ordo salutis* (q.v.). See *conversio; renovatio.*

regimen ecclesiasticum: *rule of the church;* specifically, the rule of the church exercised by human beings as distinct from and derived from the *gubernatio ecclesiae,* or governance of the church, that ultimately belongs to God in Christ. We thus distinguish the *regimen principale,* or principal rule, which is Christ's, from the *regimen ministeriale,* or ministerial rule, which is given to the *ministerium* of clergy and teachers, also known as the *ecclesia repraesentativa.* See *ecclesia.*

regnum Christi: *the rule or kingdom of Christ.* The Protestant scholastics recognize several distinctions that can be made with regard to the exercise of Christ's rule. The Lutherans tend to argue a threefold kingdom: (1) the *regnum potentiae,* or kingdom of power, according to which Christ, as divine Word and Second Person of the Trinity, rules the entire creation providentially and is the Lord of all creatures without distinction; (2) the *regnum gratiae*, or kingdom of grace, according to which Christ governs, blesses, and defends the *ecclesia militans* (q.v.) during its earthly pilgrimage (SEE *viator; in via*) for the sake of the salvation of believers; and (3) the *regnum gloriae*, or kingdom of glory, according to which Christ governs the glorious *ecclesia triumphans*, both presently in heaven and also in the *consummatio saeculi* (q.v.), when he will subdue all his enemies and bring the whole church into its triumphal reign. These divisions do not indicate several reigns but merely distinctions in the manner and exercise of rule. The *regnum potentiae* is universal and general or natural, whereas the *regnum gratiae* extends only to believers and is exercised in and through Christ's threefold office (*munus triplex*, q.v.), specifically, through the *munus regium*. The *regnum gloriae* is distinct from the other divisions of the *regnum Christi* in regard to the place and state of believers. The Reformed scholastics express essentially the same distinctions in a twofold division of the kingdom into the *regnum essentiale*, or essential rule, also called *regnum universale* or *naturale*, universal or natural rule, and the *regnum personale*, or personal rule, also called *regnum oeconomicum*, or economic, soteriological rule (SEE *opus oeconomicum*). The former set of terms corresponds to the Lutheran definition of the *regnum potentiae*, the latter to the *regnum gratiae* and *regnum gloriae*, which belong to Christ as the Mediator of salvation, and are thus both *personale* and *oeconomicum*, personal and economic. The Reformed further distinguish the *regnum personale* or *oeconomicum* of the Mediator according to the states and modes of its administration, grace and glory. The difference between the Lutherans and Reformed over the *communicatio idiomatum* (q.v.) leads the Lutherans to argue that Christ rules his entire kingdom as *theanthrōpos* (q.v.), or God-man, including the *regnum potentiae*, since the *Logos* is never apart from the human nature and works all things in and through Christ's humanity. The Reformed, however, tend to attribute the *regnum universale* specifically to the Second Person of the Trinity and only the *regnum oeconomicum* to the God-man as Mediator. The Reformed and the Lutherans agree, however, on the eternal duration of the *regnum Christi* and the cessation only of certain modes of administration. The *consummatio mundi* (q.v.) will bring about the end of administration according to the mode of grace, and the *regnum potentiae* or *regnum universale* will at that point become fully manifest. Christ will continue the mediatorial rule in the raising of the dead and in his rule of the blessed; his enemies will be subjugated, and he will turn over all things to the Father and God will be all in all (1 Cor. 15:24). Against the Socinians, who use this passage to argue an end to Christ's mediation, both the Lutherans and the Reformed argue a change merely in the divine *oeconomia* and a turning over of the kingdom which is not an *actus depositionis,* an act of deposition, but an *actus propositionis,* an act of presentation, for the glory of the Father in which the essence of the mediatorial rule will be fully revealed. Some of the Reformed argue an end of the *regnum mediatorium,* or mediatorial reign, according to its prophetic and sacrificial activities, while acknowledging the eternity of the *munus regium* and the continuance of the intercessory work of the *munus sacerdotale.*

regnum gratiae: *kingdom or rule of grace.* SEE *regnum Christi.*

regnum mediatorium: *mediatorial rule.* SEE *munus triplex; regnum Christi.*

regnum potentiae: *kingdom or rule of power.* SEE *regnum Christi.*

regula fidei: *rule of faith;* in the early church, the credal expansion of the baptismal formula used to define the apostolic tradition of faith against the Gnostics; in the age of the Reformation and Protestant orthodoxy, the canonical Scriptures themselves; also called the *regula fidei et caritatis,* "the rule of faith and love," comprising the whole of Christian belief and life.

relatio: *relation.* SEE *praedicamenta; relatio personalis.*

relatio personalis: *personal relation;* in the doctrine of the Trinity the incommunicable property or mode of subsistence that identifies the individual persons of the Trinity in relation to each other. There are, thus, three personal relations in the Trinity, the *paternitas* of the Father, the *filiatio* of the Son, and the *processio* or *spiratio* of the Spirit. *Relatio personalis* describes, then, the internal workings of the Trinity when they indicate the relationships of the persons one to the other; when these *opera Dei personalia* (q.v.), or personal works of God, are used to identify the persons individually, each is viewed as a distinct *character hypostaticus sive personalis* (q.v.) or *proprietas personalis* (q.v.). SEE *notiones personales; Trinitas.*

religio: *religion;* true religion is most simply defined by the Protestant scholastics as the right way of knowing and honoring God (*recta Deum cognoscendi et colendi ratio*), involving knowledge of God (*cognitio Dei*), love of God (*amor Dei,* q.v.), and fear of God (*timor Dei*) leading to an honoring or veneration (*cultus,* q.v.) of God. The word *religio* itself has been subject to several etymological interpre-

261

tations that the Protestant scholastics invariably rehearse and assess. Cicero (106–43 B.C.) thought that the word *religio* derived from the verb *relego, relegere*, which means "to gather together, to set aside, or to re-read." *Religio* is therefore the diligent study and observance of things pertaining to the gods. Zwingli adopted this derivation in his *Commentary on True and False Religion*. Macrobius, on the other hand, had favored derivation from *relinquo, relinquere*, "to relinquish or leave behind," inasmuch as religion demands separation from the profane. Both of these classic derivations are viewed with interest by the Protestant scholastics, though quite a few writers, following Calvin, note that Cicero's, and thus Zwingli's, view is a bit farfetched linguistically. The preferred etymology is that of Lactantius (*Divine Institutes*, IV. 28) and Augustine (*The City of God*, X.3, and *On True Religion*, 55), which derives *religio* from the verb *religo, religare*, "to fasten, bind back, or reattach." *Religio*, thus, is a binding back or reattachment of fallen humanity to God, related to the idea of a choice for God and of the divine choice for man, and thus also to the verb *eligo, eligere*, "to choose or elect." The term "religion" is, therefore, deduced from the bond of piety—*Nomen religionis a vinculo pietatis deductum est* (Baier, *Compendium*, I, p. 14, after Lactantius). The orthodox further distinguish true from false religion, the latter consisting in superstitious worship, heresy, and pagan opinion; and also from impiety or contempt of God as manifest both in open blasphemy and in hypocrisy. True religion, moreover, can be distinguished into *religio obiectiva*, objective religion, and *religio subiectiva*, subjective religion. Objective religion is religion objectively considered as man's knowledge of God as revealed in Scripture, in the law (*lex*, q.v.) and in the gospel (*evangelium*, q.v.). Subjective religion, or religion subjectively considered, is the effect of this knowledge of God in the life of man, the individual and corporate love, fear, and worship of God.

religio naturalis/religio revelata: *natural religion/revealed religion.* SEE *theologia naturalis/theologia revelata sive supernaturalis.*

remissio peccatorum: *remission of sins*, which occurs through and cannot be separated from faith in Christ, *fides in Christum.*

renovatio: *renovation;* literally, *a making new once more;* specifically, that gracious work of the Spirit after conversion (*conversio*, q.v.) by means of which the old Adam is put aside and the corrupted *imago Dei* (q.v.), or image of God, restored to its integrity. The regenerated will cooperates with the grace of the Spirit in *renovatio*, and good works proceed from the believer. The term *renovatio* is, thus, roughly synonymous with *sanctificatio* (q.v.), or sanctification, the difference being that *renovatio* indicates primarily the undoing of the effects of the fall both negatively and positively, while *sanctificatio* indicates not so much a "making new once more" as a "making holy." The scholastics further distinguish between *renovatio negativa*, the mortification of the old Adam as the believer increasingly dies to sin, and *renovatio positiva*, the vivification or renewal of the *imago Dei* (SEE *ordo salutis*). *Renovatio* can also refer to the final purgation of the world by fire when all things will be made new. When used in this sense, it is juxtaposed with *annihilatio*, the annihilation, or destruction of the world by fire. Both views of the end of the world were held by the Protestant orthodox, the majority tending toward *renovatio*. SEE *interitus mundi.*

repletivus, -a, -um (adj.): *repletive;* incapable of being judged or measured by circumscription or defined by physical limitations or spatial boundaries, but rather identified as filling space or acting upon space while at the same time transcending it. SEE *praesentia.*

reprobatio: *reprobation;* the eternal decree (*decretum*, q.v.) of God according to which he wills to leave certain individuals in their corrupt condition, to damn them because of their sin and leave them to eternal punishment apart from the divine presence. *Reprobatio* is, therefore, distinct from *damnatio:* whereas the cause of *damnatio* is the sin of an individual, the cause of *reprobatio* is the sovereign will of God. *Reprobatio* can be conceived in two ways: (1) the supralapsarians among the Reformed consider *reprobatio* a decree coordinate with *electio* (q.v.) and conceived in the divine mind apart from any consideration of the actual fall of man but only with a view toward the ultimate declaration of divine justice; and (2) as defined by the infralapsarians among the Reformed and by the Lutherans, it is a negative act of God that leaves some of the fallen in sin; the Lutherans add the reason: they are not found in Christ and do not believe. Thus, the Lutheran orthodox rest reprobation on the vindicatory justice of God (SEE *iustitia vindicativa sive punitiva*) in its relation to sin and, above all, to final unbelief. In contrast to the Reformed, the Lutheran scholastics will not define reprobation as mere preterition, or passing over (*praeteritio*, q.v.), since God has seriously offered grace and salvation to the reprobate. Nonetheless, the decree of reprobation is defined as immutable by the Lutherans as well as by the Reformed. SEE *intuitu incredulitatis finalis; praedestinatio; praeteritio.*

reprobi: *the reprobate;* the reprobate are sometimes also called the *praesciti,* or foreseen, inasmuch as God does not effectively cause their sin and damnation but foresees their failure to respond to the Word and therefore passes over them in their sins, leaving them to their just damnation. See *damnatio; reprobatio.*

res: *thing; an actual thing, a real thing; thing in the most general sense;* i.e., anything, something, or no particular kind of thing. In other words, *res* like *ens* (q.v.) indicates an existent in the most basic sense. The plural, "things" (also *res*), can simply indicate all finite reality. Secondarily, *res* can refer to the "thing in question," the "issue at hand" or the "substance" of an argument or text. Thus, the Protestant scholastics can distinguish between scriptural authority *quoad verba,* according to the words, and *quoad res,* according to the things or issues signified by the words. See *signum; universalia.*

res iustifica: *the thing that justifies.* See *bonum iustificum.*

res sacra/res sacrans: *a holy thing/a thing that makes holy.* See *sacramentum.*

res sacramenti: literally, *the thing of the sacrament;* i.e., the thing toward which the sacramental *signum* (q.v.) points. In general, for both baptism and the Lord's Supper, the *res sacramenti* is the person of Christ together with Christ's merits and benefits. Specifically, in the Lord's Supper, where the Reformed hold that bread and wine signify the presence of Christ's body and blood, the whole person of Christ whose body was broken and whose blood was shed is the *res sacramenti.* The *res sacramenti* can also be called the *res signata,* or thing signified, inasmuch as it is the referent of the *signum.* See *materia coelestis; sacramentum.*

res signata: *thing signified.* See *res sacramenti; signum.*

res testata: *the thing attested.* See *testimonium.*

resipiscentia: *repentance, a change of mind or heart;* the term used by the Reformers to translate *metanoia* rather than the traditional patristic and medieval term, *poenitentia. Resipiscentia* indicated *poenitentia* only in the sense of the penitance or contrition (*contritio,* q.v.) characteristic of conversion to faith in Christ (*conversio ad fidem Christi;* see *conversio*) and of the effects of the gracious work of the Spirit in sinners (see *gratia; sanctificatio*).

resurrectio: *resurrection;* specifically, either the resurrection of Christ or the final resurrection of all people before the final judgment. The Reformed and the Lutherans are at one against all forms of *chiliasmus* (q.v.) in arguing a single resurrection at the end of time. They disagree slightly over Christ's resurrection, the Lutherans viewing it as the second stage of Christ's *status exaltationis* (q.v.), after the *descensus ad inferos* (q.v.). Since the Reformed view the *descensus* as belonging to the *status humiliationis* (q.v.), they see the resurrection of Christ as the first stage of his *exaltatio.* The *causa resurrectionis* is the power of God which, according to both Lutherans and Reformed, in and through the *unio personalis* (q.v.) imparts new life to Christ's human nature for the sake of the salvation of believers. The *resurrectio Christi* is the victory over the power of sin and death which makes possible the resurrection of the dead.

The *resurrectio mortuorum,* or resurrection of the dead, is defined by the Protestant scholastics as the quickening and awakening from temporal death (*mors temporalis,* q.v.) of the earthly body and its reunion with the soul for the sake of the final manifestation of the remuneratory and vindicatory justice of God (SEE *iustitia remuneratoria sive distributiva* and *iustitia vindicativa sive punitiva*) in the eternal salvation of believers and the eternal damnation of unbelievers. The *subiectum quod resurrectionis,* or passive subject of the divine work of resurrection, is all mankind; the *subiectum quo,* or active, actual subject, is the body. The resurrected body is identical with the earthly body but is, by the enlivening work of the Spirit, now made spiritual, incorruptible, and glorious. SEE *adventus Christi.*

resuscitatio: *resuscitation, revival;* as, e.g., of the fallen will or fallen intellect. SEE *conversio; illuminatio; vivificatio.*

revelatio: *revelation;* a making-known specifically directed toward the intellect, as opposed to *patefactio,* or manifestation, which indicates a presentation to sight as well.

revelatio generalis/revelatio specialis: *general revelation/special revelation;* a basic distinction between the general gift of knowledge of God to all people in and through the created order and the special gift of saving knowledge in Christ in and through the prophets and the apostles and in and through the teaching or prophetic office of Christ (SEE *munus triplex*). After the fall, man's reason has proved incapable of deriving a pure or complete knowledge of God from creation. Thus *revelatio generalis* and the *theologia naturalis* (q.v.) resulting from it contain only a nonsaving truth, known only partially and imperfectly by the sinful intellect. A *revelatio specialis* was, therefore, necessary for salvation; and the *theologia revelata* or *theologia supernaturalis* based on it can alone contain true, undistorted, and saving knowledge of God.

revelatio immediata: *immediate or unmediated revelation;* a direct revelation of God by means of a theophany, a vision, a voice, or some inward inspiration, like the "inner light." The orthodox, both Lutheran and Reformed, allow an immediate revelation given to the authors of Scripture but deny the existence of all such revelations after the closing of the canon. The Holy Spirit now reveals the truth of God mediately, through Scripture. SEE *revelatio nova; testimonium internum Spiritus Sancti.*

revelatio nova: *new revelation;* i.e., a denial of the fullness of revelation in Christ and of the closure of the canon of Scripture; specifically, the assertion that new truths are given directly by God; a category of revelation affirmed by enthusiasts but denied absolutely by all the orthodox, Lutheran and Reformed alike. SEE *revelatio immediata.*

reverentia: *reverence.*

Ss

sacerdos impeccabilis: *sinless or impeccable priest;* i.e., Christ in his priestly work of self-sacrifice which required that he be a sinless offering given for the sins of the world. SEE *anamartēsia; sacerdotium.*

sacerdotium: *priestly work or priestly office;* either the priestly office in the nation of Israel under the old covenant or the priestly work of Christ as the fulfillment of the Old Testament office and his complete priestly and sacrificial offering for the sins of mankind. When applied to Christ, the *sacerdotium* or *munus sacerdotale* is one aspect of the threefold office (*munus triplex,* q.v.). The Protestant scholastics divide the *sacerdotium* into two functions, the *satisfactio Christi,* or *satisfactio vicaria,* and the *intercessio.* The former term refers to the character of Christ's death as a propitiatory and expiatory work, performed for the sake of appeasing the anger of God against sin and bearing the divine wrath in the place and on behalf of believers. The latter term refers to Christ's prayers on behalf of believers—prayers both on earth (John 17) and now in heaven at the right hand of God the Father. SEE *intercessio Christi; obedientia Christi.*

sacramentaliter: *sacramentally.* SEE *praesentia illocalis sive definitiva.*

sacramentum: *sacrament;* in churchly usage, a holy rite that is both a sign and a means of grace (SEE *media gratiae; organa gratiae et salutis*). The sacraments are also defined by the scholastics as the visible Word of God, distinct but not separate from the audible Word or Holy Scripture. In the traditional Augustinian definition, a sacrament is a visible sign of an invisible grace. The Reformers and the Protestant scholastics reject what they saw as the loose and improper view of sacraments held by the medieval doctors and the Roman Church and therefore reject also the medieval scholastic doctrine of seven sacraments. Properly and strictly (*proprie et stricte*) sacraments must have three characteristics: (1) they must be commanded by God (*a Deo mandata*), (2) they must have visible or sensible elements prescribed by God, and (3) they must apply and seal by

267

grace the promise of the gospel (*promissio evangelicae*). This strict definition applies to only two rites of the church, baptism (see *baptismus*) and the Lord's Supper (see *coena sacra*). Other rites considered sacraments by Rome—confirmation, penance, ordination, and extreme unction—do not have the *mandatum Dei*, while marriage, also counted a sacrament, lacks the *promissio evangelicae*.

Protestant orthodoxy therefore defines a sacrament as a sacred action (*actio*), instituted by God, that employs an external sign (*signum*), or element, to confer on and seal to believers by grace the promise of the gospel for remission of sins and life eternal. The Reformed orthodox develop this definition, together with the basic Augustinian definition cited above, in terms of a distinction between the visible signs and the thing signified (*res signata*), or thing of the sacrament (*res sacramenti*). Thus the visible sign points to Christ, the thing signified. This language is reflected in the Reformed view of Christ's presence in the Lord's Supper as a spiritual presence (*praesentia spiritualis*) according to which the body and blood of Christ, now in heaven, are mediated to believers by the power of the Spirit. Such language, however, is not acceptable to the orthodox Lutherans inasmuch as it allows a separation of the *signa* and the *res signata*. Lutheran theologians prefer a distinction between the visible and invisible elements of the sacrament or between the external or earthly material and the heavenly material (*materia coelestis*, q.v.) of the sacrament. Christ is not merely represented and sealed but presented under the visible elements. The Reformed do insist on a sacramental union (*unio sacramentalis*) between sign and thing signified and can argue that, sacramentally, Christ is truly and substantially (*substantialiter*) given, but they also insist that Christ's body remains locally in heaven. See *consecratio; forma sacramenti; Nihil habet rationem sacramenti extra usum a Christo institutum; praesentia illocalis sive definitiva; res sacramenti; sedes tropi; signum; unio sacramentalis; verbum institutionis.*

sacramentum confirmationis: *the sacrament of confirmation or confirmatory sacrament;* in orthodox Protestant theology, the Lord's Supper. See *coena sacra; sacramentum initiationis.*

sacramentum initiationis: *the sacrament of initiation;* i.e., baptism, as distinct from the *sacramentum confirmationis*, the sacrament of confirmation, by which Protestant theology indicates, *not* the ritual of *confirmatio* (q.v.), or confirmation, but the Lord's Supper. Thus, baptism marks the beginning of one's life as a member of the church and is the necessary prerequisite for participation in the Lord's Supper, while the Lord's Supper itself serves, not as the initial means of grace, but as the continuing means, or medium, of grace that strengthens and confirms, by grace, the faith and the justification of the Christian before God. SEE *coena sacra.*

sacramentum regenerationis: *sacrament of regeneration;* i.e., baptism. SEE *baptismus; sacramentum initiationis.*

sacrarium: *sacrarium or sacristy;* viz., a place where holy or sacred things are kept; specifically, the place where the consecrated bread remaining after the celebration of the Eucharist is reserved for adoration. This usage is directly connected with the Roman Catholic doctrine of transubstantiation (*transubstantiatio,* q.v.) and is condemned by Protestants, Lutherans and Reformed alike.

sacrificium intellectus: *sacrifice of the intellect.*

sacrificium propitiatorium: *propitiatory sacrifice;* i.e., the death of Christ considered as a sacrifice that appeases or conciliates God. SEE *obedientia Christi; satisfactio vicaria.*

saeculum: *age or era;* the Latin equivalent of αἰών. SEE *consummatio saeculi.*

salus aeterna: *eternal salvation.*

Salus extra ecclesiam non est: *[There is] no salvation outside of the church;* the famous maxim from Cyprian of Carthage. SEE *Extra ecclesiam non sit salus.*

sanctificatio: *sanctification;* viz., the gracious work of God, accomplished in believers by the grace of the Spirit following and resting on faith and justification, by means of which believers are drawn out of their corruption toward holiness of life. Sanctification is, therefore, distinct from *iustificatio* (q.v.), or justification. Whereas the medieval scholastics did *not* distinguish *iustificatio* from *sanctificatio* and viewed the former as consisting in both the reckoning righteous and the making righteous of believers (SEE *iustitia infusa*), the Reformers' teaching of justification by grace alone, through faith and apart from works, led orthodox Protestantism toward a strictly forensic concept of justification and toward the conclusion that actual righteousness or holiness in believers and the resultant good works are not part of justification but belong to a distinct aspect of the *ordo salutis* (q.v.), sanctification. Sanctification, then, represents an actual change in man, indeed, the renewal and renovation (SEE *renovatio*) of man

269

according to the *imago Dei* (q.v.), or image of God. Thus, the scholastic Protestants describe the sinful corruption of the image as the *terminus a quo* (q.v.), or beginning of sanctification, and the restoration of the *imago* as the *terminus ad quem* (q.v.), or end of sanctification. *Sanctificatio*, therefore, begins with *conversio* (q.v.), or conversion, and continues throughout the life of the believer. The mortification and vivification that belong to *conversio* also belong to *sanctificatio* as the basic form of Christian life, dying to the world and living the new life in Christ. Since it is the continuation of regeneration or conversion, sanctification is sometimes called *conversio continuata* (q.v.).

The Protestant scholastics further distinguish between sanctification broadly and strictly defined. (1) *Sanctificatio late dicta*, or sanctification loosely considered, indicates the entire gracious work of the Spirit in the believer; (2) *sanctificatio stricte dicta*, or sanctification strictly defined, refers directly to the problem of the corrupted *imago Dei* and the old Adam in believers and is defined as the negative renovation (*renovatio negativa*) according to which believers daily die to sin and set aside the old Adam; (3) *sanctificatio strictissime dicta*, or sanctification most strictly considered, is the actual renewal of the *imago Dei* or positive renovation (*renovatio positiva*) of the Christian according to which the believer is actually made holy and, by the grace of the Spirit, cooperates willingly in the renewal of life and willingly does good works (*bona opera*). The Protestant orthodox, Lutheran and Reformed, are unanimous in their teaching that perfect or total sanctification does not occur in this life.

sanctio foederis: *the sanction or ratification of the covenant;* in Reformed federalism, the divine stipulations of salvation in return for obedience and judgment in return for disobedience. See *confirmatio foederis; foedus gratiae; promulgatio foederis.*

sanctitas: *sanctity, holiness, inward or intrinsic righteousness;* the *sanctitas Dei*, or holiness of God, refers to the absolute goodness of God's being and willing. It is a *sanctitas positiva*, or positive holiness, both intrinsically, in the essential goodness and righteousness of God, and extrinsically, in the goodness and righteousness of God's will toward his creatures, specifically, in his will that all rational creatures be holy as he himself is holy. It is also a *sanctitas negativa*, or negative holiness, in the sense that the goodness and righteousness of God remain inviolate and eternally separate from all that is sinful or tainted in the created order. See *iustitia Dei.*

sanctus, -a, -um: *holy.*

Sanctus Spiritus: *Holy Spirit; the Third Person of the Trinity.* SEE *Deus; Trinitas.*

sanguis Christi: *the blood of Christ.* SEE *coena sacra; praesentia; sanguis corruptus.*

sanguis corruptus: *corrupted blood;* a term used to describe fallen humanity in contrast with the uncorrupted and cleansing *sanguis Christi,* or blood of Christ, which is the λύτρον *redemptionis,* or redemptive ransom, of corrupt humanity.

sapientia: *wisdom;* the Latin equivalent of σοφία. In scholastic philosophy and theology, *sapientia* denotes a knowledge of first principles and the conclusions which can be drawn from them, particularly a knowledge of the good and the true. Thus, *sapientia* is the basis of distinctions between true and false in any specific body of knowledge (SEE *scientia*). *Sapientia* is also numbered among the divine attributes (SEE *omnisapientia*).

satisfactio: *satisfaction; a making amends or reparation;* specifically, the making amends for sin required by God for forgiveness to take place. The work of satisfaction manifests the constancy of God's justice or righteousness (SEE *iustitia Dei*) while at the same time revealing God's mercy in the fact of forgiveness. *Satisfactio* has two meanings: (1) the satisfaction made by individual sinners according to the Roman Catholic sacrament (*sacramentum,* q.v.) of penance (*poenitentia,* q.v.), and (2) the all-sufficient satisfaction of Christ (*satisfactio Christi*) or vicarious satisfaction (*satisfactio vicaria,* q.v.) made by Christ on the cross for sin. The former meaning was held by the medieval church and its doctors, but rejected by the Reformers on the ground that Christ's obedience (*obedientia Christi,* q.v.) was sufficient payment for both our guilt (*culpa,* q.v.) and our punishment (*poena,* q.v.). In the medieval scholastic and Roman Catholic doctrine, however, Christ's satisfaction remits the guilt of sin and the eternal punishment, leaving temporal punishment to be met by works of satisfaction imposed in the sacrament of penance.

satisfactio Christi: *the satisfaction of Christ.* SEE *satisfactio vicaria.*

satisfactio vicaria: *vicarious satisfaction;* viz., Christ's work of propitiation and expiation considered as payment for sin made for the sake of believers and in their place. The scholastics define *satisfactio* as *vera debiti solutio,* true payment of debt. It is vicarious because it is performed in the place of the satisfaction that otherwise would

271

have been required by God of mankind in return for the forgiveness of sin, and because Christ stands in the place of believers and bears the full wrath of God against sin. It is characteristic of the Reformers and of the orthodox that they depart from the medieval scholastic theory of a satisfaction made for the sake of the divine honor and rest their views of satisfaction on the justice or righteousness of God (*iustitia Dei*, q.v.) which is angry and wrathful against sin. Thus Christ's satisfaction includes and implies the *obedientia Christi* (q.v.) through which Christ both fulfills the law for us vicariously and then accepts, vicariously, the punishment for sin required under the law, death.

The Lutheran and Reformed scholastics agree, against the Socinians, that a satisfaction must be made for all sin if there are to be redemption and reconciliation. It is no contradiction of the gratuitous character of redemption to make satisfaction for sin under the law, since God is not simply a merciful creditor, but also the just judge of sin. According to the Protestant orthodox, the doctrine of a vicarious satisfaction alone meets the requirements of the biblical view of God as both merciful and just, both gracious and righteous. Justice and righteousness are satisfied and, yet, in the vicarious nature of the work, mercy and grace are manifest. Since God cannot set aside his own *iustitia*, satisfaction is necessary. In further describing the *satisfactio vicaria*, the Lutherans and the Reformed both draw on the medieval satisfaction theory. Against the patristic ransom theory, the scholastics argue that the sin of mankind was a violation of God's law and that payment must therefore be made to God. The payment must, moreover, be made by a human being, inasmuch as sin is the sin of human beings. Yet, the assault of sin against infinite God demands infinite punishment and can be satisfied only through an infinite payment. Such payment cannot be made by a mere human being, but only by a being with infinite powers, namely God. The one who makes satisfaction must, therefore, be the God-man, Christ. Because the divine nature concurs with the human in the work of redemption, the merit of the work is infinite. It should be noted that Calvin had credited the all-sufficiency of Christ's merit (*meritum Christi*, q.v.) to the divine decree, a doctrine more in accord with the Reformed Christology than the scholastic Reformed view that the source of Christ's infinite merit was the infinite value of his divine-human work. The Lutheran view of Christ's merit as infinite can draw directly on the second and third *genera* of the *communicatio idiomatum* (q.v.). The infinite merit of the *satisfactio Christi* renders it the sufficient payment for all sin. Here the agreement between Lutherans and Reformed ends. The Lutherans interpret the *sufficientia satisfactionis* as a universal payment for all sins, which has as its object the personal salvation of each and every sinful man. If this sufficient payment does not become efficient for all, the cause of the inefficiency lies only in the failure of some sinners to believe in Christ. The Reformed hold the *sufficientia satisfactionis* but argue the efficiency (*efficientia/efficacia*) of Christ's satisfaction for the elect only, thus resting the inefficiency or nonapplication of Christ's work on the divine decree rather than on human sin.

Finally, we note that the concept of *satisfactio vicaria* or *satisfactio Christi* is the central issue in the orthodox discussion of the *officium Christi*, or work of Christ. *Satisfactio* has been inappositely rendered into English as "atonement." The imprecision of the word "atonement" is exacerbated when the Reformed view is characterized as "limited atonement." The Reformed never claim a limited sufficiency of the value of Christ's satisfaction, nor do the opponents of "limited atonement," either Lutheran or Arminian, ever imply an unlimited application or efficacy of Christ's satisfaction. The issue is that the Reformed argue the limitation of efficacy to the elect, whereas the Lutherans and the Arminians place the limitation in human unbelief, the Lutherans holding on to the paradox of salvation *sola gratia*, the Arminians abandoning the *sola gratia* to synergism. The Reformed also argue, in the late seventeenth century, a distinction between the worthiness of Christ's death (SEE *meritum Christi*, q.v.) and the will and intention of Christ in the accomplishment of his work. The former is infinite, since it corresponds with the sufficiency of Christ's work; the latter is limited to the elect, since it corresponds with the efficiency of Christ's work. The Reformed conclude that Christ did not die for all; the divine intention in the all-sufficient sacrifice of Christ was the salvation of the elect only and not the hypothetical universal extension of Christ's work or the universal salvation of mankind (SEE *universalismus hypotheticus*). SEE *expiatio.*

scandalum: *a stumbling block;* hence, something that causes offense or is a source of temptation or an inducement to sin.

schēma (σχῆμα): *form or shape,* plural, **schēmata;** e.g., 1 Cor. 7:31; Phil. 2:7.

schetikos (σχετικός): *incidental* or *nonessential;* used by the fathers with reference to the union of believers with God by grace and, pejoratively, with reference to the Nestorian view of the union of the two natures in Christ.

273

scientia: *knowledge;* in the most general sense of the term, synonymous with *cognitio* (q.v.) and *notitia.* It indicates knowledge generally, whether simple or complex, latent (*habitualis*) or actual, immediate (*intuitiva*) or mediate, infused or acquired. More specifically, however, *scientia* indicates a knowledge acquired by demonstration and resting on self-evident first principles (*principia per se nota*). In this restricted sense, *scientia* cannot of course be predicated of God, since God's knowledge is not acquired. It is in precisely this sense, however, that a definable body of human knowledge is called *scientia,* because it is a certain and evident knowledge (*notitia certa et evidens*) that is acquired by logical demonstration. Human *scientia* can be further distinguished into primary sciences or bodies of knowledge that rest on their own self-evident principles, and secondary or subalternate sciences that rest on principles derived from a primary science. Because of its basis in logical demonstration, *scientia* is also to be distinguished from other varieties of knowing, viz., art (*ars*), wisdom (*sapientia,* q.v.), and prudence (*prudentia,* q.v.).

scientia Dei: *the knowledge of God;* i.e., the attribute of knowledge predicated of God, which is the knowledge, identical with the divine essence (SEE *essentia*), according to which God knows himself and all his works most perfectly. The scholastics distinguish two basic categories of divine knowing, the *scientia simplicis intelligentiae,* or knowledge of unqualified intelligence, and the *scientia libera,* or free knowledge. In opposition to the Lutheran and Reformed orthodox, the Arminians follow the Jesuits in adding a third category in between the *scientia simplicis intelligentiae* and the *scientia libera,* the so-called *scientia media,* or middle knowledge. The first category, *scientia simplicis intelligentiae seu naturalis et indefinita* (q.v.), also called simply *scientia necessaria* or *scientia naturalis,* is the uncompounded, unqualified, absolute, indefinite, or unbounded knowledge that God has necessarily according to his nature and by which God perfectly knows himself and the whole range of possibility. This is an antecedent knowledge that logically precedes the eternal decrees and, thus, the free exercise of the divine will *ad extra.* By way of contrast, the *scientia libera* is a consequent knowledge resting upon the divine will. It is a *scientia libera seu visionis et definita* (q.v.), a *scientia voluntaria,* a free or visionary and definite knowledge, a voluntary knowledge, of actual things brought freely into existence by the divine will operating within the range of possibility perfectly known to God. The effect of this conception of divine knowing is to rest all divine knowledge, including the divine foreknowledge of contingent events, upon the divine will which alone can actualize what is possible. Nothing falls outside of the divine knowing because all things rest on the divine will (SEE *voluntas Dei*). Contingent events are known to God as belonging to the realm of his permissive willing and providential concurrence (*concursus*, q.v.). Against this view, in the attempt to create an area of radically free willing and moral responsibility beyond the control of the divine will, the Jesuit theologians Pedro de Fonseca and Luis Molina proposed a category of middle knowledge, or *scientia media*. The *scientia media* underlies their synergistic theory of salvation and was adopted in the seventeenth century by the Arminians for the same purpose. Middle knowledge is a conditioned and consequent knowledge of future contingents by which God knows of an event because of its occurrence. In other words, it is a knowledge eternally in God consequent on, and causally independent of, events in time. Such events are outside of the divine willing. The effect of such a doctrine upon soteriology is to allow an area of human choice, prior to the effective operation of divine grace, the results of which condition the divine activity or operation *ad extra*. God can elect individuals on the basis of his foreknowledge of their freely willed acceptance of the promises given in Christ, and this election will be grounded upon no antecedent willing or operation of God. The acts *ad extra* of the divine will and the *scientia libera* or *scientia voluntaria* will rest, then, in certain instances on a foreknowledge of future contingents which is consequent on and conditioned by the contingents themselves. Both the Lutheran and the Reformed orthodox reject the idea—the Reformed with vehemence. At very best, the *scientia media* limits divine control to the circumstances surrounding an event and provides a certain knowledge of events that lie outside of divine control; at worst it hypothesizes an uncertain knowledge of contingents on the part of God. In either case it limits the sovereignty of grace in the work of salvation. SEE *omniscientia*.

scientia experimentalis: *experimental knowledge; knowledge gained inductively from sense experience.*

scientia habitualis: *habitual knowledge;* i.e., knowledge present to the intellect as a capacity or disposition but not actually in use; the opposite of *scientia actualis*, actual knowledge, or knowledge being used. SEE *scientia*.

scientia libera seu visionis et definita: *free knowledge or visionary and definite knowledge;* the knowledge by which God knows what actually exists because of his will. This knowledge is free (*libera*) because it rests on the freedom of the divine will, as distinct from the *scientia necessaria* which rests on the nature of God himself (SEE *necessitas naturae; scientia necessaria).* It is *visionis,* visionary or of vision, since it represents the direct divine contemplation of all that is. Finally, it is *definita,* definite or defined, since it is a knowledge of actual things. Because it rests on the divine will, the *scientia libera* is also called *scientia voluntaria.* SEE *scientia Dei.*

scientia media: *middle knowledge;* a term used to describe a category in the divine knowing according to which God has a conditioned or consequent, rather than an absolute and antecedent, foreknowledge of future contingents. SEE *scientia Dei.*

scientia metaphysica: *metaphysical knowledge; metaphysics.* SEE *metaphysica.*

scientia naturalis: *natural knowledge;* i.e., the knowledge that belongs to an intelligent or rational being according to its nature. In God, *scientia naturalis* is more frequently termed *scientia necessaria* (q.v.) or *scientia simplicis intelligentiae seu naturalis et indefinita* (q.v.).

scientia necessaria: *necessary knowledge;* viz., the knowledge that God, according to his nature, must necessarily have; infinite and perfect knowledge both of the divine being itself (SEE *theologia archetypa*) and of all possibilities. *Scientia necessaria* is synonymous with *scientia simplicis intelligentiae seu naturalis et indefinita* (q.v.). SEE *scientia Dei.*

scientia simplicis intelligentiae seu naturalis et indefinita: *knowledge of uncompounded or unqualified intelligence, or natural and indefinite knowledge;* viz., that knowledge by which God knows himself and the entire realm of possibility infinitely and perfectly. This knowledge is *simplex,* i.e., uncompounded, unqualified, or absolute because it is not conditioned in any way by externals, but is itself the condition, in an absolute sense, for all things *ad extra.* Since it is one with the divine essence it must be uncompounded or noncomposite. It is a natural knowledge (*scientia naturalis*) since it belongs to the very nature of God. It is indefinite because unqualified and unconditioned; it includes all possibility and is logically prior to the definite knowledge of created (or creatable) actuality. SEE *scientia Dei.*

scientia voluntaria: *voluntary knowledge;* i.e., the knowledge by which God knows the effects of his will. SEE *scientia Dei; scientia libera seu visionis et definita.*

276

scintilla animae: *a spark of the soul;* a term typical of late medieval mysticism indicating a divine spark deep within the soul, more profound than either intellect or will, that provides the point of union between God and man in the exercise of mystic detachment from externals. The *scintilla animae* is, in effect, an uncreated spark of the divine intellect within the soul, an "interior fortress" of the unsullied divine within the human being. Because of the tendency of such a concept to deny the radicality of the fall and to deny the need for an alien righteousness (*iustitia aliena*) in justification, the concept is attacked by Protestantism. The presence of similar ideas in Protestant mystics like Jacob Boehme led to their condemnation in the systems of the Protestant scholastics.

scintilla conscientiae: *spark of conscience.* SEE *conscientia; synderesis.*

Scriptura sacra: *Sacred or Holy Scripture;* the Protestant scholastics elaborated the Reformation principle of *sola Scriptura* into an entire dogmatic *locus* in which Scripture was defined as one of the *principia theologiae* (q.v.) and then described according to its attributes, dignity (*dignitas*), clarity (*perspicuitas*), authority (*authoritas*), truth (*veritas*), holiness (*sanctitas*), and sufficiency (*sufficientia*). In addition, they follow the Reformers in defining *Scriptura sacra* strictly, as consisting in the Old Testament (*Vetus Testamentum*) and the New Testament (*Novum Testamentum*), to the exclusion of the Apocrypha or apocryphal books (*libri apocryphi*). These latter are not considered inspired, but may be read for edification. SEE *authoritas Scripturae; norma.*

Scriptura sacra locuta, res decisa est: *Holy Scripture has spoken, the issue is decided;* a maxim indicating the final authority of Scripture in all matters of faith and practice.

Scripturam ex Scriptura explicandam esse: *Scripture is to be explained from Scripture;* one of several forms of a maxim employed by both Lutheran and Reformed orthodox to indicate the normative authority and self-authenticating character of Scripture over against the Roman Catholic contention that the church has absolute authority to explain the text. The orthodox grant that Scripture cannot be interpreted outside of the church, but they insist that the authority of the church derives from Scripture and not the authority of Scripture from the church's testimony. Since Word, as such, is authoritative and effective, it must be its own standard of interpretation. Other versions of the maxim include: *Scriptura seipsam interpretatur; Scriptura Scripturam interpretatur; Scriptura sui interpres.*

secundum se: *according to itself;* as distinct from *secundum aliud,* according to another (thing). SEE *alius/aliud.*

sedes doctrinae: *a seat of doctrine;* the particular text of Scripture used as the primary foundation of a doctrine.

sedes tropi: *seat of the figure;* viz., the word or group of words in which a figure of speech is said to lie. Against the literal reading of the words of institution, "This is my body" and "This is my blood"— *hoc est corpus meum, hic est sanguis meus*—taught by the Lutherans, the Reformed argued that the words contained a figure, or trope, and variously located the trope in the copula *est* and/or in the words *corpus* and *sanguis.*

semen fidei: *seed of faith;* the ground or beginning of faith in man, brought about or implanted by the work of the Spirit in regeneration. Some of the Protestant scholastics use *semen fidei* as a synonym for the disposition of or capacity for faith, the *habitus fidei* (q.v.); others make the *semen fidei* more basic and regard the disposition, or *habitus,* of faith as a fully developed capacity arising out of the seed, or *semen.*

semen impurum: *impure seed;* a basis of the *propagatio peccati* (q.v.).

semen religionis: *seed of religion;* i.e., the rudimentary knowledge of God that arises in every human being because of the objective revelation of God in his work of creation and providence, and because of the subjective reality of a remnant of the image of God (*imago Dei,* q.v.) in each person. Because of the fall, however, the *semen religionis* gives rise, not to true religion, but to idolatry and error in the name of God.

semina virtutum: *the seed of virtue;* viz., an inherent capacity to do good; denied by the Protestant scholastics inasmuch as it implies the ability of man, unaided by grace, to perform righteous or meritorious acts. SEE *donum superadditum; peccatum originalis; status purorum naturalium.*

sensus accommodatitius: *the accommodated sense;* i.e., the sense of a text of Scripture as interpreted, not literally, but with a view toward the reconciliation of problematic statements with historical-critical discoveries. The term refers, therefore, to the impact of rationalist exegesis and is denied by all the Protestant orthodox as applicable to Scripture. SEE *accommodatio.*

Sensus allegoricus non est argumentativus: *The allegorical meaning is not argumentative or conclusive.* SEE *quadriga; Theologia symbolica non est argumentativa.*

sensus compositus: *composite sense;* also **sensus literalis compositus**: *composite or compounded literal sense;* as distinguished from a divided or isolated sense *(sensus divisus,* q.v.). SEE *sensus literalis.*

sensus divinitatis: *sense of the divine;* viz., a basic, intuitive perception of the divine existence; it is generated in all men through their encounter with the providential ordering of the world. The *sensus divinitatis* is, therefore, the basis both of pagan religion and of natural theology. Because of the fall, the religion that arises out of this sense of the divine or seed of religion *(semen religionis,* q.v.) is idolatrous and incapable of saving or of producing true obedience before God. Man's *sensus divinitatis,* thus, is capable only of leaving him without excuse in his rejection of God's truth.

sensus divisus: *the divided sense;* i.e., the meaning of a word or idea in itself apart from its general relation to other words of a text; the opposite of *sensus compositus.*

sensus irae divinae: *the sense or experience of divine wrath;* i.e., the *poena sensus,* or punishment of the senses, to which the damned are subjected. SEE *poena.*

sensus literalis: *literal sense;* the fundamental literal or grammatical sense of the text of Scripture, distinguished into (1) *sensus literalis simplex,* the simple literal sense, which lies immediately in the grammar and the meaning of the individual words, and (2) *sensus literalis compositus,* the constructed or compounded literal sense, which is inferred from the Scripture as a whole or from individual clear, and therefore normative, passages of Scripture when the simple literal sense of the text in question seems to violate either the *articuli fidei* (q.v.) or the *praecepta caritatis* (q.v.). SEE *historicus; quadriga.*

sensus mysticus: *mystical sense* or *mystical interpretation;* also called the **sensus spiritualis**: *spiritual sense;* viz., as distinct from the literal reading of a text, the reading or interpretation that finds in the words of the text types, signs, figures, tropes, or symbols of meaning not literally stated in the text. The Protestant orthodox favor a literal reading of Scripture (SEE *sensus literalis*) but allow a mystical or spiritual reading of those texts which either cannot bear a purely literal construction or are clearly intended to shadow forth a deeper, usually prophetic, meaning. The federal school of Reformed theology founded by Johannes Cocceius was given to excessive typological reading of the Old Testament and was, on that account, attacked by Reformed and Lutherans alike in the name of literal exegesis.

sententia: *sentence, sense, meaning;* the term can indicate a sentence or conclusion concerning an issue, a judgment, decision, or opinion about something, or a series of words or a discourse having a particular meaning or significance. These several meanings conjoin in the title of the famous compendium of theology by Peter Lombard, the *Libri quattuor sententiarum* (*Four Books of Sentences*), where doctrinal problems are stated in the form of distinctions and a decision is made dogmatically concerning each problem or set of distinctions.

septem peccata mortalia: *seven deadly (mortal) sins;* i.e., the seven categories of sin into which the medieval doctors divided the mortal sins (*peccata mortalia*, q.v.): *superbia* or pride; *avaritia* or greed; *invidia* or envy; *gula* or gluttony; *luxuria* or lust; *ira* or anger; and *acedia* or despair. *Superbia*, pride, is the direct opposite of *humilitas*, humility, and may be defined as an inordinate valuation of self or an inordinate love of self (*amor sui*). The scholastic doctors of the Middle Ages viewed *superbia completa*, utter or total pride, as the identifying characteristic of the entire genus *peccata mortalia* and as the sin at the root of the fall insofar as pride, in the extreme, sets the individual higher than all other goods, higher even than God, the highest good (*summum bonum*, q.v.). Such is the pride that would know good and evil, that would be as God. Such is the pride of the devil. *Superbia* is sometimes, therefore, called *omnium peccatorum mater*, "the mother of all sins." It is characterized by vainglory or vanity (*vana gloria* or *vanitas*), ambition (*ambitio*), and presumption (*praesumptio*). In the Augustinian language of rightly and wrongly directed love, *superbia* may be seen as the love of self as an end in itself (SEE *frui*). *Avaritia*, avarice or greed, is the opposite of the virtue *liberalitas*, or liberality, since it represents an inordinate appetite or desire for temporal goods (*appetitus inordinatus bonorum temporalium*), expressed both as the excessive desire to retain what one already has and as the excessive appetite to gain new possessions. *Invidia*, envy or jealousy, is opposed to *caritas*, love or self-giving love, and may be defined as sorrow over the good of another person arising from a prideful estimation of self. *Gula*, gluttony, is simply an inordinate appetite for food and drink, as opposed to the virtues of abstinence (*abstinentia*) and sobriety (*sobrietas*). *Luxuria*, or lust, strictly defined as one of the mortal sins, is the inordinate appetite for or indulgence in sexual activity. *Ira,* or anger, is the opposite of mildness or gentleness (*mansuetudo* or *clementia*), and may be defined as an inordinate appetite for revenge or simply as vengefulness, which manifests itself in aversion (*aversio*) to others and rancor (*rancor*) or indignation (*indignatio*) toward others. Finally, *acedia,* despair or morosity, strictly defined is an opposition to or sorrow in the face of the goodness, grace, and friendship (*amicitia*) of God, a rejection of the love of God (*amor Dei,* q.v.). See *appetitus inordinatus.*

septem vitia capitalia: *seven deadly sins.* See *septem peccata mortalia.*

sermo: *word;* synonymous with *verbum* (q.v.).

servum arbitrium: *enslaved or bound choice.* See *liberum arbitrium.*

sessio Christi: *the sitting or act of sitting of Christ at the right hand of the Father* (*ad dextram Patris*); apart from the basic agreement of Lutheran and Reformed that the *sessio Christi* is the highest exaltation of Christ as the God-man and that the expression, *sedet ad dextram Patris,* "he sits at the right hand of the Father," is a figurative expression, the *sessio Christi* marks a point of fundamental christological opposition between Lutheran and Reformed. The Lutherans emphasize the biblical usage of "right hand of God" as a figurative description of the exercise of divine power. Since the power of God is exercised everywhere, the exaltation of Christ to the right hand of God is an indication of Christ's *ubiquitas* (q.v.) according to his human nature, which is the subject of the exaltation. The Reformed deny this communication of a divine attribute to Christ's humanity and argue from the ascension of Christ *in coelis* that the heavenly session indicates the removal of Christ's human nature from the earth. The figurative usage, *ad dextram Patris,* the Reformed interpret as the highest exaltation of Christ as God-man, as an indication that Christ in his humanity now participates in the divine majesty and rule, not as though the right hand of God indicates a place (*ubi*), but rather an honor conferred upon Christ. For the Reformed, however, the heavenly *sessio* indicates *ubietas,* or "whereness," specifically, the location of Christ's finite humanity in heaven. See *communicatio idiomatum; praesentia illocalis sive definitiva.*

seu (conj.): *or.* See *sive.*

Si homo non periisset, Filius hominis non venisset: *If man had not perished, the Son of man would not have come;* a maxim drawn from Augustine, *Sermon* 174. The saying and the argument behind it are important in the history of the doctrine of the incarnation and its relation to the doctrines of Christ's work and of the *imago Dei* (q.v.), or image of God. During the Middle Ages in the teaching of Rupert of Deutz, Albert the Great, and Duns Scotus, and during the Reformation, in the teaching of Andreas Osiander (the Elder), the argument was put forth that the incarnation was necessary, apart from the problem of sin, as the crowning glory of the divine work of creation. Christ, as the last Adam and as the *imago Dei* in which man was originally created, must be incarnate as the actualization of the divine will for man and man's fellowship with God. Thus, the predestination of Christ to be the God-man (*praedestinatio Christi*) is viewed as an unconditional, or absolute, predestination, and only the predestination of Christ to die for the sins of the world as a conditioned or consequent will of God (SEE *praedestinatio; voluntas Dei*). Further, it would be entirely inappropriate for sin to become the reason for the fulfillment of revelation in Christ, inasmuch as the entire essence of God and the ultimate purpose of God exclude sin. Over against this view, Augustine, Thomas Aquinas, and, in the Reformation, both Lutheran and Reformed theologians argue that Scripture teaches only one purpose of the incarnation, viz., the redemption of man, and, moreover, in no way implies a work of Christ other than the work of mediation between God and the fallen creature. It is the work of mediation upon which the union of the natures in Christ is predicated. Both Lutheran and Reformed orthodox explicitly reject the Scotist and the Osiandrian views as speculative excess. SEE *praedestinatio*.

signa diei novissimi: *signs of the last day.* SEE *dies novissimus.*

signa temporis: *signs of the times.* SEE *dies novissimus.*

signum: *sign;* particularly in contrast to *res,* a thing. A *signum* is defined as a thing, i.e., an object or a word, that points beyond itself to another thing. *Res,* in this sense, is a thing considered in and of itself. Since anything in the finite universe can become a sign, the mind must make an interpretive judgment each time it encounters a thing. In the exegetical model proposed by Augustine, each word, of course, is a sign of some thing; but the thing signified by the word may also be a sign. If the latter is the case, then interpretation cannot rest with the literal meaning but must ask the question of significance by moving toward allegorical or tropological reading of the text. SEE *quadriga*.

The distinction between *signum* and *res* also obtains in sacramental theology. SEE *materia coelestis; res sacramenti; sacramentum.*

similia similibus percipiuntur: *Similar or like things are perceived by similar things;* i.e., there must be some common ground or analogy of being (*analogia entis,* q.v.) between the knower and the thing known.

similitudo: *likeness, similitude.* See *imago Dei.*

simplicitas: *simplicity;* i.e., having an uncompounded or noncomposite nature; especially, the *simplicitas Dei* according to which God is understood as being absolutely free of any and all composition, not merely physical, but also rational or logical composition. Thus, God is not the sum of the divine attributes (*attributa divina,* q.v.); the attributes are understood to be identical with and inseparable from the *essentia Dei* (q.v.). The scholastics observe that if God were even logically or rationally composite, God would necessarily be viewed as a result and in some sense contingent. Simplicity is the guarantee of the absolute ultimacy and perfection of God, so much so that it frequently appears in scholastic systems as the first divine attribute on which a right understanding of all other divine attributes depends.

simul iustus et peccator: *at once righteous and a sinner;* Luther's characterization of the believer justified by grace through faith. Since faith, not works, is the ground of our justification (*iustificatio,* q.v.), and since justification is not an infusion of righteousness that makes a sinner righteous in and of himself, the sinner is both righteous in God's sight because of Christ and a sinner as measured according to his own merits.

sine mensura: *without measure.*

sine qua non. See *conditio sine qua non.*

sive (conj.): *or;* in pairs, *either . . . or;* synonymous with *seu.*

sola fide: *by faith alone;* also **per solam fidem**: *through faith alone;* and sometimes **ex fide**: *by faith.* See *iustificatio.*

Sola fides in Christum membra ecclesiae constituit: *Only faith in Christ can establish the members of the church;* i.e., the foundation or basis of membership in the church is faith. A maxim cited by Francis Pieper (*Christian Dogmatics,* III, p. 397).

sola gratia: *grace alone; by grace alone;* viz., the teaching of the Reformers and of their scholastic successors that grace alone is the ground of salvation and that individuals are justified by grace alone through faith. The term allows only grace to be the active power in justification and leaves nothing to the human will or to human works. Synergism (*synergismus*, q.v.), or cooperation between man and God, is therefore effectively ruled out of the initial work of salvation. Even faith (*fides*, q.v.) is a result of grace and cannot be considered as the result of human effort. SEE *gratia; iustificatio; ordo salutis.*

sola Scriptura: *Scripture alone;* the watchword of the Reformation in its establishment of the basis for a renewed and reformed statement of Christian doctrine. We find the concept of *sola Scriptura*, Scripture alone as the primary and absolute norm of doctrine, at the foundation of the early Protestant attempts at theological system in the form of exegetical *loci communes* (q.v.), or common places. In the orthodox or scholastic codification of Lutheran and Reformed doctrine, the *sola Scriptura* of the Reformers was elaborated as a separate doctrinal *locus* placed at the beginning of theological system and determinative of its contents. Scripture was identified as the *principium cognoscendi,* the principle of knowing or cognitive foundation of theology, and described doctrinally in terms of its authority, clarity, and sufficiency in all matters of faith and morals. Finally, it ought to be noted that *sola Scriptura* was never meant as a denial of the usefulness of the Christian tradition as a subordinate norm in theology. The views of the Reformers developed out of a debate in the late medieval theology over the relation of Scripture and tradition, one party viewing the two as coequal norms, the other party viewing Scripture as the absolute and therefore prior norm, but allowing tradition a derivative but important secondary role in doctrinal statement. The Reformers and the Protestant orthodox held the latter view, on the assumption that tradition was a useful guide, that the trinitarian and christological statements of Nicaea, Constantinople, and Chalcedon were expressions of biblical truth, and that the great teachers of the church provided valuable instruction in theology that always needed to be evaluated in the light of Scripture. We encounter, particularly in the scholastic era of Protestantism, a profound interest in the patristic period and a critical, but often substantive, use of ideas and patterns enunciated by the medieval doctors. SEE *authoritas Scripturae; principia theologiae.*

soli Deo gloria: *glory to God alone.*

Soli Deo, non diabolo λύτρον persolvendum erat: *The ransom was* *paid, not to the devil, (but) to God alone;* a maxim adapted by Francis Pieper from Quenstedt (cf. Pieper, II, p. 380, and Baier-Walther, III, p. 112). The maxim encapsulates the central difference between the satisfaction theory of atonement held by both the medieval and the Protestant scholastics and the patristic ransom theory according to which the ransom was paid not to God, but to the devil.

solus, -a, -um (adj.): *only, alone.*

sōstikōs (σωστικῶς): *savingly;* in a saving way.

species: *species;* viz., either a group of individual things exhaustively identified as a group by a common concept or universal, or the universal itself as predicated of a group of individual things, the essence of which it fully or exhaustively identifies. SEE *genus.*

speculativus, -a, -um (adj.): *speculative;* synonymous with *contemplativus.* A concept can be identified as speculative or contemplative when it is considered as an end in, of, and by itself. Similarly, a discipline is called speculative when its truths are grasped in and for themselves and not for the sake of gaining a goal or end that is beyond the discipline in question. SEE *practicus.*

speculum electionis: *mirror of election;* a term used by Calvin in describing Christ as the one in whom individual election can be known and assurance of salvation can be found.

speranda: *things to be hoped for;* viz., the eternal or eschatological goals of Christian hope. SEE *agenda; credenda.*

spermatikos (σπερματικός): *spermatic;* i.e., like a seed; particularly, in patristic usage, the *Logos spermatikos,* or seed of the Logos, which is in the soul of man and which accounts for the truths of the universe known even to pagan philosophy.

spes meliorum temporum: *the hope of better times;* a phrase or term associated with the so-called *chiliasmus subtilis* or *subtilissimus* of the era of declining orthodoxy and pietism. The *spes meliorum temporum* is the hope for a gradual betterment of the world through the progress of God's grace, i.e., the gradual dawn of a millennial age. SEE *chiliasmus.*

sphragides (σφραγίδες; singular, σφραγίς): *seals;* specifically, seals that confirm or authenticate something; therefore, the sacraments as seals of the grace of God. SEE *baptismus; coena Domini.*

spiratio: *spiration* or *procession;* the personal property (SEE *proprietas*) of the Spirit and his personal relation (*relatio personalis,* q.v.) to the Father and the Son, strictly defined as the inward act by which the Father and the Son simultaneously and eternally produce the Spirit from their own substance, without division of substance, and entirely within the one divine essence. The scholastics also distinguish between *spiratio activa,* which is the activity of the Father and the Son spirating, and *spiratio passiva,* which is the movement of the Spirit being spirated. SEE *filiatio; generatio; notiones personales; Trinitas.*

spiritualitas: *spirituality;* i.e., immateriality of substance, an attribute of spiritual beings. SEE *spiritus.*

spiritus: *spirit; immaterial or nonmaterial substance;* any being whose substance is not material. The term *spiritus* can therefore be applied to God generally, to the Third Person of the Trinity specifically, to angelic beings, and to the soul. SEE *anima; pneumata leitourgika; spiritus completus; spiritus incompletus.*

spiritus completus: *a complete spirit;* i.e., a spirit complete in itself as spirit, the subsistence of which does not imply union with a material substance; a term applied to angels, but not to the human soul, which is *spiritus incompletus* (q.v.).

spiritus incompletus: *an incomplete spirit;* i.e., a spirit not complete in itself that requires for its proper subsistence union with a material substance; a term applied to the soul, but not applied to angels, since a soul, in order to perform its function, must be united to a body. Although they distinguish body from soul, the scholastics cannot be viewed as dualists, since they assume the incompleteness of either body or soul considered *in abstracto* (q.v.) and argue the integrity of the human being as a creature of body and soul. The soul is the *forma corporis,* or form of the body. SEE *anima; entelecheia; status animarum a corpore separatarum.*

Spiritus Sanctus: *the Holy Spirit; the Third Person of the Trinity.* SEE *Deus; Trinitas.*

sponsio: *a guarantee* or *surety;* specifically, a solemn promise between two parties. The term comes from Roman law and was adopted by the Reformed federalists as a designation for the promise made by God the Son to God the Father in the covenant of redemption, or *pactum salutis* (q.v.). The term was used by some synonymously with *fideiussio* (q.v.), which has the connotation of bond, or bail.

status animarum a corpore separatarum: *the state or condition of souls separated from the body;* viz., the so-called intermediate state. The Protestant scholastics, Lutheran and Reformed, are in agreement in their delineation of possible solutions to this question and in their doctrinal conclusions. They reject as error the teaching that the soul sleeps and is oblivious to all things, neither thinking nor feeling, i.e., *psychopannychia*, the soul-sleep, inasmuch as it contradicts Luke 23:43, "Today thou shalt be with me in paradise." They also reject the view that the soul enters a state of lethargy (*refrigerius!*) during which it has a foretaste of blessedness to come. The orthodox affirm a full and consummated blessedness of the souls of believers in which they experience the vision of God (*visio Dei*, q.v.) and have an immediate apprehension of God and God's truth (*cognitio Dei intuitiva*, q.v.). This blessedness falls short of the absolute consummation of the end-time (SEE *dies novissimus*) only because the soul itself is not complete, i.e., in union with the body (SEE *spiritus incompletus*). The place in which the souls of the blessed (*beati*, q.v.) await the end is paradise (*paradisio*, q.v.). The souls of the wicked also enter a conscious state after the death of the body, but it is a state of punishment in *Hades* (q.v.). SEE *anima; iudicium particulare et occultum; psychopannychia; purgatorium.*

status controversiae: *state of controversy;* frequently, a term for the section of a doctrinal *locus* in which debate over theological issues is surveyed. It occurs immediately before the statement of doctrinal conclusions.

status exaltationis: *state of exaltation;* i.e., the state or condition of the exalted Christ. The Lutheran orthodox begin the *status exaltationis* with the *descensus ad inferos* (q.v.), or descent into hell, whereas the Reformed begin it with the *resurrectio* (q.v.), or resurrection, of Christ. The remaining degrees of the state of exaltation are the ascension, the sitting of Christ at the right hand of God (SEE *sessio Christi*), and the final judgment (*iudicium extremum*, q.v.). The *status exaltationis*, according to the Reformed, is a state or condition that follows the *status humiliationis* (q.v.), or state of humiliation. The Lutheran orthodox, however, on the ground of their doctrine of the *communicatio idiomatum* (q.v.) and of the consequent possession (*ktēsis*, q.v.) of the divine attributes by the human nature of Christ, must regard Christ's humanity as always exalted, though in a hidden way during the *status humiliationis*. The *status exaltationis*, therefore, for Lutheran orthodoxy, is the manifestation of the full exercise of the divine attributes in and by Christ's humanity, which begins with the *descensus ad inferos*. The Reformed not only allow no concurrence of the two states, but also view the *status exaltationis* as a heavenly state of Christ. The Lutherans argue the *sessio Christi ad dextram Patris* to indicate the omnipresence of Christ's humanity.

status gloriosus: *glorious condition;* also **status coelestis**: *heavenly state or condition;* viz., the state or condition of Christ after his ascension, with particular reference to the exaltation and glorification of his human nature. See *status exaltationis*.

status gratiae: *the state or condition of grace;* also **status pacis**: *the state or condition of peace.*

status humiliationis: *state of humiliation*, sometimes called **status exinanitionis**: *state of self-emptying;* a term, together with its counterpart, the *status exaltationis* (q.v.), state of exaltation, belonging to the christological concept known as the two states of Christ, based on Phil. 2:5–11 and used as a basic structural feature in the Lutheran and the Reformed Christologies. The doctrine was first developed by the Lutherans as a reflection on the earthly suffering and humiliation of Christ in relation to the *communicatio idiomatum* (q.v.). In scholastic Lutheran theology, the incarnation itself is not considered an act of self-renunciation or self-emptying. *Kenōsis* or *exinanitio* is predicated of the God-man and not of the Word or of the Word's act of assuming flesh, since the *status humiliationis*, and not the incarnation itself, is what ends in the *status exaltationis*. The subject, therefore, of the *humiliatio* or *exinanitio* is Christ's human nature in union with the divine person, not the divine person itself. In a formal sense, the *humiliatio* consists both in the sufferings of Christ's humanity as such and in the renunciation, non-use, and concealment of the divine attributes that belong to Christ's humanity as a result of the *communicatio idiomatum*. The Lutheran view is also distinctive in its termination of the *status humiliationis* with Christ's death and burial, and in its considering the descent into hell (*descensus ad inferos*, q.v.) as the first stage of the *status exaltationis*.

In determining the beginning of the *status humiliationis* or *exinanitionis*, the Reformed make a distinction between *exinanitio*, or *kenōsis*, and *humiliatio*, or *tapeinōsis* (ταπείνωσις). The *exinanitio* or preliminary stage of the *status humiliationis* refers to the incarnation itself and the acceptance of servant-form by the Word. Nevertheless, since the Word in and of itself is in no way diminished in incarnation and since the incarnation remains in the *status exaltationis,* the *humiliatio* proper refers to the economy of ministry, earthly life, and suffering of the Incarnate One. Thus the Reformed disagree with the Lutherans by including the *kenōsis* and incarnation in the *status humiliationis.* The Reformed argue a withholding of the use of the divine attributes by Christ's divine nature from the *kenōsis* to the moment of resurrection. In addition, the Reformed view the *descensus ad inferos* as the final stage of the *status humiliationis.* See *anthrōpopatheia; exinanitio; ktēsis; occultatio.*

status integritatis: *state of integrity;* the state or condition of man before the fall when he was in full possession of the qualities of original righteousness and wisdom, and lived in the true knowledge of God in both perfect fellowship and godly service. See *imago Dei.*

status originalis: *original condition or state;* specifically, the original created condition of man and angels before the fall. See *iustitia originalis; status integritatis.*

status purorum naturalium: *the purely natural condition;* i.e., the condition of human nature unaided by grace. The concept of a *status purorum naturalium* and a resident capacity of human beings to move toward God on the basis of, or out of, purely natural abilities (*ex puris naturalibus*) was typical of the semi-Pelagian tendency in late medieval theology and was at the basis of the concept of human merit rejected by the Reformers (see *meritum de congruo*). The Protestant orthodox, both Lutheran and Reformed, follow the Reformers in rejecting the theology of merit and specifically argue that there could be no *status purorum naturalium* even before the fall, since even then human capacity for the good rested upon the grace of God. In this denial of a *status purorum naturalium,* and in the denial of the concept of a *donum superadditum* (q.v.), or superadded gift, of grace bestowed on man because of a meritorious act performed *ex puris naturalibus* prior to the fall, the orthodox stand on the fully Augustinian side of the scholastic tradition. The human nature of Adam and Eve, according to the Protestant scholastics and their Augustinian predecessors in the Middle Ages, received grace as an aspect of its original condition. See *donum concreatum.*

stipulatio: *stipulation or condition;* particularly, the *stipulatio foederis,* the legal foundation or condition for the covenant of grace. See *foedus gratiae.*

stricte: *strictly;* the opposite of *late,* loosely. *Stricte* and *late* are frequently used by Protestant scholastics as characterizations of definitions, *stricte* with reference to precise definition, *late* with reference to general or colloquial definition.

sub specie aeternitatis: *under the aspect or form of eternity;* viz., the viewing of a thing or idea in terms of the essential or universal principle that defines it; therefore, in accord with God, who is the essential or ontological ground of all things, the eternal measure of his creation.

subiectum: *subject;* anything of which either substance or any of the several categories of accident can be predicated. Therefore, in logic, a subject is the topic of predication, that about which the affirmation or denial is made in any proposition. In philosophy, the *subiectum* is that in which attributes inhere, i.e., a substance. SEE *accidens; obiectum; praedicatio; substantia.*

subiectum convertendum: *the converted subject;* viz., the individual believer considered as the *subiectum quod,* or passive subject, of conversion. SEE *conversio; subiectum quo/ subiectum quod.*

subiectum quo/subiectum quod: *the subject by which/the subject which.* The former term indicates an active subject or involvement of the subject in an activity; the latter term indicates an essentially passive subject. Thus, Christ's human nature is the *subiectum quo* of his sufferings, whereas the divine-human *persona* (q.v.) is the *subiectum quod* of the suffering.

subsistentia: *subsistence* or *subsistent;* indicating a particular being or existent, an individual instance of a given essence. In this latter sense, the Latin equivalent of *hypostasis,* and a more technical and philosophically adequate term than *persona* (q.v.) for indicating the Father, Son, and Spirit in the Trinity. SEE *modus subsistendi.*

substantia: *substance;* the underlying "stuff," material or spiritual, of things; that which exists. Emphasis here is on concrete reality as distinct from *essentia* (q.v.), which indicates simply what a thing is. In the Aristotelian perspective, *substantia* indicates a union of form and matter. Form (SEE *forma; universalia*) is the idea or actuality (*actus,* q.v.) of a thing; matter (*materia*) is the underlying corporeal substratum. Neither by itself is a thing (*res,* q.v.) or a substance, since *substantia* is the stuff of actual, individual things and is neither an abstract genus nor an unidentifiable, indeterminate material (SEE *materia prima*). Thus, substance is distinguished from essence, since it is not a universal considered in the abstract. Nonetheless, *substantia* can indicate the formal and material reality held in common by all members of a genus as well as the formal and material reality of an individual.

substantia cogitans: *thinking substance;* also **actus substantialis cogitandi** or **actus cogitandi**: *the substantial actualization of thinking* or *the actuality of thinking;* terms used as synonyms for soul in those few late-seventeenth-century Reformed authors influenced by the Cartesian dichotomization of all substance into thought and extension, the former being the basic Cartesian term for soul.

substantia individua intelligens: *an individual, intelligent substance;* a synonym for *persona* (q.v.).

suggestio verborum: *the suggestion of words;* a term used to clarify the doctrine of the verbal inspiration of Scripture, indicating that not only the minds of the *amanuenses* (q.v.), nor only the ideas in the text, but also the very words of the text are inspired, having been given to the *amanuenses* by suggestion of the Spirit. SEE *inspiratio; perfectio integralis; Scriptura sacra; theopneustos.*

summa: *the main point, principal issue,* or *substance;* hence, a textbook or compendium that gathers together in summary form the substance or principal issues of a discipline; thus, *summa theologiae,* the sum, substance, or compendium of theology.

summum bonum: *the highest good;* i.e., God as the source and end of all good.

summus princeps: *supreme ruler* or *sovereign;* a term applied to God as sovereign of the created order.

superadditum: *something superadded;* viz., something granted or given above and beyond the original constitution of a thing; also used as an adjective. SEE *donum superadditum.*

superbia: *pride.* SEE *septem peccata mortalia.*

suppositum: *supposit; a self-existent or self-subsistent thing.*

suppositum intelligens: *a thinking, self-subsistent being;* i.e., a person. SEE *persona.*

supra lapsum: *above or prior to the fall;* as opposed to *infra lapsum* (q.v.). Two basic views of predestination emerged from the development of Reformed doctrine in the late sixteenth and early seventeenth centuries: the supralapsarian view, sometimes referred to as full double predestination, and the infralapsarian view, frequently termed single predestination. Both views arise out of consideration of an eternal, logical "order of the things of the decree," or *ordo rerum decretarum*, in the mind of God. According to the supralapsarian view, the election and reprobation of individuals are logically prior to the divine decree of creation and the divine ordination to permit the fall. In the divine mind, the human subject of election and reprobation is conceived as *creabilis et labilis*, creatable and fallible, i.e., as a possibility for creation and as capable of falling. In this view, the prior purpose of God is the manifestation of his glory in the mercy of election and the justice of reprobation, while the creation itself and the decree to permit the fall are secondary purposes, or means to the end, of election and reprobation. The infralapsarian view, which is the confessional position of the Reformed churches, places the divine will to create human beings with free will and the decree to permit the fall prior to the election of some to salvation. Thus, in the divine mind the human subject of election is viewed in eternity as *creatus et lapsus*, created and fallen. In this view, the prior purpose of God is the creation of human beings for fellowship with himself, and the decree to elect some to salvation appears as a means to the end of that fellowship. The infralapsarian perspective is frequently called single predestination because its standard formulations represent God as electing some men for salvation out of the fallen mass of humanity and then, not decreeing reprobation, but merely passing over the rest, leaving them in their sin to their own damnation. The infralapsarian doctrine of predestination, therefore, arises out of the problem of the fall and salvation by grace, whereas the supralapsarian teaching arises out of a more abstract consideration of the eternity and omnipotence of God. See *causa; praedestinatio.*

sursum corda: *lift up (your) hearts;* a phrase from the liturgy of the Lord's Supper. It is especially important to the Reformed as an explanation of the union (SEE *unio sacramentalis*) between the participant in the Lord's Supper and the resurrected Christ. Rather than argue the presence of Christ's body in the elements, the Reformed will argue, in effect, the spiritual union of the believer with the exalted Christ, a participation in the thing signified (SEE *res sacramenti*) by means of faithful participation in the sign (*signum*, q.v.) and the concomitant operation of the Spirit that joins together by grace the uplifted heart of the believer and the person of Christ with all its benefits. SEE *praesentia spiritualis sive virtualis.*

sustentatio: *preservation, providential sustenance;* synonym, *conservatio.* SEE *continuata creatio; providentia.*

syllogismus practicus: *the practical syllogism;* a logical construction used by the Reformed in order to establish the *certitudo electionis* in and for an individual. Stated bluntly, it seems to rest certainty of election on the outward fruits of faith; in its usual form, however, it recognizes the exclusion of works from the causality of salvation and respects the doctrine that election occurs in Christ alone, and therefore states the logic of assurance in terms, first, of the scriptural promise, and, second, of the inward, spiritual fruits of the application of Christ's work by the Holy Spirit. As for the syllogism itself, the orthodox Reformed clearly state that the major must be read in Scripture, the external Word (*Verbum externum*), and that the minor, the internal Word (*Verbum internum*) of the Spirit, must be "read" in the heart. This formulation of the problem specifically avoids the possibility of an empirical *syllogismus practicus* as adumbrated by Theodore Beza. The basic form of the *syllogismus* (here taken from Francis Turretin) is as follows: *Quisquis vere credit et resipiscit electus sit; Atqui ego credo, etc.; Ergo electus sum:* "Whoever truly believes and becomes of a right spirit is elect; But in fact I believe, etc.; Therefore I am elect" (*Institutio theologiae,* IV. xiii.4). This basic logical form, in a multitude of varieties drawn from studies of the problems and temptations of daily life, is also found in the Puritan casuistry of "cases of conscience," all of which were developed specifically for the sake of self-examination and personal assurance of salvation. SEE *certitudo et gratiae praesentis et salutis aeternae; conscientia; incrementa fidei; terrores conscientiae.*

synaidios (συναΐδιος): *coeternal;* used by the fathers to indicate the coeternity, and therefore the equality, of the Father and the Son. SEE *Trinitas.*

synaphē (συναφή): *attachment, connection or union;* more commonly *synapheia* (q.v.).

synapheia (συνάφεια): *union* or *conjunction;* the term perhaps most often used by the fathers to indicate a union, both in trinitarian and christological statements and in statements regarding the union of believers with Christ and with one another.

synchōrētikōs (*συγχωρητικῶς*): *forgivingly;* having to do with forgiveness or concession.

synderesis: also **synteresis**: *the innate habit of the understanding which grasps basic principles of moral law apart from the activity of formal moral training;* a concept from Aristotle, used by the medieval scholastics as a synonym for the patristic term *scintilla conscientiae.* Bonaventure and Alexander of Hales viewed *synderesis* as a habit of will; Albert the Great and Thomas Aquinas placed it under the intellect. *Synderesis* can be distinguished from *conscientia* in that the latter is an act while *synderesis* is a *habitus* (q.v.), or capacity. See *conscientia.*

syneidēsis (*συνείδησις*): *conscience.* See *conscientia.*

synergismus: *synergism; i.e., a working together;* the term *συνεργός* is frequently employed in the Pauline literature to indicate a "fellow worker" or "co-worker" in the propagation of the gospel (Rom. 16:3, 9, 21), and even a "helper" of God (1 Thess. 3:2), but never to indicate a cooperation of the individual person with the grace of God in the work of salvation. When the orthodox Lutheran and Reformed theologians apply the term to the doctrine of cooperation between God and man before the grace of regeneration, they do so with the intention of indicating an unorthodox and unbiblical doctrine. A distinction ought also to be made between the Melanchthonian and Arminian forms of synergism. Melanchthonian synergism, as debated in sixteenth-century Lutheranism and excluded by the *Formula of Concord,* argues a coincidence of the Word, the Spirit, and the human will not refusing God's grace. This form of synergism emphasizes the coincident work of Word and Spirit and the openness of the will to Word and Spirit but does not set will prior to grace as an active power or faculty capable of applying grace to the individual (*facultas se applicandi ad gratiam,* q.v.). Melanchthon's teaching is synergistic, but does not deserve to be called semi-Pelagian. The Arminian view, however, not only supposes the cooperation of the will with Word and Spirit, but the ability of the will to apply or attach itself to grace. In the Arminian view, the will is the effective ground of salvation. This perspective is not only synergistic but also fully semi-Pelagian. See *cooperatio; intuitu fidei; praevisa fidei; regeneratio.*

synergoi (*συνεργοί*): *fellow workers* or *co-workers.*

syntaxia (*συνταξία*): *a collection* or *arrangement.*

Tt

ta dynata (τὰ δυνατά): *possible things;* viz., all possible existents that are defined as possible insofar as they are not in violation of the law of noncontradiction; as distinguished from *ta mellonta* (q.v.), things that are to be, the possible existents, or *possibilia,* will not necessarily be brought into being. SEE *possibilia; scientia libera; scientia necessaria; scientia simplicis intelligentiae.*

ta mellonta (τὰ μέλλοντα): *things that are to be;* viz., the possible things that God wills to make as opposed to the possible things that God wills to leave unmade; thus, only a part of the whole realm of the possible, *ta dynata* (q.v.). SEE *possibilia.*

tantus, -a, -um (adj.): *only.*

tapeinōsis (ταπείνωσις): *humiliation.* SEE *status humiliationis.*

tautotēs (ταὐτότης): *identity.*

tautousios (ταὐτούσιος): *of identical essence.* SEE *homoousios.*

teleiōsis (τελείωσις): *fulfillment* or *perfection;* e.g., Luke 1:45.

telos (τέλος): *goal.* SEE *causa finalis; finis.*

tentatio: *trial, affliction, temptation;* distinguished into (1) *tentatio seductionis,* seductive temptation, or trial of seduction, behind which lies the purpose of Satan or another evil agent to draw an individual into sin, and (2) *tentatio probationis,* probative temptation, or affliction of probation, also called *dokimasia* (δοκιμασία), which comes from God and has as its intention the testing and strengthening of an individual believer's faith and obedience. *Tentatio probationis* is distinguished also from the *castigationes paternae* (q.v.) and *paideia* (παιδεία), which teach believers the true path in life through cross and suffering.

terminus a quo: *the terminus or point from which;* i.e., the point of departure of a process.

terminus ad quem: *the terminus or point to which;* i.e., the final goal of a process; also **terminus ultimus**: *ultimate goal;* and **terminus proprius**: *proper goal.*

terminus gratiae peremptorius: *the peremptory limit of grace.* SEE *terminus salutis peremptorius.*

terminus salutis peremptorius: *the peremptory limit of salvation;* a pietist doctrine condemned by orthodox Lutheranism, according to which each individual was given a limited time to respond to the divine offer of salvation, after which time the offer would, in effect, be retracted and salvation no longer possible. As a corollary of this doctrine, its proponents argued also a limit to the offer of grace, a *terminus gratiae peremptorius.* In response, the orthodox argued the full offer of salvation throughout the life of the individual and placed the limit of grace only in the individual sinner's unwillingness to respond.

terminus vocationis ad quem: *the point to which of calling;* i.e., the church as the place or end to which men are called by the gospel. SEE *vocatio.*

terra: *earth.*

terra incognita: *an unknown land;* figuratively, a topic as yet untraversed or unmapped by the intellect.

terrores conscientiae: *terrors of conscience;* fears of the anger of God and of eternal damnation resting on a perception of one's own sinfulness and moral inability. When generated by the gracious work of the Spirit in and through the second use of the law, the *usus elenchticus, terrores conscientiae* are a preparation for the understanding and acceptance of the gospel. The term is more typical of Lutheran than Reformed orthodoxy, but represents a concept similar to—though less in danger of tending toward works-righteousness than—the idea of preparation found in seventeenth-century Puritan theology. SEE *contritio; lex Dei; praeparatio ad conversionem; usus legis.*

tertius usus legis: *third use of the law.* SEE *usus legis.*

tessera: *token or sign;* a term sometimes used with reference to the visible elements in the sacraments; more commonly, *signum* (q.v.), or sign, and *pignus* (q.v.), pledge or assurance, are used. SEE *sacramentum.*

testamentum: *testament;* like the Greek *diathēkē,* the Latin term *testamentum* has a double meaning: either covenant or a legal bequest. Thus, the Protestant scholastics will use the term to indicate the old covenant and the new covenant, in other words, the *oeconomia,* or economy, of God's covenant as fulfilled in Christ; to indicate the parts of Scripture in which these two economies or dispensations are related, the Old Testament and the New Testament; and to indicate the covenant of grace (*foedus gratiae,* q.v.) in which mankind receives the *testamentum,* or bequest, of Christ, the *testator* of the gift of salvation which is made available to his heirs upon his death. SEE *dispensatio.*

testes veritatis: *witnesses of the truth;* only the scriptural revelation can be the norm of doctrine, but the teachers and confessions of the church are aids in interpretation insofar as they are witnesses of the truth that manifest its presence and preservation in the life of the church. Lutheranism, even more than the Reformed tradition, places its confessions in the category of *testes veritatis.* SEE *norma.*

testimonium: *testimony* or *witness;* specifically, in Reformed sacramental theology, a term used with reference to the bread, the wine, and the promise of Christ in the words of institution (SEE *verbum institutionis*). The bread, wine, and promise are the *testimonium* to the offering of Christ's body and blood once for all on the cross and to the *unio cum Christo* made possible through faith by the Holy Spirit. The offering of Christ and the union with Christ are the "thing attested," or "thing witnessed," *res testata.* The distinction between *testimonium* and *res testata* parallels that between *signum* (q.v.) and *res signata,* though it tends toward a more covenantal construction than the latter.

testimonium internum Spiritus Sancti: *internal testimony of the Holy Spirit;* the inward work of the Spirit that testifies to faith concerning the truth of Scripture. The Reformers and the Protestant scholastics were adamant in their belief both that the *testimonium* is necessary to the subjective receipt of the truth of Scripture, and that the *testimonium* only ratifies the truth of the text and adds *no* new information. The *testimonium* also functions to make faith the *prin-*

cipium cognoscendi internum of theology. See *principia theologiae; revelatio immediata.*

textus receptus: *the received text;* i.e., the standard Greek text of the New Testament published by Erasmus (1516) and virtually contemporaneously by Ximenes (the Complutensian Polyglot, printed in 1514, published in 1522), and subsequently reissued with only slight emendation by Stephanus (1550), Beza (1565), and Elzevir (1633). The term *textus receptus* comes from a phrase in the Elzevir preface, *"Textum* ergo habes, nunc ab omnibus *receptum"* and was adopted as a standard usage only after the period of orthodoxy, although it does refer to the text supported by the Protestant scholastics as the authentic text *quoad verba.* See *authoritas divina duplex.*

theanthrōpos (θεάνθρωπος): *God-man;* rendered into Latin as *Deus-homo,* whence the title *Cur Deus homo?* of Anselm's famous treatise.

theologia (from θεός, God, and λόγος, word or reason): *theology;* the scholastics generally defined *theologia* as *sermo vel ratio de Deo,* a word or rational discourse concerning God, and therefore as human wisdom or knowledge concerning God. More precisely, *theologia* can indicate four things: (1) divine revelation itself given in Scripture, the sum of all knowledge necessary to salvation; given by inspiration, it is therefore free from all error; (2) the knowledge held by faith that is gained either by the direct reading of Scripture or by drawing conclusions from the text of Scripture; (3) the science (*scientia,* q.v.), or wisdom (*sapientia,* q.v.), constructed from revelation by means of reason for the explication and defense of the faith; (4) the divine self-knowledge which is the archetype (*theologia archetypa,* q.v.) of all true knowledge of God.

Theological system is primarily a representation of the third category: the science or wisdom constructed for the explication and defense of the faith. Here the Protestant scholastics distinguish between *theologia naturalis* (q.v.), or natural theology, which rests upon the light of nature or revelation of God through his effects in nature, and *theologia supernaturalis sive revelata,* supernatural or revealed theology, which rests upon divine revelation and presents the truths that are necessary to salvation and inaccessible to the unaided human reason. The Protestant orthodox systems, both Reformed and Lutheran, consist in revealed theology, and manifest little or no attention to the exposition of a positive natural theology. This characteristic is manifest in the identification of Scripture and not reason as the cognitive foundation or *principium cognoscendi* of theology (see *principia theologiae*). This revealed theology, inasmuch as it is a reflection of the divine self-knowledge or *theologia archetypa*, is also characterized as a form of *theologia ectypa* (q.v.), or ectypal theology, and as *theologia in via*, theology on the way to God, or *theologia viatorum* (q.v.), theology of pilgrims or those on the way. Finally, there is some debate among the Protestant scholastics concerning the status of theology as a science. They are virtually unanimous in arguing that theology is not a *scientia speculativa*, or speculative science, since speculative knowledge is knowledge that is properly known in and for itself, whereas theology is clearly a form of knowledge that leads believers to God. Theology is, therefore, primarily practical. Many of the orthodox, both Lutheran and Reformed, refer to theology as a *scientia practica*. Others dissent, on the ground that theology, although surely practical, is not a science properly so-called. *Scientia* indicates a body of knowledge resting on the evidences and argument of reason and characterized by demonstrative certainty (*certitudo*, q.v.). Theology, however, rests not on logical demonstration, but on divine authority accepted in faith; it may therefore be classed as a *sapientia*, or form of wisdom, not as a *scientia*. In either case, theology can be called a practical capacity, or disposition of the intellect (*habitus practicus intellectus*), the goal of which is redemption, and the material or material object of which is the *credenda* (q.v.), or articles of faith (*articuli fidei*), and the *agenda*, or things to be done as the practical result of faith, i.e., Christian morality.

Theologia a Deo docetur, Deum docet, et ad Deum ducit: *Theology is taught by God, teaches of God, and leads to God;* a phrase of Thomas Aquinas frequently cited with favor by both the Reformed and Lutheran scholastics as a basic characterization of theology.

theologia acroamatica: *higher theology;* the theology of the learned, as opposed to *theologia catechetica;* a term favored by the Lutheran scholastics as a designation for theological system taught in the university to clergy and theologians for the sake of the detailed exposition and defense of the high mysteries of the faith. See *medulla*.

theologia angelorum: *the theology of angels;* viz., a form of ectypal theology known by angels and, because of the spiritual excellence of the blessed angels and because of their proximity to God, a higher form of the knowledge of God than that which is attainable by man. See *theologia ectypa*.

theologia archetypa: *archetypal theology;* the infinite knowledge of God known only to God himself, which is the archetype or ultimate

299

pattern for all true theology. Since God is infinite and simple, the divine essence being identical with all of the divine attributes, the *omniscientia Dei* (q.v.), which is the *theologia archetypa*, is also God himself. SEE *theologia ectypa*.

theologia beatorum: *theology of the blessed;* the theology of which the blessed elect are capable in heaven according to the *liber gloriae,* the "book of glory," and the *lumen gloriae,* the "light of glory." The *theologia beatorum,* although still an ectypal knowledge of God (SEE *theologia ectypa*), is nonetheless clearer and fuller than the *theologia viatorum* (q.v.), the theology of earthly pilgrims or wanderers searching for the heavenly city. It is the perfected form of human theology, equivalent to the final vision of God (SEE *visio Dei*).

theologia catechetica: *catechetical theology;* basic theology taught to, and required of, all Christians, in which the necessary truths of the faith are set forth, specifically, the doctrines of the creed and the meaning of the sacraments, of the Decalogue, and of the Lord's Prayer.

theologia crucis: *theology of the cross;* a term used by Luther and descriptive of his insight into the nature of revelation and therefore of theology as a whole. God has chosen to reveal himself, not as human reason describes him in its rational theology of glory (*theologia gloriae,* q.v.), but in the weakness and the scandal of the cross. True knowledge of God is, therefore, a knowledge of God that rests upon the hiddenness of God in his revelation, a knowledge that humbles worldly reason and wisdom. Like Luther's distinction between God hidden and God revealed (*Deus absconditus/Deus revelatus,* q.v.), this concept of a *theologia crucis* militates against the marriage of theology and philosophy contemplated by the medieval scholastics.

theologia ectypa: *ectypal theology;* i.e., all true finite theology, defined as a reflection of the divine archetype. *Theologia ectypa* is, therefore, a broad category into which all knowledge of God available to finite minds is gathered, with the exception of false theology (*theologia falsa,* q.v.). *Theologia naturalis* (q.v.) can therefore be considered as ectypal theology insofar as it is a true reflection of the being of God. In view of the problem of human sinfulness, true natural theology must be a natural theology of the regenerate (*theologia naturalis regenitorum*); and an unregenerate natural theology, i.e., a natural theology arising outside of the church, must belong to the category of *theologia falsa* as a theology of (pagan) philosophers, a *theologia* *philosophorum.* The greater part of *theologia ectypa* concerns the varieties of supernatural or revealed theology (*theologia supernaturalis sive revelata*). The varieties of ectypal revealed theology are distinguished according to knower. Thus the scholastics identify *theologia angelorum* (q.v.), theology of angels; *theologia unionis* (q.v.), theology of union, i.e., the theology known to Jesus because of the hypostatic union; *theologia beatorum* (q.v.), theology of the blessed or heavenly saints; and *theologia viatorum* (q.v.), theology of the pilgrims, i.e., theology of temporal mankind in its search for the heavenly city. These categories serve to define the limits of human theology. It is a theology lower than that of angels or of Christ or of the blessed. The Protestant scholastics also recognize distinctions within the *theologia viatorum;* human theology has been affected by the fall and is further affected by the limits of human intelligence. Thus, there is *theologia viatorum ante lapsum,* human theology before the fall such as Adam and Eve knew in their intimate fellowship with God in the garden, and *theologia viatorum post lapsum,* pilgrim theology after the fall, limited not only by the finite intelligence of man, but also by the stain of sin and the inability of the sinner to have pure or perfect fellowship with God. All human theology is therefore *theologia viatorum post lapsum;* but not all human theology after the fall is identical, and, surely, not all human theology is conceived as well as it could be conceived. Thus, the scholastics distinguish between *theologia in se,* theology in itself, or theology ideally considered, and *theologia in subiecto,* theology in the subject, or theology as it actually exists in the works of theologians. This *theologia in subiecto* is, then, triply limited—by humanity, by the fall, and by the individual intellect. At the close of the seventeenth century, Johann Heidegger could write of the *imperfectio theologiae,* the imperfection of theology. Nevertheless, this highly limited and restricted human theology can claim to represent divine truth and to be a valid form of *theologia ectypa* insofar as it locates all authority in the revealed Word of God rather than in human reason or in the institutional church.

theologia falsa: *false theology;* viz., pagan teaching concerning God as opposed to all forms of Christian theology (*theologia Christiana*) both natural and revealed. Some of the Protestant scholastics divide all finite theology first into *theologia vera* (true theology) and *theologia falsa* in order to place all the divisions of *theologia ectypa* (q.v.), or ectypal theology, under *theologia vera.* Since false theology does not reflect the divine archetype, it cannot be classed as *theologia ectypa.* In elaborating on this model, the Protestant scholastics follow Augustine's use of the typology of theology developed by the Roman philosopher Varro. Pagan theology divides into the theology of the myths or fables (*theologia fabulosa*), the civil theology of the empire (*theologia civilis*), and the theology of the philosophers (*theologia philosophorum*). All three categories belong to *theologia falsa* as contrasted with the *theologia vera* of Christianity. SEE *theologia archetypa; theologia naturalis.*

theologia gloriae: *theology of glory;* Luther's term for the rationalistic theology of the scholastics that discussed God in terms of his glorious attributes rather than in terms of his self-revelation in suffering and cross. SEE *theologia crucis.*

theologia in se: *theology in itself;* the Scotist term for the theology known in and of itself to the divine mind. The divine mind is the only mind with a knowledge of God and God's works that is proportionate to the object of theology (*obiectum theologiae,* q.v.), i.e., proportionate to God and his works. The term is used in a different sense by the Protestant orthodox to indicate human theology in an ideal form distinct from its actual occurrence in any individual intellect. The Scotist concept of *theologia in se* appears in Protestant orthodoxy as *theologia archetypa* (q.v.), and, among the Lutherans, also as *theologia unionis* (q.v.). SEE *theologia nostra.*

theologia irregenitorum: *theology of the unregenerate;* i.e., correct doctrinal knowledge held by a person untouched by saving grace; *fides historica* (q.v.) raised to the level of a full system.

theologia naturalis: *natural theology;* viz., the knowledge of God that is available to reason through the light of nature. *Theologia naturalis* can know of God as the highest good (*summum bonum,* q.v.), and it can know of the end of man in God on the basis of perfect obedience to the natural law (*lex naturalis,* q.v.). It is therefore insufficient to save man but sufficient to leave him without excuse in his sins. The Protestant orthodox include virtually no natural theology in their systems and never view natural theology, human reason, or the light of nature as a foundation upon which revealed theology can build. SEE *revelatio generalis/revelatio specialis; theologia naturalis regenitorum; usus philosophiae.*

theologia naturalis/theologia revelata sive supernaturalis: *natural theology/revealed or supernatural theology.*

theologia naturalis regenitorum: *natural theology of the regenerate;* in the context of the universal Protestant assumption that fallen natural reason and/or pagan philosophy could produce no saving knowledge of God, the connection between natural and revealed theology was necessarily severed, raising the question of the possibility of finding truths about God in the created order. Beza is usually credited with the formal statement of a natural theology of the regenerate, a sense of the divine work in creation, useful to Christian theology, but possible only in the context of a prior saving knowledge of God. SEE *duplex cognitio Dei; theologia irregenitorum.*

Theologia non est habitus demonstrativus, sed exhibitivus: *Theology is not a demonstrative, but an exhibitive habit;* theology, considered as a human capacity or disposition, does not follow philosophy in attempting to demonstrate its truths rationally but rather exhibits or proclaims its truth to the world. The maxim in this form is Lutheran, but the Reformed scholastics concur, particularly in distinguishing theological certainty and the *genus* of theological knowledge from philosophical certainty and from the *genus* of philosophical knowledge. SEE *certitudo; genus theologiae.*

theologia nostra: *our theology;* the Scotist term for human knowledge of God and of God's essence given to us by Christ. It is generally equivalent to the Protestant orthodox *theologia viatorum* (q.v.), i.e., to human ectypal theology (*theologia ectypa,* q.v.) resting upon revelation.

theologia positiva: *positive theology;* i.e., theology positively, objectively, or thetically stated according to the logic of its doctrines, as distinguished from a negative or polemical theology stated according to the order or logic of debate with adversaries. The Lutheran scholastics favor the term as a description of a scriptural and didactic theology organized by *loci.*

theologia supernaturalis sive revelata: *supernatural or revealed theology.* SEE *theologia; theologia naturalis.*

Theologia symbolica non est argumentativa: *Symbolical theology is not argumentative;* i.e., theology that is the result of symbolical or allegorical reasoning cannot provide the foundation or presupposition of a new argument. Proper argumentation begins from simple, literal foundations. SEE *quadriga.*

theologia unionis: *theology of union;* viz., the knowledge of God that is available to Christ according to his human nature in its union with the person of the Word. The Reformed attribute this knowledge of God both to the fellowship, or *koinōnia,* of the union (SEE *communio naturarum*) and to the extraordinary gifts (*dona extraordinaria finita,* q.v.) bestowed upon Christ's human nature by the Holy Spirit. Just as the *dona extraordinaria* are *finita,* finite, and suited to the finitude of Christ's human nature, so is the knowledge bestowed finite. According to the Reformed, the *theologia unionis* is a form of ectypal theology (*theologia ectypa,* q.v.), albeit an exalted form. The Lutheran scholastics, following out the implications of their distinctive doctrine of the communication of proper qualities (*communicatio idiomatum,* q.v.), argue the infinitude of the *theologia unionis* as a result of the divine omniscience communicated to Christ's human nature in the personal union. In the Lutheran view, the *theologia unionis* is identical with the archetypal theology (*theologia archetypa,* q.v.), which is the divine mind itself.

theologia viatorum: *theology of the* viatores, *or pilgrims;* a term applied to the incomplete or imperfect theology of believers in the world, in contrast to the theology of those who have reached their end in God, the *theologia beatorum* (q.v.). SEE *in via; theologia ectypa; viator.*

theopneustos (θεόπνευστος): *God-breathed, inspired;* a term used to describe both the human authors of Scripture as acted upon by the Spirit in their work of writing and the character of the resulting written text as Word of God. SEE *inspiratio; mandatum scribendi; Scriptura sacra; Verbum Dei.*

theoprepēs (θεοπρεπής): *godly, fit for God;* hence, in scholastic usage, proper to God, viz., the virtues of goodness, holiness, and righteousness.

Theos (Θεός): *God.* SEE *Deus.*

theotēs (θεότης): *deity, divinity;* used therefore as a synonym for *deitas* and *divinitas.*

Theotokos (Θεοτόκος): *bearer of God;* a title given to the Virgin Mary by the Alexandrian and Cappadocian theologians of the fourth and fifth centuries, predicated upon a *communicatio idiomatum in abstracto* (q.v.), the communication of divine attributes to the human nature. Nestorius's polemical denial of the title *Theotokos* as an Arian or Apollinarian heresy touched off the controversy leading to the Council of Chalcedon (A.D. 451).

theseōs bebaiōsis (θέσεως βεβαίωσις): *a firm or steadfast declaration.*

thrēskeia (θρησκεία): *religion, worship, especially the religious service dedicated to God;* e.g., Acts 26:5. SEE *religio.*

timor Dei: *fear of God.* SEE *religio; timor filialis.*

timor filialis: *filial fear;* viz., a fear of God characteristic of true children who both fear God's anger and stand in loving awe of his righteousness (*iustitia Dei*, q.v.), to be distinguished from *timor servilis*, servile fear, characteristic of those who merely fear divine punishment. SEE *attritio; contritio; religio.*

totidem verbis: *in so many words.*

totus/totum: *the whole person/the whole thing;* a distinction used by the Reformed, particularly with reference to the omnipresence of Christ as defined by the *communicatio idiomatum* (q.v.). Thus, the *totus Christus*, i.e., the whole person of Christ, is omnipresent, inasmuch as the divine person is, by virtue of his divinity, omnipresent; but the *totum Christi*, all of Christ, i.e., both natures, cannot be omnipresent, since the human nature must be in one place.

traductio; also **tradux**: *a transmission* or *transfer;* specifically, the transmission of the soul by generation from parents to children, or the transfer of sin from parents to children by the act of conception. SEE *anima; propagatio peccati.*

transitivus, -a, -um (adj.): *transitive;* having to do with transition or passing over from one being to another or one condition to another. Thus, both conversion (*conversio*, q.v.) and justification (*iustificatio*, q.v.) can be described as transitive acts or actions (*actus transitivus*) inasmuch as both begin in God and pass over to the human subject. *Actus transitivus* is synonymous with *actus transiens*, transient act or action.

transubstantiatio: *transubstantiation;* viz., the doctrine of Christ's sacramental presence in the Eucharist that came into prominence in the Middle Ages, was declared *de fide* (q.v.) by the Fourth Lateran Council (1215), and explicated in the terms of the Aristotelian language of the thirteenth century. According to the theory of *transub-*

stantiatio, the substance (*substantia*, q.v.) of the bread and wine, or more precisely, the substantial form (*forma substantialis;* SEE *forma*), as distinct from the material substratum (SEE *materia prima*) of the bread and wine, undergoes a transformation (*transformatio*) or formal conversion (*conversio formalis*) and becomes, in the consecration, the true body and blood of Christ. The transformation, however, is only a transformation of substance, not of the incidental properties or accidents (SEE *accidens*) of the bread and wine. The appearance of bread and wine, therefore, remains. This transubstantiation is neither the creation of a new substance nor an annihilation of the substances initially present, but an actual conversion of the substance of bread and wine into the substance of body and blood. This conversion is entirely supernatural and therefore distinct from the two types of transformation that occur daily in nature: the *conversio accidentalis*, accidental conversion, or *transaccidentatio*, transaccidentation, as a result of which the substance remains unaltered but the incidental properties or accidents change; and the *conversio substantialis*, or substantial conversion, as a result of which one substance is changed into another, as by decay or digestion, and both the substance and the accidents which inhere in it change. *Transubstantiatio*, though not possible in the natural order, rests on the separability of substance and accidents witnessed in *transaccidentatio*, and indicates simply the third logical possibility involved in the alteration of substance and accident. The theory of transubstantiation was not without opposition even in the Middle Ages. Without denying the authority of the church or explicitly attacking the doctrine from a theological point of view, Scotus and several of the late medieval nominalists argued the philosophical improbability of substantial change apart from alteration of accidents and expressed a decided philosophical preference for consubstantiation (*consubstantiatio*, q.v.), the presence of Christ's body and blood with the bread and wine. John Wyclif even more pointedly denied the doctrine, arguing the continuance of the bread and wine after the consecration and a spiritual presence of Christ for believers only. The Reformers and the Protestant orthodox uniformly reject transubstantiation. SEE *impanatio; manducatio indignorum; praesentia realis; praesentia spiritualis sive virtualis.*

trichotomia (τριχοτομία): *trichotomy; a division into three parts.*

Trinitas: *Trinity;* viz., the existence of God as one in essence (*essentia*, q.v.) and three in person (*persona*, q.v.). The doctrine of the Trinity arises out of the church's reflection on the biblical declaration that God is one, but is known as Father, Son, and Spirit. The correlation of the way in which God is known through his self-revelation and the way in which God truly is in himself constitutes the necessary presupposition of true doctrine, i.e., of the truth of the revelation itself; therefore, the revelation that God is one and the revelation that God is three cannot be reduced to an eternal oneness and a temporal or economical threeness. Equally, the oneness cannot be defined in such a way that it ultimately abolishes the threeness, or the threeness in such a way that it ultimately abolishes the oneness. Trinity, therefore, is an attempt to avoid both a monadic oneness and a tritheistic view of God through the affirmation that God is one in essence and three in person. The terms used to elucidate this doctrine come from both the patristic and the medieval church. For convenience, we introduce the patristic terms first and then give their later scholastic equivalents and elaborations. (*N. B.* All the terms employed in this section are defined individually, some at length, in the alphabetical order of the lexicon.)

The first important set of terms was established by Tertullian (ca. 220) in his debate with the modalistic monarchian heresy. Against the notion that the monarchy, or sole rule, of God could best be explained if the Father, Son, and Spirit were modes or roles taken by the one God in his self-revelation, Tertullian argued the eternal truth of God's existence as one and as Father, Son, and Spirit: God is one in *substantia* or substance and three in *persona* (person). In the Greek church, the problem was not so much the establishment of a language of oneness and threeness as the defense of the essential oneness or numerical unity of the Godhead in the Father, Son, and Spirit. Against the subordinationistic and tritheistic view of Arius, Athanasius and the Council of Nicaea (A.D. 325) argued the consubstantiality of the Father, Son, and Spirit. The Arians viewed the persons as of different essence (*heteroousios*) and as unlike (*anomoios*); Athanasius held that the persons were of one essence, or consubstantial (*homoousios*). Although the term *homoousios* was embodied in the Creed of Nicaea, many bishops of the fourth century doubted the wisdom of speaking about God in the potentially materialistic philosophical language of essence (*ousia*). Others, accepting the language of *ousia*, thought that *homoousios*, or consubstantiality, threatened the conception of God as truly three. They found the term reminiscent of modalistic monarchianism. So they proposed to argue, against both the Arians and the Athanasians, that Father, Son, and Spirit were of like essence (*homoiousios*) or, with a view to avoiding the question of essence entirely, that Father, Son, and Spirit were like or similar (*homoios*). Final acceptance of the Athanasian language of *homoousios* was made possible by the use of that term in connection with an adequate explanation of the threeness of the

Godhead. This was the achievement of the Cappadocian fathers, Basil of Caesarea, Gregory of Nyssa, and Gregory of Nazianzus. The Cappadocians argued one *ousia* but three *hypostases,* defining *hypostasis* as a particularization, or an individual instance, of an essence, or *ousia.* Thus Peter, James, and John are three individual instances, or *hypostases,* of the essence, or *ousia,* of humanity. In order to avoid a tritheism of three essentially coequal gods, the Cappadocians further stipulated that the entire divine *ousia* is indivisibly present in the three *hypostases* or, more precisely, that the three *hypostases* are eternally subsistent relations in the one *ousia.* Expressed individually as relations, the *hypostases* of the Father (*Pater*), Son (*Hyios*), and Spirit (*Pneuma*) are the unbegottenness (*agennēsia*) of the Father, the begottenness (*gennēsia*) of the Son, and the procession (*ekporeusis*) of the Spirit, all of which occur eternally, without beginning or end, in the divine *ousia.* This trinitarian model is characterized by a unity of essence and a threeness, with relational subordination in order only. The Father is understood as the first principle (*archē*) of the Trinity and, therefore, as the unifying principle of the *hypostases.* The Son is begotten from the Father, and the Spirit proceeds from the Father through the Son.

The Western or Latin fathers recognized the validity or orthodoxy of this Greek expression but realized also the difference between it and the Western view, together with the difficulty of establishing Latin equivalents to the Greek terms used by the Cappadocians. *Ousia,* expressive of the oneness of divine essence, was viewed as the equivalent of Tertullian's *substantia,* substance. *Hypostasis,* however, was only with difficulty assimilated to *persona,* since before the Cappadocian modification of the term, it had been used synonymously with *ousia* and also translated as *substantia.* In addition, *persona,* or person, does not have a philosophical or metaphysical capability coordinate with that of *substantia.* Two terms were therefore ultimately added to the Latin vocabulary, both of which had a major impact on scholastic formulation: *subsistentia,* indicating an individual instance of a *substantia,* as the equivalent of *hypostasis;* and *modus subsistendi,* mode of subsisting or manner of subsistence, as an attempt to express the implication of *hypostasis* as a relation within the Trinity. The latter term is particularly important for the distinctive Western and Augustinian view of the coequality of the persons as modes of subsistence of the one divine substance or essence (*essentia*). In the Western view, order and relation do not indicate subordination but are rather evidences of absolute coequality. Rather than view the Father as alone proceeding the Spirit, Western trinitarian theory argues the double procession of the Spirit from the Father and the Son (*filioque,* literally, "and the Son") and views the Spirit as the bond of love between the Father and the Son (*vinculum caritatis*). The Spirit, in this view, stands as a reciprocal relation between the Father and the Son; here, in contrast to the Greek theory, he accounts for the oneness of the three persons. In both the Greek and Latin trinitarian theories, the common possession of the entire essence by the persons is described as a coinherence of the persons in the essence and in one another: *perichōrēsis* or *emperichōrēsis* in Greek, *circumincessio* in Latin. Although it became the normative Latin usage to replace *substantia* with *essentia*, *homoousios* was rendered by both *coessentialis* and *consubstantialis*, coessential and consubstantial. Trinity can thus be defined as three persons in one divine essence (*tres personae in una essentia divina*) or as one divine essence subsisting in three modes (*una divina essentia in tribus modis subsistis*), the unity of essence being guaranteed by the consubstantiality and coinherence of the persons, the distinction of persons being manifest in their relations.

This patristic terminology was drawn into the scholastic formulation of the doctrine, with Latin equivalents being established for all the Greek terms and with general categories being developed in order to understand or describe the relation of the terms one to another. All the relations of the persons and corresponding activities or operations in the divine essence are called by the scholastics *operationes* or *opera Dei personalia*, operations or personal works of God. The term serves to distinguish the begetting and the proceeding of Son and Spirit from the common work of the Godhead, the *opera Dei essentialia*, or essential works of God. The *opera Dei personalia* can be considered (1) in terms of the activity itself of begetting and proceeding, (2) in terms of the persons or *hypostases* themselves, (3) in terms of the relations between the *hypostases*, and (4) in terms of the full set of personal characteristics implied by the persons and their relations. Thus (1) the Trinity is seen in terms of two emanations (*emanationes*), the begetting (*generatio*), or generation, of the Son and the procession (*processio*), or spiration (*spiratio*), of the Spirit. *Generatio* is the Latin equivalent of *gennēsia; processio* that of *ekporeusis*. (2) The two *emanationes* imply the three *personae* or *hypostases* of the Trinity: the Father (*Pater*) who begets the Son and spirates the Spirit; the Son (*Filius*) who is begotten by the Father and who also spirates the Spirit; and the Spirit who is spirated by or proceeds from the Father and the Son. Note that the scholastics assume the Western trinitarian model and the *filioque* or double-procession of the Spirit. (3) The two emanations and three persons are related to one another in this model by four personal relations (sing., *relatio personalis*); the Father relates to the Son by his active generation (*generatio activa*) of the Son, and to the Spirit by his

309

active spiration (*spiratio activa*) of the Spirit; the Son relates to the Father by his begottenness or passive generation (*generatio passiva*), which is also termed filiation (*filiatio*), and to the Spirit by his active spiration of the Spirit, identical with the *spiratio activa* of the Spirit by the Father; and the Spirit relates to the Father and the Son by his procession, or passive spiration (*spiratio passiva*), from both Father and Son. The four personal relations, therefore, are *generatio activa*, *generatio passiva*, *spiratio activa*, and *spiratio passiva*, each active emanation being reflected in a passive reciprocal relation. (4) The trinitarian language is completed by the delineation actively and passively of the hypostatic or personal character (*character hypostaticus sive personalis*) of each of the three persons or, in other words, by the statement of the five *notiones personales* that identify the three persons individually and in their relations. The hypostatic character of the Father is his paternity (*paternitas*), which is defined by three *notiones*, or notions: *innascibilitas*, or unbegottenness, *generatio activa*, and *spiratio activa*. (*Innascibilitas* is the Latin equivalent of *agennēsia*.) The hypostatic character of the Son, loosely called *filiatio*, is defined by two *notiones: generatio passiva* or *filiatio*, strictly so-called, and *spiratio activa*. The hypostatic character of the Spirit, loosely called *processio*, is defined by one *notio*, or notion: *spiratio passiva*. The personal notions or characteristics (*notiones personales*) are thus identical with the *relationes personales* with the addition of the unbegottenness or *innascibilitas* of the Father. In describing the common work of the Godhead, scholastics observe the pattern of relations and notions by declaring that the Father, who is from none (*a nemine*), is the source of trinitarian activity (*fons actionis*); that the Son, who is from the Father (*a Patre*), is the mediating agent or means of action (*medium actionis*); and that the Spirit, who proceeds from both (*ab utroque*), is the limit of the activity or operation of the Godhead (*terminus actionis*). This pattern of operation is observed in all the essential works of the Godhead (*opera Dei essentialis*), with the sole exception of the incarnation (*incarnatio*), in which the Son is, as the Incarnate One, the *terminus actionis*. Since all three persons of the Trinity participate in this essential work, it is also called the common work (*opera communis*) of the Godhead and is described by the maxim that the externally directed works of the Trinity are undivided, *Opera Trinitatis ad extra sunt indivisa* (q.v.).

tuba: *trumpet;* especially, the *tuba ultima*, or last trumpet, which sounds at the end of time. In the words of the *Dies irae* (q.v.), *Tuba mirum spargens sonum/per sepulcra regionum/coget omnes ante thronum*—"A trumpet spreading marvellous sound/through the places of sepulchres/draws all before the throne" (cf. 1 Thess. 4:16). The *tuba* is, specifically, a straight war trumpet used to signal attack, as distinct from the *bucina,* a curved or crooked trumpet used at assembly, and the *cornu,* a large curved horn made from or resembling the horns of animals. SEE *dies novissimus; iudicium extremum.*

Uu

ubietas: literally, *whereness;* the condition of having an *ubi,* i.e., a "where"; hence, place or position. SEE *alicubitas; praedicamenta; praesentia; sessio Christi.*

ubiquitas: *ubiquity; presence everywhere; omnipresence;* specifically, the illocal, supernatural presence of Christ's human nature resulting from the communion of natures (*communio naturarum,* q.v.) and the communication of proper qualities (*communicatio idiomatum,* q.v.) in the person of Christ. The Lutheran orthodox argue that this ubiquity is not a spatial or local ubiquity such as might characterize (hypothetically) a ubiquitous or infinitely extended material substance. Christ's human nature is *not* ubiquitous with reference to its own attributes. Rather the ubiquity of Christ's humanity is illocal, supernatural, and grounded in the omnipresence of the *Logos.* Above all, it is a personal ubiquity that belongs, not to the human nature as such, but to the human nature in its union with the divine person of the Word. The personal union (*unio personalis,* q.v.) is such that the *Logos* is never apart from the flesh and the flesh never apart from the *Logos* (*Logos non extra carnem,* q.v.); and since the person of the Word fills all things, the human nature of Christ must also fill all things. The basic christological implication of ubiquity, then, is the general omnipresence (*omnipraesentia generalis,* q.v.) and repletive presence (*praesentia repletiva*) of Christ's human nature. Although this christological conclusion provides the dogmatic background of Lutheran sacramental theology and explains how, christologically, the real presence of Christ's body and blood in the Lord's Supper is possible, this general ubiquity, or omnipresence, of Christ must not be confused with the sacramental presence. The illocal and supernatural presence of Christ's body and blood in the elements is not repletive but definitive (*praesentia definitiva*), not general but specific to the sacrament. SEE *praesentia; praesentia illocalis sive definitiva.*

ubivolipraesentia: *ubivolipresence;* viz., a presence everywhere (*ubi*) according to the will of God (*voli*); specifically, the presence of

Christ's humanity in and with the Logos. SEE *communicatio idiomatum; multivolipraesentia; omnipraesentia generalis.*

ultima tuba: *last trumpet.* SEE *tuba.*

ultimus iudex: *the final judge;* viz., Christ in his regal office (*munus regium*) at the end of the age (*consummatio saeculi,* q.v.) when he returns to judge the quick and the dead in the final judgment (*iudicium extremum,* q.v.). SEE *adventus Christi; munus triplex.*

una persona geminae substantiae: *one person of two substances;* a standard Latin patristic christological formula. SEE *unio personalis.*

unio accidentalis: *an accidental or incidental union;* e.g., the occasional and temporary union of angels with bodily form. The union is accidental as opposed to a substantial or essential union (*unio essentialis,* q.v.).

unio coessentialis: *coessential union;* viz., not a union of differing essences (*unio essentialis,* q.v.), but a union in one essence, as the union of persons in the Trinity.

unio cum Christo: *union with Christ.* SEE *unio mystica; vocatio.*

unio drastikē; unio δραστική: *an efficacious union.*

unio essentialis: *essential union;* i.e., a union of two different essences, such as the union of all things with God according to the divine *omnipraesentia* (q.v.) and *omnipotentia* (q.v.) and manifest in the divine *concursus.* This union of God with all things can also be called the *unio generalis,* or general union, inasmuch as it belongs to the universal nonsaving work of God as opposed to the *unio specialis* or *unio mystica* (q.v.).

unio hypostatikē; unio ὑποστατική: *hypostatic or personal union.* SEE *unio personalis.*

unio immediata: *immediate or unmediated union;* viz., the effective union of two things brought about by the action of one or both of them, without the aid of a third thing or power. The term can be used to describe the union of the Word with its human nature (SEE *unio personalis*) and is contrasted with *unio mediata* (q.v.).

unio kata charin; unio κατὰ χάριν: *union according to grace.* SEE *unio mystica.*

unio mediata: *mediate or mediated union;* viz., a union made possible in whole or in part by the effective operation of a third thing or power in addition to the immediate subjects of the union. The term is applied to the *unio personalis* (q.v.), or union of the divine and human natures in Christ, insofar as that union is made possible by the gift of supernatural graces to the human nature by the Holy Spirit (SEE *apotelesma; communicatio gratiarum*). The personal union is, of course, primarily the effective work of the Word assuming a human nature into fellowship with itself in its own person (*persona,* q.v.), or subsistence (*subsistentia,* q.v.)—so that the *unio personalis* is not exhaustively described as an *unio mediata,* but must also be termed *unio immediata,* an immediate or unmediated union of the divine and the human.

unio mystica sive praesentia gratiae tantum: *mystical union or union by the presence of grace alone;* i.e., a union made possible and maintained by grace rather than by the interrelation of essences or accidents. It goes beyond the *unio essentialis* (q.v.) of God or, more precisely, the Logos, with all things, since it is of grace and not merely of power and presence. It is, therefore, an *unio specialis.* Specifically, the term *unio mystica,* in orthodox Lutheran and ortho- dox Reformed dogmatics, refers to the special union, founded on the indwelling grace of God in Christ, that occurs between God and the believer in and through regeneration. The union is mystical because it rests on the mystery of grace and of the unsearchable mercy of God; it can also be called *unio spiritualis,* spiritual union, since it is not physical or material but of the Spirit. The qualifying phrase, *sive praesentia gratiae tantum,* is added to the *unio mystica* in order to mark the difference between this union of believers with God and the hypostatic, or personal, union of the divine and human natures in Christ. SEE *unio personalis.*

The orthodox therefore define the *unio mystica* as the spiritual conjunction (*coniunctio spiritualis*) of the Triune God with the be- liever in and following justification. It is a substantial and graciously effective indwelling. In relation to the *ordo salutis* (q.v.), or order of salvation, the Protestant scholastics distinguish the initial *unitio* (q.v.), or uniting, of the *unio mystica,* which is the basis for the imputation of Christ's righteousness to the believer and which corresponds with the adoption (*adoptio*) of the believer, and the ongoing *unio,* or union, of the *unio mystica,* which continues concurrent with sanctification throughout the life of the believer. SEE *adoptio; iustificatio; sanctificatio.*

unio naturalis: *natural union;* as distinct from the *unio personalis, unio naturalis* is a union of two seeming disparates into one *essentia* or *natura,* such as the union of form and matter or soul and body. The essence resulting from an *unio naturalis* is a composite. Such unions occur in the normal order of nature or creation and, unlike the *unio personalis,* which is a union of two *essentiae* in one *persona,* are never between an uncreated and a created being (*ens increatum et creatum*). SEE *unio essentialis; unio personalis.*

unio parastatikē; unio παραστατική: *a helping or assisting union;* sometimes *unio per meram assistentiam,* a union merely for assistance, as, e.g., the union of two people in need, which lasts only as long as the necessity or task that unites them; also referred to as *unio sustentativa,* a sustaining union.

unio per adoptionem: *union by or through adoption;* a term used to describe the christological heresy of adoptionism. The classic adoptionist position, as enunciated by the dynamic monarchianists of the early church, argued that the union between Jesus and God occurred only at Jesus' baptism and was represented by the descent of the divine *dynamis* (δύναμις) upon Jesus. Thus a divine power, not a divine person, dwelt in Jesus. Quite a different issue was raised at the close of the eighth century by the so-called Spanish adoptionists, Felix of Urgel and Elipandus of Toledo. They had no interest in postponing the union of God and man in Christ until Christ's baptism or in arguing a divine power rather than a divine person indwelling in Christ's flesh. Rather, in the interest of stating clearly the fullness of Christ's humanity, they referred to the human nature as *homo adoptatus,* the adopted man, and spoke of a dual sonship, a sonship of the Word by nature and a sonship of Jesus' human nature by gracious adoption. Christ was thus both *Filius Dei naturalis* and *Filius Dei adoptivus,* both the natural and adoptive Son of God. The Spanish adoptionists were never accused of being dynamic monarchians or Samosatians (after Paul of Samosata), but rather of being Nestorians. In fact, they were neither; their doctrine ought to be viewed as a denial of the *anhypostasis* (q.v.) of Christ's human nature and therefore as not in accord with later christological orthodoxy. The Protestant scholastics reject both forms of adoptionism. SEE *enhypostasis; unio personalis.*

unio personalis: *personal union;* viz., the union of the two natures in the person of Christ; the Lutheran and Reformed orthodox agree on the basic Chalcedonian definition of the *unio personalis* and disagree only in the further explication of the definition in terms of the *communicatio idiomatum* (q.v.). The *unio* is defined as the assumption of a human nature by the preexistent eternal person of the Son of God in such a way as to draw the human nature into the oneness of the divine person without division or separation of natures (ἀδι-αιρέτως καὶ ἀχωρίστως), but also without change or confusion of natures (ἀτρέπτως καὶ ἀσυγχύτως); yet also in such a way that the attributes of both natures belong to the divine-human person and contribute conjointly to the work of salvation. Thus, Christ is *una persona geminae substantiae sive naturae,* one person of two substances or natures. The hypostatic, or personal, union is maintained in orthodox doctrine through the recognition that the *persona* (q.v.) is not the sum of two natures but rather is the divine person of the Son. It is the eternal person, or *subsistentia* (q.v.), of the Second Person of the Trinity which is the subsistence or independent, individual existent, Christ. The human nature, which subsists only in and for the union, has no independent subsistence of its own apart from the *unio* (SEE *anhypostasis; enhypostasis*). Thus, the union of the divine person (and nature) with the human nature does not result in the creation of a double person, but of one divine person, in whom two natures, the divine and the human, are united. The *unio* can further be described as the περιχώρησις or *circumincessio* (q.v.), viz., the coinherence of the natures. The two natures coinhere or interpenetrate in perfect union so that the human is never without the divine or the divine without the human (BUT SEE *extra calvinisticum*), yet the natures do not mix or mingle and are never confused one with the other. The results of the *unio* are described as the *communicatio gratiarum* (q.v.), the *communicatio idiomatum* (q.v.), and the *communicatio apotelesmatum* (q.v.). SEE *actus unionis; adiairetōs kai achōristōs; atreptōs kai asynchytōs; natura; unio mediata.*

unio physica: *physical or natural union;* i.e., the union of *materia* and *forma* (q.v.) in a thing.

unio sacramentalis: *sacramental union;* the union between Christ's body and blood and the bread and wine of the sacrament, taught by Lutheranism, over against both the Reformed, who accept no union of Christ's body and blood with the elements, and the Roman Catholics, who argue the transubstantiation of the bread and wine into body and blood. In the Lutheran doctrine the bread and wine remain and, during the sacramental action (*actio sacramentalis,* q.v.), are in sacramental union with the true body and blood of Christ. The Reformed scholastics argue against any physical, local, or even spiritual union of the elements with the body and blood of Christ and refer to the union as *unio relativa*, relative union, or as an *unio significativa* or *unio moralis*, a significative or moral union. The union is between the sign and the thing signified only in terms of the significance of the sign and its relation to the thing. The thing (*res* or *res sacramenti*, q.v.) is not contained in the sign. Thus the Reformed must ultimately argue that Christ is not received with the signs of bread and wine but rather that participation in the sign (*signum*, q.v.) in faith is the foundation of a spiritual participation in the thing signified. SEE *sursum corda*.

unio schetikē; unio σχετική: *an incidental or nonessential union;* viz., a union of individuals by consensus or disposition (*unio habitualis*) or a relative rather than absolute union (*unio relativa*). The orthodox use these terms negatively to identify what the union of natures in Christ *is not*.

unio spiritualis: *spiritual union;* a term used by the Reformed to indicate the union with Christ that results from the faithful reception of the Lord's Supper (SEE *coena sacra*). This *unio* is not local (*localis*), natural (*naturalis*), or bodily (*corporalis*), yet it is real (*realis*) and, since it involves the substance of Christ, *essentialis*. The Reformed prefer to use the term *unio spiritualis* in order to indicate the agency of the Spirit which joins the believer to Christ in faith through the celebration of the sacrament. They reserve *unio mystica* (q.v.) for the broader, not necessarily sacramental, union with Christ in faith and justification. The Lutherans use *unio mystica* with reference to the sacrament, but clarify the term by defining it as *unio spiritualis*, both because of the agency of the Spirit and because of the effect upon the believer of the Spirit's work.

unio substantialis: *substantial union;* a union of two substances; a term sometimes used by the Reformed to indicate the union of the substance of the resurrected Christ with the sacramental elements. Although they deny bodily presence, the Reformed insist that this *unio substantialis* is an *unio realis*, or real union, and an *unio vera*, a true union, accomplished by the power of the Spirit. SEE *coena sacra; praesentia spiritualis sive virtualis; unio sacramentalis*.

unio symbolica: *symbolic union;* used by the Reformed as a synonym of *unio significativa*, significative union; i.e., the union between the sign and the thing signified in the sacrament. SEE *unio sacramentalis*.

unitas: *unity, oneness;* especially, as an attribute of God, the *unitas Dei,* unity of God. God is one in an absolute sense because there is no other God and because the one God is an absolute unity incapable of division. *Unitas* indicates, therefore, that there is no *genus* God and that the one and only God is *simplex,* or simple. The scholastics, therefore, speak of an *unitas singularitatis,* a unity of singularity, or numerical oneness, and an *unitas simplicitatis,* a unity of simplicity, or noncomposite nature as both descriptive of the *unitas Dei.* SEE *simplicitas.*

unitas essentiae: *unity of essence.* SEE *homoousios; unitas.*

unitas operationis: *unity of operation or work.* SEE *apotelesma; opera Dei ad extra; opera Dei essentialia; unitas.*

unitio: *unition, a uniting;* specifically, the uniting of believers with Christ at the inception of the *unio mystica* (q.v.). The *uniti Christo,* those united to Christ, are the recipients, by imputation, of his righteousness, the *iustitia Christi.* SEE *iustificatio; iustitia; iustitia imputata.*

unius substantiae: *of one substance.* SEE *homoousios.*

universalia: *universals, forms, ideas;* the *universalia* are either common signs or terms that can be applied descriptively to a number of distinct things, or they are real attributes or predicables that can be found in a number of distinct things. Considered as a predicate (*praedicamentum;* SEE *praedicamenta*), a universal may therefore be further defined as the relation between several things, or as the basis in those things for the relation that exists between them. As implied in these definitions, there is a further question to be answered concerning the nature of universals. Are *universalia* things in their own right, and, if so, do they have a subsistence independent of the things of which they are predicated? Three distinct answers to the question are proposed and debated by the scholastics. (1) Universals have a real, extramental existence independent of the things of which they are predicated and therefore may be said to subsist *ante rem,* before the thing. In this view, the mind knows the universal first and then, by means of the universal, recognizes the thing as an individual instance or embodiment of the universal. This view is called realism because it holds to the independent reality of the universal; it is the Platonic position. (2) Universals have extramental existence, but only in the things of which they are predicated. *Universalia* are therefore said to subsist *in re,* in the thing, as the inseparable substantial form (*forma substantialis;* SEE *forma*) of the thing. In this view, the mind encounters the thing and from it learns the universal. The relation of the universal to knowledge of the individual can be explained in two ways. The Thomist view is that the senses receive an impression of the thing, and from this as yet unidentified phantasm (*phantasma*), the abstractive powers of the intellect elicit the universal. The universal then becomes the basis for an identification of the individual. In the Scotist view, the intellect first knows the thing as an individual by means of the senses and then abstracts the universal from the thing for the identification of other individuals of the same genus or species. Both the Thomist position and the Scotist critical simplification are called conceptualism and may be identified as Aristotelian in their placement of the universal in the thing. (3) Universals have no extramental existence and subsist only in the mind as a result of its abstractive function. Things themselves exist as individuals only, and the universal is merely a term, or name (*nomen*), used in the identification and classification of individuals by the mind. Universals are therefore said to subsist only in the mind and *post rem*, after things. Since it views universals as mere names, *nomina,* this position is called nominalism.

Each of these positions has major implications for the theology of its proponents. The realist view must be qualified theologically by the inclusion of *universalia* in the mind of God. The existence of universals independent of and outside of the mind of God would render God's intellect and will powerless over the forms of things and, in the elaboration of the doctrine of divine attributes, would render God a composite and logically derivative being. The conceptualist must similarly take care in the predication of divine attributes not to violate the divine simplicity—not, of course, by viewing the attributes as prior to God, but rather by explaining them as distinct things in God. In addition, since the conceptualist allows the reality of universals *in re*, he must allow also their real existence *ante rem* in the case of God and God's knowledge of the created order. The nominalist position has the rather different problem of being unable to argue the distinction of divine attributes anywhere but in the human mind. The Protestant orthodox tend to follow a conceptualist or Aristotelian view of *universalia* particularly in their discussion of the divine attributes (*attributa divina,* q.v.), despite the impact of nominalist theology and its categories of the absolute and ordained power of God (SEE *potentia absoluta; potentia ordinata*) on the theology of the Reformers and on Protestant scholastic theology.

universalismus hypotheticus: *hypothetical universalism;* viz., the teaching, based on the doctrine of the all-sufficient merit of Christ's obedience (SEE *meritum Christi; obedientia Christi*), that Christ's death is hypothetically universal in its extent, the extent being limited only by the failure of some to believe. *Ex hypothesi*, hypothetically, all might choose to believe and all might be saved. Thus, Christ is said to have died for all. In actuality, however, man cannot come to faith apart from grace, and the application of Christ's merit is limited to the elect. This view was proposed in the seventeenth century by the French Reformed theologian, Moses Amyraut. It was rejected by the majority of Reformed scholastics as too close an approach to Arminianism and by Lutheran scholastics as an essentially synergistic view such as had been rejected in the *Formula of Concord.* The later Reformed orthodox responded to the *universalismus hypotheticus* by arguing that the divine intention to save was limited to the elect, so that Christ's death could still be declared sufficient for all sin, but Christ could nevertheless be said also to have died for the elect only. The Lutheran scholastics argue, against both the orthodox Reformed and the Amyraldians, the all-sufficient value and the universal intention of Christ's death, without hypothetical qualification. The Amyraldian view, like that of the Arminians and the Lutheran synergists, makes the divine intention in Christ's death contingent on human belief. This orthodox Lutheranism rejected. SEE *intuitu fidei; satisfactio vicaria.*

univocus: *univocal; having a single meaning.* SEE *praedicatio.*

unus Deus: *the one God.*

usus: *use, usage, practice;* hence, a practice or rite of worship as, e.g., a sacrament. SEE *Nihil habet rationem sacramenti extra usum a Christo institutum.*

usus legis: *use of the law;* as distinguished by the Protestant scholastics, both Lutheran and Reformed, there are three basic uses of the *lex moralis.* (1) The *usus politicus sive civilis*, the political or civil use, according to which the law serves the commonwealth, or body politic, as a force for the restraint of sin. This first *usus* stands completely apart from any relation to the work of salvation and functions much as *revelatio generalis* (q.v.) in bringing some knowledge of God's will to all mankind. (2) The *usus elenchticus sive paedagogicus*, the elenctical or pedagogical use; i.e., the use of the law for the confrontation and refutation of sin and for the purpose of pointing the way to Christ. Some of the Lutheran orthodox (e.g., Hollaz) divide this second use into two parts, distinguishing the purely elenctical use of the law, which merely serves for the *peccati* *manifestatio et redargutio,* the manifestation and refutation of sin, from the *usus paedagogicus* according to which the law becomes a guide to Christ in and through the work of the Spirit, a *compulsus indirectus ad Christum,* an indirect compulsion toward Christ. This division of the second use yields, of course, four uses, in which case (3) the *usus didacticus sive normativus* would become the fourth use. Most frequently, however, the division is threefold, and this latter didactic or normative use is referred to simply as the *tertius usus legis,* the third use of the law. This final use of the law pertains to believers in Christ who have been saved through faith apart from works. In the regenerate life, the law no longer functions to condemn, since it no longer stands elenctically over against man as the unreachable basis for salvation, but acts as a norm of conduct, freely accepted by those in whom the grace of God works the good. This normative use is also didactic inasmuch as the law now teaches, without condemnation, the way of righteousness. In this model, Christ appears as the *finis legis,* or end of the law, both in the sense that the *usus paedagogicus* leads to Christ as to a goal and in the sense that the *usus normativus* has become a possibility for man only because Christ has fulfilled the law in himself. There is one major distinction between the Lutherans and the Reformed in the discussion and application of the *usus legis:* the Reformed lay heavy stress on the *tertius usus legis* on the assumption that faith must spring forth and bear the fruit of good works, as defined by the law in its normative function. The Lutherans, however, see here the danger of works-righteousness and insist that the *usus normativus* ultimately returns the believer, who remains *simul iustus et peccator* (q.v.), to the *usus paedagogicus* and from there again to Christ and his grace as the sole source of salvation. The law, for Lutheranism, can never become the ultimate norm for Christian living but, instead, must always lead to Christ who alone is righteous. This difference between the Lutherans and the Reformed arises out of the dialectical relationship of law and gospel in Lutheranism as opposed to the simple distinction of law and gospel within the one *foedus gratiae* (q.v.) held among the Reformed.

usus loquendi: *practice of speaking* or *experience of speaking; usage;* i.e., the meaning of words and phrases indicated, not by etymology or philology, but by actual use; also *modus loquendi.*

usus philosophiae: *the uses of philosophy;* the Protestant scholastics distinguish three uses of philosophy in theology, all of which conform to the traditional definition of philosophy as the *ancilla theologiae,* or handmaid of theology: (1) *usus organicus,* the organic use, i.e., the use of philosophy to train the reason, analyze arguments, and serve theology in a purely instrumental manner; (2) *usus κατασκευαστικῶς*, the use for argument or for proof, the use of philosophy to adduce ancillary arguments to support theological proof; this use is possible only in the *articuli mixti* (SEE *articuli puri/mixti*), in which both theology and philosophy have a role, e.g., the existence of God; (3) *usus ἀνασκευαστικῶς*, the use for demolition (of an argument), the use of philosophy to refute error and find logical gaps in argumentation. SEE *usus rationis*.

usus rationis: *the use of reason;* specifically, the use of reason in theology. In order to avoid what they saw as the abuse of reason in medieval scholasticism, the Protestant orthodox distinguished between the legitimate use of reason in theology, variously called *usus organicus, usus instrumentalis, usus ministerialis,* and the illegitimate use, the *usus magisterialis.* The organic, instrumental, or ministerial use of reason recognizes the inherent rationality of man and of human discourse, including theology. Reason thus is used organically, according to its place among the natural faculties of soul, and instrumentally or ministerially, as a tool or aid to logical or rational discourse. When, however, reason assumes a magisterial function and presumes to teach theology its contents, it oversteps its limits; the content of theology must rest solely on revelation. In the polemic of seventeenth-century orthodoxy, the Reformed tended to allow a broader use of reason in theology than the Lutherans, arguing, e.g., the irrationality, and therefore the error, of attributing ubiquity to Christ's body. The Lutherans in return accused the Reformed of allowing an illegitimate *usus rationis magisterialis* to enter their theology and of arguing, improperly, a normative use of regenerate reason. SEE *theologia naturalis regenitorum; usus philosophiae.*

uti: *to use;* in the Augustinian vocabulary, to love something for the sake of another or to love something for the sake of where it leads or points, i.e., a love suited to means rather than to ends, to things which are less than ultimate. SEE *frui.*

Vv

vanitas: *vanity.* SEE *septem peccata mortalia.*

variae lectiones: *variant readings;* specifically, variant readings in the several ancient codices of Scripture that lead to debate concerning the infallibility of the scriptural Word. The orthodox, Lutheran and Reformed, generally argued that the meaning of the original can be recovered by careful collation of texts. In the second half of the seventeenth century the argument was developed that inconsistencies occurred only in the copies, or *apographa* (q.v.), and not in the now lost originals, or *autographa* (q.v.), of Scripture.

velle gratiam: *to will or to wish for grace;* also **velle accipere gratiam**: *to will or wish to accept or receive grace;* a characteristic of fully actualized faith in the individual. SEE *actus fidei; fides.*

velle malum: *willing evil to be done;* specifically, in the sense of permitted evil (SEE *non-impeditio peccati* and *permissio efficax*). The scholastics make a distinction between *velle malum*, willing evil to be done, which can be said of God, particularly in terms of the divine *concursus* (q.v.), which willingly permits the evil acts of finite agents; and *male velle*, evil willing, which wills to accomplish what God has forbidden, an activity which cannot be predicated of God.

velleitas (or **velle**): *will considered as the act of willing;* the ability of a spiritual being to act without compulsion. SEE *arbitrium; voluntas.*

veracitas: *truthfulness;* **veracitas Dei**: *the truthfulness of God,* an attribute of God; the divine truthfulness is the ground on which all the promises of God and all the truths of revelation rest. Since God is infinite both in intellect and will, he can lack no knowledge and fail in none of his decrees. His promises are therefore sure and his truthfulness incapable of fault. SEE *veritas.*

verba institutionis: *words of institution.* SEE *verbum institutionis.*

Verbum ἄγραφον: *the unwritten Word.* SEE *Verbum Dei.*

Verbum Dei: *Word of God;* as distinguished by the Protestant orthodox, there are four basic and interrelated meanings of the term
Verbum Dei: (1) the eternal Word of God, the Second Person of the
Trinity, the Son; (2) the incarnate Word, Jesus Christ, the divine-
human Mediator of salvation; (3) the inspired Word of the Holy
Scripture, which is the wisdom of God given in a form accessible to
man, but nonetheless grounded in the eternal Word and Wisdom of
God, God the Son, and historically focused on Christ the Word
incarnate; (4) the internal Word of the Spirit, or *testimonium internum Spiritus Sancti* (q.v.), the *Verbum internum*, which testifies to
the human heart concerning the truth of the written or external
Word (*Verbum externum*). The Protestant scholastics further distinguish the *Verbum externum* into the *Verbum* ἄγραφον, or unwritten
Word, spoken by God to the prophets and apostles, and the *Verbum*
ἔγγραφον, the written or inscripturated Word produced by the
human penmen of Scripture under the inspiration of the Holy Spirit.
This latter distinction is crucial to the Protestant theological argument that the church does not precede and guarantee the Scriptures
but rather that *ecclesia nata est ex Dei Verbo* ("the church is born of
the Word of God"). In historical fact, there has always been a people
of God before the written Word, or *Verbum* ἔγγραφον, but the
concept of an unwritten Word, or *Verbum* ἄγραφον, that constitutes
both the call of the people and the basis of the written Word argues
for the priority of Word over church. The concept also takes into
account the centuries recounted in Genesis before any written Scripture, during which the Word of God called and led the people of
God. These sets of distinctions appear throughout the period of
orthodoxy in both Lutheran and Reformed systems. SEE *authoritas
Scripturae; Scriptura sacra; viva vox.*

Verbum ἔγγραφον: *written Word.* SEE *Verbum Dei.*

Verbum externum: *external Word.* SEE *Verbum Dei.*

verbum institutionis: *word of institution;* or **verba institutionis**: *words
of institution;* also **verbum consecratorium**: *word of consecration;* i.e.,
the words recited in the institution or consecration of the sacrament,
indicating both the establishment (*institutio*) of the sacrament by
Christ and the setting aside of the elements (*consecratio*) from a
common to a sacred use. The Protestant orthodox will also speak of
the *verbum concionale,* or word of explanation, and sometimes the
verbum sacramentale seu concionale et praedicatum, the sacramen-

tal word of explanation and preaching, indicating the clear setting forth of the biblical words of institution for the edification of the congregation. The Reformed, whose doctrine of the Lord's Supper (SEE *coena Domini*) speaks of a spiritual rather than a bodily presence of Christ, sometimes tend away from the language of *consecratio* and use terms like *verbum promissionis*, word of promise, and *verbum ordinationis*, word of ordination. Protestant scholastics often also use the plural, words of institution, *verba institutionis*, etc. SEE *Nihil habet rationem sacramenti extra usum a Christo institutum.*

Verbum internum: *internal Word.* SEE *Verbum Dei.*

verbum mentis: literally, *word of the mind;* i.e., a concept.

verbum visibile: *visible word;* a term applied to the sacraments in order to emphasize their direct relationship to the Word of God.

veritas: *truth;* in the classic definition common to the medieval and the Protestant scholastics, "Truth is the correspondence or conformity of a thing with the intellect" (*Veritas est adaequatio rei ad intellectum, sive conformitas*). In this definition, neither the thing as such nor the intellect as such is true or false; rather, the knowledge or judgment of the intellect concerning the thing will be true or false depending on its conformity to the thing. In other words, truth does not stand as an independent reality which can be known or in which the intellect can participate, but truth is lodged in the correct expression of the conformity of the thing with the knowledge of the thing in the intellect. Specifically, truth and falsehood are inseparable from the truth or falsehood of concepts, statements, or propositions. In the Protestant scholastic systems *theologia vera* and *theologia falsa,* true and false theology, are distinguished in terms of the *conformitas* of true theology to the proper object of theology (*obiectum theologiae,* q.v.), which is God as he has revealed himself. It follows also that *theologia vera* implies the correspondence of finite and derivative knowledge of God (SEE *theologia ectypa*) with the infinite and original knowledge of God which is the divine self-knowledge (SEE *theologia archetypa*). The *veritas Dei,* or truth of God, is ultimately the correspondence, indeed, the identity of the understanding (*intellectus,* q.v.) and will (*voluntas,* q.v.) of God with the *essentia Dei* (q.v.), or essence of God. God is truth itself, in an absolute sense.

veritas θεόπνευστος: *God-breathed truth; inspired truth;* a ground of the historical *authoritas Scripturae* (q.v.) or *authentia historiae* (q.v.) of Scripture. SEE *theopneustos.*

verus, -a, um (adj.): *true.*

verus Deus/verus homo: *true God, true man;* a reference to Christ as fully God and fully man.

Vetus Testamentum: *Old Testament.* SEE *foedus gratiae; Scriptura sacra; testamentum.*

via causalitatis: *the way of causality;* viz., a method of identifying the divine attributes by means of the relationship of effect to cause. Thus, God can be identified as the self-existent and necessary first cause and, by extension, as all-powerful and all-wise. SEE *aseitas; attributa divina; omnipotentia; omnisapientia; via eminentiae; via negativa.*

via eminentiae: *the way of eminence;* as opposed to *via negativa* (q.v.), *via eminentiae* is the method for the positive derivation of divine attributes (*attributa divina,* q.v.) by raising attributes of things in the finite order, particularly spiritual attributes of human beings, to the order of the infinite. E.g., power becomes omnipotence; wisdom becomes omniscience. This method rests on the *analogia entis* (q.v.).

via negativa: *negative way;* also termed the **via negationis**: *way of negation;* i.e., a method of defining or identifying the divine attributes (*attributa divina,* q.v.) by negating the attributes of the finite order. Thus, creatures are measurable, mutable, and finite; God is immeasurable or immense (SEE *immensitas*), immutable (SEE *immutabilitas*), and infinite (SEE *infinitas*). In addition, creatures are complex and temporal; God is simple and eternal. SEE *attributa divina; via causalitatis; via eminentiae.*

via salutis: *the way or order of salvation.* SEE *ordo salutis.*

viator: *pilgrim* or *sojourner;* literally, one on the way, or *in via.* The term arises in particular out of the language and implication of Augustine's *City of God* and denotes the sojourner status of the Christian who is in the world but not of the world. The *viator* has no abiding city on earth, but seeks the heavenly city, which is to come. SEE *homo; in patria; in via; theologia viatorum.*

vicarius, -a, -um (adj.): *vicarious, substitutionary, standing in the place of another person or thing.* See *satisfactio vicaria.*

Video meliora proboque, deteriora sequor: *I see and pronounce good the better things, but I follow the worse;* cited by Johannes Cocceius with reference to Romans 7 (in Heppe, *Reformed Dogmatics*, p. 575). The quotation is from the speech of Medea in Ovid, *Metamorphoses* (VII. 11.20–21), and has been viewed in the tradition as an adumbration of or preparation for the gospel. See *praeparatio evangelica.*

virtualiter: literally, *virtually;* i.e., with *virtus,* or power; powerfully, effectively.

virtus operativa: *operative power.* See *ex opere operato.*

virtutes Dei: *powers or virtues of God;* i.e., the divine attributes, or *attributa divina* (q.v.).

vis dativa mediorum gratiae: *the imparting power of the means of grace;* also **vis exhibitiva**: *exhibiting power;* **vis collativa**: *conferring power.* The means of grace, i.e., Word and sacrament, have *vis dativa* inasmuch as they are able to convey the offer of forgiveness made possible in Christ. Insofar as the sacraments are visible signs, the *vis dativa* is also a *vis exhibitiva.* See *organa gratiae et salutis.*

vis effectiva sive operativa mediorum gratiae: *the effective or operative power of the means of grace;* i.e., the gracious working of the Holy Spirit in and through the Word and the sacraments. See *organa gratiae et salutis.*

visio Dei: *the vision of God;* the final vision of God's glory and truth given to the blessed. We now see as through a glass, darkly; then we shall see face to face. The *visio Dei* is thus impossible to the *viator* (q.v.) and accessible only to the *beati* (q.v.) *in patria* (q.v.); thus it is also called *visio beatifica,* beatific vision. The scholastics note that the *visio* is not a *visio oculi,* a vision of the eye, except with reference to the perception of the glorified Christ. With reference to the saints' new perception of God, the *visio* is *cognitio Dei clara et intuitiva,* a clear and intuitive knowledge of God, an inward *actus intellectus et voluntatis,* or act of intellect and will.

vita aeterna: *eternal life;* viz., the life enjoyed by the blessed (*beati,* q.v.) in their glorified bodies after the resurrection and the judgment, in which they will experience the fullness of life and the vision of

God (*visio Dei*, q.v.). The blessings of the *vita aeterna* are described by the Protestant scholastics as both negative (*negativa*), or privative (*privativa*), and positive (*positiva*). The negative, or privative, blessing is the removal of sin and its consequences, i.e., the suffering and imperfection of earthly existence. The positive blessings are either internal (*interna*) or external (*externa*). The internal blessings consist in the complete renewal and perfecting of intellect and will, the spiritual perfecting of the body and the bestowing upon it of incorruptibility and beauty and the capacity of unimpeded local movement, together with the gift of eternal security in salvation. The external blessings consist in fellowship with God, the blessed angels, and the glorious company of believers in the church triumphant (*ecclesia triumphans;* SEE *ecclesia*).

vita Dei: *the life of God;* as a divine attribute, *vita* is considered in two ways: (1) *essentialiter* or *in actu primo,* in its primary actuality— the *vita Dei* is the divine essence itself inasmuch as God is *autozōos* (αὐτόζωος) and self-moved; and (2) *efficaciter,* effectually or ἐνεργη-τικῶς, which is to say *in actu secundo,* in its second or secondary actuality, as the immanent activity of the Godhead, the *operationes* or *opera ad intra,* which proceed from the divine nature and are the life of the divine essence. SEE *actus; attributa divina; in actu.*

vitium: *imperfection, defect, blemish;* the quality of sinfulness in human beings, particularly considered as a defect in human nature. SEE *causa deficiens; imago Dei; malum; peccata.*

viva vox: *living or spoken word;* also **viva Vox Dei**: *the living Word or speech of God.* The term is applied to the Word of God spoken directly to Israel before the Mosaic inscription of the law and to the Word of God spoken directly to the prophets. In addition, because of the Reformers' emphasis upon the power and efficacy of Scripture, the term was used by the Reformers and by the Protestant orthodox to indicate the reading aloud of vernacular Scriptures during worship. Reformation and post-Reformation interpretation of Scripture, for all of its emphasis upon a strict grammatical reading of the text, holds in common with the earlier exegesis a sense of the direct address of the text to the present-day church. The preacher is not one who applies an old word to new situations, but rather he is a servant and an instrument of the living Word, the *viva Vox Dei,* for its effective operation in the world. SEE *quadriga; Verbum* ἄγραφον.

vivificatio: *vivification, quickening;* viz., the spiritual awakening that is described in Scripture as a putting on of the new man (Col. 3:9–

10) which corresponds to *contritio activa* and *conversio activa sive actualis* (q.v.) and which follows mortification in repentance. SEE *poenitentia; sanctificatio.*

vocatio: *calling;* specifically, the call of God to be his children, which occurs by the grace of the Holy Spirit, both generally in the government of the world and the manifestation of divine *benevolentia* (q.v.) toward all creatures, and specially in and through the proclamation of the Word. Both Lutheran and Reformed scholastics make this distinction between the *vocatio generalis,* or *universalis,* and the *vocatio specialis,* or *evangelica.* General or universal calling is sometimes termed *vocatio realis,* or real calling, because it occurs in and through the things (*res*) of the world, whereas special, or evangelical, calling is sometimes termed a *vocatio verbalis,* since it comes only through the Word (*Verbum*). The Lutherans, however, argue that the *vocatio specialis* of the *Verbum Dei* (q.v.) is sufficient and effective for salvation and is presented equally to all with the divine intention that all be saved. Against the Reformed distinction between an effective (*efficax*) and ineffective (*inefficax*) *vocatio,* the Lutherans hold the sufficiency of Scripture and the efficacious character of God's call in all cases. Failure to heed the call indicates no fault in the Word but rather in the hearer. The Reformed, by contrast, distinguish *vocatio specialis* into *vocatio externa,* which is the universal call of the gospel to all men without distinction, and *vocatio interna,* which is the inward calling of the Spirit that creates the communion between man and God necessary for the *vocatio externa* also to be *vocatio efficax.* Only the elect are therefore effectively called. The Lutherans will allow no such separation of Word and Spirit and argue the necessary correspondence of the external Word with the internal testimony of the Spirit. *Vocatio* can also be distinguished into *vocatio mediata* and *vocatio immediata* (q.v.), the former referring to the call of God through intermediaries, e.g., angels or the church; the latter referring to the call of the Word itself. The Protestant scholastics also distinguish *vocatio extraordinaria,* which can take place apart from the usual service of Word and sacrament, and *vocatio ordinaria,* which occurs in and through those means. The result of God's calling is the reception of believers into the kingdom and their union with and their life in Christ, the *unio mystica* (q.v.), *unio cum Christo* (union with Christ), or *insitio in Christum* (q.v.). *Vocatio* also refers to the calling of individuals to specific office in the church, as the call to ministry or to the teaching of *sacra doctrina.* SEE *gratia; ordo salutis; potestas ecclesiae; regimen ecclesiasticum.*

vocatio efficax: *effectual calling.* SEE *vocatio.*

vocatio immediata/vocatio mediata: *immediate call/mediate call. Vocatio immediata*, the immediate call of God's Word, specifically, the call of God to the prophets and the apostles, is distinguished from the calling of ministers, which is a mediate calling, or *vocatio mediata*, a call that comes from God but is mediated by the church. The Reformed also refer to the calling of the Word to the elect as *vocatio immediata* (SEE *vocatio*).

vocatio inefficax: *ineffectual calling.* SEE *vocatio.*

voluntas: *will;* i.e., the faculty of will resident by nature in all spiritual beings; the appetitive power (*potentia appetitiva*) of a spiritual being. Will is distinct from intellect (*intellectus*, q.v.) in scholastic faculty psychology. The intellect is that which knows objects, the will is that which has an appetite or desire for them. Will and intellect are the two highest spiritual powers. The question immediately arises as to which of the faculties stands prior to the other. In the Thomistic model, intellect stands prior as the deliberative faculty; the will does not deliberate but merely inclines toward or desires that which the intellect knows as good or true. The will, thus, can be called an intellectual appetite (*appetitus intellectualis*) or a rational appetite (*appetitus rationalis*). This view was rejected by Scotus in the name of the freedom of the will. Scotus argued that the will is essentially free and, therefore, self-moved. Although the will always acts on the basis of knowledge, it is also true that we know and remember only because we will to do so. Thus, Scotus will argue that, in a limited sense, the will is dependent upon intellect and that will and intellect must act together. In this conjoint activity, however, the will is to the intellect as form is to matter. The will is more perfect and it determines the use of materials gathered by the intellect. The Protestant orthodox frequently state the problem of priority without solving it definitively; they recognize the interrelationship of intellect and will, but focus on the problem of fallen man. After the fall, the intellect is distorted in its knowing, and the will refuses the good known to the intellect. Indeed, the will follows the lower or sensual appetite (SEE *appetitus*).

Will, defined as the appetitive faculty in man, must also be distinguished from choice (*arbitrium*). The will is the faculty that chooses; *arbitrium* is the capacity of will to make a choice or a decision. Thus, the will can be viewed as essentially free and unconstrained but nonetheless limited by its own capacity to choose particular things and, in view of the restricting and debilitating effects of sin (*peccata*, q.v.), in bondage to its own fallen capacities (SEE *liberum arbitrium; velleitas*).

voluntas decernens: *decisive or deciding will.* SEE *voluntas Dei.*

voluntas decreti vel beneplaciti: *the will of the decree or of (the divine) good pleasure;* viz., the ultimate, absolute, and hidden will of God. SEE *voluntas Dei.*

voluntas Dei: *will of God;* i.e., the attribute of God according to which God may be said to have a potency or, more precisely, an appetitive potency (*potentia appetitiva*) *ad extra* that operates to bring about the good known to and desired by God as the highest end or greatest good (*summum bonum*, q.v.) of all things; it operates, also, to defeat all evil in the created order. Since the divine essence is simple and the *summum bonum* is God himself, it is also correct to say that God is what he wills, in an ultimate sense, and that the divine will is both one (*unica*) and simple (*simplex*). Nevertheless, the scholastics do make a series of distinctions in the divine will as it relates either directly or indirectly to creatures and as it can be known or must remain hidden to creatures. The Protestant scholastics here draw directly on the language of the medieval doctors, modifying it to suit the needs of Protestant systems. The Lutherans and the Reformed agree in a primary distinction between the *voluntas necessaria sive naturalis*, the necessary or natural will, and the *voluntas libera*, the free will, of God. The former term indicates the will which God must have and employ according to his nature and by which God must necessarily will to be himself, to be who and what he eternally is. Thus, God wills his own goodness, justice, and holiness, necessarily or naturally so. The *voluntas necessaria sive naturalis* indicates the precise correspondence of the divine will with the divine essence. The latter term, *voluntas libera*, indicates the utterly free will according to which God determines all things. Since it is the *voluntas libera* that is operative *ad extra*, it is also the subject of further distinction. A primary distinction in the *voluntas libera* may be made between the *voluntas decreti vel beneplaciti* and the *voluntas signi vel praecepti.* The *voluntas decreti vel beneplaciti*, the will of the decree or of (the divine) good pleasure, is the ultimate, effective, and absolutely unsearchable will of God which underlies the revealed will of God. It may therefore also be called the *voluntas arcana*, or hidden will, and the *voluntas decernens*, or decisive, deciding will of God. Lutheran orthodoxy uses the term with reference to the work of salvation only in the sense that human beings cannot know the ultimate reason in the mind and will of God for the gracious salvation of some rather than others. The Reformed, by contrast, argue a hidden will of God to bestow special saving grace irresistibly upon the elect, a *voluntas decreti sive beneplaciti arcana,* more ultimate than the revealed will of God to offer salvation to all by means of a universal grace. This distinction is denied by the Lutherans as endangering the universal grace. The *voluntas decreti vel beneplaciti,* for orthodox Lutheranism, is not an externally effective will, but rather only a will to limit the extent of revelation. The Reformed make the *voluntas decreti vel beneplaciti* the ultimate, effective will of God. The *voluntas signi vel praecepti,* the will of the sign or precept, is the *voluntas revelata,* or revealed will, of God and the *voluntas moralis,* or moral will, according to which God reveals in signs and precepts his plan for mankind both in the law and in the gospel. Here, again, the Lutherans and Reformed differ insofar as the former deny the contrast between a universally offered salvation revealed in the *voluntas signi* and a secret elective will in the *voluntas beneplaciti.*

A second set of distinctions can be made between the *voluntas Dei absoluta et antecedens,* the absolute and antecedent will, of God and the *voluntas Dei ordinata et consequens.* The Lutheran orthodox argue this distinction as a description of the effective will of God *ad extra* and juxtapose it with the previous distinction between the revelative will of God and the hidden will. The *voluntas absoluta et antecedens,* sometimes called *voluntas prima,* first or primary will, is the eternal divine will in and of itself, according to which the ultimate end or final good is willed by God apart from consideration of conditions, circumstances, and means to be encountered or used proximately in the achievement of the divine purpose. The *voluntas ordinata et consequens,* sometimes called *voluntas secunda,* second or secondary will, is the will of God according to which he orders proximate causes and effects both in terms of the universal order and its laws and in terms of the circumstances that arise out of the contingent events and the creaturely free wills resident in the order. The *voluntas ordinata,* therefore, corresponds with the *potentia ordinata* (q.v.), or ordained power of God, whereas the *voluntas consequens* is a distinct willing that rests on the divine foreknowledge. In the systems of Lutheran orthodoxy, the *voluntas consequens* is the will of God that elects *intuitu fidei* (q.v.), in view of faith. The Reformed deny the distinction between *voluntas antecedens* and *voluntas consequens* on the ground that it amounts to a denial of the freedom and independence of the divine will and implies contingency in God himself. They accept, however, the distinction between *voluntas absoluta* and *voluntas ordinata* in conjunction with that between *potentia absoluta* and *potentia ordinata,* and subsume both *voluntas absoluta* and *voluntas ordinata* under the *voluntas decreti vel beneplaciti* considered as the ultimate *voluntas Dei decernens,* the deciding will of God.

The Reformed further argue the distinction of the *voluntas decreti vel beneplaciti* or *voluntas decernens* into the categories of *voluntas efficiens,* effecting will, and *voluntas permittens,* permitting will. Under the former category, God is viewed as directly or indirectly through instrumental causes effecting his positive will, whereas under the latter category God is understood as permitting both contingent events and acts of free will even when such events and acts go against his revealed will. Since God is not a *Deus otiosus,* or idle God, the *voluntas permittens* is typically called *voluntas efficaciter permittens,* an effectively permitting will (SEE *concursus*).

Finally, the Protestant scholastics argue a series of distinctions in the *voluntas signi vel praecepti.* The *voluntas signi vel praecepti* is, first, synonymous with *voluntas revelata* and *voluntas moralis.* As such, several of the Lutheran orthodox argue that the *voluntas signi* is not truly the will of God but an effect of his will or a subsidiary willing resting on the *voluntas antecedens* and, formally, on the *voluntas consequens.* In other words, it is an effect or object of the divine will that provides a sign of what is willed in and by God. The *voluntas revelata* can be distinguished into a *voluntas legalis,* according to which God demands obedience to his will, and a *voluntas evangelica,* according to which God wills to save through grace in Christ. The Reformed occasionally allow here a distinction between *voluntas antecedens* and *voluntas consequens.* The former refers to the commands of God, the *voluntas legalis,* which ordains the conditions of human life absolutely; the latter refers to the *voluntas evangelica,* which establishes the conditions under which fallen mankind can be saved. SEE *scientia Dei; voluntas revelata Dei.*

voluntas effectiva: *effective will.* SEE *voluntas Dei.*

voluntas permissiva: *permissive will;* also **voluntas permittens**: *permitting will.* SEE *voluntas Dei.*

voluntas revelata Dei: *the revealed will of God;* viz., the will of God concerning human obedience and human salvation that is revealed in the law and the gospel, as distinguished from the *voluntas abscondita,* the hidden will of God, which is the ultimate divine purpose underlying the *voluntas revelata,* the unsearchable judgments and ways of the infinite mind of God itself (Rom. 11:33). The distinction is similar to that between the *potentia ordinata* (q.v.) and *potentia absoluta* (q.v.) and between *theologia ectypa* (q.v.) and *theologia archetypa* (q.v.) insofar as all three distinctions arise out of a theological concern for the divine transcendence, and are virtually identical with the distinction between *voluntas signi* and *voluntas beneplaciti* (SEE *voluntas Dei*).

voluntas signi vel praecepti: *the will of the sign or of the precept;* viz., the revealed will of God manifest in signs and precepts. SEE *voluntas Dei.*

vox: *voice, spoken sound,* or *word.* SEE *Verbum Dei; viva vox.*

Xx

xenium: *a gift.*

Zz

zamia: *injury* or *loss.*

zelotes: *one who is jealous;* e.g., God as a jealous God (Exod. 20:5).

zelotypia: *jealousy.*

zōopoiēsis (ζωοποίησις): *a making alive; vivification.* SEE *vivificatio.*

Soli Deo Gloria

Index to Key Terms

act: *actus*
  of faith: *actus fidei*
  of trust: *actus fiduciae*
  of union: *actus unionis*
action: *actus*
actuality: *actus*
adoption: *adoptio*
affliction: *tentatio*
allegory: see: *quadriga*
analogy: *analogia*
  of being: *analogia entis*
  of faith: *analogia fidei*
  of Scripture: *analogia Scripturae*
angels: *angeloi; pneumata leitourgika*
Antichrist: *antichristus*
apostasy: *apostasia*
assent: *assensus*
attribute: *attributum*
authority of Scripture: *authoritas Scripturae*

begetting: *generatio; genesis*
being: *ens*
birth: *genesis*
blessedness: *beatitudo*
body of Christ: *corpus Christi*

calling: *vocatio*
cause: *causa*
certainty: *certitudo*
children of the faithful: *infantes fidelium*
choice: *arbitrium*
Christ—person of: *persona Christi*
  office of: *munus triplex*
  satisfaction of: *satisfactio vicaria*
  states of: *status exaltationis; status humiliationis*

also see: *persona; Trinitas*
commands: *praecepta*
  of love: *praecepta caritatis*
  of the law: *praecepta Decalogi*
common grace: *gratia communis*
common places: *loci communes*
communication of proper qualities: *communicatio idiomatum*
communion: *communio; koinōnia*
community: *koinōnia*
concurrence: *concursus*
consubstantial: *homoousios*
contrition: *contritio; poenitentia*
conversion: *conversio*
cooperating grace: see: *gratia*
counsel of God: *consilium Dei*
covenant: *foedus; pactum*
  of grace: *foedus gratiae*
  of redemption: *pactum salutis*
  of works: *foedus operum*
covetousness: see: *septem peccata mortalia*

damnation: *damnatio*
death: *mors*
decree: *decretum*
degrees of glory: *gradus gloriae*
desire: *appetitus*
despair: see: *septem peccata mortalia*
dispensation: *dispensatio*
disposition: *habitus*
  of faith: *habitus fidei*
  of grace: *habitus gratiae*
distributive justice: *iustitia remuneratoria sive distributiva*
divine attributes: *attributa divina*

eating (sacramental): *manducatio*

336

economy: *dispensatio*
effectual calling: *vocatio efficax*
emotion: *affectio*
end of the world: *consummatio
    saeculi*
  also see: *interitus mundi*
envy: see: *septem peccata mortalia*
equivocal: *aequivocus*
essence: *essentia; quidditas*
  of God: *essentia Dei*
eternal ideas: *rationes aeternae*
eternal life: *vita aeterna*
eternity: *aeternitas*
exaltation of Christ: *status
    exaltationis*
existence: *esse*

faithfulness: *fidelitas*
fault: *culpa*
fear of God: *timor Dei*
  also see: *timor filialis; contritio*
first cause: *prima causa*
first mover: *primum movens*
foreknowledge: *praescientia*
foreknowledge of faith: *praevisa
    fidei*
foreordination: *praedestinatio*
form: *forma*
  also see: *universalia*
foundation: *fundamentum*
  of election: *fundamentum
    electionis*
  of faith: *fundamentum fidei*
  also see: *principia theologiae*
free will (i.e., free choice): *liberum
    arbitrium*
fundamental articles: *articuli
    fundamentales*
fundamental principles of theology:
    principia theologiae

general revelation: *revelatio
    generalis*
gluttony: see: *septem peccata
    mortalia*
God: *Deus*
God-man: *theanthrōpos*
good-will: *benevolentia*

goodness: *bonitas*
grace: *gratia*
  of God: *gratia Dei*
grace alone: *sola gratia*
greed: see: *septem peccata mortalia*
guarantee: *fideiussio; sponsio*
guilt: *culpa*

happiness: *felicitas*
hatred: *odium*
holiness: *sanctitas*
humiliation of Christ: *status
    humiliationis*
hypostatic union: *unio personalis*
hypothetical universalism:
    universalismus hypotheticus

ideas: *universalia; rationes aeternae*
illocal presence: *praesentia illocalis
    sive definitiva*
  also see: *praesentia*
illumination: *illuminatio*
image of God: *imago Dei*
immeasurability: *immensitas*
immortality: *immortalitas*
imperfection: *vitium*
impersonality: *anhypostasis*
imputation: *imputatio*
imputed righteousness: *iustitia
    imputata*
in view of faith: *intuitu fidei*
incarnation: *incarnatio*
inspiration: *inspiratio*
  also see: *theopneustos*
intellect: *intellectus*
intermediate state: *status animarum
    a corpore separatarum*
internal testimony of the Holy Spirit:
    *testimonium internum
    Spiritus Sancti*

justice: *iustitia*
justification: *iustificatio*

kenosis: *exinanitio*
kingdom of Christ: *regnum Christi*
knowledge: *cognitio; notitia; scientia*

last day: *dies novissimus*
last judgment: *iudicium extremum*
law: *lex*
    ceremonial: *lex ceremonialis*
    of Christ: *lex Christi*
    moral: *lex moralis*
    of Moses: *lex Mosaica*
    of nature: *lex naturalis*
liability: *reatus*
life: *vita*
light—of God: *lux Dei*
    of nature/grace/glory: *lumen naturae/gratiae/gloriae*
long-suffering: *longanimitas*
Lord's Supper: *coena sacra*
love: *amor; caritas; dilectio*
    of God: *amor Dei*
lust: see: *septem peccata mortalia*

majesty; *maiestas*
man (generic): *homo*
manifestation: *patefactio*
marks of the church: *notae ecclesiae*
means: *media*
    of grace: *media gratiae; organa gratiae et salutis*
    also see: *instrumentum*
mediator: *Mediator*
mercy: *misericordia*
merit: *meritum*
    of Christ: *meritum Christi*
metaphysics: *metaphysica*
millennialism: *chiliasmus*
miracles: *miracula*
mirror of election: *speculum electionis*
morosity: see: *septem peccata mortalia*
mystical union: *unio mystica*

names of God: *nomina Dei*
natural condition: *status purorum naturalium*
natural theology: *theologia naturalis*
necessity: *necessitas*
    absolute: *necessitas absoluta*
    of compulsion: *necessitas coactionis*

of nature: *necessitas naturae*
    relative: *necessitas consequentiae*
nothingness: *nihil; mē on*
    also see: *ex nihilo*

obedience of Christ: *obedientia Christi*
object: *obiectum*
    of election: *obiectum electionis*
    of faith: *obiectum fidei*
    of theology: *obiectum theologiae*
office of Christ: *munus triplex*
omnipotence: *omnipotentia*
order: *ordo*
    of created things: *ordo rerum creatarum*
    of decreed things: *ordo rerum decretarum*
    of salvation: *ordo salutis*
original righteousness: *iustitia originalis*

permission: *permissio*
perseverance: *perseverantia*
personal relation: *relatio personalis*
personal union: *unio personalis*
place: *locus*
power: *potentia; potestas*
    absolute: *potentia absoluta*
    ordained: *potentia ordinata*
    of the church: *potestas ecclesiae*
practical syllogism: *syllogismus practicus*
practice: *praxis*
prayer: *oratio*
predestination: *praedestinatio*
predication: *praedicatio*
preparation—for conversion: *praeparatio ad conversionem*
    for the gospel: *praeparatio evangelica*
presence: *praesentia*
prevenient grace: *gratia praeveniens*
pride: see: *septem peccata mortalia*
priestly work: *sacerdotium*
primacy: *primitas*
primary actuality: *actus primus*
prime matter: *materia prima*

procession: *spiratio; processio*
promise: *promissio*
proper qualities: *idiomata*
property: *proprietas; proprium*
prophecy: *prophetia*
providence: *providentia*
punishment: *poena*
punitive justice: *iustitia vindicativa sive punitiva*
pure act: *actus purus*

ransom: *lytron*
real presence: see: *praesentia*
reality: *actus; ens; esse; res*
received text: *textus receptus*
reconciliation: *reconciliatio*
remunerative justice: *iustitia remuneratoria sive distributiva*
repentance: *metanoia; poenitentia; resipiscentia*
reprobation: *reprobatio*
resistible grace: *gratia resistibilis*
resurrection: *resurrectio*
revelation: *patefactio; revelatio*
righteousness: *iustitia*
 of faith: *iustitia fidei*
 of God: *iustitia Dei*
rule of faith: *regula fidei*

sacrament: *sacramentum*
sacramental action: *actio sacramentalis*
sacramental union: *unio sacramentalis*
sanctification: *sanctificatio*
Scripture alone: *sola Scriptura*
second coming: *adventus Christi*
secondary causes: *causae secundae*
seed of faith: *semen fidei*
self-emptying: *exinanitio; kenōsis*
self-existence: *aseitas*
sense: *sensus*
 composite: *sensus compositus*
 of the divine: *sensus divinitatis*
 literal: *sensus literalis*
 mystical: *sensus mysticus*

seven deadly sins: *septem peccata mortalia*
sign: *signum*
simplicity: *simplicitas*
sinlessness: *anamartēsia*
sin(s): *peccatum; peccata*
 mortal: *peccata mortalia*
 actual: *peccatum actualis*
 against the Holy Spirit: *peccatum in Spiritum Sanctum*
 original: *peccatum originalis*
 propagation of: *propagatio peccati*
 imputation of: *imputatio peccati*
soul: *anima*
soul-sleep: *psychopannychia*
stain (of sin): *macula*
state of exaltation: *status exaltationis*
state of humiliation: *status humiliationis*
subject: *subiectum*
subsistence: *subsistentia*
substance: *substantia*
suffering: *passio*
surety: *fideiussio; sponsio*
synergism: *synergismus*

teaching: *paideia*
temptation: *tentatio*
theology: *theologia*
 of angels: *theologia angelorum*
 archetypal: *theologia archetypa*
 of the blessed: *theologia beatorum*
 of Christ: *theologia unionis*
 of the cross: *theology crucis*
 ectypal: *theologia ectypa*
 natural: *theologia naturalis*
 of Christians: *theologia viatorum*
thing: *res*
third use of the law: see: *usus legis*
threefold office: *munus triplex*
trial: *tentatio*
Trinity: *Trinitas*
 also see: *Deus; persona*
truth: *veritas*
truthfulness: *veracitas*

understanding: *intellectus*
union: *unio*

accidental: *unio accidentalis*
essential: *unio essentialis*
mystical: *unio mystica*
natural: *unio naturalis*
by adoption: *unio per adoptionem*
personal: *unio personalis*
sacramental: *unio sacramentalis*
universal grace: *gratia universalis*
universals: *universalia*

vicarious satisfaction: *satisfactio vicaria*
vowel points: *puncta vocalia*

will: *voluntas*
of God: *voluntas Dei*

wisdom: *sapientia*
witness: *testimonium*
wonders: *mirabilia*
Word: *Logos*
of God: *Verbum Dei*
word(s) of institution: *verbum institutionis*
work: *officium; opus*
of God: *opera Dei*
of supererogation: *opera supererogationis*
proper (as opposed to alien): *opus proprium*
work of Christ: see: *munus Christi; obedientia Christi; satisfactio vicaria*
wrath: *ira*